CAMBRIDGE LIBRARY COLLECTION

Books of enduring scholarly value

Cambridge

The city of Cambridge received its royal charter in 1201, having already been home to Britons, Romans and Anglo-Saxons for many centuries. Cambridge University was founded soon afterwards and celebrated its octocentenary in 2009. This series explores the history and influence of Cambridge as a centre of science, learning, and discovery, its contributions to national and global politics and culture, and its inevitable controversies and scandals.

Catalogue of the Books and Papers for the Most Part Relating to Cambridge

John Willis Clark, the Cambridge academic and antiquarian, began collecting literature connected with Cambridge in the 1860s. In 1910 he bequeathed to Cambridge University Library his collection of over ten thousand books, pamphlets and pieces of print relating, directly or indirectly, to Cambridge University, including some whose primary reference is to the town or county of Cambridge. Published in 1912, this catalogue documents Clark's extensive collection, listing the literature he amassed from all periods and upon every subject. Clark had a particular interest in college architecture and tracing the growth of the collegiate system, which explains the inclusion of works relating to Oxford and Eton in the collection. Arranged as a dictionary catalogue, with authors and subjects listed alphabetically, the work reflects Clark's aim to illustrate the history and development of Cambridge through its literature, from an historical and biographical point of view.

Cambridge University Press has long been a pioneer in the reissuing of out-of-print titles from its own backlist, producing digital reprints of books that are still sought after by scholars and students but could not be reprinted economically using traditional technology. The Cambridge Library Collection extends this activity to a wider range of books which are still of importance to researchers and professionals, either for the source material they contain, or as landmarks in the history of their academic discipline.

Drawing from the world-renowned collections in the Cambridge University Library, and guided by the advice of experts in each subject area, Cambridge University Press is using state-of-the-art scanning machines in its own Printing House to capture the content of each book selected for inclusion. The files are processed to give a consistently clear, crisp image, and the books finished to the high quality standard for which the Press is recognised around the world. The latest print-on-demand technology ensures that the books will remain available indefinitely, and that orders for single or multiple copies can quickly be supplied.

The Cambridge Library Collection will bring back to life books of enduring scholarly value (including out-of-copyright works originally issued by other publishers) across a wide range of disciplines in the humanities and social sciences and in science and technology.

Catalogue of the Books and Papers for the Most Part Relating to Cambridge

Bequeathed to the University by John Willis Clark, M.A.

EDITED BY A. T. BARTHOLOMEW

CAMBRIDGE
UNIVERSITY PRESS

CAMBRIDGE UNIVERSITY PRESS

Cambridge, New York, Melbourne, Madrid, Cape Town, Singapore,
São Paolo, Delhi, Dubai, Tokyo, Mexico City

Published in the United States of America by Cambridge University Press, New York

www.cambridge.org
Information on this title: www.cambridge.org/9781108015929

© in this compilation Cambridge University Press 2010

This edition first published 1912
This digitally printed version 2010

ISBN 978-1-108-01592-9 Paperback

CATALOGUE OF THE
CLARK BEQUEST

CAMBRIDGE UNIVERSITY PRESS
London: FETTER LANE, E.C.
C. F. CLAY, Manager

Edinburgh: 100, PRINCES STREET
Berlin: A. ASHER AND CO.
Leipzig: F. A. BROCKHAUS
New York: G. P. PUTNAM'S SONS
Bombay and Calcutta: MACMILLAN AND CO., Ltd.

J. W. CLARK
in the South Cloister of Gloucester Cathedral
2 July 1895

CATALOGUE

OF THE BOOKS AND PAPERS
FOR THE MOST PART RELATING TO THE

UNIVERSITY, TOWN, AND COUNTY
OF CAMBRIDGE

BEQUEATHED TO THE UNIVERSITY

BY

JOHN WILLIS CLARK, M.A.

REGISTRARY OF THE UNIVERSITY AND
FORMERLY FELLOW OF TRINITY COLLEGE

BY

A. T. BARTHOLOMEW, M.A.

OF PETERHOUSE, CAMBRIDGE

CAMBRIDGE
AT THE UNIVERSITY PRESS
1912

Cambridge:

PRINTED BY JOHN CLAY, M.A.
AT THE UNIVERSITY PRESS

TO
THE MEMORY OF
JOHN WILLIS CLARK
THIS CATALOGUE
OF HIS
CAMBRIDGE COLLECTION
IS AFFECTIONATELY
INSCRIBED

CONTENTS

PREFACE

THE collection here catalogued was bequeathed to the University by John Willis Clark, M.A., Registrary, formerly Fellow of Trinity College, in the following terms :

"I bequeath to the Chancellor, Masters and Scholars of the University of Cambridge, to be placed in the University Library, all my books, pamphlets, manuscripts and collections of views and photographs relating to the Town, County, Colleges, or University of Cambridge, or to the University of Oxford, except such views as may be found framed and glazed and hanging on the walls of my house at the time of my decease, together with the manuscript of the Architectural History of Cambridge by the late Professor Willis, his notes and lecture diagrams, and the quarto volumes of extracts from College Account Books and other documents made by myself. And I wish that the Librarian shall be in no way fettered as regards the distribution of this collection (which I do not desire kept separate unless perfectly convenient), and that if any items of such collection shall be duplicates of works already in the Library the said Librarian shall be at liberty to sell or exchange them as he thinks proper. And I declare that notwithstanding the circumstance that these books, pamphlets and manuscripts are all recorded in a manuscript catalogue, in two volumes folio, it shall be in the absolute discretion of my Executors to determine the items which pass under this Bequest whether so recorded or not."

(*Cambridge University Reporter*, 29 November 1910.)

It was accepted by Grace of the Senate, 3 December 1910 (*Reporter*, 6 December 1910).

The collection consists of upwards of ten thousand books, pamphlets, and pieces, relating for the most part to the University, and to a less extent to the Town and County, of

Cambridge. Included, however, are a certain number of books which have no direct connection with Cambridge, *e.g.* books by Cambridge men on subjects unconnected with Cambridge, and books about other Universities, and about University education.

Mr Clark's interest in Cambridge literature began about the year 1860, when, at the suggestion of Dr Luard, he resolved to collect the long series of tracts issued in connection with Dr Richard Bentley's quarrels with Trinity College, and with his various other activities and controversies. Very soon, however, he became so much interested in his task that he enlarged his plan, and set about collecting Cambridge literature of all periods and upon every subject. As is well known he was specially interested in College architecture, and in tracing the growth of the collegiate system. This explains the presence of works, particularly a series of books about Oxford colleges, and another series relating to Eton, which at first sight seem to have no proper place in a Cambridge collection.

The principal sources of the collection were these : (1) An important *Catalogue of tracts, etc., relating to Cambridgeshire* was issued by A. R. Smith, of Soho Square, in 1878, and from this Mr Clark bought extensively. (2) The Rev. Stephen Parkinson, Fellow of St John's College (B.A. 1845, M.A. 1848), was in the habit of preserving all Cambridge papers which came into his hands ; his collection was acquired by Mr Clark, and filled numerous gaps in the long series of fly-sheets, programmes, proposals, etc., which is a particularly valuable feature of the Clark Collection (see the Catalogue, *s.v.* 'Cambridge Papers' and 'Fly-Sheets'). (3) Mr Henry Bradshaw, University Librarian, added many tracts to the collection ; and at the sale which followed his death in 1886 Mr Clark acquired many more Cambridge items. (4) Dr H. R. Luard, Registrary, who died in 1891, left Mr Clark his University pamphlets and Bentleiana. (5) In 1894 Mr Robert Bowes published his remarkable *Catalogue of Cambridge Books*, and a large number of the pieces there described found their way into the Cambridge collection at Scroope House. In addition to these main sources Mr Clark rarely missed an opportunity of securing any books which came within the scope of his collection wherever and whenever he happened to see them.

Mr Clark's main idea in forming the collection was to illustrate the history and development of Cambridge by means of its literature ; he collected from an historical and biographical rather than from a bibliographical point of view. Most of the books of typographical interest which were originally included in his Cambridge collection he gave to the Library in 1902[1], in order that they might appear in Mr Sayle's *Early English Printed Books in the University Library, Cambridge.*

The present work is based on the manuscript catalogue referred to in Mr Clark's will. This was finished in 1897 by Mr Clark, assisted by Mr Alfred Rogers of the University Library. He always hoped to see it printed, but it was not until 1909 that any very definite steps were taken. Since then it has been revised throughout, and to a large extent recast with a view to publication. Each book or tract has been compared with its catalogue-entry, and a large number of additional cross-references and subject-headings have been introduced. The general plan for the printed Catalogue and the earlier part of the revision were made by Mr Clark and myself working together; but in 1910 his health broke down, and I was obliged to continue the work alone.

In form it is a dictionary catalogue, with authors and subjects in one alphabetical arrangement. The titles have been kept short ; and the main purpose has been to give an idea of the historical value of the collection rather than bibliographical descriptions of the books which compose it. To this end the subject-headings have been made as complete as possible.

[1] See Report of the Library Syndicate for the year ending 31 December 1902 (*Reporter*, 23 June 1903). Mr Clark also gave a documentary history of the University Library, arranged by himself, in six folio volumes.

As has already been stated, the collection includes a certain number of books which have no very close connection with Cambridge; but in spite of this it has been treated as a Cambridge Collection, and the headings 'Cambridge' and 'University of Cambridge' have been reduced to a minimum. (See the notes under those headings in the Catalogue.)

In the University Library the Clark Collection has been incorporated with a smaller collection of similar books already preserved there; and the whole has been arranged in chronological order as a special class (Cam.), to which Cambridge literature of every description can in future be added as it appears, and in which gaps can be filled as occasion offers. The Clark books are distinguished by a book-plate and a special stamp.

The present Catalogue, which includes only those books which came to the University under Mr Clark's will, is published as a contribution towards that complete bibliography of Cambridge which has yet to be written, and as a memorial of one who was unwearying in his efforts to advance the interests of the University Library.

Considerable pains have been taken (in some cases without success) to discover the authors of the numerous anonymous publications included in the collection, and I take this opportunity of thanking the various Cambridge publishers and booksellers to whom I have applied for information concerning some of the more recent publications of the kind.

My best thanks are also due to Mr Francis Jenkinson, University Librarian, and to Mr H. G. Aldis, Secretary of the University Library, who have read the proof-sheets of the Catalogue, and given me much help and encouragement throughout; to Mr Robert Bowes, who has placed at my disposal his unrivalled knowledge of Cambridge literature, and to whose *Catalogue of Cambridge Books* I have constantly referred; to Mr A. H. Cook, my colleague in the Acton Library, who has read all the proofs with particular care, and saved me from many errors and inconsistencies; to Mr Charles Sayle, Assistant Under Librarian, for allowing me to make use of his list of the manuscripts received under the Clark bequest in drawing up Appendix I; and to the Syndics of the University Press for the loan of the block (originally made for Mr Clark's *Care of Books*) from which the frontispiece is taken.

A. T. BARTHOLOMEW

University Library
Cambridge
15 *June* 1912

ABBREVIATIONS

When no place of publication is given Cambridge may be assumed.
When no size is given octavo may be assumed.

Bowes = A Catalogue of books printed at or relating to the University, Town, and County of Cambridge from 1521 to 1893, with bibliographical and biographical notes; by Robert Bowes. 1894.

C.A.S. = Proceedings of the Cambridge Antiquarian Society with Communications made to the Society.

ADDITIONS AND CORRECTIONS

PAGE

27 *for* Blakeney (E.P.) *read* Blakeney (E.H.).

29 *insert* Boissier (G.R.)   Notes on the Cambridgeshire Churches.

30 *heading* Bourne (V.) *for* Latina *read* Latine.

55 *heading* Clark (J.W.) *add* The Woodwardian Professor and the Sedgwick Memorial Museum. By A. Newton and J. W. Clark. 14 Feb. (1887).

63 *heading* Collegian's Guide *add* 2nd ed.   1858.

86 *heading* Essington (R.W.) *for* Cain *read* Canaan.

97 *heading* Flower (W.H.) *transfer* to p. 96.

115 *heading* Hallam (A.H.) *add* The influence of Italian works of the imagination on the same class of compositions in England.   1832.

124 *heading* Huckman (J.) *add* Original Poems.   3rd ed.   1825.

162 *heading* Mason (W.) *add* Mirth, a poem. *London,* 1774.

163 *heading* Mathias (T.J.) *add* An heroic epistle to the Rev. R. Watson. *London,* 1780.

PRINTED BOOKS
AND PAPERS

CATALOGUE

⁎ When no place of publication is given Cambridge may be assumed. When no size is given octavo may be assumed.

A

A.D.C. *See* Amateur Dramatic Club.

ABBEY DISTRICT. *See* Barnwell.

ABINGTON PIGOTTS. The Parish Registers of Abington Pigotts. Ed. by W. Graham F. Pigott. *Norwich*, 1890

ACADEMIC (The): or a disputation on the state of the University of Cambridge. [Attr. to J. Green, Bp of Lincoln, and others.] (Bowes 1193.) *London*, 1750

Remarks on the Academic. [Attr. to S. Squire.] *London*, 1751

ACADEMIC Errors; or recollections of youth. By a Member of the University of Cambridge [W. S. Gilly]. (Bowes 1576.) *London*, 1817

ACADEMICA; an occasional journal. May 1858. (Bowes 2299.) 1858

ACADEMICAL contributions of original and translated poetry. 1795

ACADEMICAL dress. *See* Almond (A.G.); Clark (E.C.); Costumes.

ACADEMICUS. *See* Crawford (Ch.); Green (J.); Kipling (T.).

ACCOUNTS. University Accounts, 1847–1877. 4° 1848–78

ACKLAND (T.G.) The Gospel the power of God unto Salvation. Commencement sermon, July 5, 1829. 1829

ACLAND (H.W.) The Oxford Museum. 2nd ed. *Oxford*, 1860
—— 4th ed. *Oxford*, 1867

Report to the Radcliffe Trustees, on the transfer of the Radcliffe Library to Oxford University Museum. *Oxford*, 1861

ACTON (*Lord*) A lecture on the study of history. *London*, 1895

Lord Acton at Cambridge. By F. J. Pollock. (*Indep. Review*, April 1904.)
The Cambridge Modern History. Account of its origin, etc. 1907
See also Library.

ACTS AND BILLS.

Acts affecting the Universities of Oxford and Cambridge. Ed. by W. B. Skene. *London*, 1894

1703. An Act for making the River Cham, alias Grant...more navigable from Clay-Hithe-Ferry, to the Queen's-Mill... (1 Anne, 27 Feb. 1702–3.) [1804?]

ACTS AND BILLS.

1724. An Act for repairing the roads from Stump Cross...to Newmarket Heath, and the town of Cambridge. (10 Geo. I. 24 April 1724.)

1725. An Act for repairing part of the road from London to Cambridge, beginning at...Foulmire...and ending...in Trumpington-Street. (11 Geo. I. 24 March 1724-5.)

1730. An Act to explain, amend, and render more effectual an Act...for repairing the roads from Stump Cross...to Newmarket Heath, and the town of Cambridge...and also an Act for repairing part of the road from London to Cambridge... (3 Geo. II. 15 May 1730.)

1742. An Act for continuing the Powers granted by Three several Acts [set forth immediately above]. (15 Geo. II. 16 June 1742.)

The last four published together.　　　　　　　12° *London*, 1755

1727. An Act for the effectual draining and preservation of Haddenham Level, in the Isle of Ely. (13 Geo. I. 24 April 1727.)
　　　　　　　　　　　　　　　　　　　F° *London*, 1727

1738. An Act for...draining...certain fens called Cawdle Fen, Waterden [etc.]. (11 Geo. II. 20 May 1738.)　F° *London*, 1738

1749. An Act for draining...certain fen lands...in the parishes of Sutton, Mepall [etc.]. (22 Geo. II. 22 March 1748—9.)
　　　　　　　　　　　　　　　　　　　F° *London*, 1749

1749. An Act for draining...certain fen lands in the bounds and precincts of Whittlesey... (22 Geo. II. 26 May 1749.)
　　　　　　　　　　　　　　　　　　　F° *London*, 1749

1749. An Act for enlarging...An Act for making a new road... between Wisbech and March... (22 Geo. II. 26 May 1749.)
　　　　　　　　　　　　　　　　　　　F° *London*, 1749

1757. An Act for draining...certain fen lands...in the parishes of Ramsey, Bury [etc.]. (30 Geo. II. 28 June 1757.)
　　　　　　　　　　　　　　　　　　　F° *London*, 1757

1763. An Act to enable the Master, Fellows, and Scholars of Clare-hall...to alter and vary the benefactions of Doctor Blyth... (3 Geo. III. 12 April 1763.)　　　　　F° [*London*, 1763]

1788. An Act for the better paving, cleansing, and lighting the town of Cambridge...To which is added a copious Index. (28 Geo. III. 8 May 1788.)　　　　　　　　　　　　1788

1790. An Act for enlarging the term of several Acts made for repairing the roads from Stump Cross to Newmarket Heath [etc.]. (30 Geo. III. 1 April 1790.)　　　　　　F° [*London*, 1790]

1794. An Act to amend and enlarge the Powers of [the Paving] Act... (34 Geo. III. 23 May 1794.)　　　　　　　　1794

Published with a re-issue of the Paving Act (1788). Interleaved copy, with notes, bearing the stamps of the 'Surveyor's Office, Cambridge Improvement Acts' and of 'R. R. Rowe, Architect and Civil Engineer, Cambridge.'

ACTS AND BILLS.

1797. An Act for dividing, allotting, and laying in severalty the common and open fields...within the parish of Great Wilbraham in the county of Cambridge. (37 Geo. III. 25 May 1797.)
F° [*London*, 1797]

1797. A Bill for dividing, allotting, inclosing, and laying in severalty the common and open fields...within the parish of Little Wilbraham in the county of Cambridge. (Annotated proof.)
F° [*London*, 1797]

1797. An Act for...Little Wilbraham [as above]. (37 Geo. III. 25 May 1797.)
F° [*London*, 1797]

1801. An Act for extinguishing the Rights of Common...over... Saint Thomas's Leys, otherwise Pembroke Leys... (41 Geo. III. 2 July 1801.)
F° [*London*, 1801]

1806. An Act to continue and amend two Acts...for repairing the road from Newmarket to Stump Cross... (46 Geo. III. 12 July 1806.)
F° [*London*, 1806]

1813. An Act for extending and amending an Act...for making the River Cham more navigable. (52 Geo. III. 21 July 1813.)
12° [1813?]

Published with the Act of 1703, *see above*.

1815. An Act for more effectually repairing the road from Jesus Lane in the town of Cambridge, to the first Rubbing House on Newmarket Heath. (55 Geo. III. 12 May 1815.)
F° [*London*, 1815]

1822. An Act to authorize the sale and conveyance of ground for the enlargement of the Public Library and Lecture Rooms in the University of Cambridge, and for the erection of an Astronomical Observatory...and of a Museum for the preservation of the pictures, books, and other articles bequeathed...by Richard Viscount Fitzwilliam, deceased. (3 Geo. IV. 24 June 1822.) F° *London*, 1822

1823. An Act for effecting an exchange between...King's College... and...Clare Hall. (4 Geo. IV. 30 May 1823.)
F° [*London*, 1823]

1823. An Act to amend an Act...intituled An Act for vesting certain...land...belonging to Sidney Sussex College...in trustees for sale... (4 Geo. IV. 4 July 1823.) F° [*London*, 1823]

1825. An Act to repeal an Act...to enable the Master, Fellows, and Scholars of Clare Hall to vary the benefaction of Doctor Blyth. (6 Geo. IV. 22 June 1825.) F° [*London*, 1825]

1828. An Act for inclosing lands in the parish of Litlington... (9 Geo. IV. 3 April 1828.) F° *London*, 1828

1834. A Bill (as amended by the Committee) to remove certain disabilities which prevent some classes of His Majesty's subjects from resorting to the Universities. (5 Will. IV. 2 July 1834.)
F° [*London*, 1834]

1845. An Act for consolidating in one Act certain provisions usually inserted in Acts authorizing the making of Railways. (8 Vict. 8 May 1845.) F° *London*, 1848

ACTS AND BILLS.

1845. An Act for consolidating in one Act certain provisions usually inserted in Acts authorizing the taking of Lands for Undertakings of a public nature. (8 Vict. 8 May 1845.)   Fᵒ *London*, 1851

1846. An Act to amend the Cambridge Improvement Acts, and to exempt the Eastern Counties Railway Company from certain Tolls thereby imposed. (9 and 10 Vict. 3 Aug. 1846.) [*London*, 1846]

1847. An Act for consolidating in one Act certain provisions usually contained in Acts with respect to the Constitution and Regulation of Bodies of Commissioners appointed for carrying on Undertakings of a public nature. (10 Vict. 23 April 1847.)   Fᵒ *London*, 1851

1851. An Act for repealing and amending the provisions of the Acts relating to the navigation of the River Cam or Cham, alias Grant... (14 and 15 Vict. 24 July 1851.)   Fᵒ *London*, 1851

The last two Acts (1847 and 1851) and those of 1845 are bound in one volume, formerly the property of the County Conservator, together with an Index (printed by Hall of Cambridge), and the Bye-Laws made by the Conservators of the Cam (printed by Naylor of Cambridge).

1854. An Act to make further provision for the good government and extension of the University of Oxford...and of the College of Saint Mary Winchester. (17 and 18 Vict. 7 Aug. 1854.)
     Fᵒ *London*, 1854

1855-6. A Bill intituled An Act to make further provision for the good government of the University of Cambridge...and of the College...at Eton. 30 March 1855.   Fᵒ *London*, 1855
—— As amended in Committee. 24 April 1855. Fᵒ *London*, 1855
—— As amended on Report. 12 June 1855. Fᵒ *London*, 1855
—— 14 March 1856.   Fᵒ *London*, 1856

1856. An Act [as above]. (19 and 20 Vict. 29 July 1856.)
     Fᵒ *London*, 1856

1856. A Bill to confirm an Award for the settlement of matters in difference between the University and Borough of Cambridge. April, 1856.   Fᵒ [*London*, 1856]
—— As amended in Committee. May, 1856. Fᵒ [*London*, 1856]

1856. An Act [as above]. (19 and 20 Vict. 5 June 1856.)
     Fᵒ *London*, 1857

1861. An Act to provide that votes at Elections for the Universities may be recorded by means of voting papers. (24 and 25 Vict. 1 Aug. 1861.)   Fᵒ *London*, 1861

1863. A Bill for stopping up certain streets [St John's Lane, etc.], and widening other streets in Cambridge. (26 Vict.) Fᵒ [*London*, 1863]
The Act received the Royal Assent, 4 May 1863.

1876. A Bill...for making further provision respecting the...University of Oxford and the Colleges therein. (39 Vict. 24 Feb. 1876.)   Fᵒ [*London*, 1876]

1876. A Bill to make further provision respecting the University of Cambridge and the Colleges therein. (39 Vict. 16 May 1876.)
     Fᵒ [*London*, 1876]

ACTS AND BILLS.

1877. A Bill to make further provision respecting the Universities of Oxford and Cambridge and the Colleges therein. (40 Vict. 9 Feb. 1877.)   F° [*London*, 1877]

1877. An Act to make further provision respecting the Universities of Oxford and Cambridge and the Colleges therein. (40 and 41 Vict. 10 Aug. 1877.)   F° *London*, 1877

1895. A Bill to enable the Master, Professors, Fellows, and Scholars of Downing College...to sell...part of their estate.... (58 Vict. 27 June 1895.)   F° *London* (1895)

ADAM (J.) R. A. Neil. A memorial article. (*Camb. Review.*) (1901)

E. S. Shuckburgh. A memorial article.   (1906)

The doctrine of the celestial origin of the Soul from Pindar to Plato. (*Praelections.*)   1906

Religious Teachers of Greece. Ed., with memoir, by A. M. Adam.
Edinburgh, 1908

ADAMI (J.G.) Physiological bearing of waist-belts and stays. (*National Review*, Nov. 1888.)

ADAMS (J.C.) An account of the discovery [by J. C. A.] of the new Planet. By J. Challis.   4° 1846

Proposal to found a Prize in his honour, 30 March 1848. 4° (1848)

John Couch Adams. By D. MacAlister. (*Eagle.*)   1892

Life. By J. W. L. Glaisher. (From *Collected Sci. Papers.*) 4° 1897

Catalogue of a collection of...books bequeathed to the University Library, by J. C. Adams.   1902

ADAMS (R.N.) The Qualifications for the Christian ministry. Commencement Sermon, July 4, 1830.   1830

ADDENBROOKE'S HOSPITAL.

Rules and orders of the public Infirmary.   1766

—— Another edition.   4° 1770

A form of prayer for the use of Addenbrooke's Hospital.   (1770)

State for the year ending Michaelmas 1771.   4° 1771

—— 1777.   4° 1777

—— 1781.   4° 1781

—— 1782.   4° 1782

For later Reports see below, 1857, etc.

Programme of Concert for benefit of Addenbrooke's Hospital, 30 June 1803.   4° 1803

—— 30 June 1808.   1808

Advertisement of Sermon and Anthem for benefit of Hospital, 27 June 1811.   4° 1811

—— 2 July 1812.   4° 1812

—— 1 July 1813.   4° 1813

Programme of Musical Festival on occasion of opening the new Wards, July 1824.   F° 1824

Cambridge Grand Musical Festival for the benefit of Addenbrooke's Hospital. Three concerts in the Senate House, June 28, 30, July 1.   1828

ADDENBROOKE'S HOSPITAL.
  Report of some cases of operation. By G. M. Humphry. *London*, 1856
  State for year ended Michaelmas 1857. 4° 1857
  Annual Report 1880, 1881, 1886, 1887, 1889–1909. 1880–1909
  Report on proposed changes, by Sir H. C. Burdett. 18 June 1898
  Report of Special Committee on above Report. 30 Sept. With
    fly-sheets. (1898)
  Case for opinion of Counsel respecting scheme of management, with
    opinion. 12 Jan. F° *n.p.* (1899)
  Report of the Committee appointed to consider the...financial position
    of the Hospital. Dec. 1899. (1899)
  Reports of the General Committee, July 1905, Nov. 1905, Feb. 1906,
    May 1906, Aug. 1906, Nov. 1906, Feb. 1907, May 1907, Jan.
    1908. 1905–8
  See also Bayes (W.).
ADDERLEY (*Hon.* J.G.) The fight for the drama at Oxford.
  Oxford, 1888
ADDRESS to the Members of the Senate...on the attention due to
  worth of character from a Religious Society. By a Master of
  Arts [John Gordon, Emmanuel]. *n.p.* 1764
ADDRESS to the Senate of the University, relative to certain pro-
  ceedings which occasionally take place therein on the Lord's Day.
  [By W. Farish.] *London*, 1823
ADIE (R.H.) Syllabus of a course of twelve lectures on Agricultural
  Chemistry. 1891
ADVENTURES of a Cambridge Pro-Proctor. By Bub. 1864
ADVICE to a young student. With a method of study for the four
  first years. [By D. Waterland.] *London*, 1730
ADVICE to the Universities of Oxford and Cambridge. 2nd ed.
  London, 1783
AESCHYLUS. Agamemnon, as played by Oxford Undergraduates
  at St George's Hall, London. 4° *n.p.* 1880
  Agamemnon, translated by W. Headlam. *London*, 1904
  See also Greek plays at Cambridge.
AGENDA; a religious and social review. Vol. I, no. I; Vol. III,
  no. 2. [Ed. by F. J. M. Stratton, Gonv. and Caius.] 1907–9
AINGER (A.) Testimonials when a candidate for the Clark Lecture-
  ship in English Literature. 1883
AINGER (A.C.) Eton Songs. 4° *London*, 1891–2
AINGER (W.) Commencement Sermon, 30 June 1822. 1822

  Circular soliciting subscriptions to bust of W. A., 12 Jan. 1841. 4° 1841
  Circular to subscribers to bust, March 1842. 4° 1842

AINSLIE (G.) Historical account of the Oaths and Subscriptions
  required in the University. (2 copies.) 1833
AIRY (*Sir* G.B.) On the draft of proposed new Statutes for Trinity
  College. 1859

  Obituary notice. By E. J. Routh. (*Proc. Roy. Soc.*) *London*, 1892
  Autobiography. Ed. by W. Airy. 1896

ALBERT, *Prince Consort.*

Address, inviting him to stand as Chancellor, with his reply, and other official papers respecting his election.   F° 1847

Poll on his election as Chancellor. (2 eds.)   1847

Ode, by William Wordsworth, performed in the Senate House, July 6, 1847, at the first Commencement after the Installation of Prince Albert.   4° 1847

—— Another ed., illuminated.   4° *London,* 1847

Per l' inaugurazione di sua altezza reale il Principe Alberto, all' officio di Cancelliere...canzone. [By the Marchese Spineto.]   1847

Accounts of his Election and Installation (*Camb. Chron., Illustr. London News, Punch,* etc.), with various notices, cards, programmes, etc.   F° 1847

—— Another series.   1847

Recollections of the Installation. By Anna H. Potts.   F° 1847

Congratulatory lines... By John Peat.   4° 1847

A few plain truths, or the late proceedings at Cambridge reviewed. By Philo Patria. (On the Chancellorship.)   *London,* 1847

Vice-Chancellor's notice that the Prince has presented a portrait of himself, 21 April, 1849; with Grace to accept, 25 April 1849.   F° 1849

The Chancellor's Letter to the Vice-Chancellor on the approaching Royal Commission, 27 May 1850.   F° 1850

Funeral Sermon, Dec. 23, 1861. By J. A. Jeremie.   1862

—— By J. G. Howes.   1862

Quis desiderio sit pudor aut modus tam cari capitis? [By W. Selwyn.]   1862

A few remarks on the most fitting material and site for the memorial statue to our late Chancellor. By a Member of the Cambridge Committee [T. Worsley].   1862

Fly-sheets, etc., on the Memorial to the Prince Consort.   1862

Cambridge University Memorial to H.R.H. the Prince Consort, Chancellor, 22 Jan. 1878. List of Subscribers.   4° 1878

University Memorial of the Prince Consort. Proceedings at the unveiling of the statue, 22 Jan. 1878. (*Reporter,* Feb. 4, 1878.)

ALBUMAZAR; a comedy presented before the King's Majesty at Cambridge. By the Gentlemen of Trinity Colledge. [By J. Tomkis.] (Bowes 2910.)   4° *London,* 1634

ALDIS (H.G.) The organisation and methods of the Cambridge University Library. (*Lib. Assoc. Record.*)   *London,* 1905

ALDIS (W.S.) University Tests.   1870

ALFORD (H.) Prælectio theologica.   4° 1850

"Audi alteram partem." A reply to a recent article in the *Christian Remembrancer.*   *London,* 1851

ALI. Sentences. Transl. by S. Ockley, and repr. by C. Sayle.   12° 1902

ALL SAINTS' CHURCH. Order of service...on laying the corner stone, 27 May.   1863

All Saints' Memorial Cross. Subscriptions, etc.   F° 1882

ALLBUTT (*Sir* T.C.)   Inaugural address...as Regius Professor of
  Physic.   (*Brit. Med. Jour.*)   *London,* 1892
Science and Medieval Thought.   (Harveian Oration, 1900.)
                                                     London, 1901
  Notes on the composition of Scientific Papers.   *London,* 1904
ALLEN (A.J.C.)   The freedom of the so-called " Free Churches."
                                                     London, 1905
ALLEN (John)   The dormant energies of our Universities.   A letter
  to the Bishop of Oxford.   *London,* 1862
ALLEN (Joseph), *Bp of Ely.*   The correspondence between the
  Ecclesiastical Commissioners and the Bishop of Ely (J. A.).
                                                     London, 1837
  A sermon preached at the consecration of the Church of St Andrew
  the Great, Cambridge, Oct. 19, 1843.   *London,* 1843
ALLEN (T.W.)   Application and testimonials for the Regius Pro-
  fessorship of Greek at Oxford.   4° *n.p.* 1908
ALMA MATER ; or seven years at the University of Cambridge.
  By a Trinity man [J. M. F. Wright].   2 vols.   (Bowes 1718.)
                                                     London, 1827
ALMA MATER.   Nos. 1-5.   Nov. 29, 1899–March 7, 1900.
                                                     4° 1899–1900
ALMOND (A.G.)   Cambridge robes and college gowns.   1909
ALTY (J.)   Epitaph.   4° *n.p.* 1815
ALUMNI Cantabrigienses.   By W. J. Harvey.   (Specimen.)   1891
AMATEUR Art Exhibition...at the Lion Hotel, 1855.   Catalogue.
                                                     4° 1855
AMATEUR DRAMATIC CLUB.
  Programmes, Menus, Letters, 1855-1909.   1855–1909
  The Seventh Shot.   By F. C. Burnand and M. Williams.   (Per-
  formed at A.D.C. Nov. 1860.)   1860
  Alonzo the Brave.   By F. C. Burnand.   3rd ed.   (Performed at
  A.D.C. May 1857, etc.)   1861
  Aladdin ; or the Wonderful Scamp.   By H. J. Byron.   (Performed
  at A.D.C. Nov. 1862.)   *London,* 1862
  —— (Performed at A.D.C. June 1864.)   *London,* 1864
  —— (Performed at A.D.C. Nov. 1867.)   1867
  The Maid and the Magpie.   By H. J. Byron.   (Performed at
  A.D.C. 1863.)   *London,* 1863
  Fra Diavolo.   By H. J. Byron.   (Performed at A.D.C. March 1864.)
                                                     London, 1864
  The Critic.   Ed. by J. W. Clark.   (Performed at A.D.C. Nov. 1864.)
                                                     London (1864)
  —— (Performed at A.D.C. Nov. 1882.)   1882
  —— (Performed at A.D.C. Nov. 1908.)   1908
  Ruy Blas.   Drama in 4 acts adapted from Victor Hugo [by J. W.
  Clark] for representation at A.D.C. 3 June 1867.   1867
  The Rivals.   [Ed. by J. W. Clark.]   (Performed at A.D.C.
  1868.)   *London,* 1868
  —— (Performed at A.D.C. 1895.)   1895

AMATEUR DRAMATIC CLUB.

Ivanhoe. By H. J. Byron. (Performed at A.D.C. 1868.) *n.p.* 1868
Paris. By F. C. Burnand. (Performed at A.D.C. May 1869.) 1869
—— (Performed at A.D.C. May 29, 1871.) 1871
The Lyons Mail. [Ed by J. W. Clark.] (Performed at A.D.C. Nov. 1870.) *London,* 1870
—— (Performed at A.D.C. 1895.) 1895
Peer? or Peasant? By J. W. Clark. (Performed at A.D.C. May 29, 1871.) 1871
The A.D.C. and the Tutors. Alteration in Rules, with letters on the subject, 1871–8. 4° 1871–8
Personal Reminiscences. By F. C. Burnand. (*Ours,* No. 1. May 1878.)
Personal Reminiscences. By F. C. Burnand. *London,* 1880
Rules, Regulations, etc. Easter Term, 1886; Lent Term, 1887; Lent Term, 1891; Lent and Oct. Terms, 1892; Lent Term, 1893; Lent Term, 1894; Lent Term, 1895; Lent Term, 1897; Easter Term, 1898. 1886–98
King Henry the Fourth, Part I. Arranged by J. W. Clark. (Performed at A.D.C., Michaelmas Term, 1886.) 1886
Jupiter, LL.D. By R. C. Lehmann. (Performed at A.D.C. May 1894.) (1894)
The A.D.C. By A. H. Marshall. (*Pall Mall Mag.,* Aug., Sep. 1896.)
Money. By Sir E. Bulwer Lytton. (Performed at A.D.C. June 1897.) 1897
Medea. By J. R. Planché. Book of Words. Feb. 1898. (1898)
—— June 1898. (1898)
The Ballad-Monger. (Performed at A.D.C. June 1898.) (Type-written.) 4°
The A.D.C., Cambridge. By W. G. Elliot. (From his *Amateur Clubs and Actors.*) (*London,* 1898)
Treasurer's Accounts, 1900. 4° 1900
Jubilee. Notices, Press reports, etc. 1905
The Newmenides, or why Orestes left home. (Performed at A.D.C. 7 Dec. 1906. A parody on the Eumenides, performed at the New Theatre, 30 Nov.–4 Dec. 1906.) (Type-written.) 4° 1906
Fellow or Felon? or the Master and the Miscreant. By 'Thomas Wentworth' and 'William Brown' [i.e. T. W. Pym and D. A. Winstanley.] (Acted at A.D.C. Feb. and Dec. 1909.) 1909
—— Type-written copy. 4°
See also, for programmes, Cambridge Papers.
AMATEUR Musical Society. Words of Concerts, 20 May 1868; 19 May 1869; 25 May 1870; 22 Dec. 1870; 7 March 1872; 25 March 1874; 20 May 1874. 1868–74
('Cambridge Musical Society') Words of Concerts, 3 June 1875; 25 Nov. 1875; 14 Nov. 1876; 20 Nov. 1878; 19 May 1879. 1875–9
AMATEUR Vocal Guild. Programme of Concert, Feb. 22. 1872

AMBULATOR, or the Stranger's Guide through Cambridge. (Bowes 1875.) 1835

AMERICAN Lectureship offered by H. Y. Thompson, 1865–66, with fly-sheets relating thereto. 1865–6

AMOS (A.) and Hough (W.W.) Cambridge Mission to South London. 1904

AMOS (Andrew) An introductory lecture on the Laws of England, delivered in Downing College, Oct. 23, 1850. 1850

A lecture on County Courts. 1851

An introductory lecture on the Law of Property. 1853

AMOS (S.) Oratio Latina præmio annuo dignata. (Members' Prize.) 1858

AMPHITHEATRE. Plan for an amphitheatre for musick and public lectures in Cambridge. F° 1768

ANATOMICAL Museum. A descriptive Catalogue, etc. (By Sir B. Harwood.) [ab. 1800]

Catalogue. (By William Clark.) (2 copies.) 1820

Catalogue of the osteological portion of the specimens contained in the Anatomical Museum. By William Clark. 1862

Analysis of the physiological series in the Gallery of the Museum of Comparative Anatomy. By G. M. Humphry. (1866)

Notes on the anthropological collection in the Museum of Human Anatomy. By W. L. H. Duckworth. 1899

ANATOMICAL Schools. Riot at the Anatomical Schools. (*Camb. Chron.*, Dec. 6, 1833.)

ANATOMY (Professorship of) Poll for the election of a Professor of Anatomy, Nov. 23, 1814. (J. Haviland elected.) 1814

ANCOURT (*Abbé* d') The lady's preceptor. Taken from the French of the Abbé d'Ancourt, and adapted to the English nation. By a Gentleman of Cambridge. 4th ed. *London*, 1752

ANDERSON-MORSHEAD (A.E.M.) The history of the Universities' Mission to Central Africa, 1859–1898. 3rd ed. *London*, 1902

ANDREW (St) the Great. History of church and parish, by Rev. J. Morgan. 12° 1910

ANDREW (St) the Less. British Empire Bazaar, 16, 17 Oct. 1901

ANGLESEA Abbey. Auctioneer's description. F° *n.p.* 1870

ANNINGSON (B.) On the progress of medicine since the time of Dr Caius. (Thruston Speech.) *London*, 1879

Report on the sanitary condition of the Cambridge Improvement Act district, June 1–Dec. 31. 1875

—— Jan. 1–Dec. 31. 1876–80

ANSELL (T.) Authentic narrative of proceedings against the W[estminste]r Club. [More probably by T. Francklin.] *London*, 1751

ANSON (F.H.) Report on disposal of sewage. F° *n.p.* 1885

ANSTED (D.T.) Geology as a branch of education. *London*, 1845

The correlation of the natural history sciences. (Rede Lecture.) 1863

ANSTEY (C.) Poetical Works. With some account of the author, by John Anstey. 4° *London*, 1808

ANSTEY (H.)   Munimenta Academica.   (Oxford.)   Parts 1, 2.
(Rolls ser.)   *London, 1868*
ANTHEMS.   A collection of all the Anthems us'd in King's College
Chappel, Trinity College Chappel, etc.   (Ed. by T. Tudway.)
1706
ANTI-PATER.   Hints to Paterfamilias.   1861
ANTI-SNARL.   No. 1.   Nov. 4, 1899.   4° 1899
ANTIQUARIAN Committee.   Report to the Senate (Oct. 22, 1884).
4° 1884
First (—twenty-third) Annual Report.   4° 1885–1908
ANTIQUARIAN SOCIETY.
*** *See* Bowes, pp. 354–6, *and lists included in annual List of Members.*
Reports, 1841–1909.   1841–1909
Publications.   Quarto series.   2 vols.   1840–1850.   4° 1846–62
Quarto Publications.   New series, 1–2.   4° 1908–9
Catalogue of coins, Roman and English, in the Museum of the
C.A.S., 1847.   1847
Publications.   Octavo series, 1–36, 38–44.   1851–1908
Antiquarian Communications : being papers presented at the meetings
of the C.A.S.   Vols. I–VI.   (Vol. III has a Suppl. in folio.)
1859–91
Proceedings of the C.A.S., with Communications.   N.S. I–XIII.
1893–1909
List of Members, 1879–1909.   1879–1909
Catalogue of the first exhibition of University and College Portraits
held in the Fitzwilliam Museum, May 1884.   First issue.   1884
—— Third issue.   1884
Catalogue of the second exhibition of University and College Portraits
held in the Fitzwilliam Museum, May 1885.   First issue.   1885
—— Second issue.   1885
Papers read at a joint meeting of the Essex Archæological Society and
the Cambridge Antiquarian Society, May 24, 1889.   1889
Catalogue of the Loan Collection of Plate, exhibited May 1895.
1895
—— Illustrated ed.   4° 1896
Report of the executive committee on the exhibition of Old Plate
held in the Fitzwilliam Museum, May 1895   1896
History of Cambridgeshire (Parishes).   Prospectus, and First Memo-
randum.   1899
Catalogue of first exhibition of Portraits in C.A.S. Collection, and
Cambridge Caricatures to 1840.   1908
APPEAL.   An inquiry into the right of Appeal from the Chancellor or
Vice-Chancellor of the University of Cambridge, in matters of
discipline.   [By T. Chapman.]   *London, 1751*
—— 2nd ed.   *London, 1752*
The opinion of an eminent lawyer [P. Yorke, afterwards Earl of
Hardwicke] concerning the right of Appeal from the Vice-
Chancellor of Cambridge, to the Senate.   By a Fellow of a College
[R. Hurd].   (Bowes 1206.)   *London, 1751*

APPEAL.
A further inquiry into the right of Appeal. [By T. Chapman.]
London, 1752
A letter to the author of *A further inquiry into the right of Appeal...*
[By John Smith, King's.]   *London*, 1752
Some considerations on the necessity of an Appeal in the University
of Cambridge. [By M. Hodgson.]   *London*, 1752
See also Regulations (1750–2).
APPEAL to the University on the subject of their Examinations...
London, 1836
APPLEYARD (E.S.) Letters from Cambridge.   *London*, 1828
APPOINTMENTS Association. Report of Meeting, Nov. 4, 1899.
4° 1899
APPOINTMENTS Gazette. Vol. 1, nos. 1–26.   4° 1899–1909
AQUATIC Notes, or sketches of the rise and progress of rowing at
Cambridge. By J. F. B[ateman].   1852
ARBUTHNOT (J.) Critical Remarks on Capt. Gulliver's Travels.
By Dr Bantley [*sic*].   1735
ARCANA: or the principles of the late petitioners to Parliament for
relief in the matter of Subscription. In VIII letters to a friend.
[By Robert Robinson.]   1774
—— New ed.   *Nottingham*, n.d.
ARCHÆOLOGICAL Institute of Great Britain and Ireland.
Annual Meeting 1854, held at Cambridge. (Plan of arrange-
ments, excursions, etc.) 6 pieces.   (1854)
Programme of Meeting held at Cambridge, 1892.   (1892)
ARCHÆOLOGY (Museum of). An account of the proceedings at
the opening of the Museum of Archæology, May 6, 1884; and
Report of the Antiquarian Committee, Oct. 22, 1884.   4° 1884
Catalogue of casts in Museum of Classical Archæology. By C.
Waldstein.   1889
ARCHÆOLOGY (Museum of General and Local) and of Ethnology.
Catalogue of the antiquities contained in the bequest of Walter
K. Foster.   4° 1892
Catalogue of the Antiquarian Collections. Roman Pottery. 1. Local
Collection.   4° 1892
Appeal for a new Museum, Dec. 1906.   4° 1906
—— Nov. 1907.   4° 1907
See also Antiquarian Committee.
ARCHER (T.) A letter to the Earl of Hardwicke on the...Steam
Dredging Engine in deepening the rivers in the Bedford Level.
Ely, 1829
ARCHITECTURAL Notes on German Churches. [By W.Whewell.]
1830
ARCHITECTURAL Society. Reports for 1851 and 1860. 1852–1861
Laws, etc.   1859
Report of the proceedings of the Congress of the Architectural
Society, held at Cambridge, May 28–31.   1860
Appeal for funds for the restoration of Stourbridge Chapel.   1865

ARCULUS. Grecia victrix. A lay of Modern Greece. [By E. W. Bowling, Joh.]   [1891]
ARISTOPHANES. The Frogs. Text and translation, as played by the Oxford Dramatic Soc., 1892.   *Oxford,* 1892
The Wasps adapted for representation at Radley.   *Oxford,* 1905
Programme of The Frogs, as played by the Oxford Dramatic Soc., 1909.   4° *Oxford,* 1909
See also Greek Plays at Cambridge.
ARKWRIGHT (J.H.) A Dream. A ballad, written about the year 1852. (By I. H. A. Etonensis.) (*See* Harcourt's *Eton bibliography,* 1902, p. 48.)   *Windsor,* 1852
ARMADILLO Oct. 1903, June 1904. [Ed. by N. L. Watson, Jesus.]   4° 1903–4
ARMSTRONG (H.E.) Testimonials when a candidate for the Jacksonian Professorship in the University of Cambridge.   (1875)
ARMSTRONG (J.) The history of the navigation of the port of King's-Lyn, and of Cambridge.   F° *London,* 1725
—— Second ed.   F° *London,* 1766
ARMYTAGE (H.) The Cam and Cambridge Rowing.   4° (1887)
ARNALD (W.) The important station of an English University. A sermon preached at Cambridge, Commencement Sunday, 1781.
                                                4° *London,* 1803
ARNOLD (E.V.) College charges on Undergraduates (Trin.).
                                                        1883
To the Master and Fellows of Trinity College. On the College accounts and the taxation of Undergraduates.   4° [*ab.* 1884]
ARNOLD (F.S.) Jordan. (Seatonian Prize Poem for 1883.)   1884
ARNOLD (T.K.) Remarks on Rev. F. Close's Church Architecture scripturally considered.   *London,* 1844
Examination of Rev. F. Close's Reply to Remarks on Church Architecture scripturally considered.   *London,* 1844
ARROWSMITH (J.) An accusation of Dr Arrowsmith, M^r of Johns College in Cambridge. By petition of Robert Waideson, Esq. With the grounds thereof.   4° *n.p.* 1649
ART of losing one's Remove : a treatise; being a preparation to the Art of Pluck. By Scriblerus Etonensis.   *Eton* [*ab.* 1845]
ART of making Tea. A poem.   1797
ARTHUR (L.) *See* Stephen (*Sir* J.).
ARTICLES. *See* Subscription; Tests.
ARTIST'S (An) Rambles in Cambridgeshire. By John S. Clarke. Series 1, 2.   4° 1894
ARTS and Crafts Society. Rules.   1906
ARUNDINES Cami. Ed. H. Drury. Editio altera.   1843
—— Editio quinta.   1860
ASHBURNHAM collection. Cambridge memorial to Trustees of British Museum.   F° 1883
ASCHAM (R.) The Scholemaster. Edited by J. E. B. Mayor.
                                                London, 1863
ASHTON (T.) A sermon preach'd in the Collegiate-Chapel at

ASHTON (T.)
  Eton, 9 Oct. 1746, the day appointed for a General Thanksgiving for
  the suppression of the late unnatural Rebellion. 4° *London*, 1746
  Letter to the Rev. Dr M[orell, on Eton]. 4° *London*, 1771
  Extract from case of the obligation on the electors of Eton College to
  supply all vacancies in that Society with...Fellows of King's
  College, Cambridge. Part 1. 4° *London*, 1771

ASPLAND (R.) Bigotry and Intolerance defeated: or, an account of
  the late prosecution of Mr John Gisburne, Unitarian Minister of
  Soham, Cambs. *Harlow*, 1810

ASQUITH (H.H.) "Eighty Club." Home Rule since 1886.
  Speech at the Lion Hotel, May 3, 1890 *London*, 1890

ASSESSOR to Vice-Chancellor. A reply to the Letter of a Master of
  Arts, inserted in the *Cambridge Chronicle*, Feb. 14, 1852, relating
  to the office of Assessor to the Vice-Chancellor. By one of the
  forty-eight. 1852

ASSOCIATION for the Care of Girls. Report. 1883

ATHENAE Cantabrigienses. Proposal to publish by subscription.
  4° [1829 ?]
  Proposals to print. By J. J. Smith. [*ab.* 1847]
  See also Cooper (C. H.).

ATKINSON (S.) Struggles of a poor student through Cambridge.
  (*London Magazine*, 1 April 1825.)

ATKINSON (T.D.) and Foster (J. E.) Illustrated Catalogue of the
  loan collection of Plate exhibited in the Fitzwilliam Museum,
  May 1895. 4° 1896
  Cambridge described and illustrated. With Introduction by J. W.
  Clark. *London*, 1897

ATTERBURY (F.) Short Review of the Controversy between
  Mr Boyle and Dr Bentley. *London*, 1701

ATWOOD (G.) A description of the experiments intended to
  illustrate a course of lectures on the principles of Natural
  Philosophy, read in the Observatory of Trinity College, Cambridge. *London* (1776)

AUDLEY END. *See* Neville (*Hon.* R. C.).

AUERBACH (B.) The Professor's Wife. [Transl. by W. Whewell.]
  London, 1851

AUFRECHT (T.) Testimonials when a candidate for the Professorship of Sanskrit in the University of Cambridge. 1867

AUSTEN LEIGH (A.) Suggestions to Statutes Committee (King's).
  1872
  King's College. (College histories.) *London*, 1899

  In Memoriam. 4° 1905
  Memoir. By W. Austen Leigh. *London*, 1906

AUSTEN LEIGH (R.A.) A list of Eton College in 1771. *Eton*, 1903
  Eton under Barnard, 1754–1765. *Eton*, 1904
  Illustrated Guide to Eton College. *Eton*, 1904
  —— 2nd ed. *Eton*, 1905

AUSTEN LEIGH (R.A.)
  Bygone Eton.   Pts. i., ii.   Fo *Eton* (1904)
  Bygone Eton.   Re-issue.   Fo *Eton,* 1906
  Bygone King's.   Fo *Eton,* 1907
  See Cambridge A.B.C.   1894.
AUSTEN LEIGH (W.) Augustus Austen Leigh.   *London,* 1906
AUTOBIOGRAPHY of a Cantab. Ed. by W. Mowbray. Nos. 1–5.
                                                            1842
AUXILIARY Bible Society.   *See* Bible Society.
AYLIFFE (J.)   The ancient and present state of the University of
  Oxford.   2 vols.   *London,* 1723

B

BAILLIE (H.D.)   A letter to the Dean of Christ Church, together with a correspondence relating to the removal of Mr Henry Baillie from that College.   *London*, 1823

BAILY (T.)   The Life and Death of John Fisher, Bp of Rochester.
(Bowes 268.)   *London*, 1655

BAINES (E.)   Funeral Sermon on John Stallan, who was executed for arson, at Cambridge, Dec. 7, 1833.   1833
—— Another ed.   1834

BAKER (A.)   The Poor against the Rich.   1910

BAKER (J.)   Military education in connection with the Universities. (4 April.)   1861
Letter to Rev. L. Neville.   (22 April.)   1861
Our Volunteer Army.   1861

BAKER (R.G.)   New Map of the University and town of Cambridge.   folded in 8o (1830)

BAKER (T.)   History of the College of St John the Evangelist, Cambridge.   Ed. by J. E. B. Mayor.   2 vols.   1869

Memoirs.   From the papers of Zachary Grey.   By Robert Masters.   1784
Index to the Baker Manuscripts.   By Four Members of the Cambridge Antiquarian Society [J. J. Smith, C. C. Babington, C. W. Goodwin, J. Power].   1848
See Fisher (J.), *Bp of Rochester,* 1708.

BALDREY (J.K.)   A dissertation on the windows of King's College Chapel, Cambridge.   1818

BALFOUR (A.J.)   The Religion of Humanity.   *Edinburgh*, 1889
Reflections suggested by the new theory of matter.   (Brit. Assoc., 1904.)   *London*, 1904
Decadence.   Henry Sidgwick Memorial Lecture, delivered at Newnham College, 25 Jan. 1908.   1908

BALFOUR (F.M.)   Preliminary account of the development of the elasmobranch fishes.   *London*, 1874
Comparison of the early stages in development of vertebrates.
London, 1875
On the development of the spinal nerves in elasmobranch fishes. (*Trans. Roy. Soc.*, 166.)   4o *London*, 1877
On the phenomena accompanying the maturation and impregnation of the ovum.   (*Q. Journal of Microscopical Science*, April 1878.)

Collection of newspaper-cuttings, letters, circulars, etc., concerning his death (July 1882) and the Balfour Memorial.
See Morphological Laboratory.

BALFOUR (R.)   Physics at Miletus, 625—525 B.C.   1900

Order of Service at his wedding, 10 July 1900.   1900
Some Reminiscences.   (*Dublin Review*, Oct. 1907.)

BALL (A.J.A.)   Business (?) at the Bunion.   1882
BALL (*Sir* R.S.)   Caricature in *The Philistine*, vol. xiv., no. 2.
12o *New York*, 1902

BALL (T.) The life of the renowned Dr Preston. Ed. by E. W.
 Harcourt.   *Oxford*, 1885
BALL (W.W.R.) Letter to the Mathematical Tripos Syndicate,
 October 1877.   4° 1877
 The origin and history of the Mathematical Tripos.   1880
 A history of the study of Mathematics at Cambridge.   1889
 List of Trinity Tutors, 1750–1889.   F° 1889
 On the formation of an Amalgamation Club at Trinity.   1898
 Notes on Trinity College, Cambridge.   1899
 Trinity College, Cambridge.   12° *London*, 1906
 A history of the First Trinity Boat Club.   1908
BALL (Wilfrid) Sketches on the Cam.   Obl. 8° *n.p.* [1884]
BALLY (G.) *See* Seatonian Prize Poems, 1754, 1756, 1758.
BANDINEL (B.) Catalogue of books bequeathed to the Bodleian by
 Richard Gough.   4° *Oxford*, 1814
BANKES (G.N.) A day of my life...at Eton. 2nd ed. *London*, 1877
 About some fellows.   *London*, 1878
 Cambridge trifles.   *London*, 1881
 A Cambridge staircase.   *London*, 1883
BANKING Houses. Declaration of confidence in those at Cambridge.
 Dec. 15, 1825.   F° 1825
BANNOCKBURN. (Unsuccessful Prize Poem. Written for Chan-
 cellor's Medal.)   *n.p.* (1839)
BAPTISM. A brief vindication of Jewel, Hooker, Ussher, Taylor,
 and Pearson from misrepresentations in the recent Baptismal judg-
 ment. By a Fellow of a College.   1850
BAPTISTS. *See* Gould.
BARBER (J.T.) and Morgan (J.H.) Account of Aurora Borealis seen
 near Cambridge.   [1847]
BARBER (R.W.) An East Anglian village (Chippenham). *n.p.* 1897
' BARD of the Forest.' *See* Wickenden (W.).
BARDE (A.C.D.) The narrative or story of Mr Jex Jex of Corpus.
                                                        1864
BARFORD (W.) In Pindari primum Pythium dissertatio.   4° 1751
 Oratio habita in funere Guilielmi George, Coll. Regal. Praepositi, VII°
 Kal. Oct. 1756.   4° 1756
BARHAM (T.F.) Elijah ; a sacred poem.   *London*, 1822
BARING-GOULD (S.) The Chorister.   12° [1854]
 —— 10th ed.   1895
BARKER (E.H.) Literary anecdotes and contemporary reminiscences
 of Prof. Porson, and others. With a Memoir. 2 vols. *London*, 1852
BARNBY (Jos.) Eton Songs. By A. C. Ainger. Music by J.
 Barnby.   4° *London*, 1891–2
BARNE (M.) Sermon preached before the King at White-Hall,
 17 Oct. 1675.   4° *London*, 1675
 Discourse concerning the Nature of Christ's Kingdom...in two
 Sermons.   4° 1682
 Sermon preached before the University of Cambridge, 9 Sept. 1683.
                                                    4° 1683

BARNE (M.)
Sermon preached before the University of Cambridge, 9 Sept. 1683.
4th ed.   4° *London*, 1683
BARNWELL, Abbey District. Appeal for new school premises. 1857
BARNWELL and Chesterton Clergy Fund. Reports for 1883 and
1885.   1884, 1886
Thirty-fourth (—forty-sixth) Annual Report, 1896–1909.
1897–1910
BARNWELL Priory. The history and antiquities of Barnwell Abbey,
and of Sturbridge Fair. [By J. Nichols.]   4° *London*, 1786
The history of Barnwell Abbey, with the origin of Sturbridge Fair.
1806
Some account of Barnwell Priory. By M. Prickett.   1837
Inventories of Religious Houses (including Barnwell Priory). By
M. Walcott. (*Archæologia*, XLIII.)   4° (*London*, 1870)
The Observances in use at the Augustinian Priory at Barnwell.
Ed. by J. W. Clark.   1897
Reviews of same in *Church Quarterly*, Jan. 1898, etc.
Liber Memorandorum ecclesie de Bernewelle.   Ed. by J. W.
Clark. With Introduction by F. W. Maitland. (2 copies.)   1907
Reviews of same, and some letters, 1907–8
BARRINGTON. On a mammaliferous deposit at Barrington. By
O. Fisher. (*Q. Journal Geol. Soc.*, Nov. 1879)
BARROW (I.) Lectiones geometricae.   4° *Londini*, 1670
The usefulness of mathematical learning explained and demonstrated.
Trans. by John Kirkby.   *London*, 1734

Barrow and his academical times as illustrated in his Latin works. By
W. Whewell. (From Barrow's *Works*, IX.)   (1859)

BARROW (J.) The case of Queen's College, Oxford. *Oxford*, 1854
BARRY (A.) Declamation in Trinity College Hall, 16 Dec. 1847.
1848
The Old which is ever New. A sermon.   1889
BARTHOLOMEW (A.T.) and Clark (J.W.) Hand-list of the
works of R. Bentley.   1906
Richard Bentley. A Bibliography.   4° 1908
BARWELL (S.) Sketches from Undergraduate life.   4° 1907
BARWICK (J.) Certain disquisitions...representing to the Conscience
the unlawfulness of the Oath... [By John Barwick and others.]
4° '*Oxford*' [*London*], 1644

Life. By his brother, Peter Barwick.   *London*, 1724

BASHFORTH (F.) Observations on some recent University build-
ings.   1853
BASILEONA. Nos. 1–8. 1 June 1900–March 1903.   4° 1900–3
BASILEON. B' No. 9; Δ No. 11; E No. 12.   4° 1907–10
BASKERVILLE Club. No. 1. Hand-list of books printed by John
Baskerville.   4° 1904

BATESON (M.)   In memoriam, by M. D. Chitty.   1907
  See Borough.   Charters of the Borough, 1901.
  See Grace Book B.
BATESON (W.)   Variation and differentiation.   1903
  The methods and scope of Genetics.   1908
BATESON (W.H.)   In memoriam. By J. E. Sandys.   (*Eagle*.)
     1881
BATTLE of Lake Mort, by the author of The Dauntless Three
  [i.e. A. de L. Hammond, Chr.].   1875
BATTLE of the Bench; or sketches from life.   Cantos ii., iv., v.
  By one of the Unwashed. (Bowes 2071.)   1844
BATTLE of the Pons trium Trojanorum. [By E. W. Bowling, Joh.]
  (*Eagle*.)   1881
BAYES (W.)   Two sides to a question.   1860
  Homœopathy.   An address to the Governors of Addenbrooke's
  Hospital.   1861
  Medical terrorism in 1862.   *London*, 1862
  Remarks upon Abp Whately's letter on Medical Trades-Unions.
     London, 1862
BAYFIELD (M.A.)   The Ion of Euripides.   Transl. by M. A. Bay-
  field.   1890
BAYLEY (H.V.)   Oratio priore praemiorum senioribus baccalaureis
  annuo propositorum donata et in curia Cantab. recitata. (Members'
  Prize.)   4° *Mancunii*, 1802
BAYNE (A.) and Pryme (J.T.)   Memorials of the Thackeray family.
     London, 1879
BAYS (E.)   Researches.   1902
BEAMONT (W.J.)   Letter to the Cambridge University Commis-
  sioners.   1859
  Fine Art as a branch of Academic study.   1863
  Opinions on Fine Art as a branch of liberal education and of Academic
  study.   1864
  Specimens of examination papers in architecture, painting, and
  sculpture.   1865
BEAR. University Magazine. [By G. O. Trevelyan.] No. 1. 3rd ed.
  (Bowes 2320.)   1862
BEARD-SHAVING, and the common use of the razor, an unnatural,
  irrational, unmanly, ungodly, and fatal fashion among Christians.
     London, 1847
BEAU Philosopher. A poem.   By a Gentleman of Cambridge
  [P. Bennet, Magd.]   *London*, 1736
BECK (E.A.)   The Holy Sepulchre. (Seatonian Prize Poem for 1874.)
     Brighton [1874]
BECKINGTON (T.)   Bishop Bekynton. A paper...by the Rev. G.
  Williams.   (1863)
BEDELL (W.)   Life. By his son. Ed. by J. E. B. Mayor. (Cam-
  bridge in the XVIIth century, iii.)   1871
BEDFORD Level. *See* Fens.
BEE-BEE. Passages in the life of an Undergraduate.   *London*, 1887

BEITH (J.H.) Young Blood. By Ian Hay [i.e. J. H. Beith].
2nd ed.   *London*, 1905
BELDAM (J.) The origin and use of the Royston cave. *Royston*, 1858
BELDRAGON : the May Week Magazine. [By M. S. Farmer,
Trin.]   1895
BELL (*Sir* H.) Who pays for Protection ?   1908
BELLAMY (J.W.) Jonah. (Seatonian Prize Poem for 1815.)
                                                 London, 1815.
Treachery of Judas and the failings of the other Apostles consistent
with the divine mission of Jesus Christ. (Norrisian Prize Essay
for 1815.)   1815
BELOE (E.M.) The making of Lynn. A lecture.   *Lynn*, 1891
BELOE (W.) The Sexagenarian, or recollections of a literary life.
2 vols.   *London*, 1817
BENEDICT. (Magazine of Corpus Christi College.) Nos. 1–45.
                                                 1898–1910
BENEDICT'S (St) Church. Enlargement and restoration of St Bene-
dict's Church, Cambridge. (Circular.)   1874
BENEFACTORS. *See* Commemoration.
BENEVOLENT Society. Annual Statement, 17 June, 1806. 1806
Annual Statement, 23 May, 1815.   1815
BENNET (P.) The Beau Philosopher. A poem.   *London*, 1736
Two Sermons...March 16, April 25, 1749.   1749
BENNETT (G.T.) The parallel motion of Sarrut and some allied
mechanisms. (*Philosophical Mag.*, June 1905.)
BENNETT (H.L.) Archbishop Rotherham.   *Lincoln*, 1901
BENNETT (W.S.) *See* Kingsley (Ch.) Ode, 1862.
BENSON (A.C.) Memoirs of Arthur Hamilton. By Christopher
Carr (really by A. C. Benson).   *London*, 1886
The late Master of Trinity (W. H. Thompson). (*Macmillan's Mag.*,
Nov. 1886.)
Thomas Gray.   4° *Eton*, 1895
Fasti Etonenses. A biographical history of Eton.   *Eton*, 1899
The Myrtle Bough.   *Eton*, 1903
The Olive Bough.   *Eton*, 1904
BENSON (E.F.) The Babe, B.A.   *London*, 1897
BENSON (E.W.) The praise of George Herbert. An Oration. 1851
BENTHAM (J.) A catalogue of the principal members of the Con-
ventual and Cathedral Church of Ely.   4° 1756
Extract of a letter from Mr Bentham, concerning certain discoveries
in Ely Minster. (*Archaeologia*, II.)   4° (*London*, 1773)
The history and antiquities of the Conventual and Cathedral Church
of Ely. 2nd ed.   4° *Norwich*, 1812
A supplement to the second edition of Mr Bentham's History and
antiquities of the Cathedral and Conventual Church of Ely. By
William Stevenson.   4° *Norwich*, 1817
BENTLEY (R.)
⁎⁎ *As a complete bibliography of Bentley, and of the various controversies
in which he was engaged, has been published (Camb. 1908), it has been*

BENTLEY (R.)

*considered sufficient to give brief entries only of his own productions
under his name in this catalogue. The works of his adversaries will be
found under their respective names. See also* Trinity College. *The
numbers following the entries are those of the Bibliography, see* p. 24.

Epistola ad cl. v. Joannem Millium, S.T.P. [On Malelas.] (137)
                                   (*Oxford,* 1691)

—— Another ed. (146)   1713

The Folly of Atheism. Sermon, 7 March 1691–2. (1)
                            4° *London,* 1692

—— 2nd ed. (2) 4° *London,* 1692

—— 3rd ed. (3) 4° *London,* 1692

—— 4th ed. (4) 4° *London,* 1693

Matter and Motion cannot Think. Sermon, 4 April 1692. 2nd ed.
(7) 4° *London,* 1692

—— Another issue. (8) 4° *London,* 1693

—— 3rd ed. (9) 4° *London,* 1693

Confutation of Atheism from Structure and Origin of Humane Bodies.
  Pt I. Sermon, 2 May 1692. (12) 4° *London,* 1692

—— 2nd ed. (13) 4° *London,* 1693

—— 3rd ed. (14) 4° *London,* 1693

—— Pt II. Sermon, 6 June 1692. (15) 4° *London,* 1692

—— 2nd ed. (16) 4° *London,* 1693

—— Pt III. Sermon, 5 Sept. 1692. 2nd ed. (19) 4° *London,* 1692

—— 3rd ed. (20) 4° *London,* 1694

Confutation of Atheism from Origin and Frame of the World Pt I.
  Sermon, 3 Oct. 1692. (21) 4° *London,* 1692

—— Pt II. Sermon, 7 Nov. 1692. (23) 4° *London,* 1693

—— Pt III. Sermon, 5 Dec. 1692. (24) 4° *London,* 1693

Folly and Unreasonableness of Atheism. Eight Sermons. 4th ed.
(26) 4° *London,* 1699

—— 5th ed. (27)   1724

—— 6th ed., with additions. (28)   1735

Of Revelation and the Messias. Sermon at Publick Commencement,
  5 July, 1696. (2 copies.) (34) 4° *London,* 1696

A Dissertation upon the Epistles of Phalaris, etc. (Appended to
  W. Wotton's *Reflections upon Ancient and Modern Learning.*
  2nd ed.) (94)   *London,* 1697

A Dissertation upon the Epistles of Phalaris. With an answer to
  the objections of the Hon. C. Boyle. (109)   *London,* 1699

—— Another ed., by S. Salter. (110)   *London,* 1777

—— Another ed. (111)   *London,* 1816

—— A new ed. (Salter's). (112)   *London,* 1817

Emendationes ad Ciceronis Tusculanas. (Appendix to J. Davies's ed.)
(140)   (1709)

The present state of Trinity College in Cambridg, in a letter from
  Dr Bentley to the Bishop of Ely. (205)   *London,* 1710

—— 2nd ed. (206)   *London,* 1710

Q. Horatius Flaccus ex recensione R. Bentleii. (149) 4° 1711

BENTLEY (R.)
—— Ed. alt. (150)   4° *Amst.* 1713
—— Ed. tertia. (151)   4° *Amst.* 1728
Q. Horatius Flaccus ad nuperam R. Bentleii editionem accurate
  expressus. Notas addidit T. Bentleius. (152)   1713
Dr Bentley's Dedication of Horace translated. (156)
                                              12° *London* (1712)
—— 3rd ed. (157)   12° *London* [? 1712]
The Life of Horace, with Dr Bentley's Preface, Latin and English.
  (158)   12° *London* (1712)
The Odes [etc.] of Horace, in Latin and English. With a trans-
  lation of Dr Bentley's notes. By several hands. 2 vols. (159)
                                        12° *London*, 1712–13
—— 2nd ed. (160)   12° *London*, 1719
Horatius Reformatus: sive emendationes omnes quibus editio Bent-
  leiana a vulgaribus distinguitur summa fide in unum collectæ.
  Editio alt. (163)   *Londini*, 1712
—— Another edition.   *Quedlinburgi*, 1825
Aristarchus ampullans in Curis Horatianis. (164) *Londini*, 1712
Five Extraordinary Letters...to Dr B. on his Horace. (165)
                                              London, 1712
Emendationes in Menandri et Philemonis reliquias, ex nupera editione
  Jo. Clerici. Ed. alt. (146)   1713
Remarks upon a late *Discourse of Free-Thinking*: in a letter to
  F[rancis] H[are]. By Phileleutherus Lipsiensis [R. Bentley]. (49)
                                              London, 1713
—— 5th ed. (53)   *London*, 1716–17
—— 6th ed. (54)   1725
—— 7th ed. (55)   1737
—— 8th ed. (56)   1743
Sermon upon Popery, preach'd before the University of Cambridge,
  5 Nov. 1715. (36)   1715
  Remarks on the *Sermon*. [By J. Cumming.] (38) *London*, 1716
  Reflections on the *Remarks*. (41)   *London*, 1717
Sermon preached before His Majesty King George...February 3,
  1716–17. (44)   4° *London*, 1717
—— Another ed. (43)   *London*, 1717
Two letters to Dr Bentley concerning his intended edition of the
  Greek Testament. Together with the Doctor's answer. (70)
                                              London, 1717
Dr Bentley's Proposals for printing a new edition of the Greek Testa-
  ment. By a member of Trinity College. [By Bentley himself.]
  (78)   4° *London*, 1721
Letter to R. Bentley on his Proposals. By Philalethes. (81)
                                          4° *London*, 1721
—— 2nd ed. (82)   4° *London*, 1721
Terentii Comoediæ [etc.] ex recensione R. Bentleii. (175) 4° 1726
—— Ed. alt. (176)   4° *Amsterdam*, 1727
An Argument to prove that the xxxixth section of the Lth chapter

BENTLEY (R.)
of the Statutes given by Q. Elizabeth...includes the Old Statutes...
[By J. Burford.] Together with a Reply to the Argument.
[By R. Bentley.] (241)   4° *London*, 1727
The Case of Trinity College. (242)   4° *London*, 1729
The Lord Bp. of Ely, Plaintiff in Error; Dr R. Bentley, Defendant.
The Case of the Plaintiff. With an Appendix. (248-9)
                                                 F° (*London*, 1732)
Emendations on the Twelve Books of Milton's Paradise Lost. (258)
                                                   London, 1732
A friendly letter to Dr Bentley, occasion'd by his new edition of
Paradise Lost. By a Gentleman of Christ-Church College, Oxon.
[Attr. to Z. Pearce.] (259)   *London*, 1732
A review of the Text of Milton's Paradise Lost: in which the chief
of Dr Bentley's Emendations are consider'd. [By Z. Pearce.]
(262)   *London*, 1732-3
M. Manilii Astronomicon ex recensione R. Bentleii. (183)
                                                  4° *Londini*, 1739
—— Another ed.   *Venetiis*, 1788
Académiques de Cicéron [transl. by D. Durand], avec les conjectures
de M. Bentley.   *Londres*, 1740
Lucani Pharsalia, cum notis Bentleii. (Ed. by R. Cumberland.) (193)
                                               4° *Strawberry Hill*, 1760
Phaedri Fabularum libri v. Acc. Publii Syri et aliorum Sententiæ,
ex recensione R. Bentleii.   12° *Etonæ*, 1789
Epistolae. Ed. by C. Burney. (279)   4° *London*, 1807
Works. Ed. by A. Dyce. 3 vols. (267)   *London*, 1836-8
Correspondence. Ed. by C. Wordsworth. 2 vols. (285)
                                                   London, 1842

Vita et colloquia R. Bentleii. (166)   *Londini*, 1712
Life. By J. H. Monk. (298)   4° *London*, 1830
—— 2nd ed. 2 vols. (299)   *London*, 1833
Richard Bentley. Von J. Maehly. (303)   *Leipzig*, 1868
Bentley. By R. C. Jebb. (306)   *London*, 1882
Hand-list of his works, etc. By A. T. Bartholomew and J. W. Clark. 1906
Bibliography of R. Bentley. By A. T. Bartholomew and J. W. Clark. 1908

BENTON (G.M.) Monumental Brasses now existing in Cambs.
[Reprint from Conybeare's *Rides round Cambridge*.]   1902
The Norman Font in St Peter's Church, Cambridge. (*Antiquary*,
Oct. 1910.)
BERESFORD (H.S.) The Death of Absalom. (Seatonian Prize
Poem for 1824.)   1825
BERESFORD HOPE (A.J.) On modern memoir writing. An
oration delivered in Trinity College Chapel, Dec. 14, 1840,
being Commemoration Day.   1840
Was George Villiers, first Duke of Buckingham, or Cardinal de
Richelieu, more deserving of the name of great?   (1840)
Essays.   *London*, 1844

BERESFORD HOPE (A.J.)
The new Government scheme of Academical education for Ireland
considered.   *London*, 1845
The condition and prospects of Architectural Art.   *London*, 1863
Speech on the second reading of the Bill to abolish Tests, 2 July 1868.
                                                        London, 1868
BERKENHOUT (J.)   A volume of letters from Dr Berkenhout to
his son at the University.   1790
BERNARD (H.H.)   The Easy Practical Hebrew Grammar [P. H.
Mason's and H. H. Bernard's] apostrophising its learned reviewer
(C. B. S[cott]) in No. 4 of the Cambridge *Journal of Classical
and Sacred Philology*.   [1855]
BERNAYS (A.E)   *See* Trinity College.   Inscriptions, 1900.
BERTHA.   [By C. E. Sayle.]   *Oxford*, 1885
BERTIE (Ch.)   *See* Smith (T.).
BESANT (W.)   Life of E. H. Palmer.   *London*, 1883
BEVERIDGE (W.)   Thoughts on Christian education.   *See* Bon-
wicke (A.)   Life, 1834.
BEVERLEY (J.)   An account of the different ceremonies observed
in the Senate House of the University of Cambridge.   1788
The Proceedings in the Court of Delegates on the appeal of William
Frend, M.A.   (1793)
BEVERLEY (R.M.)   A letter to the Duke of Gloucester, on the
present corrupt state of the University of Cambridge. *London*, 1833
—— 2nd ed.   *London*, 1833
—— 3rd ed.   *London*, 1833
A letter to the Rt Hon. H. Goulburn, on the morals and religion of
the University of Cambridge, with reference to a recent letter from
R. M. Beverley to the Duke of Gloucester.   By J. F. Russell.
                                                               1833
The University of Cambridge and the Church of England.   Letter
to Editors of *Leeds Mercury*, 10 Dec. 1833.
Mr Beverley and Cambridge University.   (Article, with extracts
from Beverley's Letter, from *Leeds Mercury*, 14 Dec. 1833.)
Remarks on Mr Beverley's Letter to the Duke of Gloucester.   By a
Member of Trinity College.   1833
A letter to the Duke of Gloucester, in vindication of the University
of Cambridge from the calumnious attacks of R. M. Beverley.
[Attr. to A. Watson.]   1833
A letter to R. M. Beverley from an Undergraduate of the University
of Cambridge.   [? By W. Forsyth.]   1833
Beverley unmaskt...   By Mr Anti-Reform High-Church Orthodox.
                                                             1833
An Anglo-Sapphic ode, dedicated (with French leave) to R. M.
Beverley, entitled, The Friend of Veracity *v.* the Lie Grinder.   Not
by a Can-ning, but a Can-tab.   1833
The Beverlëid, an epic.   By Reginald Bell.   1833
Fulmen Beverleium longè latèque exauditum.   1833
—— Editio nova.   1833

BEVERLEY (R.M.)
A letter to R. M. Beverley containing strictures on his Letter to the
Duke of Gloucester. By F. R. Hall.   1834
Letter to R. M. Beverley, in defence of his Strictures on the Uni-
versity of Cambridge. By an Undergraduate.   1834
Remarks on Mr Beverley's Letter, by Adam Sedgwick. (*Leeds
Mercury*, 18 Jan. 1834.)
Reply to A. Sedgwick, by R. M. Beverley. (*Leeds Mercury*, 25 Jan.
1834.)
[Further] Remarks by Adam Sedgwick. (*Leeds Mercury*, 8 Feb.
1834.)
Letter in *Jersey and Guernsey Record* in defence of the Univ. of
Camb. 22 Feb. 1834.
Letter in *Jersey British Press*, in support of Beverley, 25 Feb. 1834.
Reply to Prof. Sedgwick, by R. M. Beverley. (*Leeds Mercury*,
8 March 1834.)
Reply to Prof. Sedgwick's Letter in the *Leeds Mercury*. London, 1834
—— 3rd ed.   London, 1834
Mr Beverley and Cambridge University. By Edward Stanley.
(*Leeds Mercury*, 22 March 1834.)
The University of Cambridge and Mr Beverley. Signed: An
Undergraduate. (*Leeds Mercury*, 26 April 1834.)
Four letters to the Editors of the *Leeds Mercury*, in reply to R. M.
Beverley. By Prof. Sedgwick.   1836
BIBLE SOCIETY. *See* "Cambridge besieged"; Farish (W.);
Gorham (G. C.); Marsh (H.); Simeon (Ch.); Vansittart (N.).
BICKERDYKE (J.) With the best intentions. A tale of Under-
graduate life at Cambridge.   London, 1884
BICKERSTETH (E.) The Cambridge Mission at Delhi, North
India. (A letter to the Rev. Canon Westcott, D.D.)   1881
BIDDER (G.) By Southern Shore.   *Westminster*, 1899
BIDDULPH (*Lady*) Charles Philip Yorke, 4th Earl of Hardwicke.
London, 1910
BIJOU Theatre. *See* Exhibition of Pictures.
BINGLEY (R.M.) Spray.   1859
BIRCH (G.) Nineveh. (Seatonian Prize Poem for 1850.)   1850
BIRCH (S.) Remarks upon the cover of the granite sarcophagus of
Rameses III in the Fitzwilliam Museum. (*C. A. S.*)   4° 1876
BIRCH (W. de G.) Memorials of St Guthlac of Crowland.
Wisbech, 1881
BIRKS (H.A.) Samuel. (Seatonian Prize Poem for 1890.)   1891
BIRKS (T.R.) Oration on the analogy of mathematical and moral
certainty, delivered in Trinity College Chapel, Dec. 16, 1833.
1834
Faith, Hope, and Charity. (Seatonian Prize Poem for 1843.) 1843
The present importance of Moral Science. Inaugural Lecture.
London, 1872
The Bible and Modern Astronomy. (Vict. Inst., March 5.)
London, 1877

BIRTH of the Prince of Wales.   Unsuccessful Prize Poem.   ("When
  Gomer's Sons.")   [1842 ?]
—— ("Spirit that callest.")   [1842 ?]
BISSET (T.)   Suggestions on University Reform.   *London,* 1850
BLACKALL (O.)   Commencement Sermon, 30 June, 1700.   4° 1700
BLACKBURNE (F.)   Remarks on the Rev. Dr Powell's Sermon in
  defence of Subscriptions.   *London,* 1758
BLACKBURNE (J.)   A brief historical enquiry into the introduction
  of Stone Altars into the Christian Church.   1844
The Stone Altar.   1845
BLACKHALL (S.)   A letter to Dr Hallifax, upon the subject of his
  three discourses preached before the University of Cambridge,
  occasioned by an attempt to abolish Subscription to the 39 Articles.
  2nd ed.   4° 1772
BLACKIE (J.S.)   Thoughts on English University Reform.   (*Mac-
  millan's Magazine,* Dec. 1881.)
BLAGBORNE (J.)   The revenues of the National Universities
  considered, with a view to their being opened to Dissenters, being
  a reply...to the arguments of Dr Turton.   *London,* 1835
BLAKE (H.J.C.)   The Cantab.   *Chichester,* 1845
BLAKENEY (E.H.) and Panton (D.M.)   Poems by two friends. 1892
BLAKENEY (E.P.)   The Exile's Return.   1890
BLAKESLEY (G.H.)   A review of Mr Mill's Essay on Liberty.
  First English Essay Prize, King's College.   1867
BLAKESLEY (J.W.)   Thoughts on the recommendations of the
  Ecclesiastical Commission.   *London,* 1837
Seminaries of sound learning and religious education.   The Com-
  memoration sermon preached in Trinity College Chapel, Dec. 16,
  1839.   1839
Catholicity and Protestantism.   The Commemoration sermon preached
  in Trinity College Chapel, Dec. 16, 1841.   1842
Where does the evil lie?   Observations on the prevalence of private
  tuition in the University of Cambridge.   1845
Praelectio in Scholis Cantab. habita, Feb. 14, 1850.   1850
Real belief and true belief.   A sermon for St Bartholomew's Day,
  1862.   1862
BLAKISTON (H.E.D.)   Trinity College, Oxford.   (College histories.)
                                              London, 1898
BLANK-BOOK of a small Colleger.   *London,* 1834
BLIGH (R.)   The defence of the Rev. R. Bligh of Queens' College,
  Cambridge, A.B., against the Fellows of that Society, who rejected
  him as an improper person for a Fellow, 12 Jan. 1780.
                                            London (1780)
Letters which passed between R. Bligh and others, on account of his
  being rejected as a Fellow of Queens' College, Cambridge, on
  pretence of his want of Scholarship, etc.   *London,* 1781
BLOMEFIELD (F.)   Collectanea Cantabrigiensia. 4° *Norwich,* 1751
Annals of Gonvile and Caius College, Cambridge.   (Ives's *Select
  Papers.*)   4° *London,* 1773

BLOMER (R.)   Concio habita coram...Acad. Cant....Junii 28, 1712, instantibus comitiis academicis.   4° *Londini*, 1712

BLOMER (T.)   Full View of Dr Bentley's Letter.   *London*, 1710

BLOMFIELD (C.J.)   The importance of learning to the Clergy. A sermon preached before the University of Cambridge, July 2, 1820.   4° 1820

Memoir.   Ed. by his son, Alfred Blomfield.   2 vols.   *London*, 1863

BLOMFIELD (E. V.)   A memoir of E. V. Blomfield.   (By J. H. Monk.)   (From *Museum Criticum*, no. 7.)   (*London*, 1826)

—— A second copy, with MS. note by Professor Sedgwick.
     (*London*, 1826)

BLOOM (J.H.)   *See* Cartae antiquae.

BLORE (E.W.)   Three plain sermons preached in the Chapel of Trinity College, Cambridge, in 1859.   1860

Correspondence between W. H. H. Hudson, Esq. and the Rev. E. W. Blore.   1869

Prove all things.   A sermon preached in the Chapel of Trinity College, Cambridge, Feb. 2, 1871.   1871

Deliverance from the Evil one.   A sermon preached before the University of Cambridge, Feb. 5, 1882.   1882

'Ο πονηρὸς or τὸ πονηρὸν.   A reply to a friendly critic on some points in the controversy.   1882

Sermon preached at St Luke's, Chesterton, 3 Feb. 1885.   1885

BLOXAM (J.R.)   *See* Heylin (P.).

BLUE 'UN.   A Journal of University life.   Vol. 1, no. 1.   31 May, 1884.   4° 1884

BLUFFMAN (L.) *pseud.*   How we spun out the "Long," or The Cambs. Busy Bee Club Papers.   [By L. Boquel.]   (Specimen: breaks off at p. 16.)   1878

BLUNT (G.W.)   Peace in War.   In Memoriam L[ouisa] R[yder].
     1856

BLUNT (J.J.)   Vestiges of ancient manners and customs discoverable in modern Italy and Sicily.   *London*, 1823

Introduction to a course of lectures on the early Fathers, now in delivery in the University of Cambridge.   1840

Remarks on Regulation (E) recommended by the Syndicate appointed Feb. 9, 1848.   1848

A sermon preached at Great St Mary's, before the University of Cambridge, March 8, 1849.   150th anniversary of the S.P.C.K.
     1849

Ramsden Sermon, preached 23 May, 1852.   1852

A sermon in memory of the late Duke of Wellington, preached before the University [Nov. 21, 1852].   1852

BLYTH (E.H.)   In memoriam.   By his Father.   *Norwich*, 1866

BLYTHE (S.)   *See* Churchill (F.).

BOASE (C.W.)   Register of the rectors and fellows, etc. of Exeter College, Oxford.   *Oxford*, 1879

BOAT Race.   Newspaper cuttings, 1871–   1871, etc.

BOAT Race.
   Record of the University Boat Race, 1829–1880.   By J. H. D.
      Goldie and G. G. T. Treherne.   4° *London*, 1883
   See also Hutchinson (A. S. M.).
BOLLAND (W.)   Miracles.   (Seatonian Prize Poem for 1797.)
                                                          4° 1797
   The Epiphany.   (Seatonian Prize Poem for 1798.)   4° 1799
BONNEY (T.G.)   The Holy Places at Jerusalem.   *London*, 1864
   Letter of application and testimonials for Woodwardian Professorship
      of Geology.   *n.p.* 1873
   Cambridgeshire Geology.   1875
   In memoriam W. H. Miller.   (*Eagle*.)   1880
   A chapter in the life history of an old University.   1882
   The microscope's contributions to the earth's physical history.   (Rede
      Lecture for 1892.)   1892
   St Paul's Message to the Athenians.   Sermon preached before the
      University, Aug. 1904.   1904
   The Geology of [St John's] College Chapel.   (*Eagle*.)   1907
   A Septuagenarian's Recollections of St John's.   (*Eagle*.)   1909
   Evolution in Religion.   Sermon before the University.   1909
BONWICKE (A.)   A pattern for young students in the University,
      set forth in the life of A. Bonwicke.   *London*, 1729
   Life.   To which are added, Thoughts on Christian education, by
      William Beveridge, Bp of St Asaph.   *Oxford*, 1834
   Life.   By his father.   Ed. by J. E. B. Mayor.   1870
BOOK of the Cambridge Review, 1879–97.   1898
BOOK of Matriculations and Degrees.   *See* Matriculations.
BOROUGH.   Abstract of Accounts, 1836–37; 1837–38; 1839–40;
      1842–43; 1845–46; 1855–56; 1885–86; 1886–87; 1897–98.
                                                          1837–98
   Register of Electors, 1840–1.   1840
   Remarks on two recent Reports of a Syndicate of the University
      appointed to confer with a Committee of the Town Council...on
      the Borough Police Force.   1850
   Report of the Commissioners appointed to inquire into the existence
      of corrupt practices in the Borough of Cambridge.
                                               F° *London*, 1853
   Charters of the borough of Cambridge.   Ed. by F. W. Maitland and
      Mary Bateson.   1901
   See also Gas; Police; Rating; Schools.
BORTON (N.A.B.)   Vicarage of Burwell: testimonials in favour
      of N. A. B. Borton.   1885
BOTANIC Garden.   A short account of the late donation of a Botanic
      Garden to the University of Cambridge, by Dr Walker.   4° 1763
   Proposal for an annual subscription for support of Botanic Garden,
      27 Feb. 1765.   4° 1765
   Catalogus Horti Botanici Cantabrigiensis.   By Thomas Martin.
                                                             1771
   Hortus Cantabrigiensis.   By James Donn.   2nd ed.   1800

BOTANIC Garden.
  Hortus Cantabrigiensis.   By James Donn.   4th ed.   1807
  —— 9th ed.   *London,* 1819
  —— 13th ed.   *London,* 1845
  Fly-sheets, etc. relating to the Botanic Garden, from 1825.   1825–
  Considerations on the disposal of the new Botanical Garden ground.
    By J. J. Smith.   1845
  Further Considerations.... By J. J. Smith.   1845
  Address to the members of the University of Cambridge on the
    expediency of improving...the Botanic Garden... By J. S.
    Henslow.   1846
  A catalogue of hardy plants in the Botanic Garden.   By Andrew
    Murray.   1850
  Sunday opening.   Memorial, Letters, etc.   1880–2
  Delectus seminum quae Hortus Botanicus...pro mutua commutatione
    offert.   Jan. 1887, Jan. 1888, Jan. 1889, Jan. 1897, Jan. 1899,
    Jan. 1901, Jan. 1902, Jan. 1903, Jan. 1904, Jan. 1905, Jan. 1906,
    Jan. 1907, Jan. 1908, Jan. 1909, Jan. 1910.   1887–1910
  Proposed sale of part of the Botanic Garden Estate, March 1904.
    Fly-sheets on the subject.   4° 1904
BOTANICAL Museum.   *See* Gardiner (W.).
BOTTOMLEY (W.B.)   Syllabus of a course of twelve lectures on
    plant life, with special reference to agriculture.   1891
BOUGHEY (A.H.F.)   Funeral Sermon for Queen Victoria in Trin.
    Coll. Chapel, 3 Feb. 1901.   1901
  Funeral Sermon for King Edward VII in Gt St Mary's, Whit-
    sunday, 1901.   1910
BOURNE (V.)   Carmina Comitialia Cantabrigiensia.   Ed. V. B.
    (Vincent Bourne).   *Londini,* 1721
  Poematia.   Quintò edita.   12° *London,* 1764
  Miscellaneous Poems.   4° *London,* 1772
  Poemata Latina partim reddita, partim scripta.   Editio octava.
                                              12° *Oxonii,* 1808
  Poetical Works.   2 vols.   12° *Oxford,* 1808
  —— Another ed.   12° 1838
BOWDLER (C.)   *See* Queens' College.   Case of the President, 1821.
BOWEN (E.E.)   The Force of Habit.   (Burney Prize for 1858.) 1859
BOWES (R.)   The first printing in Cambridge.   Prospectus of a
    reprint of Linacre's ed. of Galen (Camb. 1521), and other early
    Cambridge books.   [1879]
  Biographical Notes on the University Printers from the commence-
    ment of printing in Cambridge to the present time. (*C.A.S.*) 1886
  The first printing in Cambridge.   Prospectus of a reprint of Bullock's
    Oratio (Camb. 1521), and other early Cambridge books.   4° 1886
  Note on the Cambridge University Press.   (*C.A.S.*)   1887
  On the first and other early Cambridge Newspapers.   (*C.A.S.*) 1894
  A Catalogue of books printed at or relating to the University, Town,
    and County of Cambridge from 1521 to 1893.   (With Index.)
                                                              1894

BOWES (R.) and Gray (G.J.)   John Siberch.   Bibliographical Notes, 1886–1905.   4° 1906
Catalogue of books issued by Bowes and Bowes, with notice of opening of new rooms, Dec. 1907.   1907
The Zodiac Club.   (*C.A.S.*)   1909
BOWLING (E.W.)   St Paul and Felix.   (Seatonian Prize Poem for 1880.)   1880
"Then He arose."   (Seatonian Prize Poem for 1881.)   1881
Battle of the Pons trium Trojanorum.   (*Eagle.*)   1881
"The Message to the Angel of the Church in Sardis."   (Seatonian Prize Poem for 1886.)   1886
"On Earth Peace."   (Seatonian Prize Poem for 1887.)   1888
Grecia victrix.   A lay of Modern Greece.   [1891]
BOX of Bonbons.   In three acts.   *n.p.* 1881
BOYCE (E.J.)   A memorial of the Cambridge Camden Society, instituted May 1839, and the Ecclesiological Society, May 1846.
London, 1888
BOYCE (W.)   *See* Mason (W.), 1749.
BOYLE (C.)   Dr Bentley's Dissertations on Phalaris, etc. examin'd.
London, 1698
—— 2nd ed.   *London*, 1698
—— 3rd ed.   *London*, 1699
—— 4th ed.   *London*, 1745
See also Phalaris.
BOYS' Brigade.   Cambridge Companies.   Annual Report, 1903–4, 1904–5, 1905–6, 1907–8, 1908–9.   1904–9
BOYS' Employment Agency.   First Annual Report.   1908
BRADFORD (C.W.V.)   *See* Natural Science Society.
BRADFORD (J.)   Memoirs of the life of J. Bradford, by W. Stevens.
London, 1832
BRADSHAW (H.)   The Printer of the Historia Sancti Albani. (Memoranda, 1.)   1868
The Skeleton of Chaucer's Canterbury Tales.   (Memoranda, 4.) (Issued November 23, 1871.)   1868
A classified Index of the fifteenth century books in the collection of the late M. J. de Meyer, which were sold at Ghent in Nov. 1869. (Memoranda, 2.)   1870
List of the founts of type and woodcut devices used in Holland in the fifteenth century.   (Memoranda, 3.)   1871
Notice of a fragment of the Fifteen Oes and other Prayers printed by Caxton.   (Memoranda, 5.)   1877
The University Library.   Papers contributed to the *Cambridge University Gazette*, 1869.   (Memoranda, 6.)   1881
Address at the opening of the fifth annual meeting of the Library Association, Sept. 5, 1882.   (Memoranda, 7.)   1882
—— Another ed.   1882
The early collection of Canons known as the Hibernensis.   (Memoranda, 8.)   1885
A half-century of notes on the Day-Book of John Dorne, as edited

BRADSHAW (H.)
   by F. Madan, for the Oxford Historical Society. (Facsimile of
   H. Bradshaw's manuscript.)   Fo 1886
   Collected Papers. Ed. by F. Jenkinson.   1889
   The early collection of Canons known as the Hibernensis. Two
   unfinished papers. Edited by F. Jenkinson.   1893
     Letters to J. W. Clark on the death of Henry Bradshaw, with the order of
     his funeral, press-notices, etc.   1886
     Catalogue of books...sold Nov. 16–18, 1886.   1886
     Memorial. Fly-sheets, etc. relating thereto.   1886
     Memoir of Henry Bradshaw. By G. W. Prothero.   *London*, 1888
     A Scholar-Librarian. By A. Leeper. (Lib. Assoc. of Australasia.)
                                          Adelaide, 1901
     See also Edwards (John); Henry Bradshaw Society; Statutes, 1883; Willis
     and Clark.
BRAHMS (J.) German Requiem, in King's College Chapel. In
   memory of Q. Victoria.   1901
BRANDRÉTH (H.) A few words with the Eton Reformers.
                                        London, 1865
   On modern education. A letter to the Senate of the University of
   Cambridge.   *London*, 1868
   Exercises for the office of College Preacher.   *Liverpool*, 1870
   Religion, education, and learning.   1903
BRASS Halo. Trinity Hall, Oct. Term, 1893; Lent Term, 1894;
   Lent Term, 1895.   1893–5
BRAYLEY (E.W.) and Britton (J.) A topographical and historical
   description of Cambridgeshire.   *London*, 1810
   Cambridgeshire; or original delineations of that county. *London*, 1818
BRERETON (J.L.) The County College.   *London*, 1872
   Cavendish College. An experiment in University Extension. (*Con-
   temporary Review*, Sept. 1878.)
BRETT *v.* Beales. *See* Toll Cause.
BREUL (K.) Greek and its humanistic alternatives in the "Little-
   Go."   1905
   Students' life and work in the University of Cambridge.   1908
   Die Universität Cambridge.   (1908)
   Willkommen in Cambridge. Schlichte Antworten auf kluge Fragen.
   (For the visit of German students.)   1910
BREWSTER (*Sir* D.) More Worlds than One.   *London*, 1854
BRIDGE (T.W.) and Clark (J.W.) List of Dissections. (Mus. Zool.
   and Comp. Anat.)   (1871)
   Illustrations of Comparative Anatomy. 2nd ed.   1875
BRIDGES (R.) Eden. An oratorio. Set to music by C. V. Stanford.
                                12o *London*, 1891
BRIDGTOWER (G.H.P.) *See* Rawdon (F.A.).
BRIEF account of the new Sect of Latitude-Men, by S. P. [? S. Patrick].
                             4o *London*, 1662
BRIGHT (E.) *See* Jacombe (S.).
BRIMLEY (G.) Essays. Ed. by W. G. Clark.   1858

BRISTED (C.A.)   Five years in an English University.   2 vols.
New York, 1852
—— 2nd ed.   *New York*, 1852
—— 3rd ed.   *London*, 1873
Cambridge life according to C. A. Bristed. By W. G. Clark. (*Fraser's Magazine*, January 1854.)
BRITANNIA depicta. Pt II. Cambridgeshire.   4° *London*, 1808
BRITISH Association, 1833. Lithographed signatures of the Members of the British Association who met at Cambridge, June 1833, and Report.   4° 1833
1833. Address...June 25. By W. Whewell.   1833
1845. Hommage d'un voyageur français, ami de l'humanité, aux grands hommes, savans...qu'a produits l'Angleterre. By M. A. Jullien.   *Londres*, 1845
British Association at Cambridge. (*Illustrated London News*, 21 and 28 June.)
Cards of Membership, etc.
Report of the fifteenth meeting held at Cambridge, June 1845.
London, 1846
1862. Thirty-second meeting, Cambridge, 1862. Journal of Sectional Proceedings. No. 3.   1862
List of Resident and Non-Resident Members.   1862
Supplementary list of Members, etc.   1862
List of Associates.   1862
Address...Oct. 1. By R. Willis.   1862
Report of the thirty-second meeting held at Cambridge, Oct. 1862.
London, 1863
1904. Congrès de la Brit. Assoc. à Cambridge. Compte rendu. (*Revue de Philosophie*, Nov. 1904.)   *Paris*, 1904
Cambridge meeting, 1904. Journal of Sectional Proceedings. (1904)
List of Members. (Aug. 16, Aug. 18, Suppl.)   1904
Local Programme. (Three issues.)   1904
Excursions.   1904
Miscellanea : Invitations, Programmes, Press-Cuttings, etc. 1904
See Balfour (A. J.); Darwin (F.); Hutton (J. A.).
BRITISH Dental Association. Eastern Counties Branch. Cambridge meeting, June 1884. Programme, etc.   1884
—— Aug. 1885. Reception at Peterhouse.   1885
BRITISH Medical Association, 1864. President's address. By G. E. Paget.   *London*, 1864
Address in Surgery. By G. M. Humphry.   *London*, 1864
1880. Programme of the 48th Annual Meeting to be held at Cambridge, 1880.   4° *n.p.* 1880
Daily Journal of the 48th Annual Meeting, Tues. Aug. 10.   1880
Soirée given to the Members of the Association in the Fitzwilliam Museum, Aug. 11, 1880. Words of the Glees.   1880
—— Programme of Music.   1880
Programme of Music at Prof. Humphry's Garden Party, 13 Aug. 1880.   1880

BRITISH Medical Association.
  Report of the 48th Annual Meeting, held at Cambridge, Aug. 1880.
  (*British Med. Journ.*)   (*London,* 1880)
BRITTON (J.) King's College Chapel. (From his *Architectural Antiquities,* 1.)   4° (*London,* 1805)
—— Another state.   4° (*London,* 1805)
  See also Brayley (E. W.).
BROADLEY (T.) An Essay on the internal evidence of the religion of Moses. (Norrisian Prize Essay.)   1805
BROCKLEBANK (T.) Remarks on income of King's College. (1857)
  Organ building at Cambridge in 1606. (*Ecclesiologist,* N. S., XVII.) 1859
  Sir Robert Rede (*C.A.S.*)   1859
BRODIE (P.B.) Letter of application for Woodwardian Professorship of Geology, 8 Feb. 1873.   4° *n.p.* 1873
BRODRICK (G.C.) Merton College before the Reformation. (*Nineteenth Century,* Sept. 1882.)
  A history of the University of Oxford. *London,* 1886
  Oxford in the Middle Ages. (*Macmillan's Mag.,* June 1887.)
  Unionism: the basis of a National Party. *Oxford,* 1888
BROOKE (Z.) Two Sermons preached before the Univ. of Camb. 1762.   4° 1763
BROWN (A.L.) Selwyn College. (College histories.) *London,* 1906
BROWN (A.W.) Recollections of the conversation parties of the Rev. Charles Simeon. *London,* 1863
BROWN (E.L.) Proposed memorial to him in Marlborough Coll. Chapel. *n.p.* 1860
BROWN (John), *D.D.,* † 1766. On liberty: a poem...on occasion of the Peace. 4° *London,* 1749
BROWN (John), † 1863. Fifty years' gleanings from life's harvest. 1858
BROWNE (E.G.) Description of an old Persian Commentary on the Kur'án. (*R. Asiat. Soc.*) *London,* 1894
  Report to Lord Cromer on Arabic tests for Candidates for Civil Services of Egypt and Súdán. 7 Aug. 1904. 4° 1904
  Memorial to Council of Senate on Oriental school, 10 Feb. 1905. 4° 1905
  Brief narrative of events in Persia. *London,* 1909
BROWNE (E.H.) The Pentateuch and the Elohistic Psalms. *London,* 1863
BROWNE (G.F.) Some there be which have no memorial. A Sermon preached at the Commemoration of Benefactors, Oct. 27, 1878. 1878
  The Old is better. An Assize Sermon...Nov. 8, 1879. 1879
  Statement respecting G. F. B.'s refusal to give evidence on the examination of Kingsbridge Grammar School, 1882. *n.p.* 1882
  On inscriptions at Jarrow and Monkwearmouth. (*Proc. of Soc. of Ant. of Newcastle-upon-Tyne.*) *Newcastle,* 1884
  On a supposed inscription upon the font at Wilne. *London,* 1885

BROWNE (G.F.)
Spiritual energy.   A Sermon preached before the University, 13 Nov. 1887.   1887
The income of a University, and how it is spent.   (*National Rev.*, Nov. 1888.)
St Catharine's College.   (College histories.)   *London*, 1902
BROWNE (I.H.)   On the Immortality of the Soul. A Poem. Transl. from the Latin by J. Cranwell.   4° 1765
Poems upon various subjects.   *London*, 1768
BROWNE (Thomas), *Master of Christ's College*.   An examination of the calumnies which have been assigned as reasons for the opposition to Dr Browne's election into the Office of Vice-Chancellor, which took place on the 4th Nov. 1809.   1810
Remarks on two pamphlets...the first entitled *An examination of calumnies, etc.* by the Master of Christ's College, the second entitled *A plain statement of facts*, by the Master of Catharine Hall. By a Member of the Senate.   *London*, 1811
See also Procter (J.).
BROWNE (Thomas)   Concio ad clerum Junii 11°, 1687.   Concio coram Acad. Cant. Julii 3°, 1687.   4° 1688
BROWNE (*Sir* W.)   Ode occasioned by Sir W. Browne's legacy of two Gold Medals.   4° *London*, 1776
New Statute for Sir William Browne's Medals, Nov. 23, 1857.
                                                                    1857
See also Prolusiones; Selwyn (W.), Battle of the Epigrams.
BROWNING (O.)   Testimonials of O. B., candidate for the Head Mastership of London University College School.   4° *London*, 1875
Considerations on the reform of the Statutes of King's College, Cambridge.   (1877)
On the Report of the Indian Civil Service Syndicate.   1883
The training by Universities of the Public Servants of the State.   1884
Address on Secondary Education, delivered at the Social Science Congress, Birmingham.   1884
Cambridge.   (*Engl. Illustr. Mag.*, Oct. 1886.)
Aspects of education.   (Monograph of the Industrial Educ. Assoc.)
                                                        New York, 1888
The proposed new Historical Tripos.   *London*, 1896
—— Another ed.   1897
Political Science.   The evolution of the family.   1905
Political Science.   Introductory lecture.   *Finedon*, n.d.
Memories of sixty years at Eton, Cambridge, and elsewhere.
                                                        London, 1910
BROWNING Society.   Introductory address to the Browning Society. By J. Kirkman.   1881
On some points in Browning's view of life.   By B. F. Westcott.
                                                                    1883
BROWNLOW (*Mrs* J.M.E.)   Syllabus of lectures on the beginnings of modern Music.   *London*, 1899

BRUNDISH (J.J.)   An elegy on a family tomb.   4° 1782
BRYCE (J.)   The future of the English Universities. (*Fortnightly Rev.*,
    March 1883.)
BRYDGES (*Sir* E.)   Vindication of pending Bill for amendment of
    the Copyright Act.   London, 1818
BRYER (H.)   *See* Copyright Act.
BUB.   The Adventures of a Cambridge Pro-Proctor.   1864
BUBBLE.   May Week Magazine, June 10, 1898.   1898
BUCHAN (J.)   Brasenose College, Oxford.   (College histories.)
                                                   London, 1898
BUCHANAN (C.)   *See* Yeates (T.).
BUCHANAN Prize.   On the restoration of learning in the East.   By
    Charles Grant.   4° 1805
    On the restoration of learning in the East.   Poem written by Fr.
    Wrangham; and published at request of the Adjudicators.   4° 1805
    Collegium Bengalense.   Poem which gained prize offered to Etonians.
    By G. P. Richards.   4° 1805
BUCKLEY (T.E.)   Geographical distribution of large mammals of
    South Africa.   (*P. Z. S.*, 7 March, 1876.)
BUCKMASTER (S.O.)   *See* Representatives.
BUDGETT (J.S.)   Biographical sketch, by A. E. Shipley.   4° 1908
BULL Hotel.   Catalogue of the collection of engravings, oil-paintings,
    etc. of the Bull Hotel, Cambridge.   4° 1888
BULLER (A.C.)   The life and works of Heberden.   (Wix Prize
    Essay, 1878.)   London, 1879
BULLOUGH (C.P.)   The Tale of a Trout.   4° [1903]
BULMER (J.)   Chrysopolis, anglicè Moneygrubbington.
                                                   Sunderland, 1882
BURDAKIN (J.)   A reply to the " Argument " of the Master of Clare
    Hall for declaring vacant the fellowship of W. L. F. Fischer.   1849
    Remarks on two recent Reports of a Syndicate of the University
    appointed to confer with a Committee of the Town Council on
    the subject of the Borough Police Force.   1850
BURDON (W.)   Three letters addressed to the Bishop of Llandaff.
                                                           1795
    A vindication of Pope and Grattan, from the attack of an anonymous
    defamer [i.e. T. J. Mathias].   Newcastle, 1799
BURFORD (J.)   *See* Bentley (R.), 1727.
BURGESS (T.)   Letter to the Rev. T. Beynon...in reply to A vindi-
    cation of Prof. Porson, by Crito Cantabrigiensis [T. Turton].
                                                   Salisbury, 1829
BURGON (J.W.)   Some remarks on art, with reference to the studies
    of the University.   Oxford, 1846
    Plea for the study of Divinity in Oxford.   (With a letter from Dean
    Burgon to Dr Luard inserted.)   London, 1875
BURIAL Grounds.   Financial statement of the Committee for the
    extension of the parish burial grounds in Cambridge, Dec. 1848.
                                                           1849
—— May 28, 1858.   1858

BURKE (E.)   The Oriental Trip.   (Footlights Dramatic Club.)
                                                          1901
BURMAN (F.)   Visit to Cambridge.   (Ed. by J. E. B. Mayor in
   Cambridge under Queen Anne.)   [1870-1]
BURN (A.E.)   Niceta of Remesiana.   1905
BURN (R.)   On the improvement of the ordinary B.A. course. 1864
   God our Refuge.   A Sermon preached in the Chapel of Trinity
   College, Cambridge, Feb. 2, 1873, being the Sunday after the
   death of the Rev. A. Sedgwick.   1873
   Letters by R. Burn and H. A. Morgan on Reform.   1876
   In Memoriam.   H. A. J. Munro.   (1885)
BURN (T.H.)   Christian Principle.   A Sermon preached in the Chapel
   of Marlborough College, 3 Nov. 1861.   *Marlborough* (1861)

   In Memoriam.   By G. E. L. C[otton].   1864

BURNAND (*Sir* F. C.)   *See* Amateur Dramatic Club.
BURNEY (R.)   Vice-Chancellor's Notice of the foundation of his
   Prize, 3 June 1846.   F° 1846
BURNEY Prize Essay, 1849.   The divine attribute of Mercy as
   deduced from the O.T.   By A. J. Carver.   1851
   —— 1850.   The Unity of design in the successive dispensations
   recorded in the Scriptures.   By G. F. Prescott.   1851
   —— 1855.   On faith in Natural and Revealed Religion.   By Jos.
   Foxley.   1855
   —— 1858.   The Force of Habit.   By E. E. Bowen.   1859
BURTON (R.)   Admirable curiosities, rarities, and wonders.   New ed.
                                        4° *Westminster*, 1811
BURWELL.   An account of a most terrible fire that happened on
   8 Sept. 1727, at a barn at Burwell, in Cambridgeshire.   By Tho.
   Gibbons.   *London*, 1769
See also Borton (N. A. B.); Charles (J. H.).
BURY (J.B.)   An Inaugural Lecture, delivered in the Divinity School,
   Cambridge, 26 Jan. 1903.   4° 1903
BUSINESS (?) at the Bunion.   By a Speaker [A.J.A. Ball, Trin.].
                                                          1882
BUTCHER (S.H.)   Testimonials for the Professorship of Greek in
   the University of Edinburgh.   1882
BUTLER (C.)   The Text of St Benedict's Rule.   (*Downside Review.*)
                                   Weston-super-Mare, 1899
BUTLER (H.M.)   Oratio Latina.   Poema Latinum.   Carmen
   Graecum.   Porson Prize.   1854
   The character of Edmund Burke.   An oration delivered in Trinity
   College on the day of the Commemoration of Benefactors, 1854.
                                                        (1854)
   Henry Martyn.   Sermon in Trinity Church, 17 Oct. 1887.   1887
   "Crossing the Bar," and a few other translations.   4° 1890
   Some observations on the proposals for enlarging the College Library.
                                                          1891
   Sermon on the death of Lord Tennyson, 16 Oct. 1892.   1892

BUTLER (H.M.)

An attempt to render Psalm cvii. in Latin elegiac verse.   1896

Relics of Whewell, 13 May, 1896.   4° 1896

College Extension.   1896

Proposed extension [of Trinity College]. Some observations by the Master.   1897

The Translation of King Edward the Confessor. A sermon...preached Oct. 13, 1897.   (1897)

The Parable of the Fig Tree. A sermon...preached Oct. 17, 1897.   (1897)

A sermon preached Oct. 24, 1897, being the Sunday after the funeral of the Rev. C. J. Vaughan, Dean of Llandaff.   1897

Address in Gt St Mary's Ch. Camb., on Sat. 28 May, 1898; at the hour of interment of Mr Gladstone.   1898

Intellectual enthusiasm. Lecture.   *Aberystwyth* (1898)

Sequelae, or the Results of an examination.   1898

Translations.   1898

Translations.   1899

The Mind of Christ. Sermon preached 29 March, 1908.   1908

Universities. An inaugural address delivered in the Senate House, 18 July, 1908.   1908

Sermon in Jesus Coll. Chapel, on the occasion of the death of King Edward VII, 8 May   1910

Address in St Michael's Ch. at a meeting of the Discharged Prisoners' Aid Soc., 11 May.   1910

BUTLER (*Mrs* H.M.) The Basis of Christian Science. Letter to C. E. Stephen. (*Friends' Quarterly Examiner*, July 1905.)

BUTLER (S.) Letter to the Rev. C. J. Blomfield, on Edinburgh Review of the Cambridge Aeschylus.   *Shrewsbury*, 1810

Life and Letters. By his grandson. 2 vols.   *London*, 1896

See also Monk (J. H.) Letter, 1810.

BUTLER (W.J.) Trinity College Prize Essay for 1839, on the Colonial Policy of the Ancients.   1840

BYROM (J.) Review of proceedings against Dr Bentley.

     London, 1719

Miscellaneous Poems. 2 vols.   *Manchester*, 1773

BYRON (H.J.) *See* Amateur Dramatic Club.

C

CAIAN. Easter Term, 1891.   1891
CAIUS (J.)   De pronuntiatione Graecae et Latinae linguae.
                                                    4° *Londini*, 1574
  Historiae Cantabrigiensis ab urbe condita liber 1.   4° *Londini*, 1574
  De antiquitate Cantabrigiensis Academiae libri duo.   4° *Londini*, 1574
  Of Englishe Dogges. (Repr. of 1576 ed.)   *London*, 1880
CAIUS (T.)   Assertio antiquitatis Oxoniensis Academiae.
                                                    4° *Londini*, 1574
CAIUS College. *See* Gonville and Caius College.
CALAMY (E.)   An historical account of my own life.   2nd ed.
  Ed. by J. T. Rutt. 2 vols.   *London*, 1830
CALDRON (The), or Follies of Cambridge. A satire. *Winchester*, 1799
CALGARTH Park Library (Bp Richard Watson). *See* Watson (R.).
CALLENDAR (H.L.)   A manual of cursive Shorthand. *London*, 1889
  A system of phonetic spelling adapted to English. *London*, 1889
  A primer of cursive Shorthand.   The Cambridge system.
                                                    London, 1889
  Reading practice in cursive Shorthand.   *London*, 1889
CALVERLEY (C.S.)   Literary remains. With a memoir by W. J.
  Sendall.   *London*, 1885
CAM (River).   A Report upon the present state of the River Cam.
  By C. Humfrey.   1829
  Report of the Cam Purification Committee, Dec. 1, 1868.   1868
  See also Acts and Bills.
CAM.   An elegy. [By E. B. Greene.]   4° *London*, 1764
CAM.   A May Week Magazine. June 9, 1894.   F° 1894
CAM.   Vol. I. Nos. 1–5; Vol. II. Nos. 6–12. Feb. 14–June 6,
  1906. (Ed. by H. A. Webb, Trin.)   4° 1906
CAMBRIDGE.

    *** For Cambridge Societies, Institutions, etc. see under the first important word of their respective titles, not being ' Cambridge ' or ' University ', *e.g.* Antiquarian Society ; Archæology (Museum of) ; Chess Club ; Female Refuge ; Library ; Mary (St) the Great ; Observatory ; Press ; Volunteers.

CAMBRIDGE. Reflections in the Cloisters of a College. *London*, 1831
CAMBRIDGE à la Poupée. By Two 'Varsity Men.   1903
CAMBRIDGE A.B.C. Nos. 1–4. (Ed. by R. A. Austen Leigh,
  Hon. Maurice Baring, and H. Warre Cornish.)   1894
CAMBRIDGE Annual, 1905—6.   F° 1906
"CAMBRIDGE besieged," or the Rehearsal of a deep tragedy at the
  Theatre, Barnwell, which is to be performed by Serious Christians
  at the next meeting of the Bible Society. By a Saint. *London*, 1818
CAMBRIDGE Christmas Annual.   1895
CAMBRIDGE Chronicle. 4 Jan. 1746, 25 Jan. 1788. (Reprints.) *n.d.*
CAMBRIDGE Confessor, or guide to the Church. No. 1.   1836

CAMBRIDGE crepuscular diversions, and broodings before bedtime.
1837
CAMBRIDGE Customs and Costumes. [By J. L. Roget.]
obl. 4° 1851
CAMBRIDGE Dionysia, a Classic Dream. By the Editor of the
Bear [G. O. Trevelyan]. 1858
CAMBRIDGE Essays, 1855–1858. 4 vols. *London*, 1855–8
CAMBRIDGE Fortnightly. Nos. 1–5. 24 Jan.–13 March 1888
CAMBRIDGE "Great-Go." By B.A. Cantab. [i.e. Gavin F. James].
(1884)
CAMBRIDGE Guides. *See* Guides.
CAMBRIDGE House. Reports 1898, 1907. *London*, 1898–1908
CAMBRIDGE in the Long Vacation. 12° *London*, 1830
CAMBRIDGE in the XVIIth century. (Ed. by J. E. B. Mayor.)
I. Nicholas Ferrar. Two lives, by his brother John and by
Dr Jebb. 1855. II. Matthew Robinson. Autobiography. 1856.
III. William Bedell. Life by his son. 1871. 1855–71
CAMBRIDGE Journal and Weekly Flying Post. 24 Jan. 1746.
(Reprint.) *n.d.*
CAMBRIDGE Magazine. Nos. 1–6, 8. *London*, 1769
—— Another periodical. No. 2. 25 March 1829. 1829
—— Another periodical. Nos. 1–15. 27 April 1899–30 Nov. 1899.
4° 1899
CAMBRIDGE Market Girl. By a Student of the University. 12° 1825
CAMBRIDGE Meteor. [Ed. by G. N. Bankes and J. A. Fabb.]
Nos. 1–7. 7 June–14 June 1882. 1882
CAMBRIDGE Modern History. Account of its origin, authorship,
and production. 1907
CAMBRIDGE Observer. Nos. 1–21. 3 May 1892–7 March 1893.
(Bowes 2869.) F° 1892–3
CAMBRIDGE Odes. By Peter Persius. 2nd ed. 12° [183–]
CAMBRIDGE Papers. 10 vols.

⁎ This collection is arranged chronologically as under, and includes
programmes, notices, reports, invitations, cuttings, etc., etc. connected
with the University, Town, and County. It includes some fly-sheets,
but not many (*see also* under Fly-Sheets).

I. 1762–1885; II. 1886–1891; III. 1892–1894; IV. 1894–
1896; V. 1895–1899; VI. 1900–1903; VII. 1904–1905;
VIII. 1906–1907; IX. 1908–1910; "Squibs and Crackers"
ab. 1778–1910, mostly facetiae.
CAMBRIDGE Portfolio. Ed. by J. J. Smith. 2 vols. in 1. 4° 1840
CAMBRIDGE Quarterly Review. Nos. 1–3. July 1833–Jan.
1834. *London*, 1833–4
CAMBRIDGE Review. Prospectus. 1879
Vols. 1–21. 4° 1879–1900
The Book of the Cambridge Review. 1898
CAMBRIDGE Scrap Book. [By J. L. Roget.] obl. 4° 1859
CAMBRIDGE Staircase. [By G. N. Bankes.] 12° *London*, 1883

CAMBRIDGE Tart. By Socius. [Ed. by R. Gooch.] *London*, 1823
CAMBRIDGE Tatler. Nos. 1–10 and no. 10 reprinted. 6 March
1877–July 1877. (Bowes 2679.)   4° 1877
CAMBRIDGE Terminal Magazine. Nos. 1–3. Dec. 1858–
April 1859.   1858–9
CAMBRIDGE Trifles. [By G. N. Bankes.]   12° *London*, 1881
CAMBRIDGE under Queen Anne. (Life of A. Bonwicke. Visits
to Cambridge of Burman and Uffenbach. Ed. by J. E. B. Mayor,
and left unfinished.)   [1870–1]

This work was indexed and published in 1911.

CAMBRIDGE University Almanac and Register. 1884, 1891, 1892.
                                                       1884–1892
CAMBRIDGE University Calendar. (Bowes 797.)   1797–1908/9

The Calendar for 1798 never appeared.

CAMBRIDGE University Gazette. Nos. 1–33. 28 Oct. 1868–
15 Dec. 1869.   F° 1868–9
CAMBRIDGE University Magazine. Vol. I. No. 1. March 1835
—— Another periodical, called The Symposium on the wrappers of
nos. 1–5. Vols. I., II., III., I. March 1839–March 1843. (Bowes
1995.)   1840–3
—— Another periodical. [Ed. by J. J. Withers, King's.] Nos. 1–15.
6 May–7 Dec. 1886.   F° 1886
CAMBRIDGE University Register and Almanac. By W. A. Warwick.
1843, 1844.   1843–4
CAMBRIDGE University Reporter. Oct. 1870–July 1910.
                                                       4° 1870–1910
CAMBRIDGESHIRE Cameos. (Leaflets of Local Lore.) (Ed. by
W. R. Brown.)   [189–]
CAMBRIDGESHIRE Farmers' Association. Reports: 4 Nov. 1836,
4 Jan. 1838, 10 Jan. 1840, 15 Jan. 1841, 20 Jan. 1843. 1836–43
CAMBRIDGESHIRE Horticultural Society. Prizes and Subscribers.
                                                       1902
CAMBRIDGESHIRE Law Society. Rules.   1871
CAMBRIDGESHIRE Parish Registers. Marriages. Ed. by W. P. W.
Phillimore, C. J. B. Gaskoin, and E. Young. Vols. 1–3.
                                                       London, 1907–9
CAMBRIDGESHIRE Rowing Association. Rules.   12° (1908)
CAMDEN (*Marquess*) Installation, July 4, 1835. Handel's Messiah.
                                                       (1835)
Installation Ode, July 7, 1835. By C. Wordsworth.   4° 1835
Installation of the Marquis Camden. Second Grand Concert to be
performed July 7, 1835, in the Senate House.   1835
Installation of the Marquis Camden. A grand selection of music to
be performed in Great St Mary's Church, July 8, 1835. 1835
Per l' installazione del nobilissimo Signor Marchese di Camden all'
ufficio di Gran Cancelliere della Università di Cambridge. [? By
the Marchese Spineto.]   1835

CAMDEN (*Marquess*).
Ode upon the death of the Marquis Camden. [? By J. Purchas, Chr.]
n.p. (1840)
Camden Medal. *See* Prolusiones.
CAMDEN Society (afterwards Ecclesiological Society).

*** *Cp.* Bowes, *pp.* 345–351.

Laws.	1839
—— Another ed.	1841
—— Another ed.	1846

A few hints on the practical study of Ecclesiastical Antiquities.

	1839
—— 2nd ed.	1840
—— 3rd ed.	1842
—— 4th ed.	1843

Circular announcing publication of work entitled : Illustrations of Monumental Brasses. 4° [1840]
Reports, 1840–1853. 1840–53
Report of Auditors. 29 April, 1840. F° *London,* 1840
A Few Suggestions to Churchwardens on Churches and Church Ornaments. No. 1. Suited to Country parishes. [By J. M. Neale.] 1841
—— 9th ed. 1841
—— 11th ed. 1842
—— No. 2. Suited to Town and Manufacturing parishes. [By J. M. Neale.] 3rd ed. 1841
—— 5th ed. 1842
The history of Pews. [By J. M. Neale.] 1841
—— Supplement. 1842
—— 3rd ed. 1843
A letter from Archdeacon Thorp, President, to the Chairman of Committees, on the desirability of recalling certain publications. 7 Dec. 1841. 1841
An argument for the Greek origin of the monogram I.H.S. [By B. Webb.] 1841
A few words to Church builders. [By J. M. Neale.] 6*d.* 1841
—— 1*s.* 1841
—— 2nd ed. 1842
—— 3rd ed. 1844
Transactions. 1839–1845. 4° 1841–5

> With fly-sheets of 1868 concerning proposed alterations to Gt St Mary's Church.

The Ecclesiologist. Vols. 1–4. 1841–7

> For fuller particulars see Ecclesiologist.

The Church of the Holy Sepulchre, or the Round Church, Cambridge. 14 July 1842. 1842
—— Another edition, with two plates. 1842
The Round Church. 31 Oct. 1842. 1842

CAMDEN Society.

The claims of the Camden Society considered in connection with the Church of England. By a member of Trinity College. 1842

The Christian Altar. Sermon, 23 Oct. 1842. By J. Scholefield. 1842

Remarks on same. By F. W. Collison. 1842

Further Remarks. By F. W. Collison. 1843

Remarks. By C. Warren. 1843

Twenty-three reasons for getting rid of Church pews. [1842]

Hints on the well-keeping and ordering of Churches. (Placard.) F⁰ [1842]

Notice " To all persons employed in the Restoration of this Church." (Placard.) F⁰ [1842]

A few words to the Parish Clerks and Sextons of country parishes. [By J. M. Neale.] 1843

The Pue system. By William Gillmor. *Halifax*, 1843

Church enlargement and Church arrangement. [By J. M. Neale.] 1843

A few words on the last publication of the C.C.S. [Church enlargement and Church arrangement.] By a late Vice-President [J. J. Smith]. 1843

The Symbolism of Churches and Church ornaments. By William Durandus, with introduction, etc. by J. M. Neale and B. Webb. *Leeds*, 1843

A Church scheme. 4th ed. F⁰ *n.d.*

—— 9th ed. F⁰ *n.d.*

—— 13th ed. F⁰ [? 1845]

The Church of the Holy Sepulchre. 3 Feb. 1844. By T. Thorp. 1844

—— 30 Mar. 1844. By T. Thorp. 1844

The Wooden Walls of England in danger. A defence of Church Pews. *London*, 1844

The Restoration of Churches is the Restoration of Popery. By F. Close. 2nd ed. *London*, 1844

Church Architecture scripturally considered. By F. Close. *London*, 1844

Remarks on the Rev. F. Close's *Church Architecture*. By T. K. Arnold. *London*, 1844

Reply to the *Remarks* of the Rev. T. K. Arnold. By F. Close. *London*, 1844

An examination of the Rev. F. Close's *Reply*. By T. K. Arnold. *London*, 1844

Parker's London Magazine. 1, 2. Jan.–Feb. 1845. (Contains reviews of the Close-Arnold controversy.) *Oxford*, 1845

The Orientator. 1844

An appeal to the Protestant Publick against the Stone Altar in the Round Church. By R. R. Faulkener. 29 Aug. F⁰ *n.p.* 1844

Brief historical enquiry into the introduction of Stone Altars into the English Church. By J. Blackburne. 1844

CAMDEN Society.

Notice that the publication of the *Ecclesiologist* is closed.   15 Nov. 1844. 1844

The Ecclesiologist's Guide to...Cambridge.   By F. A. Paley. 1844

—— Another ed. 1844

Twenty-four reasons for getting rid of Church Pews. [1844?]

Stone Altar case.   Judgment.   31 Jan. 1845. *London*, 1845

Thoughts on the proposed dissolution of the Cambridge Camden Society.   By a member of the Committee [P. Freeman].   5 March. *London*, 1845

Circular on dissolution.   24 April 1845. 4° 1845

Address of Committee with account of the 6th Anniversary Meeting.   8 May 1845. 1845

Letter to the Ven. Archdeacon Thorp, President.   By S. Lee.   9 May 1845. *London*, 1845

Statement respecting withdrawal from the Society, drawn up by C. J. Ellicott and others.   17 May 1845.   (Three copies, with corrections.) 1845

—— 13 June 1845. 4° 1845

Letters signed 'Academicus,' 'An old Camdenian,' etc. from *Camb. Chron.* 31 May 1845.

Sermon at re-opening of the Church of the Holy Sepulchre.   10 Aug. 1845.   By Rev. John Graham. 1845

A second letter to Archdeacon Thorp.   On symbolism.   By S. Lee.   23 Aug. *London*, 1845

Circular of Committee forwarding Report, 9 Dec. 1845. 4° 1845

A Reprint of a letter addressed to a member of the Cambridge Camden Society by M. le Comte de Montalembert.   By an Enquirer. *Cheltenham*, 1845

On the history of Christian Altars.   [By F. W. Collison.] 1845

The Stone Altar.   By J. Blackburne. 1845

A letter to a non-resident member of the Cambridge Camden Society, on the present position of that body.   [By C. A. Swainson.] 1845

A Christian Kalendar for the use of members of the Established Church.   By a lay member of the Cambridge Camden Soc.   [S. N. Stokes]. [1844]

A statement of particulars connected with the restoration of the Round Church.   By the Chairman of the Restoration Committee [T. Thorp]. 1845

The Widow's Lament, literally rendered into verse, and respectfully addressed to the parishioners of the parson deserted parish, called the Holy Sepulchre.   By One of the Unwashed. 1845

Churches of Cambridgeshire and the Isle of Ely. 4° 1845

Circular of Committee forwarding Report.   April 1846. 1846

Circular suggesting testimonial to Archdeacon Thorp, with list of subscriptions.   April, 1846. 1846

Circular requesting attendance at 7th Anniversary Meeting, with copy of revised laws.   2 May 1846. 1846

A Hand-Book of English Ecclesiology. *London*, 1847

CAMDEN Society.
  Instrumenta ecclesiastica. 2 series.   4° *London* (1847)–1856
  Hierurgia Anglicana.   1848
  A memorial of the Cambridge Camden Society instituted May 1839, and the Ecclesiological Society May 1846. By E. J. Boyce.
    London, 1888
CAMP of Refuge. [By Ch. Macfarlane.] 2 vols. in 1.
    12° *London*, 1844
CAMPBELL (D.A.G.) *See* Sellon (L.).
CAMPBELL (L.) On the nationalisation of the old English Universities.   *London*, 1901
  Life of James Clerk Maxwell. By L. Campbell and W. Garnett.
    London, 1882
CAMPBELL (W.F.) A letter to the Electors of Cambridge on change in the Reform Act.   *London*, 1854
CAMPION (W.M.) A plea for the liberal education of the clergy. A sermon.   1861
  On a point raised by the Studies Syndicate.   12° 1864
  " The Beauty of Holiness." A sermon preached at the opening of a new organ in the Chapel of Queens' College, Sept. 27, 1892.
    1892
CAMUS. Rules and Regulations of the Society.   4° 1823
  Cards for 1831, 1832.   12° 1831–2
CANAL. Abstract of the evidence given in support of the London and Cambridge Canal Bill, March and April 1812. (*London*, 1812)
CANDOLE (H.L.C.V.de) Brief account of Holy Trinity Church.
    1910
  —— Penny ed.   12° 1910
CANDY (T.H.) A plea for University Sermons on Sunday mornings.
    (1858)
  The Antidote; or an examination of Mr Pattison's Essay on the tendencies of Religious Thought.   1861
CANNING (G.) *See* Microcosm.
CANTAB. Vol. 1. Nos. 1, 2, April–May 1873.   1873
  —— Another periodical. Jan. 1898–Dec. 1899. 3 vols.
    4° 1898–1900
CANTALUPE (N.) Historiola de antiquitate et origine Universitatis Cantabrigiensis. (*In* Hearne's ed. of Sprott.)   *Oxford*, 1719
  —— Translated in *History and Antiquities of the University of Cambridge*.   *London*, 1721
CAPES (W.W.) University life in ancient Athens. *London*, 1877
CARLOS (E.J.) *See* Skelton (J.).
CARLYON (H.C.) Journal of two cold weather tours in the neighbourhood of Delhi. (Camb. Mission to Delhi. Occasional Paper.)   1884
CARMEN Canino-Anglo-Latinum...auctore Jacobulo Corvo, Coll. Down. schol.   *n.p.* 1837
CAROË (W.D.) King's Hostel, Trinity College, Cambridge.
    4° 1909

"CARR (Christopher)." *See* Benson (A.C.). Memorials of Arthur Hamilton.

CARR (E.T.S.) Remarks on a case of discipline at St Catharine's College. [1868 ?]

CARR (P.) The Greek Play, Oxford. (Elliot's *Amateur Clubs and Actors*). (*London*, 1898)

CARR (W.) University College, Oxford. (College histories.) *London*, 1902

CARRINGTON (R.C.) *See* Observatory, 1861.

CARTAE antiquae of Lord Willoughby de Broke. Pt 1, Cambridgeshire. Steeple Morden, Soham, Long Stanton. Ed. by J. H. Bloom. 4° *Hemsworth*, 1900

CARTER (E.) The history and antiquities of the University of Cambridge. *London*, 1753

The history of the County of Cambridge. *London*, 1819

CARTER (J.) On a skull of Bos Primigenius perforated by a stone Celt. (*Geol. Mag.*, Nov. 1874.)

CARTER (T.B.) Letter to the Provost on the subject of the Reredos in the Chapel of King's College. F° *n.p.* 1903

Letter to H. E. Luxmoore on the subject of the adornment of the sanctuary of the Collegiate Church of Saint Mary of Eton. F° *n.p.* 1903

Letter to those responsible for the Memorial to the Etonians who fell in the South African War. F° *n.p.* 1904

CARTER (T.J.P.) King's College Chapel: notes on its history and present condition. 1867

A letter on buildings at Eton. *Eton*, 1885

CARTMELL (J.) Circular on the Capitation Tax. 1860

CARUS (W.) The treasure in earthen vessels. A sermon preached Dec. 17, 1837. 1837

Memoirs of the Life of Rev. C. Simeon. 2nd ed. 1847

Two Sermons preached before the University. 1866

Reminiscences of A. Sedgwick. (*Churchman*, Feb. 1889.)

CARUS Greek Testament Prizes. Report. (1853)

CARVER (A.J.) The Divine attribute of Mercy as deduced from the Old Testament. (Burney Prize Essay for 1849.) 1851

CASE (T.) A brief history of the proposal to admit Women to Degrees at Cambridge in 1887–8. *Oxford*, 1896

CASE (T.H.) Memoirs of a King's College Chorister. 1899

CASKET. A miscellany, consisting of unpublished Poems. *London*, 1829

CASTELL (E.) Oratio in scholis theologicis habita. 4° *London*, 1667

CASTLEY (T.) Alma mater; being a short vindication, upon general principles, of the defensive authority invested in the University of Cambridge, for the support of the established doctrine of the Church, etc. 1793

CATALOGUE of tracts, etc. illustrating Cambridgeshire, on sale by A. R. Smith. *London*, 1878

CATHARINE'S (St) College.   Documents relating to St Catharine's College...collected by Henry Philpott.   1861

Fly-Sheets, Pamphlets, etc. on the election of Dr C. K. Robinson to the Mastership.   4° and 8° 1861–8

Letters between N. Moore and C. K. Robinson, M.C.   4 and 6 Nov. 1868

A narrative of the case of Mr Moore, of St Catharine's College.   By W. Elwin.   *London*, 1868

Remarks on a case of discipline at St Catharine's College.   By E. T. S. Carr.   [1868?]

A reply to the Remarks of Mr Carr.   By W. Elwin.   *London*, 1869

St Catharine's College.   By G. F. Browne.   (College histories.) *London*, 1902

See also Procter (J.).

CATLING (H.D.)   Versatile Verses on the 'Varsity.   1896

Women's Degrees.   1897

'Varsity Verses.   1901

CAUSTON (A.W.)   Newmarket Hoax!   Interesting memoirs of A. W.C., called the Fortunate Youth.   Ed. 2.   *London* [1818?]

CAUSTON (P.)   Tunbrigialia.   *See* Hill (T.).   Nundinae Sturbrigienses, 1709.

CAVENDISH College.   Report of the proceedings at the laying of the foundation stone of the College Lecture Hall, by the Duke of Devonshire, Oct. 26, 1876.   1876

Cavendish College.   An experiment in University Extension.   By J. L. Brereton.   (*Contemp. Rev.*, Sept. 1878.)

CAVENDISH Laboratory.   Programme, March 12, 1896.   12° 1896

CAVENDISH (*Lady* F.)   Address to Mothers Union, 27 May, 1887

CAYLEY (A.)   Biographical Notice, by A. R. Forsyth.   (*Coll. Papers*, VIII.)   4° 1895

CAYLEY (C.B.)   The Vision of St Brahamus touching the restoration of monasteries.   F° *n.p.* 1843

CAYLEY (H.)   The housing of Cambridge.   (*Econ. Rev.*)   *London*, 1904

CECIL (W.)   A solemn appeal to the Bishop of Ely on the disorder and profaneness at the Parish Church of St Michael's, Cambridge, on the occasion of the Confirmation there, June 20, 1833.   1833

CELIBACY.   A letter on the celibacy of Fellows of Colleges.   By a Member of the University of Cambridge.   *London*, 1794

Reflections on the cælibacy of Fellows of Colleges.   1798

Toleration of marriage in the Universities recommended.   By Ch. Farish.   1799

Letter to Members of the Senate on compulsory celibacy.   By R. Potts.   4° 1857

Memorial to Commissioners respecting Celibacy.   F° *n.p.* 1857

The pros and cons of the celibate system in the Universities.   By a Philogamous Fellow.   1871

CERES.   Testimonies of different authors, respecting the colossal statue of Ceres, placed in the vestibule of the Public Library at Cambridge, July 1, 1803.   1803

CERTAIN disquisitions...representing to the Conscience the unlawful-
nesse of the Oath.... [By John Barwick and others.]
4° "*Oxford*" [*London*], 1644
CHADERTON (L.)   *See* Dillingham (W.); Shuckburgh (E. S.).
CHAFY (W.)   A sermon preached before the University of Cambridge,
July 15, 1830, the day of the funeral of King George the Fourth.
4° 1830
CHALKLEN (C.W.)   Babylon.   A poem.   *London*, 1821
CHALLIS (J.)   Syllabus of a course of experimental lectures on the
equilibrium of fluids, and on Optics.   1838
An account of the discovery [by J. C. Adams] of the new Planet.
4° 1846

Biographical notice of James Challis.   By J. W. L. Glaisher.   *London*, 1883

CHALMERS (A.)   A history of the Colleges, Halls, and Public Build-
ings; attached to the University of Oxford.   2 vols.   *Oxford*, 1810
CHAMBERLAIN (J.)   Account of the reception of King James at
Cambridge, 1614.   (*Annual Register* for 1778.)
CHAMBERS (Temple), *pseud.*   The Family of Smith or Milk and
Eggs.   Comic Opera.   (Repr. from the *Granta*.)   *Surbiton*, 1903
CHAMPNEYS (B.)   Cambridge Divinity Schools.   Report on designs
submitted by B. Champneys.   *London* [1876]
CHANCE (F.)   Thesis medica, 1855.   1856
CHANCELLOR.   Poll at Election, 26 March, 1811.   (Duke of
Gloucester elected.)   (1811)
Poll at Election, 25–27 Feb. 1847.   (H.R.H. Prince Albert elected.)
By Henry Gunning.   1847
Poll at Election, 25–27 Feb. 1847, from the papers of the scrutineers
of the Earl of Powis.   (Earl of Powis's issue.)   1847
See also Albert, *Prince Consort* ; Camden ; Devonshire; Gloucester ;
Grafton ; Monmouth ; Powis.
CHANCELLOR'S Medal.   *See* Prolusiones.
CHANDLER (H.W.)   Remarks on the practice and policy of lending
Bodleian printed books and manuscripts.   *Oxford*, 1887
Further remarks on the same.   *Oxford*, 1887
CHANDLER (R.)   Life of W. Waynflete, Bp of Winchester.
London, 1811
CHAPEL.   A short inquiry into the tendency of Chapel.   [1841 ?]
See also Compulsory Chapel.
CHAPMAN (F.R.)   Sacrist Rolls of Ely.   2 vols.   1907
CHAPMAN (H.A.)   Handbook to the collection of Antiquities, etc.
in the Fitzwilliam Museum.   1898
—— 2nd ed.   1904
Candidature for Curatorship of the Walker Art Gallery, Liverpool.
1904
Fly-sheets connected with the conferring of a degree upon H. A.
Chapman.   4° 1906
CHAPMAN (J.)   Phlegon re-examined : in answer to Dr Sykes's
second defense of his Dissertation concerning Phlegon.   1735

CHAPMAN (T.)   An inquiry into the right of Appeal from the Chancellor or Vice-Chancellor of the University of Cambridge, in matters of Discipline.   *London*, 1751
—— 2nd ed.   *London*, 1752
Further Inquiry into the right of Appeal...   *London*, 1752
CHAPPELOW (L.)   The Traveller: an Arabic poem, intitled Tograi...now render'd into English.   4° 1758
CHAPTER and Verse. By X.Y.X. [i.e. D. P. Turner, Pemb.].   1900
CHARITY Commissioners. Report. Cambridge.   F° *London*, 1837
CHARITY Organization Society. Fifth, Thirteenth Annual Report.
                                                          1884, 1893
The Charities of Cambridge.   1898
Register of educational, economic, philanthropic, and other agencies.
                                                              1904
CHARITY Schools. Sermon, by Wm. Whiston, 25 January 170$\frac{4}{5}$
Rise, progress, and present state of the Charity Schools in Cambridge.
                                                          F° 1763
CHARLES I, *King of England*.   His Majesties Declaration, in answer to a Declaration of the Lords and Commons.   4° 1642
An extract of certain papers of intelligence from Cambridge, concerning His Majestie and the Armie.   4° *n.p.* 1647
Oratio in martyrium Caroli I. By W. Crowe.   *London*, 1720
CHARLES II, *King of England*. *See* Love (R.); Verses, 1660, 1662, 1684/5.
CHARLES (J.H.)   Vicarage of Burwell, Cambs. : testimonials of J. H. Charles.   1885
CHASE (D.P.)   University Tests.   *London*, 1869
CHASE (F.H.), *Bp of Ely*.   Sermon preached at the Commemoration of Benefactors in Peterhouse Chapel.   1907
CHATFIELD (R.)   An appeal to the British Public in the case of the persecuted Greeks.   *London*, 1822
CHATHAM (William Pitt, *1st Earl of*).   Letters written by the late Earl of Chatham to his nephew Thomas Pitt, then at Cambridge.
3rd ed.   *London*, 1804
CHAWNER (G.)   List of Incunabula in the Library of King's College, Cambridge.   1908
CHAWNER (W.)   Greek in the Previous Examination.   A letter addressed to members of the Senate.   4° 1904
Prove all things: a paper read at the first meeting of the Religious Discussion Society, Emmanuel College.   1909
Supplement to *Prove all things*.   1909
CHEMICAL Jingles for Bunglers. By one of them [i.e. A. Wormald, Trin. Hall].   1894
CHERRYHINTON. Church Restoration. Report.   1874
CHESS. A poem. By a Member of the Cambridge University Chess Club.   12° *London*, 1858
CHESS Club. Laws of the University Chess Club.   1901
CHESTER (P.)   An Occasional Letter to Dr Keen.   [Attr. to P. Chester.]   *London* (1750)

CHESTERTON. *See* Smedley (E. A.).
CHEVELEY.   Illustrations of Cheveley Church, Cambridgeshire.
By John Fairlie.   F⁰ *London* (1851)
CHICHELE (H.), *Abp of Canterbury.* Life by O. L. Spencer.
                                                    London, 1783
CHILDERS (J.W.) *See* Orford (*Lord*).
CHIPPENHAM. *See* Barber (R. W.).
CHITTY (M.D.) Mary Bateson. In Memoriam. (Reprinted from
the *Persean,* March 1907.)   1907
CHOIR Benevolent Fund. Choral Festival, King's College Chapel,
May 22, 1860.   1860
CHORAL Union. Concert in Guildhall, May 2, 1889. (Acis and
Galatea.)   1889
CHORISTER (The). [By S. Baring Gould.]   12⁰ [1854]
——— 10th ed.   1895
CHRETIEN (C.P.) A letter to the Rev. F. D. Maurice, on some
points suggested by his recent criticism of Mr Mansel's Bampton
Lectures.   *London,* 1859
CHRIST CHURCH. A Jubilee memorial of the consecration of
Christ Church, Cambridge. By W. White.   1889
CHRISTIAN (E.) Syllabus of lectures delivered in the University of
Cambridge. (Law.)   *London,* 1797
Syllabus of lectures. (Law.)   *London,* 1816
A vindication of the right of the Universities of the United Kingdom
to a copy of every new publication. 3rd ed.   1818
An explanation of the law of Elections in the University of Cambridge.
                                                        1822
CHRISTIAN Kalendar for the use of members of the Established
Church, 1845. By a lay member of the Cambridge Camden
Society [S. N. Stokes].   [1844]
CHRISTIAN warfare defended and recommended in a Sermon
intended to have been preached...28 Feb. 1794. [Attr. to
— Frith, Trin. Hall.]   *London* (1794)
CHRISTIE (W.D.) Two speeches on the Universities of Oxford
and Cambridge.   *London,* 1850
College influence and bribery in the Borough Election. A letter to
the Liberal Electors of Cambridge.   1865
CHRIST'S College. Argument in the case of the Poor's Rate. [By
Sir J. Marriott.]   (1768)
Christ's College Magazine. Easter term 1886 (No. 1)—Mich. term
1908 (No. 68).   1886–1908
Christ's College. By John Peile. (College histories.)
                                                    London, 1900
400th Anniversary, 4 July 1905. List of Guests, Service, Menu, etc.
                                                        1905
List of past and present members.   4⁰ 1905
——— 2nd ed.   4⁰ 1906
See also Marriott (*Sir* J.); Milton Tercentenary.
CHRONOLOGICAL series of Engravers. [By T. Martyn.] 1770

CHURCH Aid Association. Subscription List, etc.   4° 1878
CHURCH Congress. Cambridge, Sept. 1910 :
The Jubilee Church Congress day by day.   1910
—— 2nd ed.   1910
Illustrated Guide.   *London,* 1910
Official Programme.   *London,* 1910
Colonial Church Exhibition.   (1910)
Invitations, circulars, programmes, newspaper cuttings, etc.
CHURCH Missionary Association. Seventy-fifth Report.   1893
CHURCH Music Society. Rules.   1854
First Report.   1854
CHURCH of England Zenana Missionary Soc. Camb. Assoc. Report.   12° (1900)
CHURCH Rates. The Poor Man's case against the Church Rate Abolition Bill and the Ministry.   1837
CHURCH Reform. Memorial, Fly-sheets, etc.   1885
CHURCH Reform League. Proceedings at meeting, February 1899
CHURCH Union Society. Statement.   1842
CHURCHILL (F.) Oratio...in Aula Clarensi...memoriae S. Blythe ejusdem Aulae Praefecti.   4° 1767
CHURTON (R.) Lives of Wm. Smyth and Ric. Sutton, founders of Brasen Nose College.   *Oxford,* 1800
CICERO. Essay on the philosophical writings of Cicero.   1832
CIVIL Service. *See* Latham (H.).
CLARE College. Letter to Sir C. Isham, etc. By John Mapletoft. [The matter of Mr Freeman's Foundation.]   4° *n.p.* 1746
Letter to Sir H. Drury and others. By John Mapletoft. [The matter of Mr Freeman's Foundation.]   4° *n.p.* 1748
The practice of a College, and the Visitor's decision concerning it. [By John Mapletoft. Mr Freeman's Foundation in Clare Hall.]   4° *London,* 1755
Oratio...in Aula Clarensi...memoriae S. Blythe ejusdem Aulae Prae- fecti. By F. Churchill.   4° 1767
Sermon at Consecration of the Chapel, 5 July, 1769.   4° 1769
Petition of J. Mansfield, B.D., Fellow, to the Chancellor, with order of V.-C. 1799–1800.   [1800]
Argument of the Master on the appeal of W. F. L. Fischer, whose fellowship he had declared vacant.   1849
A reply to the "Argument" of the Master of Clare Hall, for declaring vacant the Fellowship of W. F. L. Fischer. By James Burdakin.   1849
On a bird's-eye view of Clare Hall. By J. W. Clark. (*C.A.S.*)   (1890)
Clare College. By J. R. Wardale. (College histories.) *London,* 1899
Clare College. Letters and Documents. Ed. by J. R. Wardale. 1903
Catalogue of Manuscripts. By M. R. James.   1905
See also Acts and Bills, 1763, 1823, 1825; Lady Clare Magazine.
CLARK (A.) The Colleges of Oxford : their history and traditions. Ed. by A. Clark.   *London,* 1891

CLARK (A.)

Lincoln College, Oxford. (College histories.) *London,* 1898

A Bodleian guide for visitors. 12° *Oxford,* 1906

CLARK (E.C.) Practical International Law. Introduction. 1869

Testimonials when a candidate for the Regius Professorship of Laws
in the University of Cambridge. 1872

Cambridge legal studies. 1888

Greek and other studies at Cambridge. 1891

English Academical costume. (Mediaeval.) (*Arch. Journal.*)
Exeter, 1894

College Caps and Doctors' Hats. (*Arch. Journal.*) *London,* 1904

CLARK (J.) Sketch of the professional life and character of J. Clark.
By J. R. Fenwick. *Newcastle,* 1806

CLARK (J.W.) A Long Vacation Ramble in Norway and Sweden.
By X and Y (two unknown quantities). [By J. W. Clark and
J. W. Dunning.] 1857

Annals of the Church of St Mary the Less, Cambridge. A paper
read before the Cambridge Architectural Soc., 19 March, 1857.
(*Ecclesiologist,* October.)

On the Churches in the Island of Gottland. (*Ecclesiologist,* June,
August, 1858.)

Annals of All Saints' Church, Cambridge. A paper read before the
Cambridge Architectural Soc., 8 March, 1860. (*Ecclesiologist,*
April, 1860.)

Journal of a yacht voyage to the Faroe Islands and Iceland. (*Vacation
Tourists and Notes of Travel in* 1860.) *Cambridge and London,* 1861

On the proposed change of the hour of dinner in hall. (Trin. Coll.
28 Feb. 1862.) 1862

Remarks on the Report of the Museums and Lecture Rooms
Syndicate.—Further Remarks. (March, 1863.) 1863

Clark (J.W.) and Jackson (H.) Examination paper in Shakespeare.
Trin. Coll. (5 June, 1863.) F° 1863

Clark (J.W.) and Jackson (H.) Examination paper in Shakespeare.
Trin. Coll. (8 June, 1865.) F° 1865

Report to Vice-Chancellor on the removal of the collection of Comparative Anatomy. (19 Oct. 1865.) 4° 1865

Remarks on the proposed Professorship of Zoology and Comparative
Anatomy. (4 Feb. 1866.) 4° 1866

Remarks on Trinity College Chapel. (5 Dec. 1867.) 1867

Clark (J.W.) and Newton (A.) On the condition of the Museum
of Zoology. (15 Feb. 1869.) 4° 1869

The Lyons Mail. A drama in four acts freely adapted [by
J. W. Clark] from *Le Courrier de Lyon,* for performance at the
A.D.C., Cambridge. *London,* 1870

—— Revised and enlarged. 1895

List of Dissections. (Mus. Zool. and Comp. Anat.) 1871

Peer? or Peasant? A story of 1685. A drama in four acts [by
J. W. Clark] written for performance at the A.D.C., Cambridge,
May 29, 1871. 1871

CLARK (J.W.)

On the skeleton of a Narwhal (*Monodon Monoceros*), with two fully developed tusks. (*Proc. Zool. Soc. Lond.* 17 Jan. 1871.)
London (1871)

La Comédie Française. (*Academy*, 15 July, 1871.)

How will it end? A Drama altered from *Le Cas de Conscience* of Octave Feuillet. 1872

—— Type-written copy.

Notes on the visceral anatomy of the Hippopotamus. (*Proc. Zool. Soc. Lond.* 20 Feb. 1872.) London (1872)

The Dramatic Season, French and English. (*Academy*, 15 Aug. 1872.)

On changes at the New Museums. (21 Nov. 1872.) 4° 1872

On the eared Seals of the Auckland Islands. (*Proc. Zool. Soc. Lond.* 18 Nov. 1873.) London (1874)

On the skull of a Marten from Burwell Fen, Cambs. (*Proc. Zool. Soc. Lond.* 2 Dec. 1873.) London (1874)

Clark (J.W.) and Bridge (T.W.) Illustrations of comparative anatomy, vertebrate and invertebrate. 2nd ed. 1875

On the needs of the Museum of Zoology and Comparative Anatomy. (9 Feb. 1875.) 4° 1875

The late Professor Willis. (*Camb. Chron.* 6 March, 1875.) 1875

On Seals. Report of lectures at the Zoological Gardens. (*Morning Post*, 22, 29 April, 1875.)

On Seals. Report of lectures at Zoological Gardens. (*Nature*, 29 April, 6 May, 1875.)

Sea Elephants from Kerguelen's Land at Berlin. (*Nature*, 2 Sept. 1875.)

Sea-Lions. (*Contemporary Review*, Dec. 1875.)

On the eared Seals of the Islands of St Paul and Amsterdam, etc. (*Proc. Zool. Soc. Lond.* 6 Dec. 1875.) London (1876)

Notes on a Dolphin taken off the coast of Norfolk. (*Proc. Zool. Soc. Lond.* 20 June, 1876.) London (1876)

Compulsory attendance at Professors' Lectures. (2 May, 1877.)
4° 1877

Clark (J.W.) and Newton (E.) On the osteology of the Solitaire. (*Phil. Trans. Roy. Soc.*, vol. 168.) 4° London, 1878

Notes on three stuffed specimens of the Sea-Lion of the Pribilov Islands. (*Otaria ursina.*) (*Proc. Zool. Soc. Lond.* 19 March, 1878.)
London (1878)

On proposed changes in the Statutes. (*Times*, 4 April, 1878.)

Les Fourchambault, by Émile Augier, at the Théâtre Français. (*Academy*, 27 April, 1878.)

Parisian Theatres. (*Academy*, 4 May, 1878.)

Review of W. H. Pollock's *Modern French Theatre*. (*Academy*, 17 August, 1878.)

Le Chandelier, by Alfred de Musset, at the Théâtre Français. (*Academy*, 12 Oct. 1878.)

French Theatres during the Exhibition. (*Academy*, 19 Oct. 1878.)

CLARK (J.W.)

Le Mari d'Ida, by MM. Delacour and Mancel, at the Théâtre du Vaudeville, Paris. (*Academy*, Oct. 1878.)

University Livings. (1 Dec. 1878.)   4° 1878

A Description of the Medrásen in Algeria. (*C. A. S.* 8 Nov. 1875.)
                                                          1879
Review of A. B. Cochrane's *The Théâtre Français in the reign of Louis XV.* (*Academy*, 29 March, 1879.)

Ruy Blas at the Théâtre Français. (*Academy*, 19 April, 1879.)

The French Stage. (*Saturday Review*, 15 May, 1880.)

Recent Restoration in Italy. (*Saturday Review*, 21 Aug. 1880.)

Cambridge. Brief historical and descriptive notes. F° *London*, 1881

—— Large paper copy.   F° *London*, 1881

—— Another ed.   *London*, 1890

—— Another ed.   *London*, 1893

—— New ed., with forty-six illustrations.   *London*, 1908

History of the Peal of Bells belonging to King's College, Cambridge. (*C. A. S.* 3 March, 1879.)   1881

On the old Provost's Lodge of King's College, with special reference to the furniture. (*C. A. S.* 17 March, 1879.)   1881

History of the Church of S. John Baptist, Cambridge; commonly called S. John Zachary. (*C. A. S.* 1 Dec. 1879.)   1881

London to Paris in a Snowstorm. (*Pall Mall Gazette*, 21 Jan. 1881.)

Prehistoric Peru. (Review.) (*Saturday Review*, 22 Jan. 1881.)

M. Sardou on Divorce. (*Saturday Review*, 29 Jan. 1881.)

La Princesse de Bagdad at the Comédie Française. (*Saturday Review*, 12 Feb. 1881.)

Review of J. E. Harting's *British Animals extinct within historic times.* (*Saturday Review*, 26 Feb. 1881.)

A Modern Greek Novel. (Review of *Loukis Laras.*) (*Saturday Review*, 26 March, 1881.)

The Comédie Française. (*Saturday Review*, 16 April, 1881.)

Seals. (*Saturday Review*, 23 April, 1881.)

What is a Cat? (Review of St George Mivart's *The Cat.*) (*Saturday Review*, 23 April, 1881.)

Parisian Theatres. (*Saturday Review*, 7 May, 1881.)

Die Meininger. (*Saturday Review*, 21 May, 1881.)

William Whewell. (*Saturday Review*, 28 May, 1881.)

The Great Gateway of Trinity College, Cambridge. (For an etching by R. Farren in *The Etcher*, Sept. 1881.)

Excavations at Carnac. (Review of J. Miln's book of that name.) (*Saturday Review*, 24 Sept. 1881.)

Our old Trees. (*Camb. Review*, 26 Oct. 1881.)

F. M. Balfour's *Embryology.* (Review.) (*Saturday Review*, 12 Nov. 1881.)

Austin's *Savonarola.* (Review.) (*Saturday Review*, 17 Dec. 1881.)

Feodora, by Sardou. (*Pall Mall Gazette*, 27 Dec. 1881.)

Sir Charles Lyell. (Review of his Life and Letters.) (*Saturday Review*, 4 Feb. 1882.)

CLARK (J.W.)

Romeo and Juliet at the Lyceum. (*Pall Mall Gazette*, 23 March, 1882.)

Half a century of Cambridge life. (On W. Whewell.) (*Ch. Qu. Review*, April, 1882.)

The Comédie Française. (*Saturday Review*, 15 April, 1882.)

A French Othello. (*Saturday Review*, 29 April, 1882.)

Review of E. W. White's *Cameos from the Silver Land*. (*Saturday Review*, 13 May, 1882.)

Ants, Bees, and Wasps. (Review of Sir John Lubbock.) (*Saturday Review*, 22 July, 1882.)

Prof. Balfour. (Obituary.) (*Academy*, 29 July, 1882.)

Professor Francis Maitland Balfour. (Obituary.) (*Saturday Review*, 29 July, 1882.)

The Ajax at Cambridge. (*Saturday Review*, 9 Dec. 1882.)

Bishop Thirlwall. (*Ch. Qu. Review*, April, 1883.)

The Comédie Française. (*Saturday Review*, 22 July, 1883.)

Edward Henry Palmer. (*Ch. Qu. Review*, Oct. 1883.)

Catalogue of the First (–Second) Exhibition of University and College Portraits held in the Fitzwilliam Museum May 1884, May 1885. 1884–5

Note on the tomb (in Westminster Abbey) of Margaret Beaufort, Countess of Richmond and Derby. (*C. A. S.* 7 May, 1883.) 1884

Tempora mutantur. [On the reception of Q. Elizabeth in 1564.] (*Camb. Review*, 12 March, 1884.)

On a Sea-Lion from the East Coast of Australia (*Otaria Cinerea*, Péron). (*Proc. Zool. Soc. Lond.* 18 March, 1884.) London (1884)

On the removal of Baratta's statue of Glory from the Law School to the Fitzwilliam Museum. (*Camb. Univ. Reporter*, 27 Jan. 1885.)

Clark (J.W.) and Redfarn (W.B.) Ancient Wood and Iron Work in Cambridge. Fo 1886

Address delivered 18 May, 1885, on retiring from the office of President of the Camb. Ant. Soc. (*C. A. S.*) 1887

On the sites proposed for the Sedgwick Memorial Museum. (9 May, 1887.) Fo 1887

Coutts Trotter. In Memoriam. By Michael Foster, J. W. Clark, and Sedley Taylor. 1888

On the acquisition by the University of the Perse School estate. (1 May, 1888.) 4o 1888

The Great Flood. (*Ch. Qu. Review*, Oct. 1888.)

On the skeleton of *Rhytina gigas* lately acquired for the Museum of Zoology and Comparative Anatomy. (*Proc. Camb. Phil. Soc.* 25 Feb. 1889.) 1889

Remarks when President of the Philosophical Soc. (*Camb. Univ. Reporter*, 5 Nov. 1889.)

Clark (J.W.) and Hughes (T.McK.) The Life and Letters of Adam Sedgwick. 2 vols. 1890

CLARK (J.W.)

Notes on a fire-place lately discovered in the Master's Lodge, Christ's College. (*C. A. S.* 5 March, 1888.) 1891

The foundation and early years of the Cambridge Philosophical Society. Address delivered on resigning office of President, 27 Oct. 1890. (*Proc. Camb. Phil. Soc.*) 1891

The Book of Observances of the English House of Austin Canons. (24 March, 1891.) 4° 1891

Lord Houghton. (*Ch. Qu. Review*, July, 1891.)

On a bird's-eye view of Clare Hall. (*C. A. S.* 19 Nov. 1890.) 1892

On the Canopy carried over Queen Elizabeth when she visited Cambridge, 1564. (*C. A. S.* 19 Nov. 1890.) 1892

An attempt to trace the architectural history and plan of Barnwell Priory. (*C. A. S.* 18 Feb. 1891.) 1892

On the proposed building in Senate House Yard. (11 May, 1892.) 4° 1892

The Hall of Pembroke College, Cambridge. (*Athenaeum*, 19 Aug. 1892.)

To the Electors of the Disney Professorship of Archaeology. [In favour of Mr W. H. St John Hope.] (6 Nov. 1892.) F° 1892

The proposed Sedgwick Memorial Museum. (21 Nov. 1892.) 4° 1892

On libraries at Cesena, Wells, Guildford, and Clare College, Cambridge. (*C. A. S.* 26 Oct., 11 Nov. 1891.) 1893

Guildford Grammar School Library. (*Surrey Times*, 30 Dec. 1893.)

Libraries in the Medieval and Renaissance periods. (Rede Lecture.) 1894

On libraries at Christ Church, Canterbury; Citeaux, Clairvaux; Zutphen, Enkhuizen. (*C. A. S.* 7 May, 1894.) 1895

Sir Richard Owen. (*Ch. Qu. Review*, July, 1895.)

Stranger than Fiction. [On the plot of *The Lyons Mail*.] (*Camb. Review*, 14 Nov. 1895.)

On libraries at Lincoln Cathedral; Westminster Abbey; St Paul's Cathedral, London. (*C. A. S.* 18 Feb. 1895.) 1896

Considerations on the acquisition of the Mortlock and Downing sites. (9 July, 1896.) 4° 1896

The Trinity Building Scheme. (*Granta*, 28 Nov. 1896.)

The site of the Sedgwick Memorial Museum. (7 Dec. 1896.) 4° 1896

Clark (J.W.) and Atkinson (T.D.) Cambridge described and illustrated. *London*, 1897
Press notices, etc. on the book.

On degrees for Women. (17 May, 1897.) 4° 1897

A Concise Guide to the Town and University of Cambridge. 1898

—— 2nd ed. 1902

—— —— India paper copy. 1902

—— British Assoc. issue, including Ely. 1904

—— 3rd ed. 1906

—— Suppl. issued for Church Congress. 1910
Press notices, etc. on the Guide.

CLARK (J.W.)

The Greek Play, Cambridge. (W. G. Elliot's *Amateur Clubs and Actors*.) (*London*, 1898)

The Queens' College of St Margaret and St Bernard. (1448–1898.) 4° 1898

Cambridge and its Colleges. [Review of A. H. Thompson's book of that name.] (*Camb. Review*, 20 Oct. 1898.)

On the disturbances at Lord Kitchener's visit. (*Camb. Review*, 1 Dec. 1898.)

Speech on the organization of the Library. (*Camb. Univ. Reporter*, 13 Dec. 1898.)

Museums of Science. History of the site and buildings. 18 March, 1899. (Statement of the needs of the University. Pt II.) 1899

Old Friends at Cambridge and elsewhere. *London*, 1900
Press notices, letters, etc. on the book.

The Care of Books. (Sandars Lectures. Privately pr.) 1900

M. Bouvier on Daudet and Maeterlinck. (*Camb. Review*, 31 May, 1900.)

A Medieval Monastery : its plan and its inmates. (*Guardian*, 8, 15 August, 1900.)

Speeches on the scheme for roofing in the East Court of the University Library. (*Camb. Univ. Reporter*, 5 June, 1900 ; 4 Dec. 1900 ; 31 May, 1901 ; 5 Nov. 1901.)

The Care of Books. 1901
—— 2nd ed. 1902
—— Cheaper re-issue. 1909
Press notices and criticisms on the book.

Historical Sketch of the Cambridge University Press. (Prefixed to *Specimens of types and ornaments in use at the University Press*.) (1901)

On the Vatican Library of Sixtus IV. (*C. A. S.* 6 March, 1899.) 1901

Le Roi est mort ! Vive le Roi ! [On the celebration of the accession of a Sovereign at Cambridge.] (*Camb. Review*, 7 Feb. 1901.)

Cambridge University Library. [Roofing in the East Court.] (*Times*, 8 March, 1901.)

Remarks on the scheme for roofing in the Eastern Quadrangle of the Library. (28 Oct. 1901.) 4° 1901

The University Library of the Future. Time : A.D. 2000. (*Camb. Review*, 14 Nov. 1901.)

The Needs of the Library. An open letter to T. F. C. Huddleston. (15 Nov. 1901.) 4° 1901

The Needs of the Library. (18, 19 Nov. 1901.) 4° 1901

The Needs of the Library. A second open letter to T. F. C. Huddleston. (20 Nov. 1901.) 4° 1901

The literary department at Somerset House. (*Athenaeum*, 6 June, 1903.)

On the Studies Syndicate. (23 Nov. 1903.) 4° 1903

CLARK (J.W.)

Concise Guide to Ely Cathedral. 1904

Le Roi s'amuse. A drama by Victor Hugo. Act v [translated].
4° 1904

On the work done to the Library of Exeter Cathedral in 1412 and 1413.— On two pieces of furniture in Exeter Cathedral, formerly used for the protection of books. (*C. A. S.* 3 Nov. 1902.) 1904

On two wheel-desks.—A description of the East Room of the University Library, by W. Cole. (*C. A. S.* 11 May, 1903.)
1904

Royal Visits to Cambridge. (*Camb. Review*, 18 Feb. 1904.)

The proposed sale of land. (3, 4 March, 1904.) 4° 1904

The Senate House. (*Camb. Review*, 9 March, 1904.)

Speech in favour of a new Entrance to the Library. (*Camb. Univ. Reporter*, 12 March, 1904.)

On the list of Benefactors in the Commemoration Service. (*Camb. Univ. Reporter*, 14 May, 1904.)

The origin and growth of the University of Cambridge. Lecture before British Association. (*Camb. Daily News*, 19 Aug. 1904.)

On the charitable foundations called Chests. (*C.A.S.* 25 Jan. 1904.)
1905

On some English verses written in a fifteenth century service-book. (*C. A. S.* 25 Jan. 1904.) 1905

Camb. Univ. Assoc. Appeal for the Library. Speech. (24 Jan. 1905.) 4° 1905

The University Library, Cambridge. (*University Extension*, No. 2, Feb. 1905.)

The origin and development of the Collegiate plan at Oxford and Cambridge. (*Builder*, 18 March, 1905.)

Speech from the stage on Undergraduate manners in the Theatre. (*Camb. Daily News*, 2 May, 1905.)

Trinity College, Cambridge. (*Country Life*, 4 Nov. 1905.)

Clark (J.W.) and others. The University Library, Cambridge. An Appeal. 5 editions. 4° 1905–8

The Riot at the Great Gate of Trinity College, February, 1610–11. (*C. A. S.* 8° publ. 43.) 1906

Clark (J.W.) and Bartholomew (A.T.) Hand-list of the works of Richard Bentley. 1906

On Pensions. (8 March, 1906.) 4° 1906

The Library, Merton College, Oxford. (*Country Life*, 4 Aug. 1906.)

All Souls College, Oxford. (*Country Life*, 25 Aug. 1906.)

Radcliffe Library, Oxford. (*Country Life*, 13 Oct. 1906.)

Queen's College, Oxford. (*Country Life*, 8 Dec. 1906.)

Note on the Library of the Benedictine Monastery of La Chaise Dieu in Auvergne. (*C. A. S.* 7 May, 1906.) 1907

Peterhouse Library, Cambridge. (*Country Life*, 7 Feb. 1907.)

St Paul's Cathedral Library. (*Country Life*, 23 March, 1907.)

On the plays chosen for presentation at the New Theatre. (*Camb. Review*, 27 April, 1907.)

CLARK (J.W.)

The public recitation of Prize Exercises. (*Camb. Review*, 23 May, 1907.)

Alfred Newton. (*Camb. Review*, 13 June, 1907.)

In Memoriam. Reginald Balfour. (*Camb. Review*, 24 Oct. 1907.)

Clark (J.W.) and Bartholomew (A.T.) Richard Bentley, D.D. A bibliography. 4° 1908

On two book covers, with chains, found in the tower of St Benedict's Church, Cambridge. (*C. A. S.* 24 Feb. 1908.) 1908

Clark (J.W.) and Fletcher (H.) Oxford and Cambridge delineated. 4° *London*, 1909

Memories and Customs, 1820–1860. (Extr. from *Camb. Review*.) 1909

Buckingham College. (*Camb. Review*, 4 Feb. 1909.)

Trinity Hall Library, Cambridge. (*Country Life*, 16 Oct. 1909.)

Captain Coe's Collection. (*Camb. Chronicle*, July, 1910.)

See Amateur Dramatic Club 1864, 1882, 1908; 1868, 1895; Barnwell, 1897, 1907; Elizabeth (*Queen*), 1892; Endowments, 1904; Farren (R.), 1881; Grace Book Γ, 1908; Josselin (J.), 1880; Maine (*Sir* H. S.), 1894; Matriculations, 1902; Ordinances, 1892, 1896, 1901, 1904, 1908; Statutes, 1896, 1904; Willis (R.), 1886.

CLARK (W.) Outlines of a course of lectures. n.d.

Catalogue of the Anatomical Museum in the University of Cambridge. (2 copies.) 1820

Analysis of a course of lectures on the anatomy and physiology of the human body. 1822

Report on animal physiology. 1834

Reviews. (*Brit. and Foreign Med. Rev.*, Jan. 1840.)

Catalogue of the osteological portion of specimens contained in the Anatomical Museum of the University of Cambridge. 1862

A Cambridge Professor of the last generation [W. Clark, M.D.]. By C. K. Watson. (*Macmillan's Mag.*, Jan. 1870.)

CLARK (W.G.) A score of lyrics. 1849

Gazpacho: or summer months in Spain. *London*, 1850

Cambridge life according to C. A. Bristed. (*Fraser's Magazine*, Jan. 1854.)

Peloponnesus. *London*, 1858

Four sermons preached in the Chapel of Trinity College. 1860

Naples and Garibaldi. (*Vacation Tourists and Notes of Travel.*) 1861

Knowledge and Charity. A sermon preached before the University of Cambridge, Oct. 27, 1861. 1861

On the duty of members of the English Church in the present controversies. Sermon. 1863

Speech in the Senate House, 2 June, 1864. 4° 1864

William Whewell. In memoriam. (*Macmillan's Mag.*, Apr. 1866.)

A Commemoration sermon preached in St Mary's Church, Nov. 1, 1868. *London*, 1868

CLARK (W.G.)

A few words on Irish questions. 1868

The present dangers of the Church of England. 1870

Reply, by Ch. Hebert. 1870

True and false Protestantism. *London*, 1871

See Brimley (G.), Essays; Shakespeare (W.).

CLARK Lectureship. *See* Ainger (A.).

CLARKE (C.B.) On the Moral Science Tripos. 1861

CLARKE (*Sir* E.) Royal Agricultural Society. The first two country meetings...Oxford, 1839, Cambridge, 1840. 1894

CLARKE (E.D.) Testimony of different authors respecting the colossal statue of Ceres placed in the vestibule of the Public Library at Cambridge, July 1, 1803. 1803

The tomb of Alexander. 4° 1805

A syllabus of lectures in mineralogy. 1807

Greek marbles brought from the shores of the Euxine, etc. and deposited in the Public Library, Cambridge. 1809

—— Large paper copy. 1809

A letter to Herbert Marsh, D.D., in reply to certain observations contained in his pamphlet relative to the British and Foreign Bible Society. 1812

Observations upon some Celtic remains, lately discovered near Sawston. (*Archaeologia*, XVIII.) 4° (*London*, 1817)

Announcement of a course of lectures on mineralogy, 13 Jan. 1820. F° 1820

Address read at the first meeting of the Cambridge Philosophical Society. 4° 1821

An account of some antiquities found at Fulbourn in Cambridgeshire. (*Archaeologia*, XIX.) 4° (*London*, 1821)

On Cadmium, and the habitudes of some of its ores. (*Annals of Philosophy*.) *London* (1822)

Grace to buy his collection of Minerals for £1500, 28 May, 1822. 4° 1822

Notice of Grace to accept Bust, and place it in vestibule in Library, 28 June, 1824. F° 1824

Life and Remains. By William Otter. 4° *London*, 1824

—— Another ed. 2 vols. *London*, 1825

CLARKE (G.R.) Cambridge University Election. Dissenters' Chapel Bill, alias the Socinian Endowment Bill. (1847)

CLARKE (J.) A farther examination of Dr S. Clarke's notions of space. 1734

CLARKE (J.H.) Experimental pathology explained and exemplified. (Letter from the *Spectator*, Dec. 4, 1886.)

CLARKE (J.S.) An Artist's rambles in Cambridgeshire. Ser. 1, 2. 4° 1894

CLARKE (S.) *See* Grotius (H.).

CLASSICAL Association. Proceedings at Cambridge, 1907. *London*, 1907

CLASSICAL Examination. Plans, with Graces relating thereto. May, 1822.   4⁰ 1822

CLASSICAL Examinations; or a selection of University Scholarship and other public Examination Papers.   1830

CLASSICAL studies. Fly-sheets relating thereto, from 1855.

CLASSICAL Tripos. Grace to appoint Syndicate to revise Regulations, 25 April, 1849.   F⁰ 1849

    Report of the Syndicate, 30 May, 1849.   F⁰ 1849

    On the Classical Tripos Examination. By Henry Sidgwick. (1866)

CLAY (C.J.) *See* Press.

CLAYTON (C.) Sermon preached in Trinity Church. 1 Feb. 1857

    University Tests bill.   12⁰ 1871

CLAYTON (J.R.) and Bell (A.) The stained glass of the great west window, King's College, Cambridge.   4⁰ 1879

CLEMENT'S (St) Church. A few remarks on a sermon, preached in the parish church of St Clement, Cambridge, and since printed. By a Layman.   1863

CLOSE (F.) The restoration of Churches is the restoration of Popery. 2nd ed.   *London*, 1844

    Church Architecture scripturally considered.   *London*, 1844

    Remarks [on above]. By T. K. Arnold.   *London*, 1844

    Reply to the *Remarks* of Rev. T. K. Arnold [as above]. *London*, 1844

    Examination of Close's *Reply*. By T. K. Arnold. *London*, 1844

    Review of *Church Architecture*, and other works. (*Parker's Lond. Mag.* 1, 2.)   *London*, 1845

CLOUGH (Anne J.) Suggestions for the training of Teachers. 1877

    Funeral Sermon. By H. E. Ryle.   12⁰ 1892

    Memoir. By B. A. Clough.   *London*, 1897

CLUB Law. A Comedy acted in Clare Hall, Cambridge, about 1599–1600.... With introduction and notes, by G. C. Moore Smith.   4⁰ 1907

COBB (G.F.) Our Chapel choir, and the appointment of Chaplains. (Trinity College.)   (1867)

    The Kiss of Peace. (2nd ed.)   *London* (1868)

    "Separation," not "Schism." A plea for the position of Anglican reunionists.   *London*, 1869

    A few words on reunion and the coming Council at Rome.   *London*, 1869

    Road paving. To the Paving Commissioners for the town of Cambridge.   1878

    The Sewage question, etc.   1878

    On the Sewage of Cambridge.   F⁰ 1884

    Brief history of the Organ in Trinity College Chapel.   1891

COCKAYNE (O.) Mr Cockayne's narrative. (King's College School.)   *n.p.* 1869

    Notes on Mr Cockayne's narrative.   *n.p.* (1869)

COCKBURN (W.) Saint Peter's denial of Christ. (Seatonian Prize Poem for 1802.)   4⁰ 1802

COCKBURN (W.)
  Christ raising the daughter of Jairus. (Seatonian Prize Poem for
    1803.)   4° 1803
  Letters to the Editors of the Edinburgh Review.   1805
  Strictures on clerical education in the University of Cambridge.
                                                        London, 1809
  A new system of geology ; dedicated to Professor Sedgwick.
                                                        London, 1849
COCKERELL (S.C.)   Testimonials when candidate for Directorship
  of Fitzwilliam Museum.   *London*, 1908
COCKERELL (T.D.A.)   The Darwin Celebration.   (*Popular
  Science Monthly*.)   *n.p.* 1910
CODDINGTON (H.)   A few remarks on the New Library question.
  By a Member of neither Syndicate [H. Coddington].   1831
CODEX Bezæ.   Prospectus of publication in facsimile.   F° 1897
COHEN (H.)   *See* Grimshaw (W.).
COLBATCH (J.)   A sermon preached in Trinity Colledge Chapel,
  Dec. 19, 1717, in commemoration of the Founders and Bene-
  factors.   1718
Jus Academicum.   4° *London*, 1722
Vindication of the Lord Bishop of Ely's Visitatorial Jurisdiction over
  Trinity College in General, and over the Master thereof in Particular.
                                              4° *London*, 1732
—— Another edition.   4° *n.p.* 1732
Reasons for altering the method used at present in letting Church
  and College leases.   By the Senior Fellow of a College in
  Cambridge [J. Colbatch].   1739
COLE (C.N.)   *See* Dugdale (W.) ; Elstobb (W.).
COLE (H.)   Popular Geology subversive of Divine Revelation.
  A letter to Adam Sedgwick.   *London*, 1834
A reflective letter...to the Royal Agricultural Society. *London*, 1852
The Bible a rule and test of religion and of science.   A sermon
  preached at Gt St Mary's Church, June 26, 1853.   1853
COLE (W.), † 1782.   Some observations on the Horns given by
  Henry I to the Cathedral of Carlisle. (*Archaeologia*, v.)
                                              4° (*London*, 1779)
COLE (W.), † 1806.   Oratio de ridiculo habita Cantab. primo die
  Julii, 1780. (Members' Prize.)   Accedit carmen comitiale 1774.
                                              4° *Etonae*, 1780
—— Another edition.   4° *Londini*, 1811
COLEMAN (J.)   Copies of marriage registers from the parish book of
  St Mary's Church, Whittlesey.   (*London*) 1880
COLERIDGE (A.D.)   Eton in the forties.   *London*, 1896
COLERIDGE (*Sir* J.D.)   Tests and their abolition.   *Oxford*, 1870
COLES (W.M.)   *See* Sellon (L.).
COLLECTION of Poems.   By the author of a Poem on the
  Cambridge Ladies.   1733
COLLECTION of theological tracts.   Ed. by R. Watson.   6 vols.
                                                           1785

COLLEGE Days.   Recorded in blank verse.   *London*, 1883
COLLEGE Jester.   By Balcony Stall [i.e. H. G. Meyer, Trin.].   1903
COLLEGE Meat Scandals: Report of Trial.   4° 1902
—— 2nd ed.   4° 1902
COLLEGE Recollections.   [? By S. O'Sullivan.]   *London*, 1829
COLLEGE Tuition considered in a letter to a friend.   By a Fellow,
    M.A. [J. R. Crowfoot].   1845
COLLEGIAN'S Guide ; or, Recollections of College Days.   By the
    Rev. [J. Pycroft], M.A.   *London*, 1845
COLLETT (W.R.)   A list of the Early Printed Books and an Index
    of English books printed before 1600 in the Library of Gonville
    and Caius College, Cambridge.   1850
COLLIER (J.)   Account of the death of A. Milnes Marshall.
          4° *n.p.* 1894
COLLIER (W.)   Poems on various occasions.   *London*, 1800
    See Letter from an Undergraduate, 1792.
COLLIGNON (C.)   Compendium anatomico-medicum.   4° 1756
    Tyrocinium anatomicum.   1763
    An enquiry into the structure of the human body. 2nd ed.   1764–5
    Medicina politica: or reflections on the art of physic.   1765
    Moral and medical dialogues.   1769
COLLINS (A.)   A Discourse of Free-thinking.   *n.p.* 1713
COLLINS (A.E.)   A Song of Trinity.   Music by Sedley Taylor.
          4° 1907
COLLINS (C.W.)   The Cambridge Apostles.   (*Blackwood's Magazine*,
    March, 1907.)
COLLISON (F.W.)   A vindication of the Anglican Reformers, in an
    examination of Prof. Scholefield's Discourses.   1841
    Remarks on a sermon by Prof. Scholefield entitled, *The Christian
    Altar*.   1842
    Some further remarks on *The Christian Altar*.   1843
COLQUHOUN (*Sir* P.)   An Epistola to Prince Albert...containing
    suggestions for a complete system of legal instruction.   1853
COLVIN (S.)   Brief catalogue of pictures in the Fitzwilliam Museum.
    Compiled under the direction of S. Colvin.   (Two editions.)
          1895, 1901
    See also Earp (F.R.).
COMBE (G.)   Review of *A Discourse on the studies of the University*.
    By Adam Sedgwick.   3rd ed.   (*Phrenological Journal*.)
          London, 1834
COMBINATION Papers.   [Lists of University preachers.]   1817–57
COMMEMORATION.   *Cp*. Bowes, *pp*. 260–2.
    Sermon preached 27 Oct. 1745.   By J. Garnett.   4° 1745
    Sermon preached Oct. 31, 1852.   By Harvey Goodwin.   1852
    Sermon preached Nov. 1, 1868.   By W. G. Clark.   *London*, 1868
    Form of Service for the Commemoration of Benefactors, used at
    Great St Mary's Church, Cambridge.   1873
    Sermon preached Oct. 27, 1878.   By G. F. Browne.   1878
    Sermon preached Nov. 5, 1882.   By A. F. Kirkpatrick.   1882

COMMENCEMENT. *Cp.* Bowes, *pp.* 260–2.

Two sermons...the first on 1 July, 1655, the other since. By
  W. Dillingham.   4° 1656
Sermon preached 5 July, 1696. By R. Bentley.   4° *London*, 1696
Sermon preached July 3, 1698. By F. Hutchinson.   4° 1698
Sermon preached July 3, 1698. By P. Nourse.   4° 1698
Sermon preached 2 July, 1699. By John Edwards.   4° 1699
Sermon preached 30 June, 1700. By John Gaskarth.   4° 1700
Sermon preached 30 June, 1700. By O. Blackall.   4° 1700
Concio...Junii 28, 1712. By R. Blomer.   4° *Londini*, 1712
Quaestiones una cum carminibus in magnis comitiis Cantabrigiae
  celebratis, 1714.   1714
Verses. By L. Eusden.   F° *London*, 1714
Music Speech, July 6, 1714. By Roger Long.   *London* (1714)
Carmina comitialia Cantabrigiensia. Ed. V. B. (Vincent Bourne).
                                         Londini, 1721
Sermon, 29 June, 1728. By Roger Long.   4° 1728
Quaestiones una cum carminibus in magnis comitiis celebratis, 1730.
                                            1730
Music Speech and Ode for Music, July 6, 1730. By J. Taylor.
                                      London, 1730
Concio ad clerum. 9 Oct. 1731. By P. Gretton.   1732
Sermon, July 2, 1732. By P. Gretton.   1732
Sermon, June 29, 1735. By S. Kerrich.   1735
Sermon, July 2, 1749. By Samuel Squire.   4° *London*, 1749
Sermon, July 2, 1749. By John Green.   4° 1749
Sermon, Commencement Sunday, 1757. By W. S. Powell. 3rd ed.
                                            1759
—— 4th ed.   1772
Sermon, 29 June, 1777. By Samuel Cooper.   4° 1777
Sermon, 4 July, 1784. By Edw. Oliver.   4° *London*, 1784
Sermon, 2 July, 1786. By W. Purkis.   4° 1786
Sermon, July 1, 1798. By T. Rennell.   (1798)
Sermon, Commencement Sunday, 1781. By W. Arnald.
                                 4° *London*, 1803
Programme of music in Gt St Mary's Church in aid of Adden-
  brooke's Hospital.   4° 1803
Sermon, June 29, 1806. By Edw. Maltby.   4° 1806
Sermon, July 4, 1813. By Herbert Marsh.   1813
Two Music Speeches...in 1714 and 1730. By R. Long and J.
  Taylor.   1819
Oratiuncula. J. Kaye. July, 1819.   (1819)
Sermon, 2 July, 1820. By C. J. Blomfield.   1820
Oratiuncula. J. Kaye. July, 1820.   (1820)
Sermon. By James Inman.   1820
Sermon, 30 June, 1822. By William Ainger.   1822
Sermon, 30 June, 1822. By J. H. Monk.   1822
Sermon, July 1, 1827. By John Lamb.   1827
Regulations for Commencement, 1828.   F° 1828

COMMENCEMENT.

Sermon, July 5, 1829. By T. G. Ackland.   1829
Sermon, July 4, 1830. By R. N. Adams.   1830
Sermon, June 30, 1833. By S. Lee.   *London*, 1833
Sermon, July 4, 1847. By Charles Perry.   1847
Sermon, June 16, 1861. By W. M. Campion.   1861
Sermon, June 15, 1862. By E. H. Perowne.   1862
Sermon, June 17, 1900. By J. E. B. Mayor.   1900
COMMISSION (University) Petition to Lord John Russell, presented
   10 July, 1848.   F° 1848
A letter addressed by Lord John Russell to the Chancellor explaining
   intentions of the Government (8 May, 1850).   F° (*London*) 1850
Representation presented by Vice-Chancellor (James Cartmell) to the
   Chancellor (14 May, 1850).   F° 1850
Address to the Vice-Chancellor by Members of the Senate in alarm
   at its approach (20 May, 1850).   F° 1850
Letter of Prince Albert to the Vice-Chancellor urging moderation on
   the University (27 May, 1850).   F° 1850
Appointment of Royal Commission (31 Aug. 1850).
                                                                F° lithographed.
Circular of Commissioners to Professors (30 Oct. 1850).
                                                           F° (*London*) 1850
Queries addressed by Commissioners to Professors (20 Nov. 1850).
                                                           F° (*London*) 1850
—— (14 Dec. 1850).   F° (*London*) 1850
—— (18 Feb. 1851).   F° (*London*) 1851
—— (19 Feb. 1851).   F° (*London*) 1851
The University Commission, or Lord John Russell's Postbag.
   Four instalments. [By W. Sewell.]   *Oxford*, 1850
Report of the Commission, 1850–2.   F° *London*, 1852
Documents relating to Cambridge.   3 vols.   *London*, 1852
Proposed draft of an Answer to the Remarks and Recommendations
   of Her Majesty's Commissioners for inquiring into the state of the
   University of Cambridge.   1853
Analysis of the evidence respecting a Matriculation examination con-
   tained in the Report of the...Commission.   By a White-Hood.
                                                                     1853
English University procedure. Draft of a Bill to be proposed by
   James Heywood (June 28 [1853]).   (*London*) [1853]
National Education at Oxford and Cambridge. Draft of a Bill to be
   proposed by James Heywood (Aug. 2 [1853]).   (*London*) [1853]
Letter of Lord Palmerston to Prince Albert, Chancellor, 12 Dec.
   1853. (Private copy.)   F° 1853
Answer to the Remarks...of the Commissioners so far as they relate
   to King's College.   1854
Notes on the Oxford Univ. Bill in reference to the Colleges at
   Cambridge.   (1854)
Copy of letter from four of the late Royal Commissioners on the
   University of Cambridge...to the Lord Chancellor.   F° 1855

COMMISSION (University).
  Remarks on the constitution of the University and the Bill before Parliament. [By H. A. Woodham and W. H. Bateson.]
  4° *n.p.* [1855 ?]
  Draft Statutes for certain Professorships. (June, 1860.)
  F° (*London*) 1860
  Statutes for the same. (24 Oct. 1860.)   F° (*London*) 1860
  Copies of statutes framed by Commissioners.   *London*, 1861
  Remarks on Report made to H.M. Secretary of State by Commissioners respecting Jesus College. By Dr Corrie.   1861
  Special Report from the Select Committee on the Oxford and Cambridge Universities Education Bill.   F° *London*, 1867
  Letters, Reports, Memorials, etc. 1870–80.   F° 1870–80
  Correspondence with the Commissioners. By R. Phelps.   1873
  Report of the Commissioners appointed to enquire into the income of the Universities.   F° *London*, 1874
  Returns of the University of Cambridge.   F° *London*, 1874
  Paper of queries. 6 Dec. 1877.   F° *London*, 1877
  Reply to enquiries of Commissioners. By Dr Phear.   Jan. 1, 1878
  See also Acts and Bills ; Statutes.
COMMITTEE for the study of special diseases. Bulletin. Vol. 1, Nos. 3–9. Aug. 1907.   4° 1907
COMPENDIUM of University Regulations for the use of persons in statu pupillari.   1870
  —— Another ed.   1888
  See also Statutes. Excerpta...1732, etc.
COMPETITIVE Examinations. (*Cornhill Mag.* Dec. 1861.)
COMPULSORY Chapel. A protest.   (1892)
COMPULSORY Chapel and the Universities' Test Act.   (1892)
  See also Cornford (F. M.).
CONCERT. First (–fourth) Grand Miscellaneous Concert. Words. 27 June, 28 June, 29 June, 1 July, 1811.   (1811)
  Selection of sacred music to be performed in Gt St Mary's, 28 June, 1811.   (1811)
  First (–third) Grand Miscellaneous Concert. Words. 30 June, 1, 2 July, 1814.   (1814)
  First (–third) Concert. Words. 3 July, 1819, 5 July, 1819, 6 July, 1819.   (1819)
  Cambridge Grand Musical Festival for the benefit of Addenbrooke's Hospital. Three Grand Miscellaneous Concerts. Words. 28 June, 30 June, 1 July, 1828.   (1828)
  Musical Festival. Words of Concerts. 29 June, 1 July, 1833.
  (1833)
CONFERENCE at Cambridge on the condition of School Children's teeth.   *London*, 1895
CONFRATERNITY of the Most Holy Trinity. Manual of Rules and Prayers.   1857
CONGREGATIONAL Church Year-Book, 1905, 1907, 1908, 1909.
  Sawston, 1905–9

CONINGTON (J.)   The University of Oxford and the Greek
  Chair.   *Oxford*, 1863
  A reply to Professor Conington's pamphlet on the Greek Pro-
  fessorship at Oxford.   *Oxford*, 1863
CONSERVATIVE Association.   Regulations of the Cambridge
  Conservative Association.   1835
CONSIDERATIONS on the...late Regulations.   [By J. Green.]
                                          London, 1751
CONSIDERATIONS on the Oaths required by the University
  of Cambridge at the time of taking Degrees.   [By W. Frend.]
                                          London, 1787
CONVERSATIONS at Cambridge.   [Attributed to R. A. Willmott.]
                                          London, 1836
CONWAY (*Sir* W.M.)   Testimonials when a candidate for the Slade
  Professorship of Fine Art in the University of Cambridge.   1886
  The Succession of Ideals.   An Address.   *Liverpool*, 1886
CONYBEARE (E.)   Tourist's guide to the county of Cambridge.
  By A. G. Hill.   2nd ed. by E. Conybeare.   *London*, 1892
  History of Cambridgeshire.   *London*, 1897
  Rides around Cambridge.   1902
CONYBEARE (W.J.)   *See* Freeman (P.).
COOK (J.)   An historical account of King's College Chapel, Cam-
  bridge.   1829
COOKE (A.)   Testimonials for post of Assistant Surgeon at Adden-
  brooke's Hospital.   4° *n.p.* 1897
COOKE (A.H.)   On the MacAndrew Collection of British Shells.
  (*Journ. of Conchology*, III.)   (*London*, 1882)
COOKE (G.A.)   Topographical and statistical description of the
  county of Cambridge.   *London*, 1807
COOKE (J.P.)   Memorial of W. H. Miller.   [1881]
COOKE (W.)   Praelectio ad Actum Publicum habitum Cantabrigiae
  8vo Id. Mart. 1787.   4° 1787
COOKESLEY (W.G.)   *See* Sellon (L.).
COOMBE (J.A.)   The inward witness of the Spirit to the believer's
  adoption.   The Commemoration sermon in St John's College
  Chapel, March 15, 1845.   1845
COOPER (C.H.)   Annals of Cambridge.   5 vols. (Vol. 5 edited with
  additions by J. W. Cooper.)   1842–1908
  —— Part 34 (being the first of Vol. 5).   [1853]
  Athenae Cantabrigienses.   By C. H. Cooper and Thompson Cooper.
  2 vols.   1858–61
  Memorials of Cambridge.   New ed. 3 vols. (Bowes 2030* d) 1860–66
  Memoir of Margaret, Countess of Richmond and Derby.   (Ed. by
  J. E. B. Mayor.)   1874
COOPER (S.)   Commencement sermon...29 June, 1777.   4° 1777
COOPER (T.) and Cooper (C.H.)   Athenae Cantabrigienses.   2 vols.
                                              1858–61
COPE (E.M.)   On the interpretation of the words "Governing Body"
  in the 27th Section of the Cambridge University Act.   1857

COPE (E.M.)

On the College Statutes. Trinity. 1858
Plato's Theætetus and Mr Grote's criticisms. 1866
Extracts from Introduction to Aristotle's Rhetoric. 1867
A Review of Aristotle's System of Ethics. Prelection. 1867

Notice of the life of E. M. C., by H. A. J. Munro. 1873

COPYRIGHT Act. Chancellor, Masters, and Scholars of the University of Cambridge against Henry Bryer [for failing to comply with the Copyright Act]. 2 pts. *London* (1812)
Vindication of pending Bill for Amendment of the Copyright Act. By Sir E. Brydges. *London*, 1818
A vindication of the right of the Universities of the United Kingdom to a copy of every new publication. By Edw. Christian. 3rd ed. 1818

CORNFORD (F.M.) The Cambridge Classical Course. 1903
On compulsory Chapel. 1904
Microcosmographia Academica. 1908
CORNISH (F.W.) Testimonials presented by F. W. C. to the Worshipful Company of Skinners. 4° 1875
See Johnson (W.), 1897.
CORNISH (H.W.) *See* Cambridge A.B.C. 1894.
CORONATION, 1838. A complete account of the proceedings at Cambridge. (Large paper copy.) 4° 1838
—— (Small paper copy.) 1838
The Coronation Remembrancer. An account of the proceedings... at Cambridge. 1838
CORONATION, 1902. Service for their Majesties King Edward VII and Queen Alexandra. 26 June, 1902. *London* (1902)
Coronation Festivities. (9 Aug. 1902.) Camb. Daily News souvenir. F° 1902
Celebration at Cambridge. 1902
CORPORATION. Reflections on the contentions and disorder of the Corporation of Cambridge. *London*, 1789
The Corporation of Cambridge. A digested Report of the evidence given in the Guildhall in Cambridge Oct. 28, etc., before two of H.M. Commissioners for enquiry into the existing state of Municipal Corporations in England and Wales. 1833
Extracts from a digested Report, etc. Cambridge, 1833. With a preface by H. Gunning. 1839
See also Borough.
CORPUS Christi College. Catalogus librorum manuscriptorum...quos legavit Matthæus Parkerus. [By W. Stanley.] F° *Londini*, 1722
List of names, etc. of all members of Corpus Christi College, with proposals for printing the history of the College. Dec. 1, 1749 and March 1, 1749–50. By R. Masters. 4° 1750
The history of the College of Corpus Christi...by R. Masters, B.D. 4° 1753
—— Large paper copy. 4° 1753

CORPUS Christi College.

An account of an illuminated manuscript in the Library....By
M. Tyson. (*Archaeologia*, II.)   4° (*London*, 1773)
Account of the Horn belonging to C.C.C. By M. Tyson. (*Archaeo-
logia*, III.)   4° (*London*, 1775)
Catalogus librorum manuscriptorum...quos...legavit Matthæus Parker.
Ed. Jacobus Nasmith.   4° 1777
Vice-Chancellor's Notice of ceremonial at laying first stone of New
Buildings, 2 July, 1823, with inscription on the stone.   F° 1823
Masters's History of Corpus Christi College, Cambridge. With
continuation by John Lamb.   4° 1831
Collection of Letters, Statutes, etc. from the Library of C.C.C.
Ed. by John Lamb.   *London*, 1838
A sermon preached at the Commemoration of Benefactors, Dec. 14,
1847. By J. G. Mould.   (1847)
Statuta Collegii Corporis Christi.   1861
A sermon preached at the Consecration of the Chapel, Nov. 2, 1870.
By J. G. Mould.   1870
The Library. By S. S. Lewis.   1890
Corpus Christi College. By Rev. H. P. Stokes. (College histories.)
          London, 1898
The Benedict. Nos. 1–38.   1898–1910
Story of a Ghost. (*Occult Review*, March, 1905.)
Catalogue of MSS. By M. R. James. Pts 1, 2.   1909–10

CORRIE (G.E.)   Sermon in Catharine Hall Chapel, 27 Feb. 1831.
          1831
Brief historical notices of the interference of the Crown with the
affairs of the English Universities.   1839
A list of books presented to Pembroke College, Cambridge, by
different donors during the 14th and 15th centuries. (*C. A. S.*)
          1860
Remarks on the Report by the Cambridge University Commissioners
respecting certain statutes proposed by them to Jesus College. 1861
List of early printed and other books in the possession of Dr Corrie.
          1880
List of books (not commonly met with) relating to the Family of
Love, in the possession of Dr Corrie.   1880
Catalogue of the scarcer books in the library of the Rev. G. E. Corrie.
          1883

Service to be used at the funeral of the Rev. G. E. Corrie.   16° 1885
Catalogue of the library of the late G. E. Corrie...sold May, 1886.
(Partly priced.) Two copies.   *London*, 1886
Memorials of the life of G. E. Corrie. Ed. by M. Holroyd.   1890

CORY (W.)   *See* Johnson (W.).
COSMO (Phil), *pseud.*, really G. M. Maxwell. *See* True Blue.
COSTUMES of the members of the University of Cambridge.
(Folding plates.)   *London*, n.d.
See also Almond (A. G.) ; Clark (E. C.) ; Harraden (R.).

COTES (R.) Hydrostatical and Pneumatical Lectures. 2nd ed.,
    by R. Smith, D.D.   1747
De descensu gravium. De motu pendulorum in cycloide. Et De
    motu projectilium.   4° 1770
Correspondence of Sir I. Newton and Professor Cotes. With Notes
    by J. Edleston.   *London*, 1850
COTMAN (J.S.) Antiquities of St Mary's Chapel, Stourbridge, near
    Cambridge.   4° *Yarmouth*, 1819
COTTAGE Home for little orphan girls. Reports: 9th, 10th, 11th,
    12th, 13th, 14th, 17th, 19th, 23rd.   1880–94
COTTENHAM. A sad relation of a dreadful fire...29 April, 1676.
                                          4° [*London*] 1676
COTTON (G.E.L.) T. H. Burn. In memoriam.   [1864]
COUBERTIN (P. de) L'éducation en Angleterre.   *Paris*, 1888
COULTHURST (H.W.) Sermon preached before the University.
    Trans. into English metre by H. W. Hopkins [i.e. A. Geddes].
                                          London, 1796
    See Frend (W.), 1789.
COUNCIL in the Moon. (Bowes 578.)   4° 1765
COUNCIL of the Senate. Analysis of the votes given to Prof. Stuart
    and Prof. Paget, 1879.   1879
Election, October, 1906. Tickets, Fly-sheets, and other papers.
                                            4° 1906
COUNTY School. Articles of Association.   1869
COURTHOPE (W.J.) Liberty and Authority in matters of taste.
                                          London, 1896
COUSIN Carl: a drama in three Acts. Trans. from the Swedish
    by Mrs Selwyn (wife of Prof. Selwyn) for representation at the
    Deanery, Ely.   4° *n.p.* [? 1866]
COVERDALE (M.) Wicklieffes Wicket. Ed. by R. Potts. 1851
COWELL (Elizabeth) Leaves of Memory.   *London*, 1892
COWELL (E.B.) Address to Electoral Roll. With testimonials for
    Sanskrit Professorship.   1867
An inaugural lecture, delivered Oct. 23, 1867.   *London*, 1867

Life and Letters. By G. Cowell.   *London*, 1904

COWLING (J.) The Regrets of a Cantab. (*London Mag.*, 1 Dec.
    1825.)
COWPER (J.) Adelphi. A sketch of the character...of J. Cowper.
    By his brother, W. Cowper. Ed. J. Newton. 12° *London*, 1802
COX (G.V.) Recollections of Oxford. 2nd ed.   *London*, 1870
COX (T.) A topographical, ecclesiastical, and natural history of
    [Cambridgeshire]. (Bowes 944.)   4° *London*, 1700 [1715]
COX (W.A.) C. J. Ellicott, Bp of Gloucester. (*Eagle*.)   1905
The blank window in the Chapel. Two legends of St John. (*Eagle*.)
                                                   1909
CRANAGE (D.H.S.) Syllabus of lectures on Monastic Life. 1900
CRANE'S Charity. Sermon by W. Cunningham, Oct. 8, 1889.
                                                   12° 1889

CRANWELL (E.)   An index of such books printed before the year MDC., as are now in the Library of Trinity College, Cambridge.
1847
CRANWELL (J.)   *See* Browne (I. H.).
CRAWFORD (C.)   Letters from Academicus to Eugenius on various subjects.   *London,* 1772
CREASSY (J.)   *See* Fens, 1777.
CRIBBLINGS from the Poets.   (Parodies.)   1883
CRITICA Novazealandica futura.   *See* Old Mother Hubbard.
CRITO *Cantabrigiensis, pseud.*   *See* Turton (T.).
CROMWELL (Oliver)   *See* Verses.
CROSS (T.)   The conflagration of Rome by Nero.   1837
CROSS (W.S.)   The theory of the Rainbow.   1836
CROSSE Scholarships.   Examination papers.   1833
CROWE (W.)   Oratio in martyrium Regis Caroli I, 30 die Jan. 1719.
Londini, 1720
—— Ed. altera.   4° *Londini,* 1720
CROWFOOT (J.R.)   College tuition considered in a letter to a friend.   By a Fellow, M.A. (J. R. C.).   1845
The interpretation of the Composition between the University and King's College.   By a Member of the Senate (J. R. C.).   1846
Remarks on some questions of economy and finance affecting the University of Cambridge.   1848
Prælectio theologica.   De Jeremiae cap. xxxiii. comm. 15, 16.
4° 1848
Remarks with reference to building a University Hostel.   1849
Academic notes on Holy Scriptures.   Ser. 1.   1850
Plea for a Colonial and Missionary College at Cambridge.
London, 1854
Statement of proceedings taken with reference to the election of Master in Gonville and Caius College in 1852.   1854
CROYLAND.   Observations on Croyland Abbey.   By James Essex.
(*Bibl. topographica Britannica,* xxii.)   4° *London,* 1784
The history of Crowland Abbey, digested from the materials collected by Mr Gough [by B. Holdich].   *Stamford,* 1816
A light on the historians and on the history of Crowland Abbey. By H. S. English.   *London,* 1868
Memorials of Saint Guthlac of Crowland.   Ed. by W. de Gray Birch.   *Wisbech,* 1881
Croyland and Thorney.   By G. W. Prothero.   *Spalding,* 1885
The present danger of Croyland Abbey.   *n.p.* 1888
Farren's Crowland Abbey.   (Etchings.)   F° 1889
CUMBERLAND (R.)   Memoirs.   Written by himself.
4° *London,* 1806
CUMMING (J.)   Plan of a course of chemical lectures.   1816
Notice of Calculus in the Library of Trinity College.   (*Trans. Philos. Soc. Camb.*)   4° 1822
A syllabus of a course of chemical lectures.   1825
A syllabus of a course of chemical lectures.   1834

CUNNINGHAM (G.)   Testimonials when candidate for the post of
  dental surgeon at Addenbrooke's Hospital.   1887
CUNNINGHAM (J.W.)   Cautions to continental travellers.
                                                   London, 1818
CUNNINGHAM (William)   John Crane's Charity.   A sermon
  preached Oct. 8, 1889.   1889
  On suggested alterations in Great St Mary's Church.   1891
  Sermon preached at Gt St Mary's Church, 27 Jan. 1901.   1901
  A Word to Church Reformers...18 June, 1901   1901
  Richard Cobden and Adam Smith. Two lectures.   *London*, 1904
  The Moral Witness of the Church on the investment of money and
    the use of wealth.   1909
  Socialism and Christianity.   *London*, 1909
CURZON (*Lord*)   Principles and Methods of University reform.
                                                   Oxford, 1909
CUST (L.) Candidature for the Directorship of the Fitzwilliam
  Museum, Nov. 1889.   1889
  Application for the Disney Professorship.   1892
  A history of Eton College.   *London*, 1899
  Eton College Portraits.   (Prospectus.)   Fº *London*, 1908

D

DAGLEY (R.) Takings, or the life of a Collegian. A Poem.
London, 1821

DALBY (W.) The real question at issue between the opponents and supporters of a Bill...entitled " A Bill to remove certain disabilities which prevent some classes of H.M. subjects from resorting to the Universities of England." *London*, 1834

DALE (T.) Probation for the Christian Ministry practically considered. Four discourses before the University of Cambridge, March, 1836. *London*, 1836

DALECHAMP (C.) Christian hospitalitie handled common-place-wise in the Chappel of Trinity Colledge in Cambridge. *Issued with* Harrisonus honoratus : id est...de vita et obitu Domini Harrisoni, Trinitatis Collegii nuper Vicepræfecti, narratiuncula. 4° 1632

DALTON (J.H.C.) The position of the laity in the Church of England. *London*, 1899
Cambridge today. (*Camb. Express.*) 1908

DANIEL (C.H.) and Barker (W.R.) Worcester College, Oxford.
London, 1900

DANIELL (A.E.) The Temple of Learning : or Cambridge illustrated by pen and pencil. [1890]

DARWIN (C.) Extracts from letters to Prof. Henslow, 1832–35.
1835
Foundations of Origin of Species : Sketch written 1842. Ed. F. Darwin. 1909
Foundations of Origin of Species : Essays written 1842 and 1844. Ed. F. Darwin. 1909

Catalogue of the Library of Ch. Darwin now in the Botany School, Cambridge. By H. W. Rutherford. Ed. F. Darwin. 1908

DARWIN (F.) Address to the Botanical Section of the Brit. Assoc. at Cambridge, 1904. *London*, 1904
See Darwin (C.); Jenyns (L.) 1903.

DARWIN (*Sir* G.H.) A tidal theory of the evolution of satellites. (*Observatory*, July, 1879.) 1879

DARWIN (L.) Free Trade, Work, and Wages. 1909

DARWIN Celebration. Darwin and Modern Science : Essays to commemorate Centenary. Ed. A. C. Seward. 1909
Order of Proceedings at Celebration held at Cambridge, June 22–24, 1909. With a sketch of Darwin's life. 4° 1909

DARWIN Celebration.

Catalogue of Portraits, Prints, etc. exhibited at Christ's College, June, 1909. 4° 1909

Programmes, Lists of delegates, guests, etc., Invitation cards, and newspaper reports. 4° 1909

See also Cockerell (T. D. A.).

DARWINIAN Theory of Origin of Species examined. By a Graduate of the University of Cambridge. 1868

DASHWOOD (J.) Case of the Rector of Doddington.

Wisbech, 1811

DAUBENY (C.G.B.) Fugitive poems connected with natural history and physical science. Collected by C. G. B. Daubeny.

Oxford, London, 1869

DAVID'S Prophecy relating to Cambridge. [By Wm Waller.]

1751

DAVIES (Emily) Account of proposed new College for Women (Girton). *London,* 1868

Women in the Universities of England and Scotland. 1896

DAVIES (G.S.) *See* Moslem.

DAVIES (J.) Christian Worship : its object and essential requisites. A Discourse preached before the Univ. of Camb., 23 June and 30 June, 1844. *London,* 1844

DAVIES (J.Ll.) The proposed conditions of the tenure of Fellowships in Trinity College. 1857

The things above in relation to education and science. A sermon preached in the Chapel of Trinity College, Cambridge, Dec. 13, 1877. *London,* 1877

The Working Men's College. *London,* 1904

DAVIES (M.) Athenæ Britannicæ : or a critical history of the Oxford and Cambridge writers and writings. Parts I–III.

London, 1716

DAVIS (H.W.C.) Balliol College, Oxford. (College histories.)

London, 1899

DAVIS (S.) A dissertation on Matthew xii. 7. 1834

DAWES (*Sir* W.) Sermon...at St Mary's Church, 5 Nov. 1705.

4° 1705

DAWKES (T.) Prodigium Willinghamense : or...passages in the life of a boy born at Willingham, 31 Oct. 1741. *London* (1747)

DAWKINS (W.B.) Letter of application and testimonials for Wood-wardian Professorship of Geology, 1 Feb. 1873. *n.p.* 1873

DAY in Vacation at College. A burlesque poem. [By W. Dodd.]

4° *London,* 1751

DAY (T.) Speeches at the General Meetings of the Counties of Cambridge and Essex, March 25 and April 25, 1780. *n.p.* 1780

DEALTRY (R.) Elegy on the Rev. Thomas Jones, A.M. 4° (1807)

DEALTRY (W.) Honour from God the sure portion of them that honour him. A sermon preached at Trinity Church, Cambridge, Nov. 20, 1836, on the death of the Rev. C. Simeon. 1836

—— Another edition. (*Pulpit,* xxix.) *London,* 1837

DEANE (A.C.) Frivolous verses.   1892
   The Religion of the Undergraduate. (With replies.) (*Nineteenth
   Century*, Oct., Nov., Dec. 1895.)
   St Columba. (Seatonian Prize Poem for 1905.)   1905
DEATH (C.) In Memoriam Caroline Death.   1893
DECK (Isaiah) Catalogue of strata of Alum Bay, I. of W.   1838
   Description of sectional model of Alum Bay.   (? 1838)
   Notice of remains of the Anglo-Saxon period, discovered at Little
   Wilbraham. (*Arch. Journ.* VIII.)   (*London*, 1851)
DECK (John) Ἵνα ὦσιν οἱ χρώμενοι τῷ κοσμῳ τουτῳ ὡς μὴ
   καταχρώμενοι. An essay which obtained the Porteus Medal.
                                                             1837
   Quantum momenti habeat ad veritatem Religionis Christianae con-
   firmandam, Pauli ad Christianam fidem transitio. Dissertatio Latina
   numismate Porteusiano dignata a.d. 1836.   1837
   Style and Composition of N.T. (Norrisian Prize Essay for 1836.)
                                                             1837
DECK (N.) The ecclesiology of Cambridgeshire. Paper read before
   the Camb. Architectural Society, 10 Nov. 1859.   (1859)
   Handbook for Visitors to Cambridge.   1861
   —— Another edition.   1862
   New Cambridge Guide. 2nd ed.   1868
DEFENCE of the *Observations* [of W. S. Powell] on the first chapter
   of a book [by E. Waring] called *Miscellanea analytica.* [By W. S.
   Powell.]   *London*, 1760
DEFOE (Daniel) A tour through the whole island of Great Britain.
   4th ed. 4 vols.   *London*, 1748
   —— 7th ed. 4 vols.   *London*, 1769
DEGREES. Regulations for degrees in Arts, 15 May, 1821 ; with
   Grace to confirm, 23 May, 1821.   4° 1821
DEIGHTON (F.) Testimonials when candidate for post of assistant
   Surgeon at Addenbrooke's Hospital.   1891
DE LA PRYME (A.) Diary. (Surtees Soc. publ.) *Durham*, 1871
DELHI. *See* Missions.
DELPHI. (Unsuccessful Prize Poem, 1833.)   " Where was the
   land."   (1833)
   —— " My Spirit saddens."   (1833)
   —— " The woods that wave."   (1833)
   —— " Oh ! Thou, the Morning's Author."   (1833)
DE MORGAN (S.E.) Reminiscences.   *London*, 1895
DENIFLE (H.) Die Universitäten des Mittelalters bis 1400.
   Band I.   *Berlin*, 1885
DENVER. *See* Fens.
DE PARAVICINI (F.) Early history of Balliol College.
                                                   London, 1891
DERHAM (W.) *See* Ray (J.).
DEVONSHIRE (Spencer Compton Cavendish, *Duke of*) Installation
   Ode. 13 June, 1892. Latin and English. By A. W. Verrall.
                                                             1892

DEVONSHIRE (Spencer Compton Cavendish, *Duke of*).
    Installation Ode. Latin Text. With music. By A. W. Verrall
    and C. V. Stanford.   1892
    —— Large paper copy.   4° 1892
    Memoir, by G. D. Liveing.   *London*, 1908
DEVONSHIRE (William Cavendish, *Duke of*) Fly-sheets, etc.
    relating to the candidature, election, and installation of the Duke
    of Devonshire as Chancellor.   1861–2
    Inauguration at Devonshire House. (*Illustr. London News*, 25 Jan.
    1862.)
    Ode...10 June, 1862, composed for the Installation of the Duke of
    Devonshire, Chancellor of the University. By Charles Kingsley.
    1862
    Report of a meeting for procuring a portrait of his Grace the
    Chancellor (Duke of Devonshire). (*Reporter*, Feb. 2, 1882.)
    Report of proceedings respecting the portrait of his Grace the
    Duke of Devonshire, Chancellor of the University. (*Reporter*,
    Dec. 17, 1883.)
DEWAR (J.) Testimonials when a candidate for the Jacksonian
    Professorship in the University of Cambridge.   1875
    Pamphlet respecting his wish to dismiss his Assistant, Mr Ruhemann.
    (1891)
D'EWES (*Sir* S.) Speech in House of Commons on Bill of Foure
    Subsidies, 9 March, 1641.   4° *London*, 1641
    Autobiography and Correspondence. Ed. by J. O. Halliwell. 2 vols.
    London, 1845
    College life in the time of James the First, as illustrated by an un-
    published diary of Sir Symonds D'Ewes. (Ed. by J. O. Halliwell.)
    London, 1851
DEXTER (F.B.) The influence of the English Universities in the
    development of New England. (*Proc. Mass. Hist. Soc.*)
    Camb., Mass., 1880
DIAL. Queens' College Magazine. Mich. Term, 1909; Easter
    Term, 1910.   1909–10
DIALOGUE for Tuesday, Oct. 26, 1858. [On the Statutes.]
    4° (1858)
DICAIOPHILUS *Cantabrigiensis*. *See* Long (R.).
DICKENS (C.) A dictionary of the University of Cambridge.
    London, 1884
    A dictionary of the University of Oxford. Second year.
    London, 1885
DICKINSON (G.L.) From King to King.   *London*, 1891
    Syllabus of a course of lectures on modern France.   1891
DIGBY (K.H.) The evidence of the divine origin of Christianity. 1821
DILLINGHAM (W.) Prove all things, hold fast that which is good.
    Two sermons at St Mary's Church, the first on 1 July, 1655,
    the other since.   4° 1656
    Vita Laurentii Chadertoni...una cum vita Jacobi Usserii.   1700
    Vita Chadertoni, translated by E. S. Shuckburgh.   1884

DISNEY (J.) The Fitzwilliam Museum, Cambridge, being illustrations of the Collection of Ancient Marbles, etc. in the Fitzwilliam Museum. 3 pts.   4º *London*, 1849
  Catalogue of a collection of Ancient Marbles presented to the Univ. of Cambridge. (Appended to J. H. Marsden's *Two lectures*.)
                                               1852
DISNEY (W.) A sermon preached before the University of Cambridge, June 28, 1789.   4º 1789
DISNEY Lectures. By G. F. Browne. Lent Term, 1891. Syllabus.
                                              1891

DISSENTERS. *See* Subscription; Tests.
DISTRICT Nursing. *See* Nurses.
DIVINITY School. Report on designs submitted by Basil Champneys.
                                            [1876]
  Prayers, etc. at opening, Oct. 24, 1879.   1879
DOBREE (P.P.) Greek inscriptions from the marbles in the Library of Trinity College.   [1824]
DOCUMENTS relating to the University and Colleges of Cambridge.
  3 vols.   *London*, 1852
DODD (E.) On the Additional Curates Society.   (1864)
DODD (H.R.) Joshua. (Seatonian Prize Poem for 1865.)   1865
DODD (P.S.) *See* Hints to Freshmen.
DODD (W.) A Day in Vacation at College.   4º *London*, 1751
DODDINGTON. Case of the Rector of Doddington. (Signed: James Dashwood.)   *Wisbech*, 1811
DODSON (W.) The designe for the perfect draining of the Great Level of the Fens (called Bedford Level).   4º *London*, 1665
DODWELL (H.) De Parma Equestri Woodwardiana dissertatio. Ed. Th. Hearne.   *Oxonii*, 1718
DOLPHIN. To the passengers and crew of the Dolphin. A poem [describing a fight at the Lamb Inn, Ely].   1828
DOMESDAY Book. Cambridgeshire.   Fº *London*, 1862
—— *See also* Walker (B.).
DONALDSON (J.W.) Prælectio philologica in scholis Cantabr. habita 4 Id. Oct. 1848.   1848
  Praelectionis candidatoriae quam Cantabr. in scholis publicis Prid. Kal. Feb. 1854 habuit J. G. D. excerpta quaedam.   1854
  A reply to Mr Perowne's renewed attack on the Editor of Jashar.
                                   London, 1855
  A brief exposure of the Rev. J. J. S. Perowne, by the Editor of Jashar.   *London*, 1855
  On some points connected with the Medo-Persic dualism.   1859
  See also Perowne (J. J. S.).
DONN (J.) Hortus Cantabrigiensis, or a catalogue of plants indigenous and exotic, cultivated in the Botanic Garden, Cambridge. 2nd ed.
                                            1800
—— 4th ed.   1807
—— 9th ed.   *London*, 1819
—— 13th ed.   *London*, 1845

DON'T you think so? or the Friend's Reply to the Letter. (Bowes 2014.) 1840

DOUGHTY (G.) A sermon preached before the University in King's College Chapel, March 25, 1724 [on the occasion of laying the foundation stone of Gibbs's building. With folding plate]. 2nd ed.
4° 1724

DOUGLAS (*Mrs* S.) Life and Correspondence of W. Whewell.
London, 1881

DOUTY (E.H.) Testimonials when a candidate for the post of Assistant Surgeon to Addenbrooke's Hospital. 1891
—— Amended testimonials. 1891
—— Amended testimonials. 1895
Le climat et la cure de la tuberculose. (Davos-Platz.)
Davos-Platz, 1899

DOWNING College. Observations on the plans and elevations designed by James Wyatt for Downing College. By T. Hope.
4° *London,* 1804
Charter and Statutes. 4° *London,* 1805
A few remarks on the outline of a scheme for the future constitution of Downing College. By the Master [T. Worsley]. (1860)
Menu of dinner given to Hon. Mr Justice Henn Collins. 1891
Menu of dinner given to Lord Russell of Killowen. 1897
Downing College. By H. W. Pettit Stevens. (College histories.)
London, 1899
See also Acts and Bills, 1801, 1895.

DOWNING (R.P.N.) Appeals by himself and his father, fly-sheets, and other papers connected with his case. (29 pieces.) F° 1882–3

DOWSING (W.) Journal. 4° *Woodbridge,* 1786

D'OYLY (G.) Life of W. Sancroft, Abp of Canterbury. 2 vols.
London, 1821

DRAINAGE. Report of Drainage Syndicate, 8 Jan. 1823, with Grace to confirm, 22 Jan. 1823. F° 1823
See also Turner (C.).

DRAKE (S.) Ara ignoto Deo sacra. Concio...VII. Id. Jul. 1724.
4° 1724

DRIVERS (The). A dialogue. (Bowes 611.) 4° 1770

DROSIER (W.H.) Remarks on the new regulations recommended by the Syndicate of Oct. 27, 1859, for the Moral and Natural Science examinations. 1860
On Zoology as a branch of University education. 1865
On the duties of a Professor of Zoology and Comparative Anatomy.
1866

DRURY (H.) *See* Arundines Cami.

DUCKWORTH (W.L.H.) Notes on the Anthropological collection in the Museum of Human Anatomy. 1899

DUDLEY (J.) Sermon before the University, 28 June, 1807. 4° 1807

DUELLING. Thoughts on Duelling. [Attr. to R. Hey.] 1773

DUGDALE (*Sir* W.) The history of imbanking and draining of divers Fens and Marshes. 2nd ed., by C. N. Cole. F° *London,* 1772

DUNCAN (P.M.)   Letter of application for Woodwardian Professor-
ship of Geology, 4 Feb. 1873.   4° *n.p.* 1873
DUNCOMBE (J.)   An Evening Contemplation in a College.
                                                4° *London*, 1753
Poems.   4° *London*, 1756
DUNDAS (L.)   *See* Lawson (M.); Maberley (T. H.).
"DUNDREARY (*Lord*)"   Speech in Section D on the great
Hippocampus question.   [By C. Kingsley.]   1862
DUNLOP (O.J.)   Leaves from a Cambridge [Girton] note-book.
                                                        1907
DUPORT (J.)   Musæ subsecivæ, seu poetica stromata.   1676

Memoir.   By J. H. Monk.   (Museum Criticum, viii.)   (1826)

DURELL (J.V.)   Historical account of the Church of Fulbourn
St Vigor.   1910
DURHAM (J.G.)   The Outworks of Christianity.   1805
DYER (G.)   English prologue and epilogue to...Ignoramus.
                                                London, 1797
History of the University and Colleges of Cambridge.   2 vols.
                                                London, 1814
—— Another copy (Large Paper).   2 vols.   *London*, 1814
An address to the subscribers to the *Privileges of the University of
Cambridge*.   *London*, 1823
The Privileges of the University of Cambridge.   2 vols.
                                                London, 1824
Academic unity; being the substance of a general dissertation con-
tained in the *Privileges of the University of Cambridge. London*, 1827

E

EAGLE. St John's Coll. Magazine.
  Index to Vols. 1–15.   1891
  Hundredth number.   1893
EARP (F.R.) Descriptive Catalogue of the Pictures in the Fitz-
  william Museum, from materials by S. Colvin.   1902
EASTERFIELD (T.H.) Syllabus of a course of lectures on Experi-
  mental Mechanics.   1891
EASTERN Association. The circular letter of the Eastern Association
  held at Cambridge, May 13 and 14, 1777, to the Protestant Dis-
  senting Churches usually denominated Baptists. Signed : Isaac
  Gould.   *n.p.* (1777)
EASTERN Counties. Papers in relation to the antient topography of
  the Eastern Counties of Britain. (By Arthur Taylor.)
                                         4° *London*, 1869
EAU Brink. *See* Fens.
ECCLESIASTICAL and architectural topography of England. Cam-
  bridgeshire. (By Prof. Willis, and others.)   *Oxford*, 1852
ECCLESIASTICAL Commissioners. The correspondence between
  the Ecclesiastical Commissioners and the Bishop of Ely.
                                       London, 1837
ECCLESIOLOGICAL Society. *See* Camden Society.
ECCLESIOLOGIST. 3 vols. :
  Vol. I, No. 1. Nov. 1841. 1st ed. (suppressed).   1841
  No. 1. Nov. 1841. 2nd, 3rd eds.   1842–4
  No. 2. Nov. 1841. 2nd, 3rd eds.   1842–4
  No. 3. Jan. 1842. 2nd ed.   1842
  No. 4. Feb. 1842. 2nd ed.   1842
  No. 5. March, 1842. 2nd ed.   1842
  Nos. 6, 7. April, 1842. 2nd ed.   1842
  No. 8. May, 1842. 1st, 2nd eds.   1842
  No. 9. June, 1842. 1st, 2nd eds.   1842
  Nos. 10, 11. July, 1842. 1st, 2nd eds.   1842
  Nos. 12, 13. Aug. 1842. 1st ed.   1842
  Vol. II, Nos. 14–24. Oct. 1842–June, 1843.   1843
  Vol. III. 2nd ed. Nos. 25–36. Sept. 1843–Sept. 1844.   1847
EDE (W.M.) Report to the Syndicate for conducting lectures in
  populous places.   1875
EDGCUMBE (*Sir* E.R.P.) Party Politics in the County Council.
                                         London, 1888
  Life and Letters of A. C. Hilton. *See* Hilton (A. C.). Works. 1904.

EDICT.   Edict against students frequenting taverns, 10 March, 1728.
F⁰ 1728
Edict against racing, 16 May, 1817.   F⁰ 1817
Edict to discommune John Litchfield, fruiterer, for arranging a
boxing match, 24 Feb. 1819.   F⁰ 1819
Edict against E. and J. Litchfield for having assisted in carrying into
effect a marriage between an undergraduate and a servant of J. L.
29 Nov. 1819.   F⁰ 1819
Edict against driving tandems and blowing horns, 24 Jan. 1821.
F⁰ 1821
Edict to discommune G. B. White, Attorney, for lending money,
18 Feb. 1822.   F⁰ 1822
Edict against giving false names, 3 May, 1823.   F⁰ 1823
Edict to discommune Joshua Gaywood for letting out tandems,
12 March, 1824.   F⁰ 1824
Edict against firing guns and pistols, 9 May, 1825.   F⁰ 1825
Edict against racing, 16 May, 1825.   F⁰ 1825
—— 28 Oct. 1825.   F⁰ 1825
Edict against not wearing academical dress, 10 Oct. 1825. F⁰ 1825
Edict against B. E. Duppa, B.A., 3 May, 1828.   F⁰ 1828
Edict against pigeon shooting, 1 Dec. 1842.   F⁰ 1842
Edict against disorder in the streets, 10 March, 1846.   F⁰ 1846
Edict against institution of legal proceedings against undergraduates
without notice to tutors, 11 April, 1846.   Re-issued 26 Nov.
1847.   F⁰ 1846–7
Edict against racing, 9 May, 1846.   Re-issued 26 Nov. 1847.
F⁰ 1846–7
Edict against tradesmen allowing debts to be contracted, 11 Feb.
1847.   Re-issued 19 Oct. 1847.   F⁰ 1847
EDLESTON (J.)   The Cambridge Senate before Whitgift's Statutes
and the University Bill of 1855.   1855
See Newton (Sir I.).   Correspondence, 1850.
EDMUND'S (St) House.   Proposal to affiliate.   Fly-sheets, etc.
4⁰ 1898
EDUCATION.   The new Education Act.   Report of a Public
Meeting held in the Guildhall, Cambridge, Oct. 25, 1870.   1870
The Thirty-Second Annual Report of the Board of Education for
the County and Town of Cambridge and Isle of Ely.   1872
EDWARD VI, King of England.   King Edward the Sixth on the
Supremacy.   Trans. and ed. by R. Potts.   1874
EDWARD VII, King of England.   The birth of the Prince of Wales.
A poem.   1842
—— Another poem on the same subject.   1842
Ode on the birth of the Prince of Wales.   By C. R. Kennedy.
London, 1842
A succinct and detailed account of the visit of the Prince and Princess
of Wales to the University of Cambridge.   (Camb. Chron.)   1864
Grace-papers, fly-sheets, etc. in connection with the visit.   1864
The Royal Visit.   (Illustr. Lond. News, 11 June, 1864.)

EDWARD VII.
    Speech delivered in the Senate House by the Public Orator, June 2,
      1864.   (Visit of Prince and Princess of Wales.)   4° 1864
    Visit of Prince and Princess of Wales.   9 June.   1888
    Service for the coronation of their Majesties.   1902
    Celebration of coronation at Cambridge.   1902
    Visit to Cambridge.   March 1, 1904.   Order of proceedings.   4° 1904
    Visit to Cambridge.   March 1, 1904.   Cambridge Daily News
      Souvenir.   4° 1904
    In Memoriam.   Address before Mayor and Corporation.   1910
    Funeral sermon by H. M. Butler, in Jesus Coll. Chapel.   1910
    Funeral sermon by A. H. F. Boughey, at Gt St Mary's.   1910
EDWARDS (G.M.)   Sidney Sussex College.   (College histories.)
                                 London, 1899
EDWARDS (John), *D.D.*, † 1716.   Commencement Sermon, 2 July,
    1699.   4° 1699
    A view of the state of the University in Queen Anne's reign.   Ed. by
    H. Bradshaw.   (*C. A. S.*)   1866
EDWARDS (M.E.)   Filiolo.   (Verses.)   12° (1907)
EDWARDS (T.)   A sermon preached before the University, 29 June,
    1766.   1773
EKINS (J.)   The Loves of Medea and Jason.   A poem.
                               4° *London*, 1771
ELECTION Flights.   *See* Straightforward (Timmy).
ELECTIONS.   Protest against Intimidation, 16 March, 1835.
                                   F° *n.p.* 1835
    See also Representatives.
ELECTORAL Roll, from 1856.
ELECTRIC Lighting and its advantages.   Issued by the Cambridge
    Electric Supply Company.   1892
    Prospectus of the Company, 27 May.   F° 1892
ELEGIAE tristes ad pudicitiam adhortantes.   1719
ELEGY on a family-tomb.   By J. J. B[rundish].   4° 1782
ELEGY written among the ruins of an Abbey.   By the author of
    The Nun [E. Jerningham].   4° *London*, 1765
ELIOT (George)   A College breakfast-party.   (*Macmillan's Magazine*,
    July, 1878.)
ELIZABETH (*Queen*)   Letters Patent of Elizabeth and James I
    addressed to the University of Cambridge.   Ed. by J. W. Clark.
                                1892
ELLICOTT (C.J.)   The destiny of the creature, and other sermons.
                               London, 1858

    Obituary notice, by W. A. Cox.   (*Eagle*, Dec. 1905.)   1905

ELLIOT (W.G.)   The A. D. C., Cambridge, 1861–1898.   (Extracted
    from *Amateur Clubs and Actors*.)   (*London*, 1898)
ELLIOTT (E.B.)   The Omnipresence of the Supreme Being.   (Sea-
    tonian Prize Poem for 1820.)   1821

ELLIS (H.)   The New Dean.   Produced by Footlights Club, 11 June, 1897.   *n.p.* 1897.
ELLIS (R.L.)   Some thoughts on the formation of a Chinese Dictionary, and on the best mode of printing Chinese.   (1854)

R. L. Ellis.   By J. P. Norris.   1859
Memoir.   By Harvey Goodwin.   1863
Review of his Life by Dean Goodwin.   By J. P. N[orris].   1864

ELSTOBB (W.)   The pernicious consequences of replacing Denver-Dam and Sluices, etc., consider'd in a letter to Mr John Leaford.
                                                                       1745
Observations on an address to the public, April 20, 1775, superscribed Bedford Level, and signed C. N. Cole.   *Lynn*, 1776
Remarks on the Report of Mr John Golborne...on a view taken in pursuance of an order of the Bedford Level Corporation.
                                                                Lynn, 1778
An historical account of the Great Level of the Fens called Bedford Level.   *Lynn*, 1793
ELWIN (W.)   A narrative of the case of Mr Moore of St Catharine's College, Cambridge.   *London*, 1868
A reply to the *Remarks* of Mr Carr.   *London*, 1869
ELY.   A catalogue of the principal members of the Conventual and Cathedral Church of Ely, 24 Sept. 1756.   By James Bentham.
                                                                4° 1756
Queries offered to the consideration of the...City of Ely.   [By James Bentham.]   1757
Extract of a letter from Mr Bentham concerning certain discoveries in Ely Minster.   (*Archaeologia*, II.)   4° (*London*, 1773)
Account of the late dispute between the Bp of Ely [James Yorke] and the Fellows of Peterhouse.   [1787 ?]
—— 2nd ed.   [1787 ?]
Architectural notices in reference to the Cathedral Church of Ely.   [By J. Haggitt.]   [18–]
Account of the Prior's Chapel.   By W. Wilkins.   (*Archaeologia*, XIV.)
                                                          4° (*London*, 1803)
A guide to the Cathedral Church and Collegiate buildings at Ely.   [By G. Millers.]   1805
—— 2nd ed.   1820
—— 4th ed.   *Ely*, 1833
—— 5th ed.   *Ely*, 1838
The history and antiquities of the Conventual and Cathedral Church of Ely.   By James Bentham.   2nd ed.   (With suppl. by W. Stevenson.)   2 vols.   4° *Norwich*, 1812–17
A full and correct report of the trials for rioting at Ely and Littleport, in May, 1816.   *London*, 1816
A description of the Cathedral Church of Ely.   By George Millers.   3rd ed.   *London*, 1834
Correspondence between Ecclesiastical Commissioners and Bp of Ely.
                                                           London, 1837

ELY.

Ely Cathedral as it is and as it was. With views by R. B. Harraden. (*Camb. Advertiser*, 8 July, 1846.)   (1846)
Ely Cathedral restoration. List of subscribers, etc.   4° *n.p.* 1847
Lecture on Ely Cathedral before the Archaeol. Inst. By R. Willis. (*Norfolk Chronicle*.)   *Norwich*, 1847
Liber Eliensis. (Ed. D. J. Stewart.) Vol. I.   *Londini*, 1848
Brief description of the Conventual and Cathedral Church of the Holy Trinity, Ely. By J. W. Hewett.   1848
Ely Cathedral. Works done by G. G. Scott. (*Arch. Qtly Rev.*, June, 1851.)
Statement by the Dean and Chapter of Ely of works to be done, with list of subscribers (Aug. 6, 1851).   *n.p.* 1851
Handbook to the Cathedral Church at Ely. 2nd ed.   *Ely*, 1853
Restoration of the Central Octagon and Lantern of Ely Cathedral, as a memorial of the late Dean.   *n.p.* 1859
Handbook to the Cathedrals of England. Ely, etc. By R. J. King.
                                                      London, 1862
Circular on restoration, signed by H. Goodwin.   *n.p.* 1866
Statuta ecclesiae cathedralis Eliensis.   4° 1867
The architectural history of Ely Cathedral. By D. J. Stewart.
                                                      London, 1868
St Etheldreda Festival. Summary of proceedings, Oct. 1873. By Ch. Merivale.   *Ely*, 1873
—— Illustrated edition.   *Ely*, 1873
Inquisitio Eliensis.   4° *Londini*, 1876
Handbook to the Cathedral Church at Ely. New (10th) ed.
                                                      Ely (1877)
"Restoration" in East Anglia. No. 1. Cathedrals of Ely and Norwich, and certain Churches and other buildings.
                                           12° *London*, 1879
Cathedral Cities. Ely and Norwich. By R. Farren.   4° 1883
Ely Episcopal Records. By A. Gibbons.   *Lincoln*, 1891
Order of Service on St Etheldreda's Day, Oct. 17, 1891. *Ely*, 1891
Ely gossip. By Harvey Goodwin.   *Ely*, 1892
Ely Cathedral with plans, etc. by Rev. D. J. Stewart. (*Builder*, 2 April, 1892.)
The sculptures in the Lady Chapel at Ely. By M. R. James. (*Arch. Journ.* XLIX.)   (*London*, 1892)
The sculptures in the Lady Chapel at Ely. By M. R. James.
                                                  4° *London*, 1895
Proposed repair of the exterior of the Lady Chapel.   *n.p.* 1896
Historical memorials of Ely Cathedral. By C. W. Stubbs.
                                                      London, 1897
Handbook to the Cathedral. 20th ed. By C. W. Stubbs. *Ely* (1898)
—— 21st ed.   *Ely*, 1904
Ely Cathedral. (Sketch of history.)   4° *n.p.* (1899)
The Cathedral Church of Ely. By W. D. Sweeting. *London*, 1901
The Acts of S. Audrey. The Octagon Sculptures.   *Ely* (1904)

ELY.
Concise Guide to the Cathedral, by J. W. Clark.   1904
Cromwell and the old house at Ely. By E. G. Punchard.   *Ely,* 1906
Sacrist Rolls. Ed. by F. R. Chapman. 2 vols.   1907
Re-opening of the Organ. October, 1908. Programme and history.
                                                        Ely, 1908
Diocesan Association for preventive, rescue, and penitentiary work.
First report.   *Ely,* 1909
EMERY (W.) Expenses of University education at Cambridge, past
and present. (*Journ. of Statistical Soc.*)   *London,* 1863
Church organization and efficient ministry. Charge, October, 1866.
EMMANUEL College. Argument in the case of the Poor's Rate
charged on the Colleges of Christ and Emmanuel. [By Sir J.
Marriott.]   (1768)
Index to English books and pamphlets printed before 1700 in the
Library. By J. B. Pearson.   1869
Commemoration of the three hundredth anniversary of the founda-
tion, 1884.   1885
—— Scrap-book.   4° 1884
Laws of the Amalgamated Clubs, Oct. 1893.   1893
Emmanuel College Magazine. Lent Term, 1893 ; Mich. Term,
1894 ; Easter Term, 1895.   1893–5
Notes on the College buildings. By J. B. Peace. (*Emm. Coll.
Mag.* VI.)   1894
Emmanuel College. By E. S. Shuckburgh. (College histories.)
                                                    London, 1904
See also Marriott (*Sir* J.) ; Sancroft (W.).
EMPIRE of the Sea. (Unsuccessful Prize Poem, 1836.)   (1836)
ENDOWMENTS. Trusts, Statutes, and Directions affecting the
Professorships (pp. 1–112). [Ed. by H. Philpott.]   1857
—— Affecting Scholarships and Prizes (pp. 115–166).   1857
—— Affecting certain Gifts and Endowments (pp. 169–315). 1857
—— The three parts bound together, with a general title prefixed.
                                                        1857
—— A new edition.   1876
Endowments of the University of Cambridge. Ed. by J. W. Clark.
                                                        1904
ENGLISH (H.S.) A light on the historians and on the history of
Crowland Abbey.   *London,* 1868
ENGRAVERS. A chronological series...from the invention of the
art to the beginning of the present century. [By T. Martyn.]
                                                        1770
ENTOMOLOGICAL and Natural Hist. Soc. Bye-laws.   1898
EPIGRAMS. *See* Prolusiones.
ESCREET (J.) Memoir. By Thomas Webster.   *London,* 1823
ESHER (*Viscount*) Foam. [A book of verses.]   *London,* 1893
Extracts from Journals, 1872–81. (Privately printed.)   1908
ESQUIRE Bedell. A plea for the triumvirate of Esquire Bedells.
Addressed to Members of the Senate. [By W. Nind.]   1852

ESQUIRE Bedell.
> Poll at Election, 19 Jan. 1854. (H. Godfrey elected.)   1854
> Fly-sheets, candidatures, etc. from 1865.   1865–
> Poll at Election, 7 Nov. 1873. (E. J. Gross elected.)   1873
> Poll at Election, 1 May, 1877. (A. P. Humphry elected.)   1877
> Poll at Election, 7 Feb. 1893. (W. A. Gill elected.)   1893

ESSAY on the causes that determined the order in which the several
> branches of Greek literature rose and flourished.   1833

ESSAY on the influence of the Homeric poems on the Greek nation. 1829

ESSAY on the philosophical writings of Cicero. [By A. H. Hallam.]
>   1832

ESSAY on the progressive improvement of mankind. An oration
> delivered in the Chapel of Trinity College, Dec. 17, 1798. [By
> W. Lamb, 2nd Viscount Melbourne.]   4° *London*, 1799

ESSEX (J.) Remarks on...brick and stone buildings in England.
> (*Archaeologia*, IV.)   4° (*London*, 1777)

> Some observations on Lincoln Cathedral. (*Archaeologia*, IV.)
>   4° (*London*, 1777)

> Observations on the origin and antiquities of Round Churches; and
> of the Round Church at Cambridge in particular. (*Archaeologia*, VI.)
>   4° (*London*, 1782)

> Observations on Croyland Abbey and Bridge. (*Bibl. topographica
> Britannica*, XXII.)   4° (*London*, 1784)

ESSINGTON (R.W.) The curse upon Cain. (Seatonian Prize
> Poem for 1846.)   1846

> The Legacy of an Etonian.   *Cambridge and London*, 1846

ETON College. Catalogus alumnorum...1444–1730. 4° *Eton*, 1730

> Extract from case of the obligation on the electors of Eton College...
> (By Thomas Ashton.) Part I.   4° *London*, 1771

> Letter to Dr M[orell]. By Thomas Ashton.   4° *London*, 1771

> Registrum Regale. List of the Provosts of Eton, etc. 4° *Etonae*, 1774

> The Microcosm, by Gregory Griffin of Eton. 3rd ed. 2 vols.
> (Harcourt's *Eton bibliography*, 1902, p. 18.)   12° *Windsor*, 1793

> Alumni Etonenses. By T. Harwood.   4° *Birmingham*, 1797

> The Miniature. A Periodical Paper. By Solomon Grildrig of the
> College of Eton. (April 23, 1804–April 1, 1805.) (Harcourt,
> p. 22.)   *London*, 1805

> Report of proceedings in the case of an Appeal by...King's College
> against...Eton College.   *London*, 1816

> The Appeal of King's College against the Fellows of Eton.   1817

> Statutes, 1446. (In 4th Report of Select Committee on Education.)
>   F° *London*, 1818

> An explanation of the various local passages and allusions in the
> Appeal, etc. of King's College *v.* Eton College. *London*, 1819

> The Etonian. 2nd ed. 2 vols. (Harcourt, p. 28.) *London*, 1822

> Some remarks on the present studies and management of Eton
> School. By a parent. 2nd ed.   *London*, 1834

> The Eton abuses considered in a letter addressed to the author of
> *Some remarks.* 2nd ed.   *London*, 1834

ETON College.

The Eton system of education vindicated...in reply to some recent publications. *London*, 1834

Memorials of Eton. By Charles W. Radclyffe. F° *Eton*, 1844

The Legacy of an Etonian. Ed. by R. Nolands. [By R. W. Essington.] *Cambridge and London*, 1846

Registrum Regale. List of the Provosts of Eton, etc. *Eton*, 1847

Ancient Laws...for Eton College. Collected by J. Heywood and T. Wright. *London*, 1850

Letter to the Provost of Eton on the election of scholars to the two foundations of Henry VI. By G. Williams. *London*, 1850

Thoughts on Eton, suggested by Sir John Coleridge's Speech at Tiverton. By an Etonian. *London*, 1861

Hints for Paterfamilias. By Anti-Pater. *n.p.* 1861

Eton Reform. 2 parts. By W. Johnson [Cory]. *London*, 1861

A few words with the Eton Reformers. By H. Brandreth. *London*, 1865

A history of Eton College, 1440–1875. By H. C. Maxwell Lyte. *London*, 1875

—— New ed. *London*, 1889

A day of my life...at Eton. [By G. N. Bankes.] 2nd ed. *London*, 1877

About some fellows. [By G. N. Bankes.] *London*, 1878

Eton College Library. By F. St John Thackeray. 4° *Eton*, 1881

How I stole the Block. By an old Etonian. *London*, 1883

A Visit to Eton. By Mowbray Morris. (*Eng. Illust. Mag.* Nov. 1884.)

A letter on buildings at Eton. By J. P. Carter. *Eton*, 1885

Noblesse oblige. A plea for preservation of Eton buildings. By H. E. Luxmoore. 4° *Eton*, 1885

Eton Housetops. A birdseye view. [By H. E. Luxmoore.] 4° *Eton*, 1885

Suggestions for the reorganization of the payment of Classical masters (at Eton College). *Eton* [1886]

Eton College : I. Historical and descriptive ; II. Athletics ; III. As a School. By Hon. A. Lyttelton. (*Engl. Illust. Mag.* July, 1890.)

Anniversary Celebration, 1891. Programmes, etc. *Eton*, 1891

Keate's Lane Papers. An Eton miscellany. (Harcourt, p. 87.) *Eton*, 1891

Loan collection of Portraits, etc. connected with the history of Eton, made on the occasion of the 450th Anniversary of the foundation of the College. 4° *Eton*, 1891

The Mayfly. Directed by present Etonians. 1–3. May 16–June 24. (Harcourt, p. 88.) 4° *Eton*, 1891

Eton. An Ode by A. C. Swinburne. Set to music by C. H. H. Parry. 4° *London* (1891)

Eton Songs. By A. C. Ainger. Music by Jos. Barnby. Illustrated by Herbert Marshall. 4° *London*, 1891–2

Stories of old Eton days. By C. Kegan Paul. (*Nineteenth Century*, October, 1892.)

ETON College.

Eton of old, or eighty years since, 1811–1822. By an old Colleger [W. H. Tucker]. Eton of today [by A. C. Benson].

4° *London*, 1892

Catalogue of Manuscripts. By M. R. James. 1895

Eton in the Forties. By an old Colleger [A. D. Coleridge].

London, 1896

Memoir of E. C. Hawtrey. By F. St John Thackeray. *London*, 1896

Acting at Eton. By F. Tarver. (From Elliot's *Amateur Clubs and Actors*.) (*London*, 1898)

A history of Eton College. By L. Cust. *London*, 1899

Fasti Etonenses. By A. C. Benson. *Eton*, 1899

A list of Eton College in 1771. Ed. by R. A. Austen Leigh.

Eton, 1903

Letter to H. E. Luxmoore on the subject of the adornment of the sanctuary of the Collegiate Church of St Mary of Eton. By T. B. Carter. F° *n.p.* 1903

Letter to those responsible for the Memorial to the Etonians who fell in the South African War. By T. B. Carter. F° *n.p.* 1904

Eton under Barnard, 1754–1765. Ed. by R. A. Austen Leigh.

Eton, 1904

Bygone Eton. By R. A. Austen Leigh. Parts 1, 2. F° *Eton*, 1904

—— Re-issue. 1906

Illustrated Guide to Eton College. By R. A. Austen Leigh.

Eton, 1904

—— 2nd ed. *Eton*, 1905

Etoniana. Nos. 1–3, 5. 4° *Eton*, 1904–5

Memorial. List of donations, to 31 Jan. 1904, with other papers and reports relating to the Memorial. *Eton*, 1904–9

Order of proceedings at the laying of the first stone of the Memorial Buildings, 29 July, 1905. 4° *Eton*, 1905

Lupton's Chapel. By H. E. Luxmoore. (*The Meteor*, no. 4, 23 June, 1905.) 4° *Eton*, 1905

The Frescoes in the Chapel at Eton College, with notes, by M. R. James. Obl. 4° *Eton*, 1907

Order of proceedings at opening the Memorial Buildings, 18 Nov. 1908. With press notices, and other papers. 4° *Eton*, 1908

Poets in Pupil Room. By themselves, or practically so. *Eton*, 1908

EUBULUS. A letter to Philograntus [J. H. Monk]. *London*, 1822

EUGENIUS. *See* Crawford (C.).

EUREKA ; a sequel to Lord John Russell's Post-bag. [By J. T. B. Landon.] *Oxford*, 1851

EURIPIDES. Medea. Ed. R. Porson. (With MS. note by Porson.) 1801

A translation of the Hecuba. 1828

See also Greek Plays at Cambridge.

EUSDEN (L.) Verses at the last Publick Commencement at Cambridge. F° *London*, 1714

EVANS (A.H.) *See* Turner (W.).

EVANS (J.)   On a hoard of bronze objects found in Wilburton Fen. (*Archaeologia*, XLVIII.)   4° (*Westminster*, 1883)

EVANS (R.W.)   A statement respecting the lectures at present given on the subject of the New Testament, in Trinity College, Cambridge.   4° 1834

EVANS (S.)   Sonnets on the death of the Duke of Wellington.   1852

EVENING Contemplation in a College.   Being a parody on the Elegy in a Country Church Yard.   By another Gentleman of Cambridge [J. Duncombe].   4° *London*, 1753

EVERETT (W.)   College essays delivered in Trinity College, Cambridge, Feb. and Dec. 1862.   1863
    On the Cam.   Lectures on the University of Cambridge in England. New ed.   *London*, 1869

EWING (J.A.)   University Training of Engineers.   1891

EXAMINATION Hall.   Fly-sheet in favour of building an Examination Hall.   F° 1825

EXAMINATION Papers.   Classical Examinations.   2nd ed.   1826
    Classical Examinations.   1830
    —— 2nd ser.   1831
    Mathematical Examinations.   1830
    Cambridge Theological Examination Papers.   1848

EXAMINATIONS.   *See* Jebb (J.); Middle Class Examinations; Tripos Examinations.

EXCURSIONS to Parnassus.   By a Gentleman of the University of Cambridge.   4° *London*, 1787

EXHIBITION of Modern Pictures.
    Bijou Theatre.   Nov. 1896.   Catalogue.   1896
    Bijou Theatre.   4–17 Nov. 1896.   Poster.
    The Garden Studio.   Nov. 1897.   Catalogue.   1897

EXILE'S Return, and other poems.   By E. H. B[lakeney].   1890

EXPEDITION of Napoleon into Russia.   (Unsuccessful Prize Poem.)
                                                             1828

EXPLANATION of the Tale of a Nettle, paragraph by paragraph from the best edition printed at Cambridge...   *n.p.* 1710

EXTENSION Meetings.   *See* Local Lectures.

EYRES (C.)   Observations on University Reform.   1849

F

FACETIÆ Cantabrigienses. By Socius. [Ed. by R. Gooch.]
London, 1825

—— 3rd ed. London, 1836
FAIR Statement. [On Celibacy.] [18–]
FAIRFAX (J.) Life of...O. Stockton...to which is added his funeral
sermon, 1681. (Reprint.) 12º London, 1826
FAIRFAX (Sir T.) Another Letter...June 8, 1647. 4º London, 1647
FAIRLIE (J.) Illustrations of Cheveley Church, Cambridgeshire.
Fº London, 1851
FAMILY of Smith, or Milk and Eggs. Comic Opera, in 2 Acts, by
Temple Chambers. (Repr. from Granta.) Surbiton, 1903
FANCOURT (W.L.) Sermon preached before the University of
Cambridge, 29 June, 1823. London, 1823
FANING (J.F.E.) See Matriculations, 1902.
FARDELL (H.) Observations on a Central Assize at Wisbech.
Wisbech, 1848
Observations on the Nene Valley drainage. Wisbech, 1850
View of the...sources from whence may be derived the means of
draining the Nene Valley. Ely, 1850
FAREWELL Ode on a distant prospect of Cambridge. By the author
of The Brunoniad [T. Foster]. 4º 1794
FAREWELL to Harold ! [Attack on Byron by E. Smedley.] 1816
FARISH (C.) Toleration of marriage in the Universities recommended
to the attention of the Heads of Houses. (1799)
FARISH (W.) Plan of a course of lectures on arts and manufactures,
more particularly such as relate to chemistry. 1796
Plan of a course of lectures. 1803
A report of the formation of the Cambridge Auxiliary Bible Society.
Ed. by W. Farish. 1812
A plan of a course of lectures on arts and manufactures. [With
notes by Prof. Willis.] 1821
Notice of his lectures, Lent Term, 1823 ; Lent Term, 1826 ; Lent
Term, 1827. Fº 1823–7
Oaths. [By W. Farish.] (1833)

Funeral Sermon...preached by Thomas Webster. London, 1837

FARMER (R.) A catalogue of the library of the late R. F....sold
May, 1798. (Priced.) (London) 1798
See also Shuckburgh (E. S.).

FARRAR (F.W.)   The influence of the revival of Classical studies on English Literature during the reigns of Elizabeth and James I. (Le Bas Prize Essay for 1856.)   1856

"From strength to strength." A sermon preached Jan. 1, 1860.
           Huntingdon, 1860

On some defects in Public School education.   *London*, 1867

FARREN (R.)   The Granta and the Cam.   4° 1880

[Etchings of Cambridge, for the re-issue of Cooper's enlargement of Le Keux.]   (Bowes 2030* *f*)   1880

Cambridge and its neighbourhood. (With introduction by J. W. Clark.)   F° 1881

Pencil jottings from the Ajax.   4° 1883

Cathedral Cities. Ely and Norwich. With introduction by E. A. Freeman.   4° 1883

The Birds of Aristophanes.   Obl. 1884

The Eumenides of Aeschylus.   Obl. 1886

—— Large paper copy.   Obl. 1886

The Oedipus Tyrannus of Sophocles.   Obl. 1888

Cathedral Cities. Peterborough, Crowland, and Thorney. (Peterborough wanting, and the Introduction.)   F° 1889

The Iphigenia in Tauris of Euripides.   Obl. 1895

FARREN (W.)   Redshanks in the Cambridgeshire Fens. (*Country Life*, 6 May, 1905.)

FARRINGTON (G.)   *See* Orford (*Lord*).

FAUCHON (J.)   A publick lecture to...La Butte.   4° 1749

FAULKNER (R.R.)   An appeal to the protestant public. 29 Aug. 1844.   F° 1844

FAWCETT (H.)   On the question of compulsory attendance at Professors' lectures.   1877

Life. By Leslie Stephen. 2nd ed.   *London*, 1885

FAWCETT (James)   Sermon preached before the University of Cambridge, 27 Jan. 1793.   4° 1793

FAWCETT (John)   The substance of two lectures.   1843

FAWCETT (W.M.)   An account of St Edmund's Church, Hauxton, near Cambridge. (*Ecclesiologist*, Dec. 1861.)

FAY (C.R.)   King's College.   *London*, 1907

FEEDLE (J.L.)   A letter to the Farmers of Cambridgeshire, wherein the claims of Capt. Yorke are stated and proved.   (1832)

FEES.   Grace to appoint a Syndicate to consider the present Table, 8 Dec. 1824 ; Report of this Syndicate, 19 Apr. 1825 ; Grace to confirm, 27 Apr. 1825.   F° 1824–25

Report of Syndicate appointed to consider whether Matriculation Fees should not be increased, 28 May, 1825.   F° 1825

FELLOW (The) Nos 1, 3–11. 29 Apr. 1836–15 Dec. 1836.   1836

FELLOW-Commoners and Honorary Degrees. By a Resident Fellow.
           1837

FELLOWSHIPS.   *See* Morgan (H. A.).

FEMALE Refuge. Reports 31–33, 38–42, 44, 46, 61–67.   1873–1909

FENNELL (C.A.M.)   The Parodos of Aeschylus's *Septem contra Thebas*.
 Prælection.   4º 1889
FENNER'S Cricket Ground.   Proposed purchase, 23 May, 1892.
                                                         Fº 1892
FENS.   The designe for the perfect draining of...Bedford Level.   By
 W. Dodson.   4º *London,* 1665
 History of the...state of the navigation of the Port of Kings-Lyn
 and of Cambridge...and of the...rivers...through the Fens.   By
 J. Armstrong.   Fº *London,* 1725
 —— Another ed.   Fº *London,* 1766
 The pernicious consequences of replacing Denver-Dam and Sluices, etc.
 consider'd.   By W. Elstobb, Junr.   1745
 Reasons against the Bill...for scouring out and deepening of the
 River Nene.   1754
 New method of making the banks in the Fens almost impregnable.
 By J. Harrison.   [1766]
 Report concerning the draining of the North Level of the Fens.
 Aug. 22, 1768.   By J. Smeaton.   4º *n.p.* (1768)
 The history of imbanking and draining of divers Fens and Marshes.
 By Sir W. Dugdale.   2nd ed., by C. N. Cole.   Fº *London,* 1772
 Observations on an address to the public, Apr. 20, 1775, superscribed
 Bedford Level, and signed C. N. Cole.   By W. Elstobb.
                                               Lynn, 1776
 Observations on the means of better draining the Middle and South
 Levels of the Fens.   By two Gentlemen who have taken a view
 thereof.   4º *London,* 1777
 An answer to a book intituled " An Inquiry into Facts and Observa-
 tions thereon, humbly submitted to the candid Examiner into the
 Principles of a Bill...for the Preservation of the Great Level of the
 Fens, etc."   *London,* 1778
 Remarks on the Report of Mr John Golborne...on a view taken in
 pursuance of an order of the Bedford Level Corporation.   By
 W. Elstobb.   *Lynn,* 1778
 Historical account of the Bedford Level.   By W. Elstobb. *Lynn,* 1793
 Facts and observations in favour of the Eau Brink Cut, and of its
 immediate execution.   *Wisbech,* 1809
 New system for draining the Fens.   By Jos. Scott.   *Wisbech* [1809 ?]
 Eau Brink Drainage Bill.   1818
 The joint report of Messrs Walker and Mylne, the engineers ap-
 pointed in consequence of the late intended Eau Brink Act. 1825
 A letter addressed to the owners of land under the Eau Brink
 Drainage.   1826
 Letter to the Duke of Bedford...on the works in the New Bedford
 River.   By S. Wells.   1828
 Letter to the Earl of Hardwicke on use of the Steam Dredging
 Engine in deepening Rivers in the Bedford Level.   By T. Archer.
                                                  Ely, 1829
 History of the drainage of the Bedford Level.   By S. Wells.
                                                 London, 1830

FENS.

The history of Wisbech, with an historical sketch of the Fens.
Wisbech, 1834

On the drainage of the Nene Valley. Report. *Northampton*, 1848

—— Another ed. *Northampton* (1849)

Plan of the Middle Level shewing the works to be executed under the Act of 1848. [1849 ?]

Remarks on a general improvement of the River Nene.
Northampton (1849)

View of the...sources from whence may be derived the means of draining the Nene Valley. By Henry Fardell. *Ely*, 1850

Observations on the Nene Valley drainage. By Henry Fardell.
Wisbech, 1850

Examination of the clauses of the Nene Valley Drainage Bill.
12° *Wisbech*, 1852

The drainage of Whittlesea Mere. By W. Wells. *London*, 1860

The Nene in danger. Considerations on the drainage scheme.
London, 1862

Theoretical remarks on the gravel and drift of the Fenlands. By H. G. Seeley. (*Geol. Mag.* III.) *Hertford*, 1866

The Fens. By Charles Kingsley. (*Good Words*, May 1, 1867.)

The Fen and Marshland Churches. A series of photographs, with notes. Series 1–3. 4° *Wisbech* [1867–9]

Lord Orford's Voyage round the Fens in 1774. *Doncaster* (1868)

The Fen Country. By A. S. Ruston. (*Journal of the Farmers' Club*, Nov. 1870.) *London* (1870)

On the treatment of the reclaimed bogland of Whittlesea Mere. By W. Wells. *London*, 1870

The Fenland past and present. By S. H. Miller and S. B. J. Skertchly. *Wisbech*, 1878

Fen Floods and the Lower Ouse. By J. H. H. Moxon. 1878

The Birds of the Fens. By J. H. H. Moxon. 1882

In the Fens. With illustrations by R. W. Macbeth. (*Engl. Illustr. Mag.* Nov. 1883.)

A Slip in the Fens. [By Jane Sexey.] New ed. *London*, 1885

The handbook to the Fenland. By S. H. Miller. *London* (1889)

—— 2nd ed. *London* (1890)

See also Acts and Bills.

FENTON (E.) Oxford and Cambridge Miscellany Poems.
London [1709]

FENWICK (J.R.) Sketch of the professional life and character of John Clark, M.D. *Newcastle*, 1806

FERRAR (N.) Memoirs of the life of N. F. By P. Peckard. 1790

Two lives of N. F. By his brother John and Dr Jebb. Ed. by J. E. B. Mayor. (Cambridge in the XVIIth century, I.) 1855

FESTIVAL Choir. Programme of a Glee and Madrigal Concert, 17 Feb. 1890. 1890

—— 10 Feb. 1891. 1891

—— 2 March, 1896. 1896

FESTIVAL Choir.
Bach's Passion (St Matthew). 26 Feb. 1902.   1902
FEW brief remarks on Camb. Univ. and College Reform. *London*, 1870
FEW plain truths, or the late proceedings at Cambridge reviewed. By
   Philo Patria. [On the Chancellorship.]   *London*, 1847
FEW Remarks on a Sermon preached in St Clement's.   1863
FEW Verses, English and Latin. [By E. Smedley.]   *London*, 1812
FIELD (C.) St Alban. (Seatonian Prize Poem for 1908.)
                                                    London, 1909
FINANCE. Appointment of Syndicate to consider plan for increasing
   the pecuniary resources of the University (Grace 5 May, 1847);
   prolongation of Syndicate (Grace 26 May, 1847); Report of
   Syndicate, 10 Dec. 1847, with notice of Grace to confirm,
   6 March, 1848.   F⁰ (1847–48)
FINCH (G.B.) Legal education, its aim and method.   1885
FINES. The reasonableness of Church and College Fines asserted.
   [By H. Gally.]   *London*, 1731
FIRTH (J.B.) The Minstrelsy of Isis.   *London*, 1908
FISCHER (W.F.L.) *See* Burdakin (J.); Webb (W.).
FISCHER-TREUENFELD (R. von) Lord Johan Fyssher, Master of
   Queen's [*sic*] College.   *London*, 1894
FISHER (E.H.) The Goth and the Saracen. (Le Bas Prize, 1859.)
                                                          1859
FISHER (G.W.) Testimonials of G. W. Fisher, a candidate for the
   Rectory of Ovington.   1883
FISHER (J.) The funeral sermon of Margaret, Countess of Richmond
   and Derby. [Ed. T. Baker.]   *London*, 1708
—— Ed. J. Hymers, B.D.   1840

Life. By T. Baily.   *London*, 1655
Life. By John Lewis. 2 vols.   *London*, 1855
Handlist of portraits of Blessed John Fisher. [By C. Sayle.] (*Eagle*.) 1890
Lord Johan Fyssher...An historical research. By R. von Fischer-Treuenfeld.
                                                   London, 1894

FISHER (Osmond) Notes on the art of growing roses out of doors.
                                                   London, 1869
Letter of application and testimonials for Woodwardian Professorship
   of Geology, 1 Feb. 1873.   1873
On a mammaliferous deposit at Barrington, Cambs. (*Qtly Journ.
   Geol. Soc.*)   (*London*, 1879)
FISHER (W.W.) A letter to the members of the Cambridgeshire
   Horticultural Society.   1850
FITCH (J.G.) University work in great towns. (*Nineteenth Century*,
   Nov. 1878.)
FITS of Folly; or the aberrations of a Philosopher. By Anybody.
                                                          [1832]
FITTON (F.C.) Testimonials when a candidate for the rectory of
   Ashley-cum-Silverley.   (1868)
FITZWILLIAM Hall Magazine. Vol. I. 1908–1910.   1910

FITZWILLIAM Museum. Fly-sheets, etc. from 1819.   1819–
Report of Syndicate on site.   Fº (1834)
Catalogue of paintings, etc. bequeathed...by Daniel Mesman, Esq.
By John Massey.   1835
—— Another ed.   1846
Regulations for future management, 27 March, 1849; Graces to
confirm, 25 April.   Fº (1849)
The Fitzwilliam Museum, Cambridge, being illustrations of the
collection of ancient marbles, etc. formerly in the possession of
John Disney.   3 pts.   4º 1849
Hand-book to the marbles, casts, and antiquities.   1855
Correspondence between the Vice-Chancellor (Dr Whewell) and
the Syndics on his alteration in the arrangement of the pictures,
1856 (several pieces).   4º 1856
Proposed purchase of the coins collected by Col. Leake (six pieces).
   4º 1863–4
Proposal to grant the use of the building for a ball to the Prince and
Princess of Wales (five pieces).   4º 1864
Verses against the proposal, by Prof. Selwyn.   4º 1864
Catalogue of a selection from Col. Leake's Greek coins exhibited
in the Fitzwilliam Museum.   By C. Babington.   4º 1867
Catalogue of a selection from the British and English coins in the
Fitzwilliam Museum.   By C. Babington.   4º 1867
Report of the Syndics on Mr Kerrich's bequest, 26 Oct. 1872.
   (1872)
The illuminated manuscripts in the library of the Fitzwilliam
Museum.   By W. G. Searle.   1876
Catalogue of the gems in the Fitzwilliam Museum.   By J. H.
Middleton.   1891
Annual Report for years ending 31 Dec. 1891, 31 Dec. 1904–31 Dec.
1909.   4º 1892, 1905–10
Brief catalogue of the pictures.   By Sidney Colvin.   1895
—— Revised ed.   1901
A descriptive catalogue of the manuscripts in the library of the
Fitzwilliam Museum.   By M. R. James.   1895
Illustrated catalogue of the loan collection of plate exhibited in the
Fitzwilliam Museum, May 1895.   By J. E. Foster and T. D.
Atkinson.   4º 1896
A catalogue of the Greek vases in the Fitzwilliam Museum.   By
E. A. Gardner.   1897
Handbook to the collection of antiquities [etc.].   By H. A. Chapman.
   1898
—— 2nd ed.   1904
Catalogue of a loan exhibition of pottery and porcelain held in the
Fitzwilliam Museum.   1902
Descriptive catalogue of the pictures in the Fitzwilliam Museum.
By F. R. Earp.   1902
Catalogue of a collection of modern Greek embroideries exhibited at
the Fitzwilliam Museum.   By A. J. B. Wace.   1905

FITZWILLIAM Museum.
> List of the fifteenth-century printed books bequeathed to the Fitz-
> william Museum by F. McClean. By S. Gaselee.   (1905)
> Catalogue of a loan collection of oriental enamels exhibited at the
> Fitzwilliam Museum.   1905
> Report (21 May 1907) of the Fitzwilliam Museum Syndicate on the
> Directorship, and recommending an Assistant-Directorship, with
> fly-sheets relating thereto.   4° 1907–8
> Letters respecting Mr Cockerell's candidature for the Directorship.
> April 1908.   *London*, 1908
> *See also* Acts and Bills, 1822.

FITZWILLIAM (J.)   A sermon preached at Cottenham, 9 Sept.
1683.   4° *London* (1683)

FLANAGAN (L.)   A letter to the free and independent electors of
Cambridge. [An attack on Spring Rice.]   4° *London* (1832)

FLEAM Dyke.   Account of excavations, 1852.   By R. C. Neville.
(*Arch. Journ.*, IX.)   (*London*, 1852)

FLEETWOOD (E.)   An enquiry into the customary-estates and
tenant-rights of those who hold lands of Church and other foundations, by the tenure of three lives and twenty-one years.
> *London*, 1731
> The rights of Churches and Colleges defended.   In answer to a
> pamphlet...by E. Fleetwood.   By Dicaiophilus Cantabrigiensis
> (R. Long).   *London*, 1731

FLEETWOOD (W.), *Bp of Ely*.   Sermon before the University in
King's College Chapel, 25 March, 1689, being the anniversary for
commemoration of Henry VI.   4° 1689
> Charge delivered at Cambridge, 7 Aug. 1716.   4° 1716

FLETCHER (C.R.L.)   Henry VI.   A lecture delivered at Eton,
5 Dec. 1891.   *Eton*, 1891

FLETCHER (H.)   Oxford and Cambridge delineated.   Introd. by
J. W. Clark.   4° *London*, 1909

FLETCHER (W.M.)   Eustace Talbot.   (By W. M. F. and others.)
4° 1908

FLORISTS' Society.   Rules, etc.   (1857)

FLOWER (B.)   National sins considered in two letters to the Rev.
Thos. Robinson.   1796
> The proceedings of the House of Lords in the case of B. F., printer
> of the Cambridge Intelligencer, for a supposed libel on the Bishop
> of Llandaff.   1800
> An address to the Freeholders of Cambridgeshire, on the General
> Election.   1802

FLY-SHEETS.
> Chronological series, 1817–1910.   1817–1910
> Classified series under the following heads:.

Addenbrooke's Hospital.	Edmund's (St) House.
American Lectureship.	Esquire Bedell.
Botanic Garden.	Fitzwilliam Museum.
Classical studies.	Jacksonian Professorship.

FLY-SHEETS.

Legal Studies.	Previous Examination.
Library.	Professors.
Local Government.	Public Orator.
Mary (St) the Great.	Reform.
Mathematical Tripos.	Registrary.
Medicine.	Representatives, University.
Moral Sciences Tripos.	Russian Lectureship.
Museums and Lecture Rooms	Sewage.
Syndicate.	Sites.
Observatory.	Studies Syndicate.
Presentation to University	Theology.
livings.	Women.
Press.	Woodwardian Museum.

See also Cambridge Papers.

FLOWER (W.H.) Report on the Oxford Museums, 14 March, 1891

FOAM. [By Viscount Esher.]   *London*, 1893

FOOTLIGHTS DRAMATIC CLUB.

Alma Mater, Comedy-Burlesque.   (1892)
The New Dean. By Harold Ellis. Produced 11 June 1897. (1897)
The Freshman. Poster.   (1899)
The Oriental Trip. By Eric Burke. Produced 7 June 1901. (1901)
—— Poster.
The Agricultural Trip. Poster.   (1903)
Paying the Piper. By H. Brodie and J. Heard. Produced 9 June
  1905.   (1905)
—— Poster.
The Classical Trip. Poster.   (1906)
The Honorary Degree. By H. Rottenburg. Produced 7 June 1907.
                                           (1907)
—— Poster.
The 'Varsity B.C. By H. Rottenburg. Produced June 1908. (1908)
—— Poster.
A Reading Party. By H. Rottenburg. Produced June 1909. (1909)
—— Poster.

See also, for programmes, Cambridge Papers.

FORDHAM (*Sir* H.G.) Notes sur la cartographie des provinces
  anglaises et françaises des xvie et xviie siècles.   *Gand*, 1907
Notes on the cartography of the counties of England and Wales.
                     Hertford, 1908
John Cary, Engraver and Map-seller. Paper read at C. A. S. Dec.
  1909.   1910
An Itinerary of the 16th century. Paper read at C. A. S. Dec. 1909.
                              1910

FOREMAN (F.W.) Soils of Cambridgeshire. (*Journ. of Agric. Sc.*)
                              1907

FORSTER (R.H.) and Harris (W.) The history of the Lady Margaret
  Boat Club, 1825–1890.   1890
Soapsuds, or Washings from the Wollerer.   1890

FORSTER (R.H.)   The Postgraduates.   1895
  Down by the River.   1901
FORSYTH (A.R.)   Arthur Cayley.   (Cayley's *Coll. Papers*, VIII.)
                                                                $4°$ 1895
  Addresses to Mathematical and Physical Section, British Assoc.,
    Toronto, 1897.   *London*, 1897
  Edward John Routh.   (*Proc. Lond. Math. Soc.*, ser. 2, vol. 5, pt 7.)
                                                                London, 1907
FORSYTH (W.)   The Great Fair of Nijni Novogorod.   *London*, 1865
FORTUNATE Youth.   *See* Causton (A. W.).
FOSTER (John), † 1774.   Oratio habita...in Coll. Regali, iv Non. Febr.
  die Fundatoris memoriæ sacro.   Accedit etiam, ab eodem scriptum,
  carmen comitiale. $4°$ 1752
Dissertatio quae premium a...Ed. Finch et Tho. Townshend pro-
  positum retulit...1754.   (Members' Prize.) $4°$ *Londini*, 1758
FOSTER (John), *Trin.*   An Essay on the method of illustrating
  Scripture from the relations of modern travellers in Palestine and
  the neighbouring countries.   1802
FOSTER (J.E.) and Atkinson (T.D.)   Illustrated Catalogue of the
  loan collection of Plate exhibited in the Fitzwilliam Museum,
  May 1895. $4°$ 1896
FOSTER (*Sir* M.)   Studies from the Physiological Laboratory in the
  Univ. of Camb.   Ed. by M. Foster.   Pt I.   1873
—— Pt II.   1876
—— Pt III.   1877
On medical education at Cambridge.   *London*, 1878
Coutts Trotter.   In Memoriam.   1888
T. H. Huxley.   (*Proc. Roy. Soc.* LIX.)   *London* [1895]

In Memoriam.   (*Journal of Physiology*, 25 March, 1907.)   (*London*) 1907
The late Professor Sir Michael Foster.   By A. E. Shipley.   (*Proc. Linnaean Soc.*)
                                                             London, 1907
Michael Foster (1836–1907).   By W. H. Gaskell.   (*Proc. Roy. Soc.*)
                                                             (*London*) 1908

FOSTER (M.G.)   Testimonials when a candidate for a post as surgeon
  in the Orient Company's Service.   1888
Meteorological observations...at the Kursaal Maloja during the summer
  of 1891.   *n.p.* (1891)
FOSTER (T.)   A farewell ode on a distant prospect of Cambridge...
  By the author of the Brunoniad (T. F.) $4°$ 1794
FOSTER (W.K.)   *See* Archæology (Museum of General and Local)
  and of Ethnology.
FOSTER Brothers (The) ;   being a history of the school and college
  life of two young men.   [By James Payn.]   *London*, 1859
FOWLER (E.J.)   History of Gamlingay.   *Gamlingay*, 1905
FOWLER (T.)   Corpus Christi College, Oxford.   (College histories.)
                                                             London, 1898
FOX (R.)   The history of Godmanchester, in the county of Huntingdon.
                                                             London, 1831

FOXLEY (J.)   On faith in natural and revealed religion.   (Burney
   Prize Essay, 1855.)   1855
Secularism, scepticism, ritualism, liberationism.   (Hulsean Lectures,
   1881.)   (1881)
FRAGMENT (A)   [Attr. to H. Stebbing.]   (Bowes 1182*.)
                                                           London (1751)
——— 2nd ed.   *London* (1751)
——— 3rd ed.   *London* (1751)
A key to the Fragment.   By Amias Riddinge [Wm King].
                                                        London, 1751
Another Fragment.   [Attr. to H. Stebbing.]   *London* (1751)
Fragmentum est pars rei fractae.   [By Z. Grey.]   *London*, 1751
FRANCIS (*Miss*)   Santa Maura, and other poems.   *London*, 1821
FRANCIS (Alban)   The Cambridge Case, being an exact narrative of
   all the proceedings against the Vice-Chancellour...for refusing to
   admit Alban Francis, a Benedictine monk, to the degree of M.A.
                                            Fº *London*, 1689
Attempt of James II to compel the University to admit Alban Francis
   to M.A. degree.   Proceedings against the Vice-Chancellor and
   University of Cambridge.   1687.   n.d.
Attempt of King James the Second to force a Dissenter upon the
   University of Cambridge, Feb. 1687.   *Oxford*, 1834
FRANCIS (H.T.)   The Vedabbha Jātaka transl. from the Pali, and
   compared with " The Pardoner's Tale."   1884
FRANCKLIN (T.)   The Epistles of Phalaris.   Transl. by T. F.
                                          London, 1749
Authentic narrative of proceedings against the W[estminste]r Club.
   [Probably by T. Francklin.]   *London*, 1751
Translation; a poem.   2nd ed.   4º 1757
FRANKS (J.C.)   Internal evidence of the genuineness and authenticity
   of the Gospels.   (Norrisian Prize Essay, 1817.)   1817
The special study of the theory of public reading and preaching
   recommended.   1857
The morning University Sermon.   1858
FRAUS honesta.   *See* Stubbs (E.).
FREE Library.   Annual Reports, 15, 16, 29, 31, 32, 37, 39, 42, 43,
   46, 47, 50, 51.   1870–1905
Catalogue of books, etc. in the Reference Department.   (Together
   with a catalogue of the Cambridge collection.)   By John Pink.
   Pts I, II, III, IV.   1874–99
After fifty years.   Retrospect of the Free Library.   By J. Pink.   1905
FREE Thoughts upon University education.   By a sincere well-wisher
   to our Universities.   Part I.   *London*, 1751
FREEMAN (A.)   The Portrait Pictures in St John's College,
   Cambridge.   4 parts.   (*Eagle*, XI., XII.)   1881–3
The College Pictures at the Tudor Exhibition.   (*Eagle*, XVI.)   1890
FREEMAN (E.A.)   *See* Farren (R.).   Cathedral Cities, 1883.
FREEMAN (G.E.)   The Transfiguration.   (Seatonian Prize Poem
   for 1882.)   1883

FREEMAN (G.E.)
Jericho. (Seatonian Prize Poem for 1888.)   1889
Damascus. (Seatonian Prize Poem for 1893.)   1894
The Broad and Narrow Way. (Seatonian Prize Poem for 1894.)
                                                              1895
FREEMAN (P.) Church principles as bearing upon certain Statutes
of the University of Cambridge.   1841
Remarks on...*Church Principles*. By W. J. Conybeare.   1841
Theses ecclesiasticae : sive orationes in Curia Cantabrigiensi habitae
A. S. 1844.   1844
Thoughts on the proposed dissolution of the Cambridge Camden
Society.   1845
Proportion in Gothic architecture.   1848
FREEMEN. Copy of Register of Freemen of the Borough of
Cambridge for year ending 1 Nov. 1833.   1832
—— for year ending 31 Oct. 1835.   1834
FRENCH (W.) An address to the Senate.   1823
Observations upon Prof. Sedgwick's Reply to Dr French's address
to the Senate.   1824
See also Sedgwick (A.).
FREND (W.) Considerations on the Oaths required by the University
of Cambridge at the time of taking Degrees.   *London,* 1787
An address to the inhabitants of Cambridge and its neighbourhood.
                                               St Ives, 1788
Second address.   *St Ives,* 1789
Thoughts on subscription to Religious Tests.   *St Ives,* 1788
—— 2nd ed.   *London,* 1789
—— Appendix.   *St Ives,* 1789
An address to the members of the Church of England. *London,* 1788
A second address to the members of the Church of England. 3rd ed.
                                               London, 1789
Address to the congregation of St Mary's...on the subject of the
sermon preached by the Rev. W— F—, M.A. 28 Dec. 1788.
By a Questionist of St John's College.   1789
Mr Coulthurst's blunders exposed.   *London,* 1789
An account of some late proceedings of the S.P.C.K. addressed to
the members thereof.   *n.p.* (1789)
Peace and Union recommended to the associated bodies of Republicans
and Anti-Republicans.   *St Ives,* 1793
—— 2nd ed.   1793
The trial of W. F., Fellow of Jesus College, Cambridge for writing
and publishing *Peace and Union*. By J. Beverley.   (1793)
An account of the proceedings in the University of Cambridge
against W. F. for publishing *Peace and Union*.   1793
The proceedings in the Court of Delegates on the appeal of W. F.
from the sentence of the Vice-Chancellor's Court. By J. Beverley.
                                                             (1793)
Extracts from writings published in the name of Mr Frend. By a
Friend to the Established Church.   *n.p.* (1793)

FREND (W.)
  A sequel to the Account of the Proceedings in the University of
    Cambridge, against the author of *Peace and Union*.   London, 1795
  A letter to the Vice-Chancellor of the University of Cambridge,
    by W. F., candidate for the Lucasian Professorship.   1798
  Principles of taxation.   London, 1799
  Animadversions on *The Elements of Christian Theology*, by the Rev.
    G. Pretyman, Bp of Lincoln.   London, 1800
FRERE (B.) Poematia...A.D. 1798. (Sir W. Browne's Medal.) [1798]
FRERE (J.A.)   Pietas et doctrina.   A sermon delivered in the Chapel
  of Trinity College, Cambridge, Dec. 16, 1845, being the Com-
  memoration of Founders.   1846
FRERE (J.H.)   *See* Microcosm.
FRERE (P.H.)   Suggestions submitted to the meeting to be held to
  consider the draft Statutes of Trinity and St John's Colleges. 1858
FRERE (W.)   Poematia numismatibus annuis dignata et in Curia
  Cantabrigiensi recitata, 1796-7. (Sir W. Browne's Medal.) [1797]
FRESH Hints; or a new Cambridge guide.   London, 1815
FRESHER'S Don't.   By a Sympathiser (B.A.) [i.e. A. J. Story, Joh.].
                                                             (1896)
  More Don'ts for Freshers.   By One of their Number [i.e. H. S.
    Goodhart Rendel, Trin.].   (1905)
FRESHMAN'S Progress.   An Interlude.   By a D.D.   2nd ed.
                                             12° London, 1882
FRESHMEN.   Ten minutes advice to Freshmen.   1785
  Hints to Freshmen.   From a Member of the University of Cambridge
    [P. S. Dodd].   London, 1796
  —— 3rd ed.   London, 1807
  —— 4th ed.   London, 1822
  —— 5th ed.   London, 1855
  A few words to Freshmen.   [By T. Thorp.]   1841
  —— No. 2.   [By T. Thorp.]   1841
  —— Another ed. of the two tracts.   1842
    A few more words to Freshmen.   By the Rev. T. T.   [A skit on
      Thorp's tracts.]   1841
  He cometh up as a Freshman.   By One who was once a Freshman.
                                                             1872
  Address to Freshmen of Oxford and Cambridge Universities.   By a
    Graduate.   2nd ed.   London (1892)
  See also " Shall I be an Evangelical ? "
FRIDAY Club.   Rules.   May 1868.   (1868)
  Rules and list of members.   Jan. 1, 1869.   (1869)
FRIENDLY and honest advice of an old Tory to the Vice-Chancellor
  of Cambridge.   London, 1751
FRIENDS in Pencil : a Cambridge sketch book.   By Herbert Jones.
                                                  Obl. 4° 1893
FROWDE (H.)   *See* Press.
FUGITIVE Poems.   Ed. by C. G. B. Daubeny.
                                   Oxford and London, 1869

FULBOURN.   An account of some antiquities found at Fulbourn in
  Cambridgeshire.   By E. D. Clarke.   (*Archaeologia*, xix.)
                                                4º (*London*, 1821)
Account of Church of Fulbourn St Vigor.   By J. V. Durell.   1910
FULLER (T.)   The history of the University of Cambridge.
                                                Fº *London*, 1655
  The history of the University of Cambridge.   Ed. by M. Prickett
  and Th. Wright.   1840
  The history of the University of Cambridge, and of Waltham Abbey.
  New ed.   By James Nichols.   *London*, 1840
  The history of the Worthies of England.   Ed. by P. A. Nuttall.
  3 vols.   *London*, 1840
  The Holy State and the Profane State.   Ed. by James Nichols.   3 vols.
                                                  London, 1841
  The Church History of Britain.   Ed. by James Nichols.   *London*, 1842
FULLEYLOVE (J.)   Catalogue of a collection of drawings of Oxford.
                                                  London, 1888
  Catalogue of a collection of drawings of Cambridge and the Riviera.
  With a note by J. W. Clark.   *London*, 1890
FURNISS (H.)   *See* Pictures at Play.
FURTHER Inquiry into the Right of Appeal from the Chancellor...
  in matters of Discipline.   [By T. Chapman.]   *London*, 1752
FUZWHISKIANA.   Dedicated to the shaven, shorn, and whiskerless.
                                                            1838
  See also Rape of the Whisker, 1838.

G

GADFLY. No. 1. Nov. 15, 1888. (Bowes 2851.) 4° 1888
GALEN. *See* Bowes (R.).
GALLY (H.) The reasonableness of Church and College Fines asserted.
London, 1731
GALTON (F.) Vacation tourists and notes of travel in 1860. Ed.
by F. Galton. 1861
GALVANIST. A periodical paper by Hydra Polycephalus, Esq.
Nos. 1–11. [Ed. by W. D. Whittington, and others.] [1804]
GAMLINGAY. History of Gamlingay, by E. J. Fowler.
Gamlingay, 1905
GANDOLPHY (P.) A congratulatory letter to the Rev. H. Marsh,
on his judicious inquiry into the consequences of neglecting to give
the Prayer Book with the Bible. *London*, 1812
GARDEN (F.) An inquiry into the advantages which have accrued
to Christianity in consequence of its narrative form. (Hulsean
Prize for 1832.) 1833
GARDINER (R.B.) The Registers of Wadham College, Oxford,
1613–1719. Ed. by R. B. G. *London*, 1889
The Letters of Dorothy Wadham, 1609-1618. Ed. by R. B. G.
London, 1904
GARDINER (W.) An account of the foundation and re-establishment
of the Botanical Museum of the University of Cambridge. 4° 1904
GARDNER (E.A.) Application for Disney Professorship. 4° 1892
A catalogue of the Greek vases in the Fitzwilliam Museum. 1897
GARNETT (J.) Sermon…14 July 1741. 4° 1741
Sermon…at Gt St Mary's Church at the Commemoration of Bene-
factors, 27 Oct. 1745. 4° 1745
GARNETT (W.) and Campbell (L.) Life of James Clerk Maxwell.
London, 1882
GARNHAM (R.E.) Sermon in the Chapel of Trin. Coll. Camb. at
the Commemoration of Benefactors, 19 Dec. 1793. (1793)
—— (2nd ed.) 1794
GARRATT (W.A.) An essay delivered in the Chapel of Trinity
College, Cambridge, on the day appointed for the Commemoration
of Benefactors, 1801. 4° *London* (1801)
GARRICK Club. Play Bills, 1833–1842. 1833–1842
The Album of the Cambridge Garrick Club. 12° 1839
Article on the Club. (*Sat. Rev.*, 6 May, 1893.)
GAS. Contract for lighting the town with gas. 1841
—— Another Contract. 1854

GAS.
   Report of Appeals of the Cambridge Gaslight Company *v.* the
      Guardians of the Poor.   *London,* 1857
   Correspondence of the Gas mediation.   *n.p.* 1868
   See also Phelps (R.).
GASELEE (S.)   List of fifteenth-century printed books bequeathed to
   the Fitzwilliam Museum by F. McClean.   (1905)
GASKARTH (J.)   Commencement Sermon, 30 June, morning.
                                                        4° 1700
GASKELL (W.H.)   Obituary notice of Sir Michael Foster.   (*Proc.*
   Roy. Soc.)   *London,* 1908
GEDDES (A.)   *See* Hopkins (H. W.).
GENERAL Medical Council.   Poll for the election of a representative
   of the University of Cambridge, 7 Nov. 1889.   (Dr Donald
   MacAlister elected.)   1889
GENERAL Theorem for a ******* [Trinity] Coll. Declamation.
   By —— With copious notes by Gronovius.   [By C. V. Le Grice.]
                                                          1796
GENT (M.)   Oratio Latina altera præmio annuo dignata.   (Members'
   Prize.)   1855
GENTLEMAN'S Magazine Library.   Ed. by G. L. Gomme.   English
   topography.   Cambridgeshire.   *London,* 1892
GEOLOGICAL Museum.   *See* Sedgwick Museum ; Woodwardian
   Museum.
GEORGE III., *King of England.*   Vice-Chancellor's notice of [funeral]
   sermon at Gt St Mary's, etc. 14 Feb. 1820.   F° 1820
   Words of funeral anthem in Gt St Mary's Church, 16 Feb. 1820.
   Funeral sermon, by W. Mandell.   1820
GEORGE IV., *King of England.*   Vice-Chancellor's notice of sermon,
   etc. on day of his funeral, 13 July, 1830.   F° 1830
   A sermon preached...15 July 1830, the day of the funeral of King
   George IV.   By W. Chafy.   4° 1830
GEORGE (W.)   Oratio habita in funere Guil. George, Coll. Regal.
   Præpositi, vii° Kal. Oct. 1756 a G. Barford.   4° 1756
GIBBONS (A.)   Ely Episcopal records.   Ed. by A. Gibbons.
                                                   London, 1891
GIBBONS (T.)   An account of a most terrible fire that happened on
   8 Sept. 1727, at Burwell.   *London,* 1769
GIBSON (A.C.)   Joe and the Geologist.   *Carlisle,* 1866
GIBSON (J.)   His manuscript, printed and illustrated by G. C. M.
   Smith.   (*Eagle,* June, 1892.)   1892
GIBSON (M.D.)   Do you confess ?   *n.p.* [1901]
GIBSON (W.)   Conscience: a poetical essay.   (Seatonian Prize Poem
   for 1772.)   4° 1772
   Jerusalem destroyed.   (Seatonian Prize Poem for 1781.)   4° 1781
GILES'S (St) Parish.   A narrative of the proceedings on the St Giles's
   Inclosure Bill.   *London,* 1802
GILL (A.)   An answer to a late pamphlet, entitled, *The Experiment*
   [by Defoe].   4° *London,* 1707

GILLESPIE (C.G.K.)   Testimonials : candidate for vicarage of
    Ilketshall St Margaret.   *n.p.* 1893
GILLMOR (W.)   The Pue system.   *Halifax*, 1843
GILLY (W.S.)   Academic Errors; or Recollections of Youth.
                                                        London, 1817
GIRDLESTONE (W.H.)   The Poll course considered from another
    point of view.   *London*, 1862
GIRLS' Friendly Society.   5th, 6th, 15th, 17th Annual Report.
                                                           1886–98
    Ely Diocesan G.F.S. Lodge.   First—Seventh Annual Report.
                                                           1902–9
GIRTON College.   Proposed new College for women. (*Lit. Churchman*).
                                                      (*London*) 1868
    Some account of proposed new College for women. By Emily Davies.
                                                        London, 1868
    Prospectus, etc. 1870; February, 1872; July, 1872.   *n.p.* 1870–2
    Entrance Examination.   *n.p.* 1872
    Reports.   August 1873; July 1875; for year ending 30 June, 1897;
    1901.   1873–1901
    Examinations for Certificates, 1873.   1873
    Life at Girton College.   By a Girton Student.   *London*, 1882
    The Electra of Sophocles literally translated for performance at
    Girton, Nov. 22–24, with programme.   1883
    Girton and Newnham Colleges.   By E. A. Brayley Hodgetts.
    (*Strand Magazine*, Nov. 1894.)
GISBORNE (T.)   The substance of the speech of T. G., April 8,
    1812...at a meeting convened for the purpose of forming a
    Staffordshire Auxiliary Bible Society.   *London*, 1812
GISBURNE (J.)   Bigotry and intolerance defeated; or an account of
    the late persecution of Mr J. G., Unitarian Minister of Soham,
    Cambs.   By R. Aspland.   *Harlow*, 1810
GLAISHER (J.W.L.)   Biographical notice of the late J. Challis.
    (*Monthly Notices R. Astron. Soc.*, 43.)   *London*, 1883
    The Mathematical Tripos.   Presidential address before Lond. Math.
    Soc., Nov. 11, 1886.   *London*, 1886
    Address delivered before the Royal Astronomical Society, Feb. 11,
    1887.   *London*, 1887
    Life of J. C. Adams. (From his *Collected Scientific Papers*.) 4° 1897
GLAZEBROOK (R.T.)   Application for Cavendish Professorship
    of Experimental Physics.   1884
    Application for Professorship of Mechanism and Applied Mechanics
    in Univ. of Cambridge.   1890
GLEE and Madrigal Concerts.   *See* Festival Choir.
GLEES.   Collection of Glees and Rounds...composed by the Members
    of the Harmonic Society of Cambridge.—Eighth Book of Glees.
    —Second Collection of Glees.   Obl. [c. 1796]
GLOUCESTER (Mary, *Duchess of*) Reception of the Duchess of
    Gloucester and Princess Sophia, July, 1819. Grace, Plan of enter-
    tainment, etc.   1819

GLOUCESTER (William Frederick, *Duke of*) Poll at election of
    Chancellor, 26 March, 1811.   1811
Selection of sacred music to be performed at Gt St Mary's Church,
    June 28, 1811.   1811
Installation Ode...June 29, 1811.   1811
Miscellaneous Concerts (1–4) June, July, 1811.   (1811)
Words of music performed at visit of...the Chancellor, July 1819.
Sermon on the death of the Duke of Gloucester. By T. Turton.
                                                       4° *n.p.* 1834
GLOVER (W.) The Memoirs of a Cambridge Chorister. 2 vols.
                                                     London, 1885
GLUCK (C.W. von) Orpheus and Eurydice. As performed at the
    Theatre Royal, Cambridge, May 13–17, 1890.   1890
—— Announcements, programmes, cuttings, photographs, etc. 1890
GLYNN (R.) The Day of Judgment. 3rd ed. (Seatonian Prize
    Poem for 1757.)   4° 1758
—— Another ed.   1800
Narrative...concerning the late frenzy of the Rev. R. Watson.
                                             4° *London,* 1781
GODDARD (P.S.) A sermon preached at the consecration of Clare
    Hall Chapel, in Cambridge, July 5, 1769.   4° 1769
GODMAN (W.) Filius Heröum, the Son of Nobles, set forth in a
    sermon preached at St Mary's in Cambridge, 24 May, 1660.
                                             4° *London,* 1660
GODMANCHESTER. The history of Godmanchester. By Robert
    Fox.   *London,* 1831
GOETHE (J.W. von) Herman and Dorothea. Translated (by W.
    Whewell).   Obl. 8° [1839]
GOFFLOT (L.V.) Le Théatre au Collège.   *Paris,* 1907
GOLBORNE (J.) *See* Elstobb (W.).
GOLDIE (J.H.D.) and Treherne (G.G.T.) Record of the University
    Boat Race, 1829–1880.   4° *London,* 1883
GOLDSCHMIDT (E.Ph.) Seventy-five books from a library formed
    by E. Ph. G.   4° 1909
GOMME (G.L.) *See* Gentleman's Magazine Library.
GONVILLE and Caius College. Excerpta e statutis Collegii de
    Gonville et Caius.   1724
Annals. By Francis Blomefield. (Ives's *Select Papers.*) (Bowes 1275.)
                                             4° *London,* 1773
Thoughts suggested by the new Caius gown.   1837
 Answer to *Thoughts suggested by the new Caius gown.*   1837
Excerpta e statutis Collegii de Gonville et Caius.   1843
Trifolium Caianum in adventum Reginae et Principis viii. Kal. Nov.
    1843. (C. G. Prowett, G. B. Trevelyan, A. G. Day.) 4° (1843)
Report respecting the Library.   1847
Odes (500th Anniversary, 28 Jan. 1848). By C. D. Marston and
    J. Hamblin Smith.   F° 1848
A catalogue of the manuscripts in the Library of Gonville and Caius
    College. By J. J. Smith.   1849

GONVILLE and Caius College.

A list of the early printed books (and an index of English books printed before 1600) in the Library of Gonville and Caius College. By W. R. Collett. 1850

List of books added to the Library in 1850. [1851 ?]

Pictorial illustrations of the Catalogue of manuscripts in Gonville and Caius College Library. By J. J. Smith. 4° 1853

Statement of proceedings taken with reference to the election of Master...in 1852. 1854

Office for the Commemoration of Founders and Benefactors. 4° 1856

Admissions to Gonville and Caius College...March 1558–9 to Jan. 1678–9. Ed. by J. Venn. *London,* 1887

The Caian. No. 1. Easter Term, 1891. 1891

Precamini Felicitatem. Grace Anthem. By C. Wood.
London, 1892

Carmen Caianum. By B. H. Drury and C. Wood. 4° 1894

Biographical History. By J. Venn. 3 vols. 1897–1901

Account of proceedings at 550th anniversary of foundation. 1898

Caius College. By John Venn. (College histories.) *London,* 1901

Descriptive catalogue of the manuscripts. By M. R. James. 2 vols.
1907–8

GOOCH (W.) General view of the agriculture of the County of Cambridge. 1811

GOODALL (H.) The duties attending a proper discharge of the ministry. A Sermon...28 April, 1748. 4° 1748

GOODHART (H.C.) Testimonials, May, 1891, when a candidate for the Chair of Humanity at Edinburgh. 2 series. 1891

GOODLIFFE (W.) Testimonials when a candidate for the rectory of Ovington. 1883

GOODMAN (N.) Address to Congregational Union. 1869

Clerical Fellowships. *London,* 1875

GOODWIN (C.W.) Index to the Baker MSS. [By C. W. G. and others.] 1848

GOODWIN (H.) Considerations respecting the Exercises in the Schools...for the Degree of B.A. 1845

A defence of certain portions of *An elementary course of Mathematics.*
1850

Plain thoughts concerning the meaning of Holy Baptism. A sermon.
1850

Reasonable service. A sermon preached Oct. 31, 1852, being the day appointed for the Commemoration of Benefactors. 1852

Education for Working Men. An address delivered in the Town-Hall, 29 Oct. 1855. 1855

Guide to the Parish Church. 12° 1855

The Glory of the Only Begotten of the Father. (Hulsean Lectures, 1856.) 1856

Peacock Memorial. (Circular.) 1860

Memoir of Robert Leslie Ellis. (From *Mathematical and other writings of R. L. Ellis,* ed. by W. Walton.) 1863

GOODWIN (H.)
Review of his Memoir of R. L. Ellis.   By J. P. N[orris].   1864
Ely Cathedral.   (Circular.)   (*Ely*) 1863
Memoir of Bishop Mackenzie.   1864
Miss Green.   A tragedy in one act (and that a rather foolish one).
                                                   1865
On restorations in the Cathedral at Ely.   (Circular.)   (*Ely*) 1866
Adam Sedgwick.   (*Macmillan's Mag.*, April, 1880.)
Memoir of his life, by himself.   1880
Mrs Stair Douglas's Life of William Whewell.   (Review.)   (*Macmillan's Mag.*, Dec. 1881.)
Trifles for my grandchildren.   1885
The late Master of Trinity (W. H. Thompson).   (*Macmillan's Mag.*, March, 1887.)
Ely gossip.   *Ely*, 1892
See also Harvey Goodwin Home for Boys.
GORDON (J.)   Address to the Members of the Senate...on the attention due to worth of character from a Religious Society.   1764
Sermon...2 July, 1767.   4° 1767
GORHAM (G.C.)   Proceedings of the Public Meeting, 18 Nov. 1813, being the second anniversary of the Cambridge Auxiliary Bible Society.   Ed. by G. C. Gorham.   1813
Memoirs of John Martyn and of Thomas Martyn, Professors of Botany in the University of Cambridge.   *London*, 1830
GOUDY (A.P.)   *See* Russian Lectureship.
GOUGH (R.)   Anecdotes of British Topography.   4° *London*, 1768
British Topography.   2 vols.   4° *London*, 1780
The history of Crowland Abbey, digested [by B. Holdich] from materials collected by Mr Gough, etc.   *Stamford*, 1816

Catalogue of books bequeathed to the Bodleian in 1799.   4° *Oxford*, 1814

GOULD (I.)   The circular letter of the Eastern Association held at Cambridge, May 13 and 14, 1777.   (To the Protestant Dissenting Churches usually denominated Baptists.)   (1777)
GOULD (S. Baring)   *See* Baring Gould (S.).
GOVERNMENT scheme of Education in Univ. of Camb.
                                        London, 1850
GOWER (S.)   A slight reminiscence of Cambridge.   (*Hood's Magazine*, Oct. 1846.)
GOWNSMAN.   Vol. II. Nos. 2–17.   1829–30.   (Bowes 1761.)   1830
—— Another periodical.   Vol. I.   (21 Oct. 1909–15 June, 1910.)   (Ed. by R. B. Johnson.)   F° 1910
GRACE Book A...1454–1488.   Ed. by S. M. Leathes.   (Luard Memorial ser., I.)   1897
—— B...1488–1544.   2 vols.   Ed. by M. Bateson.   (Luard Memorial ser., II, III.)   1903–5
—— Γ...1501–1542.   Ed. by W. G. Searle and J. W. Clark.   1908
—— — Proof of J. W. Clark's part of Introduction.   1908
GRACE Papers, from 1841.

GRADUATI Cantabrigienses. 1659–1823. (Ed. W. Hustler.)
                                                          1823
—— 1760–1856. (Ed. J. Romilly.)   1856
—— 1800–1872. (Ed. H. R. Luard.)   1873
—— 1800–1884. (Ed. H. R. Luard.)   1884
See also Matriculations and Degrees, 1902.
GRADUS ad Cantabrigiam.   *London,* 1803
GRADUS ad Cantabrigiam. By a Brace of Cantabs. *London,* 1824
GRAFTON (Augustus Henry Fitzroy, *Duke of*) Installation Ode.
    By Tho. Gray. The music by Dr Randal.   1769
GRAHAM (J.) A sermon preached at Gt St Mary's Church Jan. 21,
    1827, being the day after the funeral of the Duke of York. 1827
Sermon preached at Gt St Mary's Church, 5 Nov. 1831.   1831
Discourse delivered at Gt St Mary's Church, 13 Jan. 1837. 1837
Sermon preached in Gt St Mary's Church, 16 March, 1841, being
    the day on which the foundation stone was laid of the Victoria
    Benefit Societies' Asylum.   1841
A sermon preached at the re-opening of the Church of the Holy
    Sepulchre, Cambridge, Aug. 10, 1845.   1845
GRANT (A.R.) A sermon preached in Trinity College Chapel at
    the annual Commemoration of Benefactors, Dec. 14, 1850. 1851
The Next Step. [On University studies.]   1849
GRANT (C.) A poem on the restoration of learning in the East
    which obtained Mr Buchanan's Prize.   4° 1805
GRANT (R.) The Little Tin Gods-on-Wheels ; or, Society in our
    modern Athens. 9th ed.   *Cambridge, Mass.,* 1881
GRANTA ; or a page from the life of a Cantab. [Attributed to D. G.
    Osborne, Magd.]   1836
Reply to Granta. By a Member of the University.   1838
Granta : a fragment, by a Freshman. Ed. by the Rev. J. Snodgrass.
    2nd ed.   *London,* 1841
Granta (Second Series), pointing out a few of the chief merits of that
    delightful little work.   1841
GRANTA (The) Vols. 1–13. 18 Jan. 1889–9 June, 1900.
                                              4° 1889–1900
—— 500th number, 12 June, 1909.   4° 1909
GRANTCHESTER. History of Grantchester, by S. P. Widnall.
                                         Grantchester, 1875
GRAY (A.) A College Chronicle, 1557–1643. (*Chanticlere.*) (1893)
The Chapter-House and some interior views thereof. (*Chanticlere.*)
                                                        (1893)
Jesus College. (College histories.)   *London,* 1902
The dual origin of the town of Cambridge. (*Camb. Chron.*) 1907
GRAY (A.B.) A note upon early Cambridge binders of the sixteenth
    century.   1901
GRAY (G.J.) Bibliography of the works of Sir Isaac Newton. 1888
—— 2nd ed.   4° 1907
A bibliography of the writings of Christopher Smart, with biographical
    references.   4° *London,* 1903

GRAY (G.J.)

The earlier Cambridge Stationers and Bookbinders, and the first Cambridge Printer. (Bibliogr. Soc. monograph.) 4° *Oxford*, 1904

Gray (G.J.) and Bowes (R.)   John Siberch.   4° 1906

GRAY (J.H.) Queens' College. (College histories.)   *London*, 1899

GRAY (T.) Ode...for Installation of the Duke of Grafton, 1 July, 1769. The music by Dr Randal.   4° 1769

Poems. New ed.   *London*, 1770

Ode Pindarica pro Cambriæ vatibus Latino carmine reddita. (Signed E. B. G[reene].)   4° 1775

Elegy written in a country churchyard. (Transl. into Latin by H. A. J. Munro.)   4° 1875

The Elegy reproduced in facsimile from the original MS. at Pembroke College.   F° 1897

GREEK. On the Report (Parts II. and VII.) of the Syndicate on the Previous and General Examinations (for making Greek *or* Latin optional). By H. Latham.   1872

On a proposed amendment of the scheme for Pass Examinations. By H. Latham.   1873

Greek as an optional subject. By R. Potts. (*Indep. Press*, 1 Feb. 1873.)   1873

Report of the Syndicate appointed...to consider the memorial...on the subject of passing an examination in Greek. (*Reporter*, April 9, 1880.)

Grecia victrix. A lay of modern Greece. By Arculus [E. W. Bowling].   1891

List of Members of the Senate who voted, 3, 4 March, 1905. (Greek question.)   1905

See also Breul (K.).

GREEK Plays performed at Cambridge.

Ajax. Text, and translation by R. C. Jebb.   1882

—— Scrap Book with photographs and reviews.

Birds. Text, and translation by B. H. Kennedy.   1883

—— Translation by J. H. Frere.   1883

—— *Scrap Book.

Electra, literally translated for performance at Girton, with programme.   1883

Eumenides. Text, and translation by A. W. Verrall.   1885

—— *Scrap Book.

Oedipus Tyrannus. Text, and translation by R. C. Jebb.   1887

—— Scrap Book.

Ion. Text, and translation by M. A. Bayfield.   1890

—— Scrap Book.

Iphigenia in Tauris. Text, and translation by A. W. Verrall.   1894

—— *Scrap Book.

Wasps. Text, and translation by B. B. Rogers.   1897

—— *Scrap Book.

Agamemnon. Text, and translation by A. Swanwick.   1900

—— 'Granta' Souvenir.   1900

GREEK Plays performed at Cambridge.
 Agamemnon.   *Scrap Book.
 Birds.   Text, and Translation by B. H. Kennedy.   1903
 —— Music by C. H. H. Parry, with English version of the songs by
   A. W. Verrall.   1903
 —— *Scrap Book.
 Eumenides.   Text, and translation by A. W. Verrall.   1906
 —— *Scrap Book.
 Wasps.   Text, and translation by B. B. Rogers.   1909
 —— Scrap Book.

   The Scrap Books marked with an asterisk are the property of the Greek
 Play Committee.   By their permission these books are for the present deposited
 in the University Library with Mr Clark's Cambridge Collection.

   See also Clark (J. W.), 1882, 1898 ; Farren (R.) ; Jebb (*Sir* R. C.),
     1884 ; Pastor of Dulichium ; Speed (L.).
   For Greek Plays performed at Oxford and Radley *see* Aristophanes ;
     Carr (P.).
 GREEK Types : being a proposal for altering the character in which
     Greek is usually written and printed.   1838
 GREEN (A.H.)   Letter of application and testimonials for the Wood-
     wardian Professorship.   1873
 GREEN (J.)   Commencement Sermon...2 July, 1749.   4° 1749
   The Academic.   (Attr. to J. Green.)   (Bowes 1193.)   *London,* 1750
   Considerations on the...late Regulations.   (Attr. to J. Green.)   (Bowes
     1198.)   *London,* 1751
   The principles and practices of the Methodists farther considered.
     (Signed: Academicus, and attr. to J. Green.)   1761
 GREEN (W.)   The Song of Deborah reduced to metre.   4° 1753
 GREEN (W.C.)   Women's Degrees: a Report in Greek and English.
                                                           1897
   Memories of Eton and King's.   *Eton,* 1905
 GREENE (E.B.)   *See* Gray (T.)
 GREENWOOD (W.)   A poem written during a shooting excursion
     on the moors.   4° *Bath,* 1787
 GRENVILLE (*Lord*)   Oxford and Locke.   2nd ed.   *London,* 1829
 GRESWELL (R.)   On education in the principles of art.   *Oxford,* 1844
 GRETTON (F.E.)   Memory's harkback through half a century,
     1808 to 1858.   *London,* 1889
 GRETTON (P.)   Two Discourses.   1732
 GREY (Z.)   Vindication of the University of Cambridge.
                                                 London, 1722
   Fragmentum est pars rei fractae.   *London,* 1751
   See Masters (R.)   Memoirs of...T. Baker, 1784.
 GRIFFIN (Gregory)   *See* Microcosm.
 GRIFFITHS (E.H.)   Lyra Fumosa.   (1900)
 GRIFFITHS (John)   Enactments in Parliament specially concerning
     the Universities of Oxford and Cambridge.   *Oxford,* 1869

GRIFFITHS (Jos.) Testimonials : candidate for post of assistant
surgeon at Addenbrooke's Hospital. (1891)
—— 1 Oct. 1894. 1894
GRILDRIG (Solomon) *See* Miniature.
GRIMSHAW (W.) Trial of W. Grimshaw and R. Kidman...and
H. Cohen. 1801
GRINFIELD (T.) Epistles and miscellaneous poems.
12º *London*, 1815
GRONOVIUS, *pseud.* *See* Le Grice (C. V.).
GROSE (F.) Cambridgeshire. (From *Antiq. of Engl. and Wales.*)
4º *London*, 1783
GROTE (J.) The Commemoration sermon preached in Trinity
College Chapel, Cambridge, Dec. 15, 1848. 1849
A few remarks on a pamphlet by Mr Shilleto, entitled *Thucydides or
Grote ?* 1851
Remarks on Mr Grote's proposal " That in all cases where it is
provided by the Statutes, with reference to the elections of the
Master and Seniors..." (Trinity College.) 1857
A few words on Statute XVIII of the new body of Statutes (for
Trinity College). (1859)
Draft scheme of examination in Moral Sciences. 1860
Remarks on the proposals made by the Syndicate...appointed in
reference to the Moral Sciences Tripos. 1860
A few words on criticism : being an examination of the article in
the Saturday Rev., Ap. 20, 1861, upon Dr Whewell's *Platonic
Dialogues for English readers.* 1861
Essays and Reviews. An examination of some portion of Dr
Lushington's judgment...in the case of the Bishop of Salisbury *v.*
Williams. 1862
A few words on the new Educational Code and the Report of the
Education Commissioners. 1862
Plato's Theætetus and Mr Grote's criticisms. By E. M. Cope. 1866
GROTIUS (H.) Synopsis compendiaria librorum Hugonis Grotii de
jure belli et pacis ; Samuelis Clarkii de Dei existentia et attributis ;
et Joannis Lockii de intellectu humano. 1751
GRYLLS (A.C.) Random Ramblings. 12º 1888
GUEST (E.) On the etymology of the word Stonehenge. (*Proc.
Philological Soc.*, vol. VI., no. 130.) (*London*, 1854)
An essay on the four Roman Ways. (*Arch. Journ.*, vol. XIV.)
(*London*, 1857)
On the northern termination of Offa's Dyke. (Repr. from *Archaeologia
Cambrensis*, 3rd ser. vol. IV.) (*London*, 1858)
On the boundaries that separated the English and Welsh races during
the 75 years which followed the capture of Bath, A.D. 577. (*Arch.
Journ.*, XVI.) (*London*, 1859)
On Welsh boundaries. (Repr. from *Archaeologia Cambrensis*, 3rd ser.
vol. VII.) (*London*, 1861)
The English conquest of the Severn Valley. (Repr. from *Arch.
Journ.*, XIX.) (*London*, 1862)

GUEST (E.)
 On the fall of Uriconium. (Repr. from *Archaeologia Cambrensis*,
  3rd ser. vol. 10.)   (*London*, 1864)
 University Tests.   1871
GUIDE.   The Foreigner's Companion through the Universities of
  Cambridge and Oxford. By Mr Salmon.   12° *London*, 1748
 Cantabrigia Depicta.   1763
 —— Another ed.   1776
 A concise and accurate description of the University, Town, and
  County of Cambridge. New ed.   [1785]
 A description of the University, Town, and County of Cambridge.
                                                      1796
 —— Another ed., defective.   (1799)
 A guide through the University of Cambridge. New ed.   (1804)
 The New Cambridge Guide ; or, a description of the University,
  Town, and County of Cambridge.   1804
 A guide through the University of Cambridge. New ed.   (1807)
 The New Cambridge Guide.   1809
 A guide through the University of Cambridge. New ed.   1811
 The New Cambridge Guide.   2nd ed., defective.   1812
 A guide through the University of Cambridge. New ed.   1814
 A guide through the University of Cambridge. New ed.   1820
 The New Cambridge Guide.   5th ed.   1821
 The Stranger's Companion and guide through the University and
  Town of Cambridge.   2nd ed.   1825
 The Cambridge Guide.   New ed.   (2 states.)   (1830)
 Ambulator: or, the Stranger's Guide through Cambridge.   1835
 The Cambridge Guide.   New ed.   1845
 The tourist's souvenir of Cambridge. [Views.]   *London* [1851 ?]
 A hand-book for visitors to Cambridge. By Norris Deck.   1861
 —— Another ed.   1862
 Cambridge: its University and Colleges. By G. M. Humphry.
                                          London, 1864
 The New Cambridge Guide.   2nd ed. [By N. Deck.]   1868
 The Railway Traveller's Walk through Cambridge.   5th ed.   1873
 Guide to Cambridge.   By G. M. Humphry.   (1880)
 —— Another ed.   (1883)
 —— Another ed.   (1886)
 The Railway Traveller's Walk through Cambridge.   7th ed.
                                                [*Ab.* 1886]
 The illustrated guide to Cambridge and neighbourhood. By a
  Resident Trinity M.A.   (Jarrold's.)   *London* [*Ab.* 1888]
 The People's guide to Cambridge.   (Spalding's.)   [1888]
 The Railway Traveller's Walk through Cambridge. 8th ed. = The
  Cambridge Visitor's Guide.   By W. White.   [1893]
 —— 9th ed.   [*Ab.* 1897]
 Cambridge Guide and View book.   12° *n.p.* [1909]
 See also Clark (J. W.) Concise Guide, 1898, etc. ; Harraden (R.);
  Harraden (R. B.).

GUNNING (H.)   Reminiscences of Cambridge.   2 vols.   *London*, 1854
  Reminiscences of Cambridge.   2nd ed.   2 vols.   *London*, 1855
  See Corporation, 1839 ; Wall (A.) Ceremonies, 1828.
GWATKIN (H.M.) and Watson (F.)   The Theological Tripos
  scheme in its relation to scholarship.   1871
GWYER (M.L.)   The Westminster Play.   (From W. G. Elliot's
  Amateur Clubs and Actors.)   (*London*, 1898)

H

HADDENHAM. *See* Acts and Bills, 1727.
HADDON (A.C.) The Aran Islands, Co. Galway. (*Irish Naturalist.*)
Dublin, 1893
HADLEY (J.) Plan of a course of Chemical lectures. 1758
HAGGITT (J.) Architectural notices in reference to the Cathedral
Church of Ely. [*Ab.* 1800]
Two letters to a Fellow of the Society of Antiquaries...containing a
refutation of Dr Milner's objections to Mr Whittington's survey
of the ecclesiastical edifices of France. 1813
HAILSTONE (E.) History of Swaffham Bulbeck. [Proofs of a work
never completed.] (*C.A.S.*) 1884
HALF Blue. May Term, 1896. 1896
HALL (F.R.) A letter to the Heads of Houses, and the Senior Fellows
in the University of Cambridge, on the defective state of theological
instruction in the University. 1833
HALL (H.) Heaven ravished. 4° *London,* 1644
HALL (H.T.) Yᵉ latest edition of yᵉ Rye House Plot. 1867
Cambridge Dramatic Album. 1868
HALL (R.) Modern infidelity considered...in a sermon preached at
the Baptist Meeting, Cambridge. 7th ed. *London,* 1811
A sermon occasioned by the death of H.R.H. the Princess Charlotte
of Wales. 12th ed. *Leicester,* 1822
HALLAM (A.H.) Essay on the philosophical writings of Cicero. 1832
Remains in verse and prose. *London,* 1863

Personal Recollections, by W. E. Gladstone. (*Daily Telegraph,* 5 Jan. 1898.)
See also Shelley (P. B.).

HALLAM (H.F.) Memoir. By H. S. M[aine] and F. L[ushington.]
(Privately pr.) *London* [1851]
HALLIFAX (S.) St Paul's doctrine of justification by faith. Dis-
courses preached before University, 1760. 1760
—— 2nd ed. 1762
Two sermons before the University. 4° 1768
Sermon...28 June, 1770. 4° 1771
Three sermons preached before the University. 2nd ed. 4° 1772
—— 3rd ed. 1772
See also Ogden (S.).
HALLIWELL-PHILLIPPS (J.O.) Brief account of...Sir Samuel
Morland. 1838
The manuscript rarities of the University of Cambridge. *London,* 1841

HALLIWELL-PHILLIPPS (J.O.)
The Jokes of the Cambridge Coffee-Houses in the seventeenth
   century.   1841
—— Another ed.   1842
See also D'Ewes (*Sir* S.) Autobiography and correspondence, 1845.
See also Sherman (J.) Historia Collegii Jesu, 1840.
HALSTED (C.A.) Life of Margaret Beaufort, Countess of Richmond
   and Derby.   *London*, 1839
HAMILTON (J.) Verse Extracts. Extracted from *Thoughts on Truth
   and Error*.   1856
HAMILTON (N.E.S.A.) Inquisitio comitatus Cantabrigiensis. Cura
   N. E. S. A. Hamilton.   4° *Londini*, 1876
HAMILTON (S.G.) Hertford College, Oxford. (College histories.)
                                          London, 1903
HAMLET; or, Not such a Fool as he looks. By the author of, and
   with extracts from, The Light Green. [By A. C. Hilton.] 1882
HAMMOND (A. de L.) The Battle of Lake Mort.   1875
HAMMOND (B.E.) Greek constitutions.   1891
HAMMOND (H.) Last Words. *See* Smith (T.).
HAMMOND (J.L.) Outline of a letter in answer to the draft of
   proposed Statutes, etc. (Trinity.)   1858
On the Sizarships, etc. at Trinity, Dec. 1866.   (1866)
On proposed combination of offices of Steward and Junior Bursar in
   Trinity College.   (1869)
HANDBOOK of ten miles round Cambridge, with Map.   12° 1852
HANDEL (G.F.) Saul. (King's College Chapel, June 11, 1888.) 1888
Acis and Galatea. (Guildhall, May 2, 1889.)   1889
Israel in Egypt. (King's College Chapel, June 12, 1889.)   1889
Messiah. (King's College Chapel, June 13, 1894.)   1894
Israel in Egypt. (King's College Chapel, June 8, 1899.)   1899
HANDSWORTH. Poll for election of a Clerk to be presented to
   the living, Nov. 16, 1870. (J. Mowat elected.)   1870
HANKINSON (T.E.) Venice. Written for the Chancellor's Medal,
   1826.   1826
The Druids. A poem. Written for the Chancellor's Medal, 1827
David playing the harp before Saul. (Seatonian Prize Poem for 1831.)
                                        1831
St Paul at Philippi. (Seatonian Prize Poem for 1833.)   1833
Jacob. (Seatonian Prize Poem for 1834.)   1834
Ethiopia stretching out her hands unto God. (Seatonian Prize Poem
   for 1838.)   1838
The Call of Abraham. (Seatonian Prize Poem for 1841.)   1841
The Cross planted upon the Himalaya mountains. (Seatonian Prize
   Poem for 1842.)   1842
Poems. Edited by his brothers. 2nd ed.   12° *London*, 1847

Life. (Printed for private circulation.)   2 vols.   *Norwich*, 1861

HAPPINESS. An Epistle to a Friend.   4° 1763
HARCOURT (E.W.) *See* Ball (T.) Life of Dr Preston, 1885.

HARDWICK (C.)   An historical inquiry touching Saint Catharine of Alexandria. (*C.A.S.*)   4° 1849

Reasons why the University should not surrender its jurisdiction over Gt St Mary's pulpit.   1857

Robert Woodlark, Founder...of St Catharine's Hall. (*C.A.S.*)   1858

HARDWICKE (Charles Philip Yorke, *4th Earl of*)   Life, by Lady Biddulph.   *London*, 1910

HARDY (E.G.)   Jesus College, Oxford.   (College histories.)
                                          London, 1899

HARDY (J.F.)   Things we have eaten. (*Fraser's Mag.*, June, 1874.)

HARE (F.)   Sermon preached at St Mary's, 6 Jan. 1709. *London*, 1709

The Clergyman's Thanks to Phileleutherus [Bentley].   *London*, 1713

Epistola critica...[Bentley's Phaedrus].   *London*, 1726

HARE (J.C.)   The Children of Light.   Sermon preached before the University, Advent Sunday, 1828.   1828

A vindication of Niebuhr's History of Rome from the charges of the Quarterly Review.   1829

On tendencies towards the subversion of Faith. (Reviewing and attacking Hare. *English Review*, Dec. 1848.)

" Thou shalt not bear false witness against thy neighbour."   Letter to the Editor of the English Review.   *London*, 1849

Fragments of two essays in English philology. (Ed. by J. E. B. Mayor.)
                                          London, 1873

The Victory of Faith. 3rd ed., by E. H. Plumptre.   *London*, 1874

HARMER (J.R.)   The paradox of the Gospel.   A sermon preached in King's College Chapel, Founder's Day, 1888.   1888

HARMER (S.F.)   President's address before the Museums Association at Norwich, 1904. (*Museums Journ.*)   *n.p.* 1904

HARMONIA Musarum, containing Nugae Cantabrigienses...Edited by Alumnus Cantabrigiensis (T.F. [T. Forster]). [? *Bruges*] 1843

HARMONIC Society. *See* Glees.

HARPER (F.W.)   On some of the changes proposed in the course of study pursued within the University.   1848

HARRADEN (R.)   Picturesque views of Cambridge. (Bowes 841.)
                                       Obl. F° 1798–1800

Descriptive Guide through...Cambridge. (Defective.)   1798–1800

—— Another issue.   (Defective.)   [1800 ?]

Costume of the various orders in the University of Cambridge. (Bowes 1459.)   4° 1803–5

HARRADEN (R.B.)   Cantabrigia depicta. (Bowes 1490.) 4° 1809–11

—— 2nd ed.   (Bowes 1541.)   1814

See also Ambulator ; Ely, 1846.

HARRIS (W.) and Forster (R.H.)   History of the Lady Margaret Boat Club, 1825–1890.   1890

Soapsuds, or Washings from the Wollerer.   1890

HARRISON (F.)   Byzantine History. (Rede Lecture, 12 June, 1900.)
                                          London, 1900

HARRISON (Jane E.)   Homo Sum.   Letter to an Anti-Suffragist.
                                       Uxbridge [1909]

HARRISON (John)   A new method of making the banks in the Fens
almost impregnable.   [1766]
HARTLEY (W.N.)   Testimonials when a candidate for the Jacksonian
Professorship.   1875
HARTSHORNE (C.H.)   The book rarities of the University of
Cambridge.   1829
On the drainage of the Nene Valley.   *Northampton*, 1848
The Parliaments of Cambridge. (*Archæol. Journ.*, XIII.) (*London*, 1855)
HARVEST (G.)   A letter to Mr S. Chandler : being a defense of the
Church of England's requiring subscription to explanatory Articles
of Faith.   2nd ed.   *London* (1748)
HARVEY (G.)   The Trimming of Thomas Nash, Gentleman, by
the high-tituled patron Don Richardo de Medico Compo, Barber
Chirurgeon to Trinity College, in Cambridge.   Ed. by Charles
Hindley.   *London*, 1871
HARVEY (W.J.)   Alumni Cantabrigienses. (Specimen.)   1891
HARVEY (W.W.)   Prælectio theologica in Prov. VIII. 22, 23.   4° 1848
HARVEY Goodwin Home for Boys, Cambridge.   Reports, 1906,
1907.   1906–7
HARWOOD (*Sir* B.)   A plan of a course of lectures on domestic
medicine.   (With his Notice prefixed.)   1807
A synopsis of a course of lectures on Comparative Anatomy and
Physiology.   1807
A descriptive catalogue [of the Anatomical Museum].   n.d.
HARWOOD (T.)   Alumni Etonenses.   4° *Birmingham*, 1797
HATFIELD (W.)   The trial and acquital of W. H., on a false charge
of riot and misdemeanour, at the Cambridge Sessions, 14 Jan. 1820.
                                                      12° (1820)
HAUSTED (P.)   Senile odium.   Comœdia Cantabrigiae publicè
Academicis recitata in Collegio Reginali ab ejusdem Collegii
juventute.   12° 1633
HAUXTON.   An account of St Edmund's Church, Hauxton, near
Cambridge.   By W. M. Fawcett.   (*Ecclesiologist*, Dec. 1861.)
HAVILAND (J.)   A letter to the Members of the Senate on the
subject of the subscriptions required of medical graduates in the
University of Cambridge.   (1833)
HAWEIS (T.)   *See* Milner (I.).
HAWKINS (J.S.)   *See* Ruggle (G.)   Ignoramus, 1787.
HAWTREY (E.C.)   Memoir.   By F. St John Thackeray.
                                                 London, 1896
HAY (Ian), *pseud.*   *See* Beith (J. H.).
HAYES (S.)   Prophecy.   (Seatonian Prize Poem for 1776.)   4° 1777
Prayer.   (Seatonian Prize Poem for 1777.)   4° 1777
The Nativity of our Saviour.   (Seatonian Prize Poem for 1778.)
                                                        4° 1778
The Ascension.   (Written for Seatonian Prize.)   4° *London*, 1781
Hope.   (Seatonian Prize Poem for 1783.)   4° 1783
HAYTER (T.)   Remarks on Mr Hume's Dialogues concerning
Natural Religion.   1780

HAZLITT (W.C.)   *See* Randolph (T.) Works, 1875.

HE cometh up as a Freshman.   1872

HEADLAM (W.)   On editing Æschylus.   A criticism.   *London,* 1891
  Greek translation of " God save the King."   (*Class. Rev.,* June, 1902.)
  The Agamemnon of Æschylus translated.   *London,* 1904
  The second chorus of the Agamemnon.   (*Praelections.*)   1906
  A book of Greek verse.   1907
  Restorations of Menander.   1908
  Letters and Poems.   With Memoir by C. Headlam, and Bibliography
    by L. Haward.   *London,* 1910

  Catalogue of his Library on sale by E. Johnson, Cambridge.   1908

HEARD (J.B.)   History of the extinction of Paganism.   (Hulsean
  Prize Essay, 1851.)   1852

HEARNE (T.)   *See* Dodwell (H.) ; Sprott (T.).

HEBERDEN (W.)   Life and works.   Essay for Wix Prize at
  St Bartholomew's Hospital.   By A. C. Buller.   *London,* 1879

HEBERT (C.)   Theological Colleges and the Universities.
                                                   Burslem, 1853
  A reply to the pamphlet of the Rev. W. G. Clark, entitled, *The
  dangers of the Church of England.*   *London and Cambridge,* 1870

HEDLEY (J.C.)   Sermon at the opening of the Church of Our Lady
  and the English Martyrs, Cambridge, Oct. 15, 1890.   *London,* 1890

HEFFER and Sons.   Photographs and history of their business.
                                               Obl. 8o [1909]

HEITLAND (W.E.)   A Letter to a Lady.—A Letter to Mr Heitland
  [by F. Seeley].—The Skirts of the Question.   (Woman Suffrage.)
                                        Camb. and Lond., 1908–9

HELP (The)   A 'Varsity Operetta.   *London,* 1891

HENDERSON (B.W.)   Merton College, Oxford.   (College histories.)
                                                   London, 1899

HENLEY (J.)   History of Queen Esther, a poem in four books.
  2nd ed.   *London,* 1715

HENRY VI, *King of England.*   Will.   Now printed in full for the
  first time, for 450th anniversary of laying the first stone of King's
  College Chapel, 25 July, 1896.   (1896)
  See also Fletcher (C. R. L.).

HENRY Bradshaw Society.   Reports, 1–3 and 6–19.
                                          London, 1890–1909

HENRY Martyn Library.   Appeal for funds.   *London,* 1897

HENSLEY (L.)   A sermon preached in the Chapel of Trinity College,
  Dec. 15, 1856, on the occasion of the Commemoration of Benefactors.   1857

HENSLOW (J.S.)   A syllabus of a course of lectures on Mineralogy.
                                                              1823
  Henslow (J.S.) and Lamb (J.)   Remarks upon the payment of the
  expenses of out-voters at an University election.   (9 April,
  27 April, 1826.)   1826
  Observations...occasioned by *Remarks.*   1826

HENSLOW (J.S.)

A catalogue of British plants.	1829
—— 2nd ed.	1835
Sketch of a course of lectures on Botany for 1833.	1833
Address to the Reformers of the town of Cambridge.	1835

A Reformer's duty. An address to the Reformers of the town of
Cambridge.   1837
Letters to the farmers of Suffolk.   *London and Hadleigh* (1843)
The Roman tumulus, Eastlow Hill, Rougham. (Repr. from the
Bury Post.)   1844
On the materials of two sepulchral vessels found at Warden, Co. Beds.
(*C.A.S.*)   4° 1846
Address to members of the University of Cambridge, on the ex-
pediency of improving the Botanic Garden.   1846
Syllabus of a course of lectures on Botany.   1848
Questions on the subject matter of sixteen lectures in Botany, required
for a Pass examination.   1851
Syllabus of lectures on Botany.   1853
On typical series of objects in Natural History adapted to Local
Museums.   *London,* 1856
Roman antiquities found at Rougham in 1843 and 1844. Repr. by
C. C. Babington.   *Beccles,* 1872

Memoir. By Leonard Jenyns.   *London,* 1862

HENTZNER (P.)   Travels in England during the Reign of Queen
Elizabeth. (Repr. by H. Morley.)   12° *London,* 1892
HERVEY (*Lord* Arthur)   A suggestion for supplying the Literary,
Scientific, and Mechanics' Institutes of Great Britain and Ireland
with lecturers from the Universities.   1855
HERVEY (T.)   Life of the Rev. Samuel Settle.   (Privately pr.)
Colmer, 1881
HEWETT (J.W.)   A brief history and description of the Conventual
and Cathedral Church of the Holy Trinity, Ely.   1848
The arrangement of Parish Churches considered.   1848
HEWETT (W.)   Memoirs of Tobias Rustat.   *London,* 1849
HEY (J.)   The Redemption. (Seatonian Prize Poem for 1763.) 4° 1763
The nature of obsolete ordinances.   A Sermon preached at the
University Church in Cambridge, 10 Mar. 1773.   1773
Sermon preached before the University of Cambridge on 5 Nov. 1774.
To which are added two others.   1774
Sermon preached before the Governors of Addenbrooke's Hospital,
26 June, 1777.   1777
The substance of a sermon preached at H.M. Chapel at Whitehall,
27 Feb. 1778.   1778
Thoughts on the Athanasian Creed.   A sermon preached at Stony
Stratford, 12 April, 1790.   1790
Heads of lectures in Divinity, delivered in the University of Cam-
bridge.   1792
—— 3rd ed.   1794

HEY (R.)   Thoughts on Duelling.   [Attr. to R. Hey.]   1773
    A dissertation on the pernicious effects of Gaming.   2nd ed.   1784
    A dissertation on Duelling.   1784
    —— 2nd ed. by W. Smith of Durham.   1801
    A dissertation on Suicide.   1785
    Some principles of Civilization.   1815
HEYLIN (P.)   Memorial of Bishop Waynflete.   Ed. J. R. Bloxam.
    (Caxton Soc. publ.)   *London,* 1851
HEYWOOD (J.) and Wright (T.)   The ancient laws of the fifteenth
    century, for King's College, Cambridge, and for Eton College.
                                      London, 1850
    Cambridge University Transactions during the Puritan controversies
    of the 16th and 17th centuries.   2 vols.   *London,* 1854
    Academic Reform and University Representation.   *London,* 1860
    See Commission [1853] ; Statutes, 1840, 1855.
HIERURGIA Anglicana.   Edited by Members of the Ecclesiological
    (late Cambridge Camden) Society.   *London,* 1848
HIGGINS (G.)   *See* Hughes (T. S.)   Letter, 1826.
HIGGINS (H.)   Testimonials : candidate for post of assistant surgeon
    to Addenbrooke's Hospital.   4° 1895
    —— Another series.   4° 1897
HIGH Steward of the University.   Poll for election, 11–13 Nov. 1840.
    By H. Gunning.   (Lord Lyndhurst elected.)   1840
    —— Another ed.   (Pr. at Office of Camb. Chronicle.)   1840
    Circular concerning the candidature of Lord Lyttelton.   *n.p.* 1840
HIGHTON (E.G.)   Classical education and the Westminster play.
                                        London, 1878
HILDYARD (H.S.)   Five sermons on the Parable of the Rich Man
    and Lazarus, preached before the University of Cambridge,
    January, 1841.   *London,* 1841
    The obligation of the University to provide for the professional edu-
    cation of its members designed for Holy Orders.   A sermon.   1841
HILDYARD (J.)   The University system of private tuition examined.
                                        London, 1844
    Further consideration of the University system of education.
                                        London, 1845
HILL (A.)   Plan of the central nervous system.   Thesis for degree of
    M.D.   1885
    The chrome-silver method.   Presidential address delivered before the
    Neurological Society.   *London,* 1896
    The acquisition of language and its relation to thought. *London,* 1906
HILL (A.G.)   Architectural and historical notices of the Churches of
    Cambridgeshire.   *London,* 1880
    Tourist's guide to the County of Cambridge.   *London,* 1882
    —— 2nd ed., by E. Conybeare.   *London,* 1892
HILL (T.)   Nundinae Sturbrigienses, anno 1702.   *Dublinii* (1702)
    —— Another edition.   *Londini,* 1709
    —— Another edition.   (+ Tunbrigialia, authore P. Causton ; Incen-
    dium Palatinum.)   *Londini,* 1709

HILLHOUSE (W.)   Application and testimonials when a candidate for the Chair of Botany, etc. in the Mason Science College, Birmingham.   4° *Birmingham*, 1882
HILTON (A.C.)   Works.   Together with his life and letters, by Sir R. P. Edgcumbe.   1904
See also Hamlet ; Light Green.
HINDUISM.   Proposal for a Prize to refute Hinduism.   30 March, 1846.   F° 1846
HINGESTON (R.)   Προγυμνάσματα ἑλληνικά.   1753
HINTS for Paterfamilias.   By Antipater.   *n.p.* 1861
HINTS for the introduction of an improved course of study in the University.   1835
HINTS to Freshmen from a Member of the University of Cambridge. [By P. S. Dodd.]   *London*, 1796
—— 3rd ed.   *London*, 1807
—— 4th ed.   *London*, 1822
—— 5th ed.   *London*, 1845
HISTORICAL Society.   First Prospectus.   1859
HISTORICAL Tripos.   The establishment of a Historical Tripos. By H. R. Luard.   1866
Suggestions towards the establishment of a History Tripos.   By A. W. Ward.   1872
The proposed new Historical Tripos.   By O. Browning.
                          London, 1896
—— Another edition.   *London*, 1897
Report of Special Board for History and Archaeology on regulations for the Tripos, 3 Mar. 1908, and fly-sheets.   4° 1908
HISTORY, Gazetteer, and Directory of Cambridgeshire.
                          Peterborough, 1851
HITCHIN.   College for Women at Hitchin.   *See* Girton College.
HODGETTS (E.A.B.)   Girton and Newnham Colleges.   (*Strand Mag.*, Nov. 1894.)
HODGSON (F.)   Memoir.   By J. T. Hodgson.   2 vols.
                          London, 1878
HODSON (G.)   Elisha at the waters of Jordan.   A sermon preached in Trinity Church, Cambridge, Nov. 20, 1836, on the occasion of the death of Charles Simeon.   1836
—— Another ed.   (*Pulpit*, xxix.)   *London*, 1837
HOLDICH (B.)   History of Crowland Abbey digested.   *Stamford*, 1816
HOLDSWORTH (R.)   A sermon preached in St Maries in Cambridge, 27 March (1642).   4° 1642
HOLLINGWORTH (J.B.)   Heads of lectures in Divinity delivered in the University of Cambridge.   *London*, 1825
—— 2nd ed.   1831
—— 3rd ed.   1835
HOLMES (A.)   A sermon preached in the Chapel of Clare College, Nov. 18, 1866.   1866
The Nemeian Odes of Pindar with especial reference to Ode the Seventh.   Thesis, Feb. 16, 1867.   1867

HOLROYD (J.) Two sermons preached at Great St Mary's Cambridge, 1870.   12° *Leeds*, 1870
HOLROYD (M.) Memorials of G. E. Corrie, D.D.   1890
HOLY Sepulchre (Church of the) *See* Round Church.
HOME (J.) Sketches of Cambridge in verse. Ser. 1. *London*, 1879
HOMER for the English. Iliad v.   *London*, 1860
HOMERTON College. Report of the Congregational Board of Education. 1902, 1903, 1904.   1902–4
HOPE (A.J. Beresford) *See* Beresford Hope.
HOPE (T.) Observations on the plans and elevations designed by James Wyatt, for Downing College.   4° *London*, 1804
HOPE (W.H.StJ.) Seals and armorial insignia of the University and Colleges of Cambridge. Pt I. The University.
                                                   4° *London* (1881)
Letters and testimonials when candidate for Disney Professorship of Archæology, Nov. 1892.   1892
HOPKINS (B.) Sculpture. A poem written for the Chancellor's Medal, at the Cambridge Commencement, July, 1825. (1825)
HOPKINS (E.) The power of womanhood.   *London* (1900)
HOPKINS (H.W.), *pseud.* A sermon preached before the University of Cambridge, by H. W. C[oulthurs]t, D.D. Translated into English metre by H. W. Hopkins [i.e. A. Geddes]. *London*, 1796
HOPKINS (W.) Remarks on certain proposed regulations respecting the studies of the University, etc.   1841
Remarks on the mathematical teaching of the University of Cambridge.   1854
HOPKINS (W.B.) Some points of Christian doctrine considered with reference to certain theories recently put forth by Sir J. Stephen.
                                                              1849
HOPPER (R.) An account of a late rustication from Peterhouse in the University of Cambridge.   *London*, 1776
A postscript to An Account of a late rustication from Peterhouse.
                                                   London, 1776
HORNBUCKLE (T.W.) On the duties and difficulties of the pastoral office in the present time. A sermon preached June 20, 1817, in the parish church of St Michael, Cambridge.   1817
HORNE (T.H.) A catalogue of the library of Queens' College, Cambridge. 2 vols.   *London*, 1827
HORT (F.J.A.) A letter to the Rev. J. Ll. Davies on the tenure of Fellowships and on Church patronage in Trinity College. 1857
Sermon...at the consecration of B. F. Westcott as Bp of Durham.
                                                   London, 1890

Memoir. By J. O. F. Murray. (*Emm. Coll. Mag.*)   1893
Catalogue of his library...sold...May, 1893.   1893
Life and Letters. By his son. 2 vols.   *London*, 1896

HOSPITAL Inkstand. No. 001. Nov. 1888.   4° 1888
HOTHAM (C.) Corporations vindicated in their fundamental liberties...
                                                   12° *London*, 1651

HOTHAM (C.)
The petition and argument of Mr Hotham, Fellow of Peterhouse in
Cambridge, before the Committee for reformation of the Universities,
April 10, 1651. 12º *London*, 1651
A true state of the case of Mr Hotham, late Fellow of Peterhouse.
4º *London*, 1651
----- Another edition. 12º *London*, 1651
HOTHAM (H.J.) A sermon preached in the Chapel of Trinity
College, Cambridge, on Commemoration Day, Dec. 15, 1864.
1865

Funeral sermon. By Coutts Trotter. 1885
In memoriam. By Coutts Trotter. 1885

HOUGH (J.) Injustice of *The Times*. (Statement respecting his
conduct when H. J. Purkiss, B.A. was drowned, 17 Sept. 1865.)
1865
HOUGH (T.) The happiness and advantages of a liberal and virtuous
education. A sermon preach'd in the Cathedral of St Paul on
25 Jan. 1728. 4º (1728)
HOUGH (W.W.) The Cambridge Mission to South London. Ed.
by A. Amos and W. W. Hough. 1904
HOUGHTON (*Lord*) Life. By T. W. Reid. 2nd ed. 2 vols.
London, 1890

See Shelley (P. B.).
HOW I stole the Block. By an Old Etonian. *London*, 1883
HOW I was rusticated from Cambridge. (*Temple Bar*, April, 1872.)
HOW to read. By a Wrangler. *London*, 1860
HOW wĕ spun out the "Long," or the Cambs. Busy Bee Club Papers.
By L. Bluffman [i.e. L. Boquel]. (Specimen : breaks off at p. 16.)
1878
HOWES (J.G.) Sermon on the death of the Prince Consort, 23 Dec.
1861. 1861
Sermon in St Mary's the Less, 11 April, 1869. 1869
HOWSON (J.S.) Five lectures on the character of St Paul. (Hulsean
Lectures for 1862.) *London*, 1864
HOYLE (C.) Paul and Barnabas at Lystra. (Seatonian Prize Poem
for 1806.) 4º 1806
HUBBARD (H.) Sermon preached before the Governors of the
Charity for relief of poor widows and orphans of Clergymen in
the County of Suffolk. 4º 1750
----- 2nd ed. 4º 1763
HUBER (V.A.) The English Universities. Ed. by F. W. Newman.
2 vols. in 3. *London*, 1843
HUCKMAN (J.) Original Poems. 4th ed. 1825
HUDDESFORD (G.) Defence of the Rector and Fellows of Exeter
College, Oxford, from accusations brought against them by Dr
Huddesford. [By F. Webber.] *Oxford*, 1754
HUDSON (J.) Saint Augustine. (Seatonian Prize Poem for 1899.)
1900

HUDSON (W.H.H.)   Correspondence between W. H. H. H. and
the Rev. E. W. Blore (on the Previous Examination).   1869
HUGH (Evans)   The Freshman at Cambridge.   1899
HUGHES (Tho.), *M.A.* (*Joh.*)   The Ascension. (Seatonian Prize Poem
for 1780.)   4° 1780
HUGHES (Tho.), † 1896.   Memoir of D. Macmillan.   *London*, 1882
HUGHES (T.McK.)   Testimonials for Woodwardian Professorship
of Geology.   2 series.   1873
Biographical notice of A. Sedgwick.   Paper read before Yorks. Geol.
and Polytechnic Soc., 1883.   *n.p.* 1883
The Sedgwick Memorial Geological Museum.   (1886)
Life and Letters of Adam Sedgwick.   By T. McK. Hughes and
J. W. Clark.   2 vols.   1890
The race represented in the archaic statues of Athens. (*Camb.
Review*, 28 April, 1898.)   1898
Herculaneum.   Paper read before the C. A. S., 19 Nov. 1906. (*Camb.
Chron.*)   1906
Hughes (T. McK.) and Mrs Hughes.   Cambridgeshire. (Camb.
County Geographies.)   1909
HUGHES (T.S.)   Mors Nelsoni.   Ode Latina...in Curia Cantabr.
recitata. (Sir Wm Browne's Medal.)   4° 1806
Belshazzar's Feast. (Seatonian Prize Poem for 1817.)   1818
An address to the people of England in the cause of the Greeks.
London, 1822
Considerations upon the Greek Revolution.   *London*, 1823
A letter to Godfrey Higgins, of Skellow Grange, on the subject of his
Horæ Sabbaticæ.   1826
HULBERT (C.A.)   On the genius of Milton.   12° *Shrewsbury*, 1834
HULSEAN Lectures.   *See* Foxley (J.), 1881 ; Goodwin (H.), 1856 ;
Howson (J. S.), 1864 ; Trench (R. C.), 1845, 1846.
HULSEAN Prize Essays.   1801.   An essay tending to show that the
Prophecies...are an evidence of the truth of the Christian religion.
By J. B. Sumner.   1802
1806.   The propagation of Christianity was not indebted to any
secondary causes.   By S. B. Vince.   1807
1817.   Dissertation on probable causes of neglect with which some
writers of antiquity treated the Christian religion.   By John
Weller.   1818
1819.   A dissertation on the fitness of the time when Jesus Christ
came into the world.   By E. White.   1820
1821.   The expedients to which the Gentile philosophers resorted in
opposing the progress of the Gospel.   By W. Trollope. *London*, 1822
1825.   In what respects the Law is a schoolmaster to bring men to
Christ.   By A. T. Russell.   1826
1832.   An inquiry into the advantages which have accrued to
Christianity in consequence of its narrative form.   By F. Garden.
1833
1851.   The history of the extinction of Paganism viewed in relation
to Christianity.   By J. B. Heard.   1852

HUMBLE Address to the Clergy of England recommending a method for the...augmentation of the income of their indigent Brethren. [By Rev. — Hutchinson, of Holywell, Hunts.]   1764
HUMFREY (C.)   Report upon the present state of the River Cam.
1829
A letter to the Electors of Cambridge.   1835
A letter to Viscount Melbourne, containing facts and practical observations relating to the currency.   1836
HUMPHRY (A.P.)   The student's handbook to the University of Cambridge.   1877
Old College Plate at Cambridge. (*Art Journal*, June, 1883.)
HUMPHRY (*Sir* G.M.)   Report of some cases of operation.
London, 1856
Cambridge : its University and Colleges. (His guide to Cambridge in its earliest form.   Written for the visit of the British Medical Assoc.)   *London*, 1864
Address in Surgery at the Meeting of the British Medical Association at Cambridge.   *London*, 1864
Analysis of the physiological series in the Gallery of the Museum of Comparative Anatomy.   1866
Address in Physiology before the...British Association at Nottingham.
1866
The Hunterian Oration...14 Feb. 1879.   1879
Address delivered at the 48th annual meeting of the British Medical Association at Cambridge, August, 1880.   4° 1880
—— Another edition.   1880
Cambridge : the Town, University, and Colleges. (Visit of British Medical Association.)   1880
Guide to Cambridge.   (1880)
—— Another edition.   (1883)
—— Another edition.   (1886)
Old age and changes incidental to it.   1885
HUMPHRY (W.G.)   Verses at Tercentenary of Trinity College, 22 Dec. 1846.   4° 1846
HUNSTANTON Convalescent Home.   24th, 27th, 28th, 30th, 31st Annual Report.   *v.p.* 1895–1909
HUNT (P.)   Narrative of what is known respecting the literary remains of the late John Tweddell.   *London*, 1826
HUNTER (J.)   *See* Thoresby (R.).   Diary, 1830.
HUNTINGTON (G.)   Random recollections.   *London*, 1893
HURD (R.)   The opinion of an eminent Lawyer [P. Yorke] supported.
London, 1751
HUSTLER (J.D.)   The case of Mr Hustler's presentation to a living in the gift of Trinity College.   (7 pieces.)   1822
HUSTLER (W.)   *See* Graduati, 1823.
HUTCHINSON (A.S.M.)   From Fresher to Blue. (*Royal Mag.*, April, 1905.)
HUTCHINSON (F.)   A sermon preached at the Public Commencement at Cambridge, July 3, 1698.   4° 1698

HUTTON (J.A.)   The Cotton Crisis.   Paper read before Brit. Assoc.,
1904.   *Manchester*, 1904
HUTTON (W.H.)   St John's College, Oxford.   (College histories.)
                                             London, 1898
HUXLEY (*Sir* T.H.)   Obituary by M. Foster.   (*Proc. Roy. Soc.*,
vol. 59.)   *London* [1895]
HYMENÆUS; a Comedy.   Ed. by G. C. Moore Smith.   4° 1908
HYMERS (J.)   *See* Fisher (J.).   Funeral sermon of Margaret, Countess
of Richmond and Derby, 1840.

I

IMPROVEMENT Act. Abstract of Accounts for the year ended
March 25, 1882. 1882
See also Anningson (B.).
IMPROVEMENT Commissioners. Bye-laws, etc. 1889
IN statu Pupillari. [By Miss Fanny Johnson.] *London*, 1907
—— Cheap ed. *London*, 1909
INDIVIDUAL. Nos. 1–15. 25 Oct. 1836—14 March, 1837.
(2 copies.) 1836–37
INDUSTRIAL School. Fourth annual report. 1854
INFLUENCE of the Homeric poems on the language...of the Greeks.
[By Tho. Myers.] 1830
INGE (W.R.) Death the Fulfilment of Life. A Sermon preached
before the University, 3 March, 1907. *London*, 1907
INGLEBY (C.M.) Reflections historical and critical on the revival
of Philosophy at Cambridge. 1870
INGLEBY (H.) The Shade of a Pageant (King's Lynn, 1908).
4° (1908)
INGLIS (*Sir* R.H.) Speech in the House of Commons, 26 March,
1834, in reference to a petition from certain Members of the
Senate. *London*, 1834
INGRAM (J.) Memorials of Oxford. 3 vols. 4° *Oxford*, 1837
Memorials of the Colleges and Halls in the University of Oxford.
2nd ed. 2 vols. *Oxford*, 1847
Memorials of the public buildings of Oxford. New ed. *Oxford*, 1848
INGRAM (R.A.) The necessity of introducing Divinity into the
regular course of Academical studies considered. *Colchester*, 1792
Syllabus...of a system of Political Philosophy : [with] a dissertation
recommending that the study of Political Economy be encouraged
by the Universities. 1799
INMAN (J.) The Scriptural doctrine of Divine Grace. A sermon
preached before the University of Cambridge, on Commencement
Sunday, 1820. 1820
INMAN (J.W.) Necessity of a Royal Commission of Inquiry into
the condition of the Universities. *London*, 1850
INQUIRY into the right of Appeal from the Chancellor or Vice-
Chancellor of the University of Cambridge, in matters of Discipline.
[By T. Chapman.] *London*, 1751
—— 2nd ed. *London*, 1752
INQUISITIO comitatus Cantabrigiensis. Cura N. E. S. A. Hamilton.
4° *London*, 1876

INSPECTOR. Nos. 1–3. *See* Student, 1750–1.

INSTRUMENTA Ecclesiastica. Edited by the Ecclesiological, late Camden Society. Two series. 4° *London*, 1847–56

INTERCEPTED correspondence of Phelim O'Cutaway, a Cambridge Bull-Dog. No. 1. Feb. 1, 1840. 1840

INTER-COLLEGIATE Christian Union, its past, present, and future. By R. L. Pelly. (1910)

INTERNATIONAL Congress of Zoology, 1898. *See* Zoology.

IRENEO (Silvio), *pseud. See* Spineto (*Marchese*).

IRISH Church Bill. The names of Members of the Senate of the University of Cambridge, in support of the petition...against the Irish Church Bill, June, 1869. Arranged by R. Potts. 1869

IVES (J.) Select papers chiefly relating to English antiquities : published from the originals in the possession of J. Ives.
4° *London*, 1773

J

JACK (W.)   Additions and emendations to draft of statutes proposed for St Peter's College.   1860

JACK-DAW. (St John's College.)   Nos. 1–5.   May 19–Dec. 1, 1900.   4º 1900

JACKSON (C.)   *See* De la Pryme (A.).

JACKSON (H.)   On some passages in the seventh book of the Eudemian Ethics.   1900

Plato's Cratylus. (*Praelections.*)   1906

JACKSON (T.G.)   Wadham College, Oxford, its foundation, architecture, and history.   4º *Oxford*, 1893

The Church of St Mary the Virgin, Oxford.   4º *Oxford*, 1897

JACKSONIAN Professorship of Experimental Philosophy, 1875. Report of the Council of the Senate, Fly-sheets, Candidates' notices, including that of J. Dewar, who was elected, etc.   1875

JACOMBE (S.)   Moses his death...Sermon at Christ Church, in London, Dec. 23, 1656, at the funeral of Mr Edward Bright, M.A., Fellow of Emmanuel Colledge.   4º *London*, 1657

JAHN (J.)   Sylloge librorum orientalium.   1821

JAMES I, *King of England*.   Account of the reception of King James, at Cambridge, in the year 1614.   By John Chamberlain. (*Annual Register* for 1778.)

Letters Patent of Elizabeth and James I addressed to the University of Cambridge.   Ed. by J. W. Clark.   1892

JAMES (M.R.)   Athens in the fourteenth century.   1887

The Sculptures in the Lady Chapel at Ely.   Lectures delivered, 16 Aug. 1892. (*Arch. Journ.*, XLIX.)   (*London*, 1892)

The Sculptures in the Lady Chapel at Ely.   4º *London*, 1895

A descriptive Catalogue of the Manuscripts in the Fitzwilliam Museum.   1895

A descriptive Catalogue of the Manuscripts in the library of Eton College.   1895

A descriptive Catalogue of the Manuscripts in the library of Jesus College.   1895

A descriptive Catalogue of the Manuscripts other than Oriental in the library of King's College.   1895

A descriptive Catalogue of the Manuscripts in the library of Peterhouse.   With an Essay on the history of the Library, by J. W. Clark.   1899

A Guide to the Windows of King's College Chapel. (2 copies corrected.)   *London*, 1899

On two series of paintings at Worcester Priory. (*C. A. S.*)   1904

JAMES (M.R.)
On the Sculptures at Malmesbury. (*C. A. S.*) 1904
A descriptive Catalogue of the Manuscripts in the library of Pembroke
College. 1905
A descriptive Catalogue of the Western Manuscripts in the library of
Clare College. 1905
A descriptive Catalogue of the Western Manuscripts in the library of
Queens' College. 1905
Facsimiles of the Frescoes in Eton College Chapel. F⁰ *Eton*, 1907
A descriptive Catalogue of the Manuscripts in the library of Trinity
Hall. 1907
A descriptive Catalogue of the Manuscripts in the library of Gonville
and Caius College. 2 vols. 1907–8
Eustace Talbot. (By M. R. J. and others.) 4° 1908
A descriptive Catalogue of the Manuscripts in the library of Corpus
Christi College, Cambridge. Parts 1, 2. 1909–10
See also McBryde (J.).
JAMESON (F.J.) Reply to a statement...relative to the last election
to the Mastership of St Catharine's College. 1868
JANEWAY (James) Invisibles, realities, demonstrated in the holy
life and triumphant death of Mr John Janeway, Fellow of King's
Colledge in Cambridge. 6th ed. 8⁰ *London*, 1702
JANEWAY (John) An extract of the life and death of John Janeway.
By James Wheatley. 12⁰ *London*, 1775
—— Another edition. 12⁰ *Leeds*, 1797
See also Janeway (James).
JEAFFRESON (J.C.) Annals of Oxford. 2nd ed. 2 vols.
Oxford, 1871
JEBB (E.) Cambridge ; a brief study in social questions. 1906
JEBB (J.) A short account of theological lectures now reading at
Cambridge. 4° 1770
—— 2nd ed. 4° 1772
Letters on...Subscription to the Liturgy and...Articles of the Church
of England. *London*, 1772
The excellency of the spirit of benevolence. A sermon preached
before the University of Cambridge, Dec. 28, 1772. 1773
Remarks upon the present mode of education in the University of
Cambridge. 1773
—— 2nd ed. 1773
—— 3rd ed. 1773
—— 4th ed. 1774
A Proposal for the establishment of public examinations in the
University of Cambridge. *London*, 1774
An Observation on the design of establishing annual examinations
at Cambridge. [By W. S. Powell.] 1774
A letter to the author of the Proposal for the establishment of
public examinations. 1774
Letter to the author of An Observation, etc. [By Ann Jebb.]
[1774 ?]

JEBB (J.)
An Address to the Members of the Senate.   (1775)
A short state of the reasons for a late resignation. To which are
added occasional observations. And a letter to the Bp of Norwich.
                                                             1775
—— 3rd ed.   1776
   Letter to Rev. J. Jebb occasioned by his Short state. *London*, 1776
   Resignation no Proof. [By E. Tew.]   *London*, 1776
   Works...with Memoirs by John Disney. 3 vols.   *London*, 1787
JEBB (*Sir* R.C.) Testimonials when a candidate for the Professorship
of Greek in the University of Glasgow.   1875
Speeches delivered as Public Orator, 16 June, 1874.   1875
Inaugural address delivered in the University of Glasgow, Nov. 4,
1875.   *Glasgow*, 1875
The Attic Orators from Antiphon to Isaeos. 2 pts.   *London*, 1876
Modern Greece. Two lectures.   *London*, 1880
—— (2nd ed.)   *London*, 1901
Old Comedy on a new Stage. (The Birds.) (*Fortnightly Review*,
1 Jan. 1884.)
Erasmus. (Rede Lecture, 1890.)   1890
The work of the Universities for the nation.   1893
Humanism in education. (Romanes Lecture, 1899.)   *London*, 1899
Macaulay. A lecture.   1900

Life and Letters. By Caroline Jebb.   1907

JELF (R.W.) Grounds for laying before the Council of King's
College, London, certain statements contained in a recent publica-
tion, entitled *Theological Essays*, by the Rev. F. D. Maurice.
                                                     Oxford, 1853
JENKINSON (F.J.H.) Address delivered at the twenty-eighth
Annual Meeting of the Library Association of the United
Kingdom, at Cambridge, 22 Aug. 1905.   1905
See Bradshaw (H.), 1889, 1893.
JENNER (C.) The Destruction of Nineveh. (Seatonian Prize Poem
for 1768.)   4° 1768
JENNINGS (E.N.) His case under the Insolvent Act. *Oxford* (1847)
JENYNS (L.) Systematic Catalogue of British Vertebrate Animals.
                                                             1835
Observations in natural history.   *London*, 1846
Memoir of Rev. J. S. Henslow.   *London*, 1862
A Naturalist's Calendar. Ed. F. Darwin.   1903
JEPHSON (T.) Notice of Grace to present petition to the Visitor of
St John's College, praying him to expel T. J., Dec. 8, 1823.
                                                         F° 1823
Report of the trial of the Rev. T. J., at the Cambridge Assizes, 1823.
                                                           (1823)
JEREMIE (J.A.) The Office and Mission of St John the Baptist.
(Norrisian Prize Essay for 1823.)   1824

JEREMIE (J.A.)

No valid argument can be drawn from the incredulity of the heathen philosophers against the truth of the Christian religion. (Norrisian Prize Essay for 1825.)   1826

Commemoration sermon preached in the Chapel of Trinity College, Cambridge, Dec. 16, 1834.   *London*, 1835

A sermon delivered in the Chapel of Trinity College, Cambridge, Dec. 13, 1842, being the Commemoration of Founders and Benefactors.   *London*, 1842

The third Centenary of Trinity College, Cambridge. A sermon preached in the Chapel, Dec. 22, 1846, being the Commemoration of Benefactors.   1847

Christian Benevolence; a Sermon preached in the chapel of the East-India College, 28 March, 1847.   1847

A sermon preached in the Chapel of Trinity College, Cambridge, Dec. 14, 1849, being the Commemoration of Founders and Benefactors.   1850

A sermon preached before the University of Cambridge, April 26, 1854; being the day appointed for general humiliation and prayer. 2nd ed.   1854

A sermon preached before the University of Cambridge, March 21, 1855. 2nd ed.   1855

A sermon preached before the University of Cambridge, Dec. 23, 1861, being the day of the funeral of H.R.H. the Prince Consort. 1862

A sermon preached before the University of Cambridge, Feb. 2, 1864, at the re-opening of Great St Mary's Church.   1864

JERNINGHAM (E.) An Elegy written among the ruins of an abbey.   4° *London*, 1765

JERWOOD (J.) A lecture on the new Planet Neptune and its discovery.   *London*, 1849

JESSOPP (A.) The Middle Class examinations; what will they do for us?   *London*, 1860

The Layman's position in the Church of the first four centuries.
                                                                     London, 1898

See North (*Hon.* R.).

JESUS College. Historia Collegii Jesu Cantabrigiensis, a J. Shermanno. Ed. J. O. Halliwell.   *Londini*, 1840

Remarks on the Report by the Cambridge University Commissioners respecting certain Statutes proposed by them to Jesus College. By G. E. Corrie.   1861

The Chapter House, and some interior views thereof. By A. Gray. (*Chanticlere.*)   1893

A College chronicle, 1557–1643. (*Chanticlere.*) By A. Gray. 1893

Catalogue of Manuscripts. By M. R. James.   1895

Jesus College. By A. Gray. (College histories.)   *London*, 1902

JOHN'S (St) College. Statutes, 1580. (Fifth Report of the Select Committee on Education.)   F° *London*, 1818

Specification of work and materials for new buildings according to the designs of Rickman and Hutchinson.   *Birmingham*, 1827

JOHN'S (St) College.

The inward witness of the Spirit to the believer's adoption. Commemoration Sermon in St John's College Chapel, March 15, 1845.
1845

Some account of St John's College Chapel, Cambridge. By F. C. Woodhouse.
1848

Early Statutes of the College of St John the Evangelist in the University of Cambridge. Ed. by J. E. B. Mayor.
1859

Order of Service...on laying the foundation stone of the New Chapel, 6 May, 1864.
1864

Oaths of Qualification, 1715–1765.
1867

The New Chapel. By G. F. Reyner.
4° 1869

The New Chapel. May 6, 1861. By W. Selwyn.
4° 1869

The New Chapel of St John's College and the consecration of it. (*Eagle*, June, 1869.)
1869

Consecration of the Chapel of St John the Evangelist, May 12, 1869.
1869

History of the College of St John the Evangelist, Cambridge. By T. Baker. Ed. by J. E. B. Mayor. 2 vols.
1869

Replies of College lecturers to the inquiries of the Master and Seniors of St John's College, Cambridge.
1872

The Portrait Pictures in St John's College, Cambridge. By A. Freeman. (4 parts.) (*Eagle*, XI., XII.)
1881–3

Our College grounds. By A. J. Poynder. (*Eagle*, Jan. 1882.) 1882

Admissions to the College of St John the Evangelist in the University of Cambridge. Part I. Jan. 1630–July, 1665. Ed. by J. E. B. Mayor. Part II. July, 1665–July, 1715. Ed. by J. E. B. Mayor. Part III. July, 1715–November, 1767. Ed. by R. F. Scott.
1882–1903

The Pilgrimage to Parnassus, etc. Comedies performed in St John's College, 1597–1601. Ed. by W. D. Macray. *Oxford*, 1886

Founders and Benefactors of St John's College, Cambridge. By A. F. Torry.
1888

A hand-list...relating to the portraits, etc. of Blessed John Fisher, Bp of Rochester. By C. Sayle. (*Eagle*.)
1890

The College Pictures at the Tudor Exhibition. By A. Freeman. (*Eagle*, XVI.)
1890

The history of the Lady Margaret Boat Club, 1825–90. By R. H. Foster and W. Harris.
1890

Notes from the College Records. By R. F. Scott. Two series. (*Eagle*.)
1890–1906

Index to the Eagle. Vols. 1–15.
1891

Bibliotheca loquitur. (Notes on the Library.) By C. Sayle. (*Eagle*.)
(1892)

The Eagle. Hundredth number.
1893

List of past occupants of rooms. By G. C. Moore Smith.
1895

The Jack-Daw. Nos. 1–5. May 19–Dec. 1, 1900.
1900

St John's College. By J. B. Mullinger. (College histories.)
London, 1901

JOHN'S (St) College.
The Geology of the College Chapel.   By T. G. Bonney.   (*Eagle.*)
1907
A Septuagenarian's Recollections of St John's.   By T. G. Bonney.
(*Eagle.*)   1909
The blank window in the Chapel.   Two legends of St John.   By
W. A. Cox.   (*Eagle.*)   1909
JOHN'S (St) Hospital.   On some remains of the Hospital of St John
the Evangelist.   By C. C. Babington.   (*C.A.S.*)   1864
JOHNSON (F.)   In Statu Pupillari.   *London*, 1907
—— Cheap ed.   *London*, 1909
JOHNSON (G.)   On a bronze vessel recently discovered in the Isle
of Ely.   (*Archaeologia*, XXVIII.)   4° (*London*, 1840)
JOHNSON (J.)   Nature inverted.   Sermon...18 July, 1670. 4° 1670
JOHNSON (R.)   Aristarchus Anti-Bentleianus. *Nottinghamiae*, 1717
JOHNSON (R.B.)   The Cambridge Colleges.   *London* [1909]
JOHNSON (S.)   Account of Dr Johnson's visit to Cambridge, in
1765.   (*New Monthly Magazine*, Dec. 1, 1818.)
JOHNSON (W.) *of Llandaff House Academy.*   Thoughts on Education.
London, 1830
JOHNSON *afterwards* Cory (W.) Eton Reform. 1, 2. *London*, 1861
Early Modern Europe.   1869
Observations on the proposals of the Syndicate for establishing a
Professors' and Public Teachers' Fund.   (1870)
Extracts from Letters and Journals.   Selected and arranged by
F. W. Cornish.   *Oxford*, 1897
JOKES of the Cambridge Coffee-Houses in the seventeenth century.
Ed. by J. O. Halliwell.   1841
—— Another edition.   1842
JONES (E.L.)   Application and Testimonials for post of Assistant-
Physician to Addenbrooke's Hospital.   1899
JONES (H.)   Friends in Pencil : a Cambridge sketch book. 4° 1893
JONES (H.L.)   *See* Le Keux (J.).   Memorials, 1847.
JONES (J.H.)   If they hear not Moses and the Prophets...(Norrisian
Prize Essay for 1846.)   1846
JONES (T.)   A sermon upon duelling, preached before the University
of Cambridge, Dec. 11, 1791.   4° 1792

Elegy on the Rev. T. J.   By Robert Dealtry.   4° (1807)
Memoir.   By Herbert Marsh.   (1808)

JOSSELIN (J.)   Historia Collegii Corporis Christi.   Ed. J. W. Clark.
(*C.A.S.*)   1880
JOWETT (B.)   Suggestions for an improvement of the Examination
Statute.   [By B. Jowett and A. P. Stanley.]   *Oxford*, 1848
JOYCE (J.)   An analysis of Paley's View of the evidences of
Christianity.   4th ed.   *Harlow*, 1810
JUBILEE (1887) Celebrations in Cambridge and surrounding villages.
12° 1887
Thanksgiving service in King's Coll. Chapel.   1887

JUBILEE (1897)   Diamond Jubilee.   Programme of festivities in Cam-
    bridge.   1897
    Jubilee Celebrations.   Official Programme.   1897
    Thanksgiving service in King's Coll. Chapel.   1897
JUDE (R.H.)   A systematic course for the analysis of a mixture of
    Acids.   1877
JUKES-BROWNE (A.J.)   Post-Tertiary Deposits of Cambridgeshire.
    (Sedgwick Prize Essay, 1877.)   1878
JULLIEN (M.A.)   À l'Angleterre savante et littéraire.   *Londres* (1845)
JUS academicum : or a defence of the peculiar jurisdiction which
    belongs of common right to Universities.   [By J. Colbatch.]
                                              4° *London,* 1722

K

K.P. Vols. 1–3. 1 Feb. 1893—7 Dec. 1894. (Ed. by N. W. Paine, Trin., and E. A. Sutherland, Tr. Hall.)   4° and 8° 1893-4
KAYE (J.) A sermon preached before the University of Cambridge, Nov. 19, 1817, being the day of the funeral of the Princess Charlotte Augusta of Wales. 2nd ed.   4° 1817
—— 3rd ed.   1818
Oratiuncula Cantabrigiæ in comitiis habita, prid. Non. Julii 1819.
   (1819)
Oratiuncula Cantabrigiæ in comitiis habita, iv Non. Julii 1820.
   (1820)
KEARY (H.) Sermon on the death of H. Keary. By C. J. Vaughan.
   London, 1852
KECK (B.A.) Sermon on occasion of his death, by W. Mandell.
   1815
KEENE (C.) See Vaughan (H.) The Cambridge Grisette.
KELLETT (E.E.) Jetsam.   1897
Carmina ephemera.   1903
KELSALL (C.) Phantasm of an University : with prolegomena.
   4° London, 1814
KELTY (M.A.) Visiting my Relations, and its results. (By M. A. Kelty.) 2nd ed.   London, 1852
Reminiscences of thought and feeling. By the author of Visiting my Relations (M. A. Kelty).   London, 1852
KEMBLE (J.M.) History of the English language. (Syllabus of lectures.)   1834
KEMP (E.) Sermon preached at St Maries...to the Universitie, Sept. 6, 1668, the Sunday before Sturbridge Fair.   4° 1668
KEMPE (J.E.) Prologue before the tragedy of Othello performed at Cambridge, March 16, 1832. By J. E. K. (J. E. Kempe).
   4° London (1832)
KENDALL (F.) The trial of F. K. for setting fire to Sydney College.
   1813
KENNEDY (B.H.) Shrewsbury School, past and present.   1882
KENNEDY (C.M.) Testimonials when a candidate for Whewell Professorship of International Law.   London, 1888
KENNEDY (C.R.) Classical education reformed.   London, 1837
Ode on the birth of the Prince (of Wales).   London, 1842
KENNEDY (G.J.) Remarks on Mr Mitchell's edition of the Comedies of Aristophanes.   1841
KENNEDY (W.R.) Cambridge University and College reform.
   London, 1870

KENNICOTT (B.) An Answer to a letter from the Rev. T. Rutherforth, D.D. *London*, 1762
KERRICH (R.E.) Report of Syndics of Fitzwilliam Museum on his bequest, 26 Oct. 1872. 1872
KERRICH (S.) A sermon preached before the University...on Commencement Sunday in the morning, 29 June, 1735. 1735
KERRICH (T.) Account of some lids of stone coffins discovered in Cambridge Castle in 1810. (*Archaeologia*, XVII.) 4° (*London*, 1813)
KEY to the Fragment. *See* Fragment.
KIDD (J.) An introductory lecture to a course in Comparative Anatomy, illustrative of Paley's Natural Theology. *Oxford*, 1824
KIDD (T.) *See* Porson (R.). Tracts, 1815.
KIDMAN (R.) *See* Grimshaw (W.).
KILNER (J.) An account of Pythagoras's School in Cambridge. (Bowes 1341.) F° (1790)
KING (C.W.) On the use of Antique Gems in the Middle Ages. (*Arch. Journ.*) (*London*, 1865)
Epitaph of M. Verrius Flaccus. (*American Philos. Soc.*) *n.p.* 1887
KING (E.) Justa Edouardo King, naufrago, ab amicis mœrentibus, amoris et μυείας χάριν. (+Obsequies...) 4° Cantabrigiae, 1638. (Reprints. Ed. by W. J. Thornhill.) *Dublinii*, 1835
KING (R.J.) Handbook to Cathedrals. Eastern division.
London, 1862
KING (William), †1712. A Journey to London in 1698.
London, 1698
Short Account of Dr Bentley's Humanity and Justice. [By W. King and others.] *London*, 1699
Dialogues of the Dead. *London*, 1699
KING (William), †1763. *See* Fragment.
KING (William), *D.Sc.* Application for Woodwardian Professorship of Geology, 6 Feb. 1873. 4° 1873
KING'S College. Sermon preached, 25 March, 1689. By Wm Fleetwood. 4° 1689
Collection of...Anthems us'd in King's Coll. [etc.]. (Ed. by T. Tudway.) 1706
Sermon preached, 25 March, 1724. By G. Doughty. 2nd ed.
1724
Catalogus alumnorum, 1444–1730. 4° *Etonae*, 1730
Oratio habita Cantabrigiae in Coll. Regali. By John Reade.
4° (1742)
Oratio habita in funere Guil. George, Coll. Regal. Praepositi, VII° Kal. Oct. 1756. By Wm Barford. 4° 1756
An account of King's College Chapel. By H. Malden. (Pp. 96. No errata.) 1769
Registrum Regale. 4° *Etonae*, 1774
Account of the Chapel. (From Britton's *Architectural Antiquities*.)
4° 1805
—— Another state.
Report of the proceedings in the case of an Appeal preferred by the

KING'S College.

Provost and Scholars of King's College, against the Provost and Fellows of Eton College, to the Bishop of Lincoln. By Philip Williams. *London*, 1816

The Appeal of King's College against the Fellows of Eton, respecting their holding ecclesiastical preferment with their Fellowships, etc. 1817

Dissertation on the windows of King's College Chapel. By J. K. Baldrey. 1818

Explanation of the various local passages and allusions in the Appeal, etc. of King's College *v.* Eton College. *London*, 1819

Exhibition of designs for completing King's College, Cambridge... (Advertisement.) *London*, 1823

—— Catalogue. 4° *London*, 1823

An historical and descriptive account of King's College Chapel. By James Cook. 1829

Delineations of the Chapel of King's College. By J. and H. S. Storer. F° [*ab.* 1830]

Statement of the question between the Provost and Fellows of King's College, and the executors of the late Mr Cory. 1831

A correct statement of the transactions between the Commissioners for Paving and Lighting the Town of Cambridge, and the Provost and Fellows of King's College. Signed: Ed. Randall, Clerk to the Commissioners. (8 Feb.) F° 1831

Reply of King's College to the statement of the Commissioners for Paving, etc. the town of Cambridge. 1831

Documents to shew the state of the question now pending between the Commissioners of Paving and King's College, relative to the purchase of Mr Cory's premises. 1831

To the Provost and Fellows of King's College. [On the position of King's College in the University.] (1837)

An address to the Fellows of King's College, Cambridge, on the subject of examinations for Degrees. *London*, 1838

Observations on the construction of the roof of King's College Chapel. By F. Mackenzie. 4° *London*, 1840

The interpretation of the composition between the University and King's College. By a Member of the Senate [J. R. Crowfoot]. 1846

A few remarks on the present system of Degrees at King's College, Cambridge. [By E. Thring.] 1846

Registrum Regale. A list of the Provosts of Eton, the Provosts of King's College, etc. *Eton*, 1847

Further remarks on Statutes, and the present system of King's College, Cambridge. [By E. Thring.] 1848

Letter to the Provost of Eton on the election of Scholars to the two foundations of Henry VI. By G. Williams. *London*, 1850

The ancient laws of the fifteenth century, for King's College, Cambridge, and for Eton College. Collected by James Heywood and Thomas Wright. *London*, 1850

KING'S College.

Instrument under seal relinquishing right to proceed to B.A. degree without examination, 2 May, 1851. With Report of Syndicate appointed to consider the question. F° 1851–2

Proposed draft of an answer to the remarks and recommendations of H.M. Commissioners for inquiring into the state, etc. of the University of Cambridge. 1853

An answer to the remarks and recommendations of H.M. Commissioners ...so far as they relate to King's College. 1854

The Chorister. A Tale of King's College Chapel in the Civil Wars. [By S. Baring Gould.] [1854]

—— 10th ed. 1895

An account of King's College Chapel. By Charles Neve. 1855

—— Another ed. n.d.

Artistic notes on the windows of King's College Chapel. By Geo. Scharf. (*Arch. Journal*, XII., XIII.) *London*, 1855–6

A letter to the Provost of King's College concerning two votes given in Congregation, 17 Dec. 1856. By George Williams, Vice-Provost. 1856

Statement of the property of King's College. By G. Williams. 1857

Further statement of property. By G. Williams. 1857

Remarks upon the sources of income of King's College. By T. B[rocklebank]. (1857)

Report of the Financial Committee. 1860

Statement relative to the financial matters of King's College. By G. Williams. 1860

Anthem, June 3, 1864. (I have surely built thee an house.—*Boyce.*) 1864

Notes on the history and present condition of King's College Chapel. By T. J. P. Carter. *London*, 1867

Catalogue of the Oriental MSS. in the library of King's College. By E. H. Palmer. (*Roy. Asiatic Soc.*) (*London*, 1867)

Mr Cockayne's narrative. [On his dismissal from the mastership of King's Coll. Choir School.] *n.p.* (1869)

—— Notes to same. *n.p.* (1869)

Suggestions to the Committee appointed to amend the Statutes. By A. Austen Leigh. 1872

Documents relating to the additional endowments and trust funds of King's College, Cambridge, 1869. Re-issued with Appendix. 1875

Fellowships and Lectureships (King's College). By G. W. Prothero. 1877

Considerations on the reform of the Statutes of King's College, Cambridge. By Oscar Browning. (1877)

Description of stained glass in West window of Chapel by J. R. Clayton and A. Bell. 22 April, 1879. 4° 1879

Proposed union of King's with St Catharine's College. Report of the Committee appointed, Nov. 25, 1879. (16 March, 1880.) 4° 1880

Report of College meeting held 13 April, 1880 to consider complete union with St Catharine's College. 4° 1880

KING'S College.
On King's College Chapel, by G. Gilbert Scott. (Extr. from his
   Hist. of Engl. Church Architecture.) London, 1881
Cambridge University. King's College. Statute B for University.
   Petition and Case of the Provost and Scholars of the Governing
   Body and Case of the University of Cambridge Commissioners.
                                  4° London (1881–2)
Report of the Council under D. III. 10. Nov. 17, 1883. 4° 1883
—— Nov. 15, 1884. 4° 1884
Performance of Mendelssohn's "St Paul," 14 March, 1884. 4° 1884
Festival Service, 20 June, 1887. Queen Victoria's Jubilee. 1887
Festival service to be held in King's College Chapel, June 11, 1888
   when will be performed Handel's Oratorio "Saul," in aid of
   Addenbrooke's Hospital. 1888
Sermon on Founder's Day, by J. R. Harmer. 1888
Special service on the occasion of the re-opening of the Organ, Feb. 8,
   1889. 1889
Festival Service, 12 June, 1889. Handel's "Israel in Egypt." 1889
—— 11 June, 1890. Mendelssohn's "Elijah." 1890
—— 13 June, 1894. Handel's "Messiah." 1894
Catalogue of Manuscripts other than Oriental. By M. R. James.
                                           1895
Report of Committee appointed to consider arrangement of east end
   of Chapel. (26 Apr.) 1896
Festival Service, 17 June, 1896. Mendelssohn's "Elijah." 1896
Will of Henry VI. now first printed in commemoration of the
   450th anniversary of the laying of the foundation stone of King's
   College Chapel, 25 July, 1896. 4° 1896
Order of Service in Chapel, 25 July, 1896. 4° 1896
Jubilee Thanksgiving Service, 16 June, 1897. 1897
Festival Service, 9 June, 1898. Stanford's "Requiem." 1898
—— 8 June, 1899. Handel's "Israel in Egypt." 1899
King's College. By A. Austen Leigh. (College histories.)
                                       London, 1899
Guide to the windows of King's College Chapel. By M. R. James.
   (2 copies corrected.) 1899
Brahms's German Requiem. Feb. 28, 1901. 1901
Festival Thanksgiving Service, 11 June, 1901. Mendelssohn's "Elijah."
                                        1901
Dedication of new altar in Chapel, Advent Sunday. 1902
Register of Admissions, 1850–1900. By J. J. Withers. London, 1903
Letter to the Provost on the subject of the Reredos in the Chapel,
   by T. B. Carter. F° 1903
Handlist of trees and shrubs, grown in the gardens and grounds of
   King's College, Cambridge. By A. A. Tilley. 4° 1904
The Limit, or Nothing Personal. A satirical melodrametta by
   A. D. K[nox] and M. A. Y[oung], performed in King's. 1907
King's College, Cambridge. By C. R. Fay. 12° London, 1907
Bygone King's. By R. A. Austen Leigh. F° Eton, 1907

KING'S College.
List of the Incunabula in the library of King's College. By G. Chawner.   1908
See also Acts and Bills, 1823.
KING'S LYNN. *See* Lynn.
KINGSBRIDGE Grammar School.   Statement respecting G. F. Browne's refusal to give evidence on the examination of Kingsbridge Grammar School.   1882
KINGSBURY (T.L.)   On the connexion between the Prophetic, and the other evidences of Christianity.   (Norrisian Prize Essay for 1847.)   1847
KINGSLEY (C.)   Alton Locke.   3rd ed.   *London,* 1852
Phaethon.   3rd ed.   1859
The limits of exact science as applied to history.   An inaugural lecture.   1860
Ode...10 June, 1862, composed for the Installation of the Duke of Devonshire, Chancellor of the University.   1862
Mr Kingsley and Dr Newman.   A Correspondence on the question whether Dr Newman teaches that truth is no virtue ? *London,* 1864
What then does Dr Newman mean ?   3rd ed.   *London,* 1864
The Fens.   (*Good Words,* May, 1867.)
God's Feast.   A sermon preached for the Industrial School, Cambridge, March 7, 1869.   *London,* 1869
In Memoriam.   F. D. Maurice.   (*Macmillan's Mag.,* May, 1872.)

Sermon preached in Westminster Abbey, Jan. 31, 1875, being the Sunday after the funeral of C. Kingsley.   By A. P. Stanley.   *London,* 1875
See also Newman (J. H.).

KINGSTON (A.)   East Anglia and the Great Civil War.
London, 1897
KIPLING (T.)   The Articles of the Church of England proved not to be Calvinistic.   1802
Remarks on *The Articles,* etc.   By Academicus.   1802
Reply to Academicus.   By a Friend of Dr Kipling.   [Probably by Kipling himself.]   *London,* 1803
KIRKBY (J.)   *See* Barrow (I.).   The Usefulness of Mathematical Learning, 1734.
KIRKMAN (J.)   Introductory address to the Browning Society. 1881
KIRKPATRICK (A.F.)   Our hopes for the future.   A sermon preached before the University in Great St Mary's Church, Nov. 5, 1882.   1882
KNIGHT (S.) Sermon...at St Bridget's Church, London, 9 April, 1729.
(1729)
KNIGHT (W.)   The missionary secretariat of Henry Venn.
London, 1880
KNOWLES (C.)   *See* Smedley (E. A.).
KNOX (V.)   Liberal education ; or a practical treatise on the methods of acquiring useful and polite learning.   10th ed.   2 vols.
London, 1789

L

LABOUCHERE (H.) Statement in his own defence when accused of copying in the Previous Examination, April, 1852.   4° 1852

LABUTTE (R.) A French Grammar. 2nd ed.   1790
See also Fauchon (J.).

LADIES' Association in Aid of Young Servants. 4th, 6th, 8th, 11th, 13th, 14th, 15th, 16th, 17th, 19th, 28th, 30th, 31st, 32nd, 33rd Annual Report.   1872–1901

LADIES' Battle. Fought at Cambridge, Feb 23, 1881.   (1881)

LADIES' Book Society. Rules.   4° 1835

LADIES' Discussion Society. Rules, etc.   1887
Rules and Report.   1907

LADY Clare Magazine. Vols. 1–9. Lent Term 1902–Easter Term 1910.   4° 1902–1910

LADY Margaret Professorship of Divinity, 1895. Notices of candidates including that of A. J. Mason who was elected.   1895

LADY'S Preceptor. By a Gentleman of Cambridge. 4th ed.
London, 1752

LAELIA. A Comedy acted at Queens' College. Ed. G. C. Moore Smith.   1910

LAKE (P.) Syllabus of a course of lectures on Agricultural Geology.   1891

LAMB (J.) and Henslow (J.S.) Remarks upon the payment of the expenses of out-voters at an University election. (9 April, 27 April, 1826.)   1826
Observations...occasioned by *Remarks...*   1826
A sermon preached before the University on July 1, 1827, being Commencement Sunday.   1827
A Christian admonition to young students, delivered Nov. 17, 1833, in the Chapel of Corpus Christi College.   1833
Review of Dr Lamb's work on Hebrew Hieroglyphics. (*Camb. Univ. Mag.* for April, 1835.)
A collection of letters, etc. in the MS. library of Corpus Christi College, illustrative of the history of the University of Cambridge from 1500 to 1572.   *London*, 1838
See also Masters (R.).

LAMPETER College. Proposal to found, by Bishop of St David's, with Grace to grant £200 from the University Chest towards it, May 14, 1822.   F° 1822

LAND. Proposed sale of land, 1904. *See* Botanic Garden.

LANGLEY (J.N.) Sir Michael Foster. In Memoriam. (*Journal of Physiology.*)   (*London*) 1907

LANKESTER (E.R.)   The relation of Universities to medicine.
London, 1878
LANTERN of the Cam.   Nos. 1–3.   Feb.–April, 1871.   4° 1871
LATHAM (H.)   Considerations on the suggestions of the University
 Commissioners with respect to Fellowships and Scholarships. 1857
 —— Revised impression.   1857
On the establishment in Cambridge of a school of practical science.
(1859)
On the Report of the Syndicate appointed to consider the examina-
 tions for the Ordinary Degree of B.A.   1864
On the regulations for the competitive examination for the Civil
 Service in India.   [1865]
A sermon preached in the Chapel of Trinity Hall, March 13, 1870,
 the Sunday after the funeral of the Rev. T. Markby.   (1870)
On the propositions made by the Head Masters of schools to the
 University of Cambridge.   1871
 Letter in reply.   By Geo. Ridding.   *Winchester,* 1871
On Parts II. and VII. of the Report of the Syndicate on the Previous
 and General Examinations (which provide for making Greek or
 Latin optional).   1872
On a proposed amendment of the scheme for Pass Examinations.
1873
On the action of examinations considered as a means of selection.
1877

Sale catalogue of his furniture and books at Southacre.   1903

LATHAM (R.G.)   A grammatikal sketch of the Greek language.
1835
LAUGHTON (R.)   A sermon preached in King's College Chapel,
 Oct. 6, 1717.   4° 1717
 —— 2nd ed.   1717
LAURIE (S.S.)   Lectures on the rise and early constitution of Uni-
 versities.   *London,* 1886
LAW Society.   Rules.   1871
LAW (E.)   Discourse upon the life and character of Christ.   1749
LAWRENCE (T.J.)   Appeal for an International University Extension
 Congress, to be held at Cambridge, 20 Jan. 1894.   (1894)
LAWSON (M.)   A few exercises composed on various public occasions.
4° *London,* 1814
 Translation of a Latin Ode to Sculpture, written for one of Sir
 William Browne's Gold Medals in the University of Cambridge,
 by M. Lawson.   (By C. H. R.)   *Oxford,* 1816
 Strictures on the Rev. F. H. Maberley's account of the melancholy
 and awful end of Lawrence Dundas, of Trinity College.
London, 1818
LAY of the last Commemoration dinner.   By a disappointed guest.
 (Trinity College.)   1880
LAYARD (C.P.)   Charity.   (Seatonian Prize Poem for 1773.)
4° 1773

LAYARD (D.P.)   An account of the Somersham water in the County
of Huntingdon.   *London*, 1767
LAYS of Modern Oxford.   By Adon.   4º *London*, 1874
LEAFLETS of Local Lore.   *See* Cambridgeshire Cameos.
LEAKE (W.M.)   A brief memoir of the life and writings of
W. M. Leake.   By J. L. Marsden.   4º *London*, 1864
See also Fitzwilliam Museum, 1863–4, 1867.
LEATHES (S.M.)   *See* Grace Book A.
LE BAS (C.W.)   Proposals for prize to commemorate him, 10 Nov.
1848.   Fº (1848)
LE BAS Prize.   1849.   The Greek Kingdoms of Bactria...By C. B.
Scott.   1849
1856.   The influence of the revival of classical studies on English
literature.   By F. W. Farrar.   1856
1859.   The Goth and the Saracen.   By E. H. Fisher.   1859
LE CLERC (J.)   Judgment and censure of Bentley's Horace.
                                              London, 1713
LEE (S.)   A letter to Mr John Bellamy on his new translation of the
Bible.   1821
A vindication of certain strictures on a pamphlet [by R. Laurence]
entitled *Remarks*, etc. Oxford, 1820.   In answer to *A Reply*, etc.
Oxford, 1821.   1822
The duty of observing the Christian Sabbath, enforced in a sermon
preached before the University of Cambridge, June 20, 1833.
                                              London, 1833
Some remarks on the Dean of Peterborough's tract, entitled, "Thoughts
on the admission of persons, without regard to their religious
opinions, to certain degrees in the Universities of England."   1834
Dissent unscriptural and unjustifiable.   1834
A letter to Archdeacon Thorp.   *London*, 1845
A second letter to Archdeacon Thorp.   On symbolism.   *London*, 1845
LEEPER (A.)   A Scholar-Librarian (Henry Bradshaw).   (*Library
Assoc. of Australasia.*)   *Adelaide*, 1901
LEFROY (G.A.)   The leather-workers of Daryaganj.   (Camb.
Mission to Delhi.   Occasional Papers.)   1884
LEGAL Studies.   Fly-sheets relating thereto from 1856.   1856–
LEGISLATIVE Ignorance. An address to the V.-C., etc. *London*, 1837
LEGRAND (Martin), *pseud.*   *See* Rice (James).
LE GRICE (C.V.)   A prize declamation, spoken in Trinity College
Chapel, May 28, 1794.   1795
A general theorem for a ******* [Trinity] Coll. Declamation.
By —— With copious notes by Gronovius. [By C. V. Le Grice.]
                                                       1796
—— (2nd ed.)   *Penzance*, 1835
Analysis of Paley's Principles of moral and political philosophy.
7th ed.   *London*, 1820
An imitation of Horace's First Epistle.   *Penzance*, 1824
LEHMANN (R.C.)   In Cambridge Courts.   *London* [1892]
Jupiter, LL.D.   Written for performance at A.D.C.   (1894)

CL. C.   10

LEIGH.   *See* Austen Leigh.

LE KEUX (J.)   Proposals for publishing his views of Cambridge.
(1827)

Memorials of Cambridge.   With historical and descriptive accounts by Thomas Wright.   Nos. 1–6.   (Trinity College ; Christ's College.)   *London*, 1837–38

Memorials of Cambridge.   Ed. by T. Wright and H. L. Jones. 2 vols.   *London*, 1847

Memorials of Cambridge.   New ed. by Charles Henry Cooper. 3 vols.   1860–66

See also Farren, R., 1880; Oxford Handbook, 1875.

LENG (J.)   Sermon preached before the King at Newmarket, 16 April, 1699.   4° 1699

A sermon preached at the consecration of the Chappel of St Katherine's Hall, Sept. 1, 1704.   4° 1704

LEO, *pseud.   See* Pemberton (C.).

LEO (C.)   Examination of the fourteen verses selected from Scripture by Mr J. Bellamy as a specimen of his emendation of the Bible.
1817

LETTER.   Letter from a gentleman of the Isle of Ely...to Col. Roderick Mansel containing an account of the discovery of the pretended Presbyterian Plot at the Assizes at Wisbech...23 Sept. 1679.   F° *n.p.* (1679)

Letter from an Undergraduate to the Rev. *. C****** [W. Collier] M.A., Fellow of Trinity College, Cambridge.   4° *London*, 1792

Letter on the Celibacy of Fellows of Colleges.   *London*, 1794

Letter to a Friend upon the proposed addition to the Academical system of Education.   1848

Letter to a Member of the Senate of the University of Cambridge. By the author of Discourses to Academic youth [E. Pearson].   1799

Letter to a Member of the Senate of the University of London on the examination for B.A.   *London*, 1838

Letter to a Student on entering the University.   12° 1835

—— Another ed.   12° 1836

—— Another ed.   1849

Letter to [T. Chapman] the Author of a Further Inquiry into the Right of Appeal from the Chancellor...   [By J. Smith.]
London, 1752

Letter to the Author [W. S. Powell] of An Observation on the design of establishing annual examinations at Cambridge.   [1774 ?]

Letter to the Author [R. Robinson] of the History and Mystery of Good-Friday.   1782

Letter to the author [J. Jebb] of the proposal for the establishment of Public Examinations.   1774

Letter to the Electors of Cambridge touching...the Poor-Laws.   1837

Letter to the Electors of the University of Cambridge.
London, 1827

Letter to the Queen from a Lay Non-Resident Member of the Senate of the University of Cambridge.   *London*, 1831

LETTER.

Letter to the Rev. H. Marsh in confutation of his opinion, That the Dissenters are aiming at the subversion of the religious establishment of this country. By a Protestant Dissenter and a Layman.
London, 1813

Letter to the Rev. John Jebb, occasioned by his Short state of the reasons for a late resignation. *London*, 1776

Letter to the Rev. Richard Watson. [By W. Vincent.] *London*, 1780

Letter to the University of Cambridge, on a late resignation. By a Gentleman of Oxford. *London*, 1756

LETTERS from Academicus [Ch. Crawford] to Eugenius on various subjects. *London*, 1772

LETTERS from Cambridge illustrative of the studies, habits, and peculiarities of the University. [By E. S. Appleyard.] *London*, 1828

LETTERS from Italy and Vienna. [By W. Nind.] 1852

LETTERS of Peter Platitude on Cambridge and the Cantabs. Parts I., II. 1841–2

LETTICE (J.) The Conversion of St Paul. (Seatonian Prize Poem for 1764. 4° 1765

LEVER (T.) Sermons, 1550. Ed. by E. Arber. (English Reprints.) *London*, 1870

LEWIS (J.) Life of John Fisher, Bishop of Rochester. 2 vols. *London*, 1855

LEWIS (J.D.) Sketches of Cantabs. (Bowes 2161.) *London*, 1849
—— 2nd ed. *London*, 1850

Our College. Leaves from an Undergraduate's "Scribbling-Book." *London*, 1857

LEWIS (S.S.) The Library, Corpus Christi College. 1890
Three last sermons. 1891

Life. By A. S. Lewis. 1892

LEWIS (W.J.) Testimonials when a candidate for the Professorship of Mineralogy in the University of Cambridge. 1881

LEWKENOR (S.) A discourse...of all those citties wherein do flourish at this day priviledged Universities. 4° *London*, 1600

LEYS Fortnightly. Special number. Old Leysian Football Club, 1878–99. 1899

LEYS School. Speech Day, June, 1891. 1891

LIBERAL Club. Speech of Sir C. Russell, 26 Feb. 1890.
London, 1890
Speech of H. H. Asquith, 3 May, 1890. *London*, 1890
Fancy Fair in aid of Liberal Club, etc. Programme. Obl. 8° 1904

LIBERATION of Abd-el-Kader. An Ode. 1856

LIBRARY. Bibliothecae Cantabrigiensis ordinandae methodus. By Conyers Middleton. 4° 1723

Carmina ad nob. Thomam Holles Ducem de Newcastle inscripta cum Academiam Cantabrigiensem Bibliothecae restituendae causa inviseret Prid. Kal. Maias 1755. (+ Oratio...a Joanne Skynner.) F° 1755

LIBRARY.

Two poems presented to the Duke of Newcastle, Chancellor...
April, 1755, at the laying of the first stone of the new building
(East façade). By J. Marriott.   4° *London*, 1755
Poll for election of Librarian, 26 March, 1822. (J. Lodge, Magd.,
elected.)   1822
Notice of Grace to confirm Report of Warming Syndicate, 8 Dec.
1823.   F° 1823
Grace to suspend election of Librarian, in the event of Mr Lodge
being elected Protobibliothecarius, in order to make new regulations
for the office (21 May, 1828).   F° (1828)
Observations on the plans for the new Library. By a Member of the
first Syndicate [G. Peacock]. (1 Jan.)   1831
Reply to *Observations on the plans for the new Library*. By a
Member of both Syndicates [W. Whewell].   1831
An answer to *Observations on the plans for the new Library*.
Birmingham, 1831
Remarks on the replies to the *Observations on the plans for the new
Library*. By a Member of the first Syndicate [G. Peacock].
1831
A few remarks on the " New Library " question. By a Member of
neither Syndicate [H. Coddington].   1831
Letter to the Members of the Senate of the University of Cambridge
[on the plans for the University Library] (9 Feb.). By William
Wilkins.   1831
An appeal to the Senate, on the subject of the plans for the University
Library (15 April). By William Wilkins.   1831
Observations upon the Report made by a Syndicate appointed to
confer with the architects who were desired to furnish the Uni-
versity with designs for a new Library. By George Peacock.
1835
Subscriptions for building a new Library.   1836
Poll on the election of Librarian, April 17, 1845. (J. Power, Cla.,
elected.)   1845
Fly-sheets, reports, etc. relating to the Library from 1846.   1846–
Observations on some recent University Buildings, together with
remarks on the management of the Public Library and Pitt Press.
By F. Bashforth.   1853
A catalogue of the MSS. preserved in the Library of the University
of Cambridge. 5 vols. and Index.   1856–67
University Library extension. By G. Williams.   1862
A letter to the Senate on the proposal to transfer the charge of the
Principal Librarian's stipend from the University Chest to the
Library Subscription Fund. By J. E. B. Mayor. (18 Nov.) 1863
On the funds of the Library. By G. Williams. (21 Nov.)   1863
On the Library Catalogues. By J. B. Pearson. (2 Dec.)   1863
On the Library Catalogues. By J. E. B. Mayor. (9 Dec.)   1863
On the extension of the Library and the building of a new Divinity
School. By George Williams. (6 Dec.)   1864

LIBRARY.

Notes on the Statute and Ordinances affecting the Library. By the Librarian, J. E. B. Mayor. (6 Feb.) 1865

Statement by the Librarian, J. E. B. Mayor, on the Catalogue, etc. (18 Nov.) 1865

Statement made to the Syndics of the Library, 7 March, 1866, by the Librarian, J. E. B. Mayor. 1866

Notice by the Librarian of non-placet of a Grace for 14 April. [On the Library-tax.] 1866

Notes on the Statute and Ordinances affecting the Library. By the Librarian, J. E. B. Mayor. (Reissued 5 May, 1866.) 1866

Circular on the Library, May 30, 1866. By J. E. B. Mayor, in answer to Dr Cookson. 1866

A chronological list of Graces, etc. in the University Registrary which concern the University Library. By H. R. Luard. (3 copies, annotated by J. W. Clark.) 1870

List of current Foreign Periodicals received at the University Library. 1870

Report on the University Library, 1880, 1881. By H. R. Tedder. 4° 1880–1

The University Library. By H. Bradshaw. 1881

Design for a library, by E. Magnússon, 1885. 1885

Election of F. J. H. Jenkinson, M.A., Trin. Coll., as Librarian. Statement and list of supporters. (3 issues.) Fo 1889

Catalogue of a Collection of Books on Logic presented to the Library by John Venn, Sc.D. (Bulletin. Extra Series.) 1889

The University Library, Cambridge. [By C. Sayle.] 1895

—— (2nd ed.) 1905

Early English Printed Books in the University Library, Cambridge. By C. Sayle. 4 vols. and Suppl. 1900–7

Report on organization, with a complete collection of the fly-sheets down to 21 Nov. 1901, when the Grace for roofing the East Quadrangle was rejected. Together with other papers on the new entrance, the alterations in Cockerell's building, and the question of adapting the East Room for a reading-room, down to Feb. 1906. 1901–6

Catalogue of the Adams Collection of Early Printed and other books. (Bulletin. Extra Series.) 1902

Annual Report for years ending Dec. 31, 1902, 1903, 1904, 1905, 1906, 1907, 1908, 1909. 4° 1903–10

List of current Foreign Periodicals. 1904

Organisation and methods. By H. G. Aldis. (*Lib. Assoc. Record.*) (*London*, 1905)

Notes for Readers. 12° 1905

First (—second) list of books wanted to complete sets in the Acton Library. 1905, 1910

Library Bulletin. Extra Series. Acton Coll. Spain and Portugal. 1908

—— —— Germany, Austria, Hungary. 1908

LIBRARY.

The University Library at Cambridge. By C. Sayle. (*Country Life*, 24 Sept. 1910.)

LIBRARY Association. Twenty-eighth Annual Meeting at Cambridge. Proceedings and papers.   *London*, 1905

—— Programme, invitations, press cuttings, etc.   1905

See also Aldis (H. G.); Bradshaw (H.), 1882; Jenkinson (F. J. H.); Pink (J.).

LICENCES. Vice-Chancellor's notice respecting licences for Alehouses, 16 Feb. 1847.   F° 1847

LIGHT Blue. A Cambridge University Magazine. Vols. 1–4. (Bowes 2464.)   1866–70

LIGHT Blue. Incorporated with the Light Green. Nos. 1–4. May, 1873–May, 1875. (Bowes 2611.)   1873–75

LIGHT Green. Nos. 1, 2. (Bowes 2588.)   1872

Light Greens. A Freshman's Diary, etc. No. 1.   1875

Reprints from the Light Green, Nos. 1, 2; and Light Greens, No. 1.   1882

See also Hamlet, 1882; Hilton (A. C.).

LIGHTFOOT (J.B.) On the Celibacy question.   1857

On the Report of the Syndicate appointed to regulate the examination of students not members of the University.   1860

Rejoinder to Mr Roberts, 8 March, 1860.   1860

Christian Progress. Sermon at Commemoration, Trin. Coll., Dec. 15, 1860.   1861

In memory of William Whewell. A sermon preached March 18, 1866.   1866

A sermon preached before the University Church Society.   1872

Sermon preached in Trin. Coll. Chapel, Sexagesima Sunday, 1873.   1873

On the Grace for abolishing compulsory attendance at Professors' lectures.   1877

Bought with a price. A sermon preached in Great St Mary's Church, on the first Sunday in Lent, 1879.   1879

Address at re-opening of the chapel at Auckland Castle, Aug. 1, 1888.   *Bishop Auckland* (1888)

Sermon by B. F. Westcott at J. B. Lightfoot's consecration to the see of Durham.   1879

Report of meeting for procuring a memorial in Cambridge of J. B. Lightfoot, 29 Jan. 1890. (*Reporter.*)

LIMIT (The), or Nothing Personal. A satirical melodrametta by A. D. K[nox] and M. A. Y[oung] performed in King's Coll.   1907

LINACRE (T.) *See* Bowes (R.); Osler (W.).

LINWOOD (W.) Remarks on the present state of Classical scholarship and distinctions in the University of Oxford.   *Oxford*, 1845

LION. Nos. 1–3. May, 1858–May, 1859. (Bowes 2311.)   1858–9

LISTEN, or a few words to Undergraduates.   *London*, 1862

LISTER (J.J.)   Letter of application and testimonials as candidate for
    Professorship of Natural History in the Univ. of Aberdeen.   1899
LITLINGTON.   *See* Acts and Bills, 1828.
LITTLEPORT.   Full and correct Report of the Trials for Rioting
    at Ely and Littleport, May, 1816.   *London*, 1816
LIVEING (G. D.)   Professors' Lectures.   (1877)
The University of Cambridge.   (*Brit. Med. Journ.*, June 19, 1897.)
                                                   (*London*, 1897)
Spencer Compton Cavendish, Duke of Devonshire, 1833–1908.
                                                         (1908)

Portrait and bust of Prof. Liveing.   Subscribers.   4° (1901)

LIVINGSTONE (D.)   Cambridge lectures.   Ed. by William Monk.
                                                           1858
——— 2nd ed.   1860
David Livingstone and Cambridge.   A record of three meetings in
    the Senate House.   1857, 1859, 1907.   *London*, 1908
LLOYD (T.)   An essay on the literary beauties of the Scriptures.
                                                        4° 1784
LLOYD (W.)   Chronological account of the life of Pythagoras.
                                                   London, 1699
LOCAL Examinations.   Examination of students who are not
    members of the University.   First (–fifteenth) Annual Report of
    Syndicate.   1859–73
Regulations, 1863, 1869.   1863–9
Proposed admission of girls.   Memorial.   *n.p.* (1864)
Report of a discussion on the proposed admission of girls.
                                                   London, 1864
The proposed admission of girls to the University Local Examinations.
    Committee's statement.   *London* [1864]
Reasons for the extension of the University Local Examinations to
    girls.   *n.p.* [1864]
Results of the University Local Examinations in Liverpool.
                                                   n.p. 1865
Proposed admission of girls.   (Repr. from *The Museum and Engl.
    Journ. of Education.*)   *London*, 1865
Examination for women.   Report of Syndicate, 1869, 1870, 1871.
                                                        1869–71
——— Examination Papers and Regulations, 1870–1, 1871–2.   1871–2
Examination Papers and Regulations, 1869–70, 1870–71, 1881–2.
                                                        1870–82
Class Lists.   Dec. 1868, Dec. 1869, Dec. 1870 (Boys only).
                                                        1869–71
——— Dec. 1871.   1872
——— Dec. 1873.   1874
——— Dec. 1874.   (Girls only.)   1875
Regulations for the promotion of home study.   1888
LOCAL Government in Cambridge.   1885
    Fly-sheets relating to Local Government in Cambridge, 1884–1888

LOCAL Lectures. Report to the Syndicate for conducting lectures in
populous places. By W. M. Ede. 1875
Report of a Conference in the Senate House, 9 March, 1887. 1887
Syllabus of lectures on English poets of the modern school. By
G. C. Moore Smith. 1889
Report of Syndicate on course of study in the Long Vacation of
1891. 1891
Syllabus of a course of six lectures on elementary principles of
Chemistry. By R. S. Morrell. 1891
Syllabus of a course of twelve lectures on elementary principles of
Chemistry. By J. Percival. 1891
Syllabus of a course of twelve lectures on plant life. By W. D.
Bottomley. 1891
Syllabus of a course of twelve lectures on plant and animal life. By
T. B. Wood. 1891
Syllabus of a course of twelve lectures on Agricultural Chemistry.
By R. H. Adie. 1891
Syllabus of a course of lectures on Agricultural Geology. By P. Lake.
1891
Syllabus of a course of lectures on injurious Insects. By C. Warburton.
1891
Syllabus of a course of lectures on Experimental Mechanics. By
T. H. Easterfield. 1891
Syllabus of a course of lectures on Modern France. By G. Lowes
Dickinson. 1891
Third Annual Report of Local Lectures Association. 1891
Report on instruction in technical science given under the County
Councils of Devonshire and Norfolk. 1891
Programme of fourth Summer meeting to be held at Cambridge,
29 July–26 Aug. 1893. 1893
—— 2nd ed. 1893
Report of the fourth Summer meeting, 29 July–26 Aug. 1893.
1893
Table of Lectures, etc. for fourth Summer meeting at Cambridge,
29 July–26 Aug. 1893. 1893
Work of the Universities for the nation. Inaugural lecture at
Guildhall, 29 July, 1893. By R. C. Jebb. 1893
Syllabus of a course of twelve lectures on the making and sharing of
wealth. By A. Milner. 1895
Programme of Summer meeting to be held at Cambridge, 30 July–
24 Aug. 1896. 1896
Report of a Conference in the Senate House, 6, 7 July, 1898. 1898
Syllabus of a course of ten lectures on the beginnings of modern
music. By Mrs J. M. E. Brownlow. 1899
Time-table of Summer meeting, Aug. 2–Aug. 27, 1900. 1900
Programme of Summer meeting, Aug. 2–Aug. 27, 1900. 1900
Syllabus of a course of lectures on Monastic life in the Middle Ages.
By D. H. S. Cranage. 1900
Time-table of Summer meeting, Pt 2, Aug. 14–26. 1902

LOCAL Lectures.

Programme of Summer meeting, Aug. 1–26.   1902
Syllabuses of Lectures, etc.   1902
Time-table of Summer meeting, Aug. 2–28.   1906
Time-table of Summer meeting, July 18–Aug. 13.   1908

LOCK (J.B.) On the planning of collegiate buildings. (*Journ. Roy. Inst. Brit. Architects.*)   4° *London*, 1904

LOCKE (J.) A syllabus of Locke's Essay on the human understanding. 7th ed.   *London*, 1820
See also Grotius (H.).

LODGE (J.) Oratio Procuratoris senioris (4 Nov. 1833).   1833

LODGING Houses. Alphabetical list of persons licensed by the V.-C., 1819.   (1819)
Request of Vice-Chancellor and Proctors that Tutors will examine, 13 May, 1823.   4° 1823

LOITERER. 1789–90. 2 vols.   *Oxford*, 1790
—— Another periodical. Vol. I. Nos. 1–8. Nov. 12–Dec. 31, 1796.
                                                 n.p. 1796

LONG (R.) The music speech spoken at the Public Commencement, July 6, 1714. 3rd ed.   *London* (1714)
Commencement Sermon. 30 June, 1728 (afternoon).   4° 1728
—— Another ed.   1728
The rights of Churches and Colleges defended. By Dicaiophilus Cantabrigiensis [i.e. R. Long].   *London*, 1731
Two music speeches at Cambridge spoken at Public Commencements in the years 1714 and 1730. By R. Long and John Taylor. Ed. by John Nichols.   *London*, 1819

LORD (H.W.) The Highway of the Seas in time of War.   1862

LORT (M.) *See* Projecte, 1769.

LOSEBY (P.J.) Elijah. (Seatonian Prize Poem for 1901.)   1902
Barnabas. (Seatonian Prize Poem for 1907.)   1907

LOTOS Club. A Wreath of Songs. By the Cambridge Lotos Club.
                                                         1880
New songs. By the Cambridge Lotos Club. (Bowes 2747.) 1881

LOVE (R.) The Watchman's Watchword. Sermon...30 March, 1641.   4° 1642
Oratio habita in Academia Cantabrigiensi in solenni magnorum Comitiorum die, anno Domini MDCLX.   4° 1660
Oratio habita...anno 1660. 2ª ed., cui adjungitur Oratiuncula qua Dr Love...Regem allocutus est, cum legati Acad. Cant. Aulam Regiam primum gratulatum accederent...   4° 1660

LOWNDES (G.A.) The history of Hatfield Broad Oak. (*Trans. Essex Arch. Soc.*, N.S., I.)   *n.p.* 1874

LOWTH (R.) Life of William of Wykeham, Bp of Winchester.
                                                Oxford, 1777

LUARD (H.R.) Porson. (*Cambridge Essays.*)   *London*, 1857
On the Proposal that the Fellowships [of Trinity College] be open to all B.As of the College who have obtained a place in the first class of any Tripos.   (1857)

LUARD (H.R.).
Remarks on the Cambridge University Commissioners' draft of
proposed new statutes for Trinity College.   1858
Remarks on the present condition and proposed restoration of the
Church of Great St Mary's.   1860
On the proposed title A.C., to be given to those who pass the Middle
Class examination.   (1860)
Suggestions on (1) the election of the Council; (2) the duties of the
Vice-Chancellor; (3) the establishment of a Historical Tripos.
1866
A chronological list of documents in the University Registry which
concern the University Library. (3 copies, annotated by J. W.
Clark.)   1870
The Victory that overcometh the World. Sermon on death of
F. D. Maurice.   1872
Sermon on recovery of Prince of Wales, Feb. 27, 1872.   1872
A list of the documents in the University Registry from 1266 to 1544
(*C. A. S.*)   1876
On the relations between England and Rome during the reign of
Henry III.   1877

Funeral sermon for H. R. Luard, by J. E. B. Mayor.   12° (1891)
Catalogue of his library, sold Nov. 1891.   *London*, 1891
Luard Memorial series. *See* Grace Book.
See also Graduati, 1873, 1884; Rud (E.), Diary, 1860; Shakespeare,
Richard the Second, 1860.

LUCKOCK (H.M.) In piam memoriam Jacobi Russell, Episc.
Eliensis.   *n.p.* (1885)
LUCY (E.) A Loyal Whig's Reflections upon the late Elections.
1886
LUDERE quæ vellem Calamo.   (*London*, 1822)
LUDLAM (W. and T.) Remarks by T. Ludlam on the scurrilous
reflections cast upon W. and T. Ludlam, by Dr Milner, Master of
Queens' Coll.   *Leicester* (1801)
LUND (T.) An exposure of a recent attempt at book-making [Tod-
hunter's Algebra] in the University of Cambridge. 4° *London*, 1858
Reply to above, by I. Todhunter.   1858
LUSHINGTON (F.) Points of War.   1854
LUSHINGTON (H. and F.) Two battle-pieces.   1855
La Nation boutiquière and other Poems.—Points of War.   1855
LUXMOORE (H.E.) Noblesse oblige. A plea for the preservation
of Eton buildings.   4° *Eton*, 1885
Some Views and Opinions of Sparrow on House-tops, extracted by
Peccator Maximus [H. E. Luxmoore].   4° *Eton*, 1885
LYNAM (C.) Architectural notes on Thorney Abbey.   (*Journ. Brit.
Arch. Assoc.*, xxxv.)   (*London*, 1878)
LYNN. The history of the...navigation of the port of King's-Lyn, and
of Cambridge. By John Armstrong.   F° *London*, 1725
—— Another ed.   F° *London*, 1766

LYNN   LYTTELTON   155
LYNN.

The history of Lynn. By William Richards. 2 vols. *Lynn,* 1812

The making of Lynn. A lecture. By E. M. Beloe. *Lynn,* 1891

LYONS (I.) An Hebrew Grammar. 1735

Observations relating to Scripture history. 1768

LYSONS (D.) and Lysons (S.) Magna Britannia. Cambridgeshire.
4° *London,* 1808

LYTE (H.C.M.) A history of Eton College, 1440-1875. *London,* 1875

—— New ed. 1440–1884. *London,* 1889

A history of the University of Oxford from the earliest times to the year 1530. *London,* 1886

LYTTELTON (A.T.) List of subscribers to his portrait, by Furse, given to Selwyn College, 3 Dec. 1894. 1894

Order of Service at his funeral, 24 Feb. 1903. 1903

LYTTELTON (E.) Athletics in Public Schools. (*Nineteenth Century,* Jan. 1880.)

M

MABERLEY (F.H.) The melancholy and awful death of Lawrence Dundas, an undergraduate of Trinity College, Cambridge.
London, 1818
—— 2nd ed. *London*, 1818
    An answer to the Rev. F. H. Maberley's pamphlet on the death of Lawrence Dundas. 2nd ed. *London*, 1818
    Remarks on the Maberleyan controversy. By R. C. *London*, 1818
    See also Lawson (M.).
MACALISTER (A.) Testimonials. Candidate for the Professorship of Anatomy in Univ. of Dublin. *Dublin*, 1879
    Report on the Oxford Museums, 14 March, 1891. *n.p.* 1891
    On the arrangement, etc. of the Oxford Museum of Science.
n.p. 1891
    History of the study of Anatomy in Cambridge. Lecture. 1891
    James Macartney. A memoir. *London*, 1900
MACALISTER (*Sir* D.) Testimonials. Physician to Addenbrooke's Hospital. 1884
    Biographical notice of Prof. J. C. Adams. (*Eagle*, March, 1892.) 1892
    Advanced Study and Research in the University of Cambridge. 1896
    Echoes. (Verses.) 1907
MACANDREW Collection of British Shells. *See* Cooke (A. H.).
MACARTNEY (J.) Memoir. By Alex. MacAlister. *London*, 1900
MACAULAY (J.) Prof. Adam Sedgwick. (*Leisure Hour*, October, 1890.)
MACBETH (R.W.) In the Fens. (*Engl. Illustr. Mag.*, Nov. 1883.)
McBRYDE (J.) The Story of a Troll-Hunt. (Ed. by M. R. James.)
4° 1904
McCLELLAN (J.B.) The Fourth Nicene Canon. 1870
MACFARLANE (C.) The Camp of Refuge. 2 vols. in 1.
12° *London*, 1844
MACKENZIE (C.F.) Memoir. By Harvey Goodwin. 1864
MACKENZIE (F.) Observations on the construction of the roof of King's College Chapel, Cambridge. 4° *London*, 1840
MACKENZIE (F.L.) Early death not premature. A memoir of F. L. M. By C. P. Miles. *London*, 1856
—— 4th ed. *London*, 1863
MACLAURIN (C.) Account of Sir I. Newton's Philosophical Discoveries. Publ. by P. Murdoch. 4° *London*, 1748

MACLEANE (D.)   Pembroke College, Oxford.   (College histories.)
London, 1900
MACLEOD (H.D.)   Thoughts on the forthcoming election of a
Professor of Political Economy.   1863
Address, Oct. 8, 1863.—Poll, 27 Nov. 1863.   F° 1863
MACMILLAN (A.)   Letters.   Edited by G. A. Macmillan.
London, 1908
MACMILLAN (D.)   Memoir.   By Thomas Hughes.   *London*, 1882
MACRAY (W.D.)   Notes from the muniments of St Mary Magdalen
College, Oxford, from the twelfth to the seventeenth century.
Oxford, 1882
See Parnassus Plays.
McTAGGART (J.M.E.)   Dare to be wise.   Address before the
" Heretics."   1910
MADAN (F.)   Rough list of manuscript materials relating to the
history of Oxford.   *Oxford*, 1887
See also Neale (T.).
MAGDALENE College.   Magdalene College.   By E. K. Purnell.
(College histories.)   *London*, 1904
Magdalene College Magazine.   Nos. 1–4.   1909–10
MAGNÚSSON (E.)   Design for a Library.   1885
MAGPIE and Stump Debating Society.   New Court Circulars, March,
1892.   4° 1892
Verbatim Report of mock trial held 2 Dec. 1892.   1893
Comic handbill, 21 Nov. 1896.   1896
Comic poster, 24 Nov. 1899.   1899
Poster " Vote for Gordon."   n.d.
MAGRATH (J. R.)   University Reform.   *Oxford*, 1876
MAINE (*Sir* H.J.S.)   The early history of the property of married
women.   *Manchester*, 1873
The effects of observation of India on modern European thought.
(Rede Lecture.)   *London*, 1875
Plato.   Unsuccessful Prize Poem, 1843.   (Reprinted by J. W. Clark.)
1894
MAINWARING (J.)   Sermon...29 May, 1775.   4° 1775
Sermon...18 May, 1776.   4° 1776
Sermon...30 Nov. 1777.   4° 1778
Sermon...3 May, 1795.   4° 1795
MAITLAND (F.W.)   Why the history of English law is not
written.   Inaugural lecture.   *London*, 1888
Township and Borough.   1898
The Life and Letters of Leslie Stephen.   *London*, 1906

Bibliography, by A. L. Smith.   *Oxford*, 1907
Report of the proceedings at a meeting for promoting a memorial to
F. W. M., 1 June, 1907.   (*Reporter.*)
F. W. Maitland.   Two Lectures and a Bibliography.   By A. L. Smith.
Oxford, 1908
See Barnwell, 1907 ; Borough Charters, 1901.

MALDEN (H.)   An account of King's College Chapel, in Cambridge.
(Pp. 91.   9 errata.)   1769
—— Another state.   (Pp. 96.   No errata.)   1769
MALDEN (H.), *Trin.*   On the origin of Universities and Academical
Degrees.   *London*, 1835
MALDEN (H.E.)   Trinity Hall.   (College histories.)   *London*, 1902
MALTBY (E.)   A sermon preached before the University of Cam-
bridge, June 29, 1806, being Commencement Sunday.   4° 1806
MANDAT-GRANCEY (*Baron* E. de)   Chez John Bull.   *Paris*, 1895
MANDELL (W.)   Preparation for death...A sermon preached in
Queens' College, Cambridge, on occasion of the death of B. A.
Keck, Scholar of that Society.   1815
Blessedness of dying in the Lord.   A sermon preached in Queens'
College on occasion of the death of King George III.   1820
The Victorious Christian's Reward.   A sermon preached before the
University of Cambridge, 19 Jan. 1823.   1823
The vanity of man as mortal.   A sermon on occasion of the death
of H.R.H. the Duke of York, preached in the parish church of
Histon, Jan. 21, 1827.   1827
Youthful religion recommended.   A sermon preached in the Chapel
of Queens' College, Cambridge, Nov. 18, 1832.   1832
The example of eminent Christians a pattern for imitation.   A
sermon preached...Nov. 20, 1836, on occasion of the death of the
Rev. C. Simeon.   1836
MANNING (C.R.)   Monuments of the De Burgh and Ingoldsthorpe
families, in Burgh Green Church.   (*Arch. Journ.*, xxxiv.)
(*London*, 1877)
MANNING (G.W.)   Whittlesey revisited, with a special reference to
the restored church of St Andrew.   *Whittlesey*, 1874
MANNINGHAM (T.)   Concio...Jul. 3, 1724.   4° *Londini*, 1724
MANSEL (H.L.)   Scenes from an unfinished drama entitled Phron-
tisterion, or Oxford in the 19th century.   4th ed.   *Oxford*, 1852
—— 5th ed.   *Oxford*, 1861
Examination of F. D. Maurice's Strictures on the Bampton Lectures
of 1858.   *London*, 1859
MANSEL (W.L.)   Gulielmum Lort Mansel, A.M. Oratorem pub-
licum Cantabrigiensem, servuli sui versicoloris in Anglia jam
commorantis diutius negligentem, iambo armatus proprio compellat
Psittacus Pseudo-Archilochæus.   (Signed T. M., Nov. 1793.)
4° *n.p.* (1793)
MANSFIELD (J.)   Petition to the Chancellor, 15 July, 1799.
F° 1799
MAPLETOFT (J.)   *See* Clare College, 1746, 1748, and 1755.
MARCUS (O.C.)   Testimonials.   1864
MARGARET, *Countess of Richmond and Derby.*   Funeral sermon.
By Bishop Fisher.   Ed. by T. Baker.   *London*, 1708
—— —— Ed. by J. Hymers.   1840
Life.   By Caroline A. Halsted.   *London*, 1839
Memoir.   By C. H. Cooper.   1874

MARILLIER (H.C.)   University Magazines and their makers.   (Odd
  Volumes opuscula, XLVII.)   12º *London*, 1899
  —— Another ed.   12º *London*, 1902
MARKBY (T.)   Funeral sermon, by H. Latham.   (1870)
MARLOWE (C.)   The Tragical History of Dr Faustus, as performed
  at Cambridge by the Elizabethan Stage Soc., 1 Nov. With
  programme.   *London*, 1904
MARR (J.E.)   The classification of the Cambrian and Silurian rocks.
  (Sedgwick Prize Essay.)   1883
  The earth history of the remote past compared with that of recent
  times.   1886
  Marr (J.E.) and Shipley (A.E.)   Handbook to the Natural History
  of Cambridgeshire.   1904
MARRIOTT (C.)   Letter to...W. E. Gladstone...on some of the
  provisions of the Oxford University Bill.   *Oxford*, 1854
MARRIOTT (C.H.)   A glance at Cambridge Undergraduates.
  2nd ed.   1890
MARRIOTT (*Sir* J.)   Two poems presented to his Grace the Duke of
  Newcastle, Chancellor...April, 1755.   4º *London*, 1755
  Poems written chiefly at the University of Cambridge ; together with
  a Latin Oration.   *n.p.* 1760(–1)
  The rights and privileges of both the Universities and of the Uni-
  versity of Cambridge in particular defended...Also an Argument in
  the case of the Colleges of Christ and Emmanuel.   1769
MARSDEN (J.H.)   Two introductory lectures delivered in the
  University of Cambridge.   1852
  Memoir of W. M. Leake.   4º *London*, 1864
MARSH (F.H.)   Inaugural Lecture as Professor of Surgery.   1904
MARSH (H.)   The authenticity of the five Books of Moses con-
  sidered.   4º 1792
  Letters to Archdeacon Travis, in vindication of one of the translator's
  notes to Michaelis's Introduction, etc.   *Leipzig*, 1795
  A Dissertation on the origin and composition of our three first canonical
  Gospels.   1801
  Letters to the anonymous author [J. Randolph] of Remarks on
  Michaelis and his Commentator.   *London*, 1802
  An Illustration of the hypothesis proposed in the Dissertation on the
  origin and composition of our three first Canonical Gospels. 1803
  A defence of the Illustration of the hypothesis proposed in the
  Dissertation on the origin...of the Gospels.   1804
  Memoir of Thomas Jones.   1808
  A course of lectures [on Divinity].   Part 1.   1809
  A letter to the conductor of the Critical Review on the subject of
  Religious Toleration.   1810
  A course of lectures [on Divinity].   4 parts in 1 vol.   (Pts. 1, 2 are
  of 2nd ed.)   1810–16
  Address to the Senate...occasioned by the proposal to introduce in
  this place an Auxiliary Bible Society, 25 Nov. 1811.   (Farish's
  Report, p. 56.)   1812

MARSH (H.).

Letter to H. M., occasioned by his Address to the Senate.   By
N. Vansittart.   *London*, 1811
—— Another ed.   (Farish's Report, p. 61.)   1812
The question examined, whether the friends of the Duke or
Gloucester...are the enemies of the Church.   1811
Remarks submitted to the readers of Dr Marsh's pamphlet.   1811
A defence of The question examined...   1811
A Vindication of Dr Bell's System of Tuition, in a series of letters.
                                                     London, 1811
A letter to the Hon. N. Vansittart.   Being an answer to his second
letter on the British and Foreign Bible Society.   *London*, 1812
An inquiry into the consequences of neglecting to give the Prayer
Book with the Bible.   1812
—— 2nd ed.   *London*, 1812
—— 4th ed.   *London*, 1812
A history of the translations which have been made of the Scriptures...
                                                     London, 1812
A course of lectures [on Divinity].   Part 3.   1813
A letter to the Rev. Peter Gandolphy, in confutation of the opinion
that the vital principle of the Reformation has been lately conceded
to the Church of Rome.   1813
A letter to the Rev. H. M., in confutation of his opinion, That the
Dissenters are aiming at the subversion of the religious establish-
ment of this country, in order to possess its honours and emoluments
etc.   By a Protestant Dissenter, and a Layman.   *London*, 1813
A letter of explanation to the Dissenter and Layman, who has lately
addressed himself to the author on the views of the Protestant
Dissenters.   1813
A reply to the strictures of the Rev. I. Milner.   1813
—— 2nd ed.   1813
A letter to the Rev. C. Simeon, in answer to his pretended con-
gratulatory address, in confutation of his various mis-statements,
etc.   1813
A second letter to the Rev. C. Simeon, in confutation of his various
mis-statements, etc.   1813
A sermon preached before the University of Cambridge on Commence-
ment Sunday, July 4, 1813.   1813
A course of lectures [on Divinity].   Part 4.   1816
A Charge delivered at his primary visitation, Aug. 1817.   1817
A course of lectures [on Divinity].   Part 6.   1822
See also Bible Society; Clarke (E. D.); Gandolphy (P.); Milner (I.);
Simeon (C.).

MARSH (W.)   Remarks on the University system of education as
affected by the adoption of the late Syndicate Report.   (2 editions.)
                                                          1848
Remarks addressed to the Studies Syndicate.   1853

MARSHALL (A.)   A plea for the creation of a curriculum in
Economics and associated branches of Political Science.   1902

MARSHALL (A.).

Selection of letters recommending an Economics Tripos.   1903

The new Cambridge curriculum in Economics.   *London,* 1903

Introduction to the tripos in Economics and associated branches of Political Science.   1906

MARSHALL (A.H.) The "A.D.C." (*Pall Mall Magazine,* Aug. and Sept. 1896.)

Peter Binney, Undergraduate.   *London,* 1899

MARSHALL (A.M.) Account of his death. By Joseph Collier. (*Owens Coll. Union Mag.,* N.S., No. 2.)   4° *Manchester,* 1894

MARSHALL (B.A.) Byzantium and other Poems.   1831

MARTIN (B.) The Natural History of England. Cambridgeshire. *London* [1763 ?]

MARTIN (F.) On the tenure of the Lucasian Professorship with a lay-fellowship.   1857

On sizarships and subsizarships at Trinity College.   1857

On Mr Clark's proposal 1. That the vacant sizarships be competed for by persons not yet resident. 2. That the subsizarships be abolished, etc.   1857

Remarks on the...passage in Bp Monk's life of Dr Bentley (p. 610, 4to ed. ; Vol. II. p. 352, 8vo ed.) relating to words occurring in the 40th Chapter of the Statutes of Trinity College.   1857

Table of students who were matriculated and who took the B.A. degree...in Trinity College...1831–1840.   1862

On composition for annual payments to the University, College, and Town.   1866

MARTYN (H.) Memoir. By John Sargent. 3rd ed. *London,* 1819

—— 10th ed.   *London,* 1830

Henry Martyn. A sermon by H. M. Butler, 17 Oct. 1887.   1887

MARTYN (J.) The first lecture of a course of Botany ; being an introduction to the rest.   *London,* 1729

Memoirs of J. Martyn and of Thomas Martyn, Professors of Botany in the University of Cambridge. By G. C. Gorham.   *London,* 1830

MARTYN (T.) Chronological series of engravers.   1770

Catalogus Horti Botanici Cantabrigiensis. (+ Mantissa.)   1771–2

Elements of Natural History.   1775

Thirty-eight plates, with explanations, intended to illustrate Linnæus's System of Vegetables.   *London,* 1799

Rousseau's Letters on the elements of botany. Transl. with additional Letters by T. Martyn. 8th ed.   *London,* 1815

MARY'S (St) the Great. Selection of sacred music to be performed, 28 June, 1811.   (1811)

Anthem by F. A. Rawdon, performed...30 June, 1811.   (1811)

Fly-sheets, notices, etc. from 1828.   1828–

St Mary's Chimes. No. 1. [By R. W. Belt.]   1840

An apology for standing during the singing at Gt St Mary's Church.   (1840)

Great St Mary's and the Union, or shall we stand or sit?   1840

MARY'S (St) the Great.

    Observations on *Great St Mary's and the Union.*   1840
    Letter to the Author of *Great St Mary's and the Union.*   1840
    Why should we stand ?   Letter...   1840
    Don't you think so ?   Answer to above.   1840

Annals of the Church of St Mary the Great.   By E. Venables.
                                              London, 1856

Reasons why the University should not surrender its jurisdiction with respect to Great St Mary's Pulpit.   By C. Hardwick.   1857

Plea for University Sermons on Sunday mornings.   [By T. H. Candy.]   (1858)

The Morning University Sermon.   By J. C. Franks.   (1858)

Remarks on the present condition and proposed restoration of the Church of Great St Mary's.   By H. R. Luard.   1860

On the proposed alterations in Great St Mary's Church.   By W. Whewell.   1860

A sermon preached before the University of Cambridge, Feb. 2, 1864, at the re-opening of Great St Mary's Church.   By J. A. Jeremie.   1864

Suggested alterations.   By W. Cunningham.   1891

Accounts for repairs, 6 Jan. 1894.   1894

MARY'S (St) the Less.   Annals of the Church of St Mary the Less.   By J. W. Clark.   (*Ecclesiologist*, Oct. 1857.)

    Form of service for opening new vestries, etc.   1892

    Appeal for funds to pay off building debt, March, 1894.   1894

MASON (A.J.)   *See* Lady Margaret Professorship, 1895.

MASON (G.E.)   Steetley Chapel, 2 June, 1883.   *Worksop,* 1883

    Claudia.   A tragedy.   *London,* 1897

MASON (J.)   John the Baptist.   (Seatonian Prize Poem for 1868.) 1868

MASON (P.H.)   Strictures upon an article (signed C. B. S[cott]) in No. 4 of the Cambridge Journal of Classical and Sacred Philology.   1855

    Letters on various subjects.   Letter 1.   On supposed cruelties of 2 Sam. XII. 31.   1887

MASON (W.)   Ode performed in the Senate House, 1 July, 1749, at Installation of the Duke of Newcastle.   4° 1749

    Odes.   4° 1756

    Odes.   2nd ed.   4° 1756

    Memoirs of W. Whitehead.   (Whitehead's *Plays and Poems,* 3.)   12° *York,* 1788

MASSEY (J.)   A catalogue of paintings, drawings, etc. bequeathed to the University by Daniel Mesman in 1834.   1835

    —— Another ed.   1846

MASTERS (R.)   List of names [etc.] of all...members of Corpus Christi College.   With proposals for printing the history of the College.   (Dec. 1, 1749 and March 1, 1749–50.)   4° 1750

The history of the College of Corpus Christi in the University of Cambridge.   4° 1753

    —— Large Paper copy.   4° 1753

MASTERS (R.)
Memoirs of the life of T. Baker, from the papers of Z. Grey.   With
Catalogue of his MS. collections.   1784
Short account of...Waterbeach.   *n.p.* 1795
History of the College of Corpus Christi, Cambridge.   With con-
tinuation by John Lamb.   4° 1831.
MATHEMATICAL Tripos.   Report of the Syndicate suggesting
changes in the Mathematical Tripos, 4 June, 1827.   F° 1827
Report of Syndicate appointed to consider the possibility of corre-
spondence between Mathematical and Classical examinations,
25 Feb. 1843.   F° 1843
Fly-sheets etc. relating to the Mathematical Tripos, from 1846.
                                                      1846–
The Mathematical Tripos.   By H. A. Morgan.   1871
Letters to the Mathematical Tripos Syndicate, Oct. 1877.   By
W. W. R. Ball.   4° 1877
The Mathematical Tripos.   By H. W. Watson.   *London,* 1877
The origin and history of the Mathematical Tripos.   By W. W. R.
Ball.   1880
The Mathematical Tripos.   By J. W. L. Glaisher.   *London,* 1886
Fly-sheets called forth by the Reports of the Special Board for
Mathematics, dated 7 Nov. 1899, 20 Jan. 1900.   4° 1899–1900
MATHEMATOGONIA.   Μαθηματογονια.   The mythological birth
of the nymph Mathesis.   [By T. S. Evans.]   1839
MATHEWS (C.M.) and Mathews (W.C.)   Everyman's Education.
A morality play.   *Birmingham,* 1903
MATHIAS (G.H.D.)   English B.A.'s and Prussian Freshmen.
                                                London, 1868
MATHIAS (T.J.)   Latin essay (Members' Prize).   4° 1775
Oratio habita in sacello Coll. Trin. Cant. festo S.S. Trinitatis
redeunte, 1779.   4° 1779
The Pursuits of Literature.   8th ed.   *London,* 1798
——— 14th ed.   *London,* 1898
Remarks [by John Mainwaring] on the Pursuits of Literature
[of T. J. Mathias].   1798
MATHISON (M.)   Letters.   *London,* 1875
MATRICULATIONS.   The Book of Matriculations and Degrees,
1851–1900.   (Ed. by J. W. Clark and J. F. E. Faning.)   1902
MATTHEW & Son.   Tariff at Café, 14, Trinity Street.   (1905)
MATTHEW (H.J.)   Shops or stores?   1879
MATTHEW'S (St) Parish.   Annual Report 1896–1903, 1906, 1908,
1909.   1896–1909
MATTHEWS (J.B.)   Testimonials.   Candidate for the Rectory of
Ovington.   1883
MATTY (H.)   Oratio...septimo Kal. Julias.   4° 1766
MAUDSLAY (A.G.)   Explorations in Guatemala.   (*Proc. Roy. Geog.*
Soc.)   (*London,* 1883)
Explorations of the ruins and site of Copan, Central America.   (*Proc.*
Roy. Geog. Soc.)   (*London,* 1886)

MAURICE (F.D.) Subscription no bondage. By Rusticus (F.D.M.).
Oxford, 1835
Reasons for not joining a party in the Church. A letter to the
Ven. Sam. Wilberforce.   *London*, 1841
Three letters to the Rev. W. Palmer, Fellow of Magd. Coll. Oxford,
on the name " Protestant," etc.   *London*, 1842
—— 2nd ed.   *London*, 1842
Letter on the attempt to defeat the nomination of Dr Hampden.
London, 1847
Thoughts on the duty of a Protestant in the present Oxford Election.
London, 1847
Queen's College, London. Letter to the Bp of London in reply
to article in Quarterly Review.   *London*, 1850
The word " Eternal " and the punishment of the Wicked. Letter
to Dr Jelf.   1853
King's College and Mr Maurice. No. 1. The Facts. By a
Barrister of Lincoln's Inn [J. M. Ludlow]. *London*, 1854
The faith of the Liturgy and the doctrine of the Thirty-nine
Articles. Two sermons.   1860
Address of congratulation to the Rev. F. D. M. on his nomination
to St Peter's, Vere St, with his reply.   1860
Casuistry, moral philosophy, and moral theology. A lecture.
12° *London*, 1866
The Light of Men. A sermon preached in Great St Andrew's
Church, Cambridge, Advent Sunday, 1868, in behalf of the
Industrial School.   1868
Christian Education. Two sermons preached on behalf of the Old
Schools, 20 Nov. 1870.   1870

The character of the writings of F. D. Maurice. By C. Perry, Bp of
Melbourne.   *n.p.* 1859
In memoriam F. D. Maurice. By Charles Kingsley. (*Macmillan's Mag.*,
May, 1872.)
The Victory that overcometh the World. A sermon preached at St Edward's
Church, Cambridge, on the Sunday after the death of the Rev. F. D.
Maurice. By H. R. Luard.   1872
See also Chretien (C. P.); Jelf (R. W.); Mansel (H. L.).

MAXWELL (G.M.) *See* True Blue.
MAXWELL (J.C.) Introductory lecture on Experimental Physics,
Oct. 25, 1871.   *London*, 1871

Life. By L. Campbell and William Garnett.   *London*, 1882

MAY BEE. Nos. 1–7. June 4–11, 1884.   4° 1884
The May Bee and other Bees. Including gems from the May Bee,
Cambridge Meteor, and Friends in Pencil. May, 1906. 4° 1906
MAY Term and Maidens. By " Growler " [i.e. B. B. Watson, Trin.].
1901
MAYFLY. Directed by present Etonians. Nos. 1–3. May 16, 1891–
June 24, 1891. (Harcourt's *Eton bibliography*, p. 88.) *Eton*, 1891

MAYOR (J.B.) Remarks on the proposal to grant the Degree of
B.A. to persons who have obtained honours in the Moral Sciences
Tripos. 1860
Considerations upon the Poll course. 1862
Further considerations upon the Poll course. 1863
Affiliation of local Colleges to the Universities of Oxford and Cam-
bridge. *London*, 1874
The End of the Century. Sermon. *London*, 1901
MAYOR (J.E.B.) On placing a bust of the late Town-Clerk
(C. H. Cooper) in the Guildhall. Letter to Swann Hurrell, Mayor.
1866
Facts and documents relating to the persecutions endured by Old
Catholics. 1875
Scholarships and Fellowships. A letter to the University of Cam-
bridge Commissioners. 1878
Modicus cibi medicus sibi, or Nature her own physician. 1880
The Peace of God. A sermon. St John's, 22 Oct. 1882. 1882
Luther and good works. 1883
In Memoriam : Isaac Todhunter. (*Camb. Review.*) 1884
Mutato nomine. [On the teaching of the Classics.] 1891
Σπειρεται σωμα ψυχικον, εγειρεται σωμα πνευματικον. [On
Registrary H. R. Luard. From a Commemoration Sermon
at St John's College, 6 May, 1891.] 1891
Memoir of Charles Cardale Babington. (*Eagle.*) 1895
A Goodly Heritage. Commencement Sermon, 17 June, 1900.
(1900)
F. H. Reusch. 1901
Commemoration Sermon. St John's, 4 May, 1902. (*Eagle.*) 1902
An Infant School. 1905
The Church of Scotland. Sermon...6 Dec. 1908. 1908
See Ascham (R.), 1863 ; Bonwicke (A.), 1870; Cambridge in the
xviith century, 1855–71 ; Cambridge under Queen Anne
[1870–1]; Cooper (C. H.), 1874 ; Hare (J. C.), 1873; John's (St)
College, 1859, 1869, 1882; Library, 1863–6; Williams (J.), 1866.
MEAT Scandals. *See* College Meat Scandals.
MEDE (J.) Diatribæ. iii Part. Or, a continuation of certaine dis-
courses on sundry texts of Scripture. 4° *London*, 1650
Παραλειπομενα. Remaines on some passages in the Revelation.
4° *London*, 1650
A paraphrase and exposition of the prophesie of St Peter. 3rd ed.
4° *London*, 1652
Opuscula Latina ad rem apocalypticam fere spectantia. 4° 1652
MEDICAL Society. Proceedings of the Cambridge Medical Society,
1880–81, 1884–1889. 1880–89
MEDICINE. Regulations for procedure in, 30 May, 1821. Graces.
1821
Fly-sheet signed "A Member of the Senate" against a Grace to
exclude from M.B. degree those who have practiced *pro mercede*
while *in statu pupillari*, 22 May, 1822. F° 1822

MEDICINE.

Report of the Syndicate on additional regulations for the M.B. degree, Oct. 8, 1827.   1827

Letter to the Members of the Senate on the subject of the subscriptions required of Medical Graduates in the University. [By J. Haviland.]   [1833]

Fly-sheets, reports, etc. relating to Medical studies in the University from 1866.   1866–

MELISSA.   Sizar MacShandy.   A legend of St Bede's College.   1885

MELVILL (H.)   The Fall of Jericho.   A sermon preached before the University of Cambridge, Nov. 26, 1848.   *London*, 1848

MEMBERS' Prize.   *See* Prolusiones.

MENDELSSOHN-BARTHOLDY (F.)   St Paul.   (King's College Chapel, March 14, 1884.)   4º 1884

Elijah.   (King's College Chapel, June 11, 1890.)   1890
Elijah.   (King's College Chapel, June 17, 1896.)   1896
Elijah.   (King's College Chapel, June 6, 1901.)   1901

MENDICITY.   Resolutions carried at a meeting held at Magdalene College, 8 May, 1819, to consider the establishment of a Society for the suppression of Mendicity.   Fº 1819

Special appeal on behalf of the Society, March, 1852.   (1852)

See also Charity Organization Society.

MERCURIUS Rusticus : or, the Countries complaint of the barbarous outrages begun in the year 1642...[By B. Ryves.]   4th ed.   [With] Querela Cantabrigiensis [by J. Barwick] [and] Mercurius Belgicus [by B. Ryves].   *London*, 1723

MERIVALE (C.)   The Church of England...Four Sermons preached before the University of Cambridge in November, 1838.   1839

A few words on University taxation.   1848

Open Fellowships.   Letter to Philip Frere.   1858

Competition, Pagan and Christian.   A sermon preached in St John's College Chapel, 6 May, 1868.   1868

St Etheldreda Festival.   Summary of proceedings at Ely, Oct. 1873.
                                                                    Ely, 1873

—— Illustrated ed.   *Ely*, 1873

Obituary notice.   By J. E. Sandys.   (*Eagle*, March, 1894.)   1894
Autobiography and Letters.   Ed. by Judith Anne Merivale.   *Oxford*, 1898

MERTON (W. de)   Sketch of the life of Walter de Merton.   By Edmund [Hobhouse], Bp of Nelson.   *Oxford*, 1859

MESMAN (D.)   Catalogue of paintings, drawings, etc. bequeathed by him to the University of Cambridge, in the year 1834.   By John Massey.   1835

—— Another ed.   1846

MICHAEL'S (St) Church.   Description.   (*Gentleman's Mag.*, April– May, 1814.)   (Bowes 1546.)

A solemn appeal to the Bishop of Ely on the disorder and profaneness at St Michael's Church, Cambridge, on the occasion of the Confirmation there, June 20, 1833.   By W. Cecil.   1833

MICHELL (J.)   Treatise on magnets.   1750
MICKLEBOROUGH (J.)   The great duty of labour and work.
   Sermon preached...27 Jan. 1750–51.   1751
MICROCOSM.   By Gregory Griffin [i.e. Geo. Canning, John Smith,
   Rob. Smith, J. H. Frere] of Eton.   3rd ed.   2 vols.   (Harcourt's
   Eton bibliography, 1902, p. 18.)   *Windsor*, 1793
MICROCOSMOGRAPHIA Academica, being a guide for the
   young academic politician.   [By F. M. Cornford.]   1908
MIDDLE Class Examinations.   Letter, signed M.A., respecting use
   of arithmetic.   (*Camb. Chron.*, 1857.)
   Examination of Students not Members of the University.   First
   Report of the Syndicate.   1859
See also Jessopp (A.); Lightfoot (J. B.); Luard (H. R.); Roberts (J.);
   Shilleto (R.); Wratislaw (A. H.).
MIDDLETON (C.)   Full and Impartial Account of all the late
   proceedings against Dr Bentley.   *London*, 1719
—— 2nd ed.   *London*, 1719
Second Part of the Full and Impartial Account.   *London*, 1719
Some Remarks upon a pamphlet [by A. A. Sykes] entitled, The Case
   of Dr Bentley farther stated...   *London*, 1719
True Account of the present state of Trinity College.   *London*, 1720
Remarks upon Bentley's Proposals for a new edition of the New
   Testament.   4° *London*, 1721
—— 2nd ed.   4° *London*, 1721
Farther Remarks.   4° *London*, 1721
Bibliothecae Cantabrigiensis ordinandae methodus.   4° 1723
Oratio de novo physiologiae explicandae munere, ex celebr. Wood-
   wardi testamento instituto.   4° *Londini*, 1732
A Dissertation concerning the origin of Printing in England.
                                                        4° 1735
A free inquiry into the Miraculous Powers...in the Christian Church.
                                                   Dublin, 1749
Miscellaneous Works.   4 vols.   4° *London*, 1752
Miscellaneous Tracts.   4° *London*, 1752
MIDDLETON (J.H.)   The engraved gems of classical times.   With
   a catalogue of the gems in the Fitzwilliam Museum.   1891
Illuminated manuscripts in classical and mediaeval times, their art
   and their technique.   1892
MILES (C.P.)   Early death not premature.   A memoir of F. L.
   Mackenzie.   *Edinburgh*, 1856
—— 4th ed.   *London*, 1863
MILL (W.H.)   Observations on the attempted application of pantheistic
   principles to the theory of the Gospel.   1840
Prælectio theologica in scholis Cantabrigiensibus habita prid. Kal.
   Feb. 1843.   4° 1843
Analysis of Pearson on the Creed.   1843
Five sermons on the temptation of Christ.   1844
Sermons preached in Lent 1845, and on several former occasions.
                                                              1845

MILL (W.H.).
Five sermons on the nature of Christianity. *London,* 1848
Four sermons preached before the University of Cambridge on
5 Nov. and the three Sundays preceding Advent, in 1848. 1849
Human Policy and Divine Truth. Sermon before the University,
17 March, 1850. 1850
Sermon preached on the foundation of Mrs Ramsden, before the Uni-
versity of Cambridge, 22 May, 1853. 1853
MILLER (E.) Some remarks upon *The Present State of Trinity College*
by R. Bentley. *London,* 1710
An account of the University of Cambridge, and the Colleges there.
London, 1717
MILLER (S.H.) and Skertchly (S.B.J.) The Fenland, past and
present. *Wisbech,* 1878
Review, by A. Newton, from the *Zoologist,* Feb. 1879.
The handbook to the Fenland. *London* (1889)
—— 2nd ed. *London* (1890)
MILLER (W.H.) In Memoriam : W. H. Miller. By T. G. Bonney.
(*Eagle,* Oct. 1880.) 1880
Memorial. By J. P. Cooke. [1881]
Memorial (with Letters). By his Wife. [1881 ?]
MILLERS (G.) A guide to the Cathedral Church and Collegiate
buildings at Ely. 1805
—— 2nd ed. 1820
—— 4th ed. *Ely,* 1833
—— 5th ed. *Ely,* 1838
A description of the Cathedral Church of Ely. 3rd ed. *London,* 1834
MILLINGTON (W.) Memoir. By G. Williams. 1858
MILLS (E.J.) To the Electors of the Jacksonian Professor of Experi-
mental Philosophy in the University of Cambridge. Address.
London, 1875
MILLS (J.W.) Judas Maccabæus. (Seatonian Prize Poem for 1877.)
London, 1877
MILNER (I.) A plan of a course of Chemical Lectures. 1784
Animadversions on Dr Haweis's...History of the Church of Christ...
being Preface to 2nd ed. of vol. I. of Jos. Milner's History of the
Church of Christ. 1800
Further animadversions on Dr Haweis's misquotations and mis-
representations of Mr Milner's History of the Church of Christ. 1801

Life. By his niece, Mary Milner. *London,* 1842
See also Ludlam (W. and T.).

MILNER (J.) View of Bentley's Dissertation upon...Phalaris.
London, 1698
MILNES (A.) Syllabus of a course of lectures on the making and
sharing of wealth (C. U. Local Lectures). 1895
MILTON (J.) *See* King (E.).
MILTON Tercentenary. The portraits, prints, and writings of
John Milton. Published in connection with the exhibition at

MILTON Tercentenary.
> Christ's College, Cambridge. By G. C. Williamson and Charles
> Sayle.   4° 1908
> —— 2nd ed.   4° 1908
> —— Special edition.   4° 1908
> Invitation cards, notices, cuttings, etc.   4° 1908

MINERALOGY (Professorship of) The King *v.* the Vice-Chancellor
> of Cambridge. A Report of the above cause, in the Court of
> King's Bench : with the proceedings in the University in opposition
> to the right of nominating to the Professorship of Mineralogy
> claimed by the Heads of Colleges.   1824
> Grace to appoint Syndicate with reference to Sir John Richardson's
> award in the matter of the Professorship of Mineralogy, 14 Nov.
> 1827.   F° (1827)

MINIATURE. A periodical paper. By Solomon Grildrig of the
> College of Eton. (April 23, 1804–April 1, 1805.) (Harcourt's
> *Eton bibliography*, p. 22.)   *London*, 1805

MINNS (E.H.) Early Printed books to the year 1500 in the Library of
> Pembroke College. (Appended to Catalogue of MSS.)   1905
> Application for directorship of Fitzwilliam Museum.   4° 1908
> *See also* Russian Lectureship.

MIRTH, a poem in answer to Warton's *Pleasures of Melancholy*. By
> a Gentleman of Cambridge (W. M[ason]).   4° *London*, 1774

MISCELLANEOUS Pieces, original and collected. By a Clergyman
> of Northamptonshire.   *London*, 1787

MISS Green. A tragedy in one act (and that a rather foolish one).
> [By Harvey Goodwin.]   1865

MISSIONS. Mission to North India. Second Report.   1880
> —— Report of London meeting, 22 June, 1885.   1885
> Mission to South London. By A. Amos and W. W. Hough.   1904
> —— Cambridge in South London.   *London*, 1910
> *See also* Anderson-Morshead (A. E. M.) ; Cambridge House ;
> Carlyon (H. C.) ; Lefroy (G. A.) ; Rowe (J. T.) ; Trinity Coll.
> Mission ; Universities' Mission.

MOBERLY (G.) A few remarks on the proposed admission of
> Dissenters into the University of Oxford.   *Oxford*, 1834

MOBERLY (G.H.) Life of William of Wykeham.
>   *Winchester and London*, 1887

MOMUS. Nos. 1–3. March 3, 1866—March 15, 1869. [Ed. by
> E. H. Palmer, Joh., G. A. Critchett, Cai., G. W. D. S. Forrest, Joh.,
> W. H. Pollock, Trin., and others.]   4° 1866–69

MONK (J.H.) Letter to the Rev. S. Butler, M.A., with Mr Butler's
> answer.   1810
> A sermon preached in the Chapel of Trinity College, Cambridge,
> Dec. 16, 1817, being the day appointed for the Commemoration
> of Benefactors of that Society.   (1817)
> A vindication of the University of Cambridge from the reflections of
> Sir J. E. Smith.   *London*, 1818
> —— 2nd ed.   *London*, 1818

MONK (J.H.).
Appendix to same.   1819
Memoir of E. V. Blomfield. (From *Museum Criticum*, no. 7.)
(Two copies.)   (*London*, 1821)
Statement against the view that no Greek Professor can proceed D.D.
without vacating his professorship.   5 March, 1822.   Fᵒ 1822
The duty of attention to the original objects of academical institutions.
A sermon preached before the University of Cambridge, June 30,
1822.   4ᵒ 1822
A letter to Philograntus [J. H. Monk], by Eubulus : being a sequel
to a pamphlet, entitled *Thoughts on the present system of Academic
education in the University of Cambridge.*   *London*, 1822
A letter to John, Bishop of Bristol, respecting an additional examina-
tion of students in the University of Cambridge.   By Philograntus
[J. H. M.].   1822
Memoir of Dr James Duport.   (From *Museum Criticum*, no. 8.)
                                                        (*London*, 1826)
The life of Richard Bentley.   4ᵒ *London*, 1830
—— 2nd ed.   2 vols.   *London*, 1833
A sermon preached before the University of Cambridge, July 5, 1835,
on occasion of the Installation of the Marquis Camden.
                                                     4ᵒ *London*, 1835
   See also Smith (*Sir* J. E.).
MONK (W.)   *See* Livingstone (D.).
MONMOUTH (James, *Duke of*)   To...Prince James...on the happy
solemnity of His Grace's inauguration in the Chancellorship of
the University of Cambridge.   Fᵒ *In the Savoy*, 1674
MONTAGU (F.)   Oratio in laudes Baconi.   1755
MONTALEMBERT (C. F., *Comte de*)   A reprint of a letter addressed
to a member of the Cambridge Camden Society, by M. le Comte
de Montalembert.   Accompanied with a few Remarks and Queries.
By an Enquirer.   *Cheltenham*, 1845
De l'avenir politique de l'Angleterre.   3ᵉ éd.   *Paris*, 1856
MONTMORENCY (J.E.G. de)   Paul before Nero.   (Seatonian
Prize Poem for 1909.)   *London*, 1910
MOON (R.)   An appeal to the Cambridge Philosophical Society in
connexion with a recent decision of the Council.   *London*, 1872
MOORE (N.)   The President of the College of Physicians.
                                                       London, 1899
Principles and practice of medicine.   *n.p.* 1899
An address on Medical books.   (Repr. from the *Lancet*.)
                                                       London, 1906
The history of the study of medicine in the British Isles.
                                                       Oxford, 1908
The Schola Salernitana.   (Finlayson Memorial lecture.)
                                                      Glasgow, 1908
   See also Catharine's (St) College, 1868-9.
MOORE (Walter)   Cambridge.   (Corporation Guides ser.)
                                                  London [1909 ?]

MOORE (William)   *See* Smith (T.).
MORAL Sciences Tripos.   Report of Syndicate on Regulations,
   9 April, 1851.   Fo 1851
   Fly-sheets, etc. from 1859 relating to the Moral and Natural Sciences
   Tripos.   1859–
   See also Clarke (C. B.); Drosier (W. H.); Grote (J.); Mayor (J. B.);
   Roby (H. J.).
MORE (H.)   Life [and] Letters by Richard Ward.   *London,* 1710
MORGAN (A.C.O.)   Aladdin.   Jesus College Hall, 3 Jan. 1899.
                                                        12o 1899
MORGAN (C.)   Six philosophical dissertations.   4o 1770
MORGAN (H.A.)   The tenure of Fellowships considered, especially
   with reference to College Tutors and Lecturers.   1871
   The Mathematical Tripos.   1871
   Morgan (H. A.) and Burn (R.)   Letters on Reform.   Fo 1876
   The Church and Dissent in Wales.   1895
MORGAN (J.)   History of St Andrew's the Great.   12o 1910
MORGAN (J.H.) and Barber (J.T.)   Account of Aurora Borealis
   seen near Cambridge, 1847.   [1847]
MORLAND (*Sir* S.)   A brief account of the life, writings, and
   inventions of Sir S. Morland. [By J. O. Halliwell-Phillipps.] 1838
MORPHOLOGICAL Laboratory.   Studies from the Morphological
   Laboratory in the University of Cambridge.   Vols. 1–6.   Ed. by
   F. M. Balfour and A. Sedgwick.   *London,* 1880–1896
MORRELL (R.S.)   Syllabus of course of lectures on the elementary
   principles of Chemistry.   1891
MORRIS (J.)   Letter of application for Woodwardian Professorship
   of Geology, 3 Feb. 1873.   4o *n.p.* 1873
MORRIS (M.)   A Visit to Eton.   (*Engl. Illustr. Mag.,* Nov. 1884.)
MORTLOCK (J.F.)   A short history of J. F. M., detailing particulars
   of his life.   1835
   Experiences of a Convict.   5 pts.   *London,* 1864–5
   Imaginary dialogues in Cambridge.   *London,* 1866
   Startling disclosures ! for the benefit of needy Chancery suitors.
                                               London, 1867
   Three dialogues.   *London,* 1868
   Eighteen imaginary dialogues.   Second Series.   1868
   How I came to be a bankrupt.   Respectfully dedicated to the
   Master of the Rolls.   *London,* 1868
MOSLEM in Cambridge.   May 1, 1890 [prophetic].   Nos. 1–3.
   Nov. 1870–April, 1871.   (Ed. by G. S. Davies.   Bowes 2557.)
                                                      4o 1870–1
MOTHERS' Union.   Address by Lady Frederick Cavendish.   1887
—— (Ely diocese.)   11th Report.   *Ely,* 1907
MOULD (J.G.)   A sermon preached at the Commemoration of
   Benefactors in the Chapel of Corpus Christi College, Dec. 14, 1847.
                                                        (1847)
   A sermon preached at the Consecration of the Chapel of the College
   of Corpus Christi, Cambridge, Nov. 2, 1870.   1870

MOULE (H.C.G.)   Christian Self-denial.   (Seatonian Prize Poem
    for 1869.)   1869
The Beloved Disciple.   (Seatonian Prize Poem for 1870.)   1870
Tyre.   (Seatonian Prize Poem for 1871.)   1871
The Gospel in Polynesia.   (Seatonian Prize Poem for 1872.) 1872
The Brazen Serpent.   (Seatonian Prize Poem for 1873.)   1873
The Victory that overcometh the World.   (Seatonian Prize Poem
    for 1876.)   1876
Charles Simeon.   *London*, 1892
On the Holy Communion.   A Sermon.   1898
Her children bless her.   A sermon.   1901
"Wise Men and Scribes."   A Commemoration sermon at Trinity.
                                                            1907
Our Great High Priest.   A sermon.   n.d.
See also Ridley (N.).
MOULTON (R.G.)   Syllabus of a course of lectures delivered 1887,
    1888.   Ancient tragedies for English audiences.   (Univ. Extension.)
                                            Sheffield, 1887–88
MOULTRIE (J.)   Dream of Life.   *London*, 1843
See Walker (W. S.).
MOWAT (J.)   *See* Handsworth.
MOWBRAY (M.)   Autobiography of a Cantab.   Nos. 1–5.   1842
MOXON (J.H.H.)   Fen floods and the lower Ouse.   1878
The Birds of the Fens.   1882
MOZART (W.A.)   A record of the Cambridge Centenary Com-
    memoration.   Ed. by Sedley Taylor.   *London*, 1892
MOZLEY (H.N.)   The stealthy advance of Vivisection.   The John
    Lucas Walker Studentship.   (With covering letters.)
                                            London (1886)
MUDDLEHEAD (Ignotus Ignoramus)   *See* Pilgrimage.
MULLINGER (J.B.)   Cambridge characteristics in the seventeenth
    century.   *London*, 1867
The University of Cambridge from the earliest times to the Royal
    Injunctions of 1535 (—to the accession of Charles I).   2 vols.
                                                    1873–84
Election to Clark Lectureship, Trinity College, Cambridge.   Testi-
    monials of J. B. M.   4° 1883
A history of the University of Cambridge.   *London*, 1888
St John's College.   (College histories.)   *London*, 1901
Was Ben Jonson ever a member of our College?   (*Eagle*, June, 1904.)
                                                        1904
MUNRO (H.A.J.)   Remarks on the Master of Trinity's criticism of
    Aristotle's account of Induction.   4° 1850
Reply to C. B. Scott's Remarks on the same subject.   4° 1850
Explanation of a Latin Inscription given in Blakesley's *Four months in
    Algeria*, p. 285.   4° 1860
Notice of the life of E. M. Cope.   1873
Translation of Gray's *Elegy* into Latin hexameters.   4° 1875
Translations into Latin and Greek verse.   4° 1884

MUNRO (H.A.J.).
In Memoriam. By R. Burn.   1885
Memorial sermon...by Coutts Trotter, Ap. 26, 1885.   1885
Memorial article. By W. H. Thompson. (*Journ. of Philology*, xiv.)
                                                        (*London*, 1885)
Catalogue of his library...sold...Nov. 16, 1885.   1885

MURCHISON (R.I.) Address delivered at the anniversary meeting
    of the Geological Society of London, 17 Feb. 1843. *London*, 1843
MURDOCH (P.) *See* Maclaurin (C.).
MURRAY (A.) A catalogue of hardy plants in the Botanic Garden,
    Cambridge.   1850
MURRAY (J.) Gideon. (Seatonian Prize Poem for 1839.)   1839
MURRAY (J.O.F.) F. J. A. Hort. (*Emm. Coll. Mag.*)   1893
MUSAE Anglicanae. Editio 4ᵃ. Vols. i., ii.   *London*, 1721
—— Vol. iii.   *Oxford*, 1717
—— Editio 5ᵃ.   12ᵒ *London*, 1741
MUSAE Cantabrigienses, 1810. *See* Prolusiones.
MUSAE Seatonianae. *See* Seatonian Prize Poems.
MUSEUM Criticum; or Cambridge Classical Researches. Vols. 1, 2.
    (Bowes 1544.)   1826
MUSEUM of Archaeology. *See* Archaeology.
MUSEUMS and Lecture Rooms Syndicate. Fly-sheets, etc. from
    1853.   1853–
Remarks on the Report of the Museums and Lecture Rooms Syndicate.
    By J. W. Clark.   1863
Reports for 1866–78, 1892, 1893, 1895.   4ᵒ 1866-95
Accounts, 1900.   4ᵒ 1901
MUSHROOM. A May Week Magazine. June 8, 1894.   4ᵒ 1894
MUSIC. *See* Concerts.
MUSICAL Fund. Programme of two Concerts in the Town Hall,
    14 and 15 Nov. 1826.   Fᵒ 1826
MUSICAL Society. Programmes of Concerts.   141, 147, 148, 150–
    179, 180, 185, 189, 190, 192, 194, 197, 198, 199, 200, 203, 204,
    206, 211, 212, 214, 215, 220, 221, 222, 224, 225, 226, 229, 231,
    245, 248, 251, 252.   1876–1906
Programmes. Wednesday Popular Concerts.   1876–1883
—— Another series.   1889–1903
Proposition to perform Mendelssohn's "St Paul" in King's College
    Chapel, and Order of the Service.   1883–4
Accounts, 1885, 1889–90, 1895–6.   Fᵒ 1885–96
The Passion according to St Matthew. By J. S. Bach. King's
    College Chapel, 10 March, 1887.   4ᵒ 1887
Dinner to Dr Joachim. Menu, list of guests, etc.   1889
The Passion according to St John. By J. S. Bach. Performed
    6 March, 1890.   4ᵒ 1890
Concert in Trinity College Chapel, 2 Dec. 1893.   4ᵒ 1893
Rules. Easter Term, 1903.   1903
List of Members and Associates, 1904–5.   1905

MUSICAL Society.
  See also Amateur Musical Society ; Amateur Vocal Guild ; Choral Union ; Church Music Society.
MYERS (F.W.H.)   St Paul and Felix.   (Written for the Seatonian Prize, 1867.)   (1867)
  In memory of Henry Sidgwick.   (*Proc. Soc. Psychical Research.*)
                                                        London, 1900
  Fragments of Prose and Poetry.   Ed. by his Wife.   *London*, 1904
MYERS (T.)   Essay on the influence of the Homeric Poems on the Greek nation.   1829
  The influence of the Homeric Poems on the language, etc. of the Greeks.   1830
  On the intent and use of the gift of tongues.   (Norrisian Prize Essay for 1832.)   *London*, 1833

N

NAPLETON (J.) Considerations on...degrees in the University of Oxford. *n.p.* 1773

NAPOLEON'S Invasion of Russia. (Unsuccessful Prize Poem.) (1828)

NARRATIVE or story of Mr Jex Jex of Corpus. Done into English Verse...by A. C. D. Barde. 1864

NASHE (T.) *See* Harvey (G.).

NASMITH (J.) Catalogus librorum manuscriptorum quos Collegio Corporis Christi legavit Matthæus Parker. 4° 1777

NATIONAL League for physical education and improvement. Cambridge branch. Second annual report. 1909

NATURAL Science Club. Programme of conversazione at Physiological Laboratory, 12 March, 1894. Obl. (1894)

NATURAL Science Society. President's (W. H. Spencer's) Report, Easter Term, 1863. 1863

Annual Report, 1863, with retiring address of President (C. W. V. Bradford), Michaelmas Term, 1863. 1863

NATURAL Sciences Tripos. Report of Syndicate on Regulations, 9 April, 1851. Fo 1851

See also Moral Sciences Tripos.

NEALE (C.M.) The Senior Wranglers of the University of Cambridge from 1748 to 1907. *Bury St Edmunds*, 1907

The early Honour-lists (1498–9 to 1746–7) of the University of Cambridge. *Bury St Edmunds*, 1909

NEALE (J.M.) Hierologus ; or the Church tourists. *London*, 1843

Ayton Priory. 1843

Edom. (Seatonian Prize Poem for 1849.) 1849

Mammon. (Seatonian Prize Poem for 1852.) 1852

Judith. (Seatonian Prize Poem for 1856.) 1856

Sinai. (Seatonian Prize Poem for 1857.) 1857

Egypt. (Seatonian Prize Poem for 1858.) 1858

The Disciples at Emmaus. (Seatonian Prize Poem for 1859.) 1859

Ruth. (Seatonian Prize Poem for 1860.) 1860

Notes ecclesiological and picturesque on Dalmatia, etc. *London*, 1861

King Josiah. (Seatonian Prize Poem for 1862.) 1862

The Seven Churches of Asia. (Seatonian Prize Poem for 1863.) 1863

Seatonian Poems. 1864

See also Camden (afterwards Ecclesiological) Society.

NEALE (Thomas), *of Trin. Coll., Camb.* 'Ενυπνιον : or the Vision. Fo *London*, 1706

176 NEALE NEWMARKET

NEALE (Thomas), *Professor of Hebrew at Oxford.* Collegiorum Scholarumque Academiæ Oxoniensis topographica delineatio. *Appended to* Dodwell (H.). De Parma equestri Woodwardiana dissertatio. *Oxonii,* 1718
—— Another ed. Ed. F. Madan. 4º *Oxonii,* 1882
NEALE (Thomas), *Rector of Manea.* The ruinous state of the parish of Manea. *n.p.* 1748
NEATE (C.) Observations on College leases. *Oxford,* 1853
NEIL (R.A.) A memorial article. By J. Adam. (*Camb. Rev.*) (1901)
Sale of his books, Nov. 12, 1901. (1901)
Sale of his wine, Nov. 19, 1901. (1901)
NENE (River) *See* Fens.
NEUBERG (V.B.) A Green Garland. *Bedford,* 1908
NEVE (C.) An account of King's College Chapel. 1855
A succinct history of King's College Chapel. n.d.
NEVILE (T.) The Fourteenth Satire of Juvenal imitated.
4º *London,* 1769
NEVILLE (*Hon.* R.C.) Antiqua explorata ; being the results of excavations made in and about Audley End. *Saffron Walden,* 1847
Examination of a group of barrows in Cambridgeshire. (*Archaeologia,* XXXII.) 4º (*London,* 1847)
Sepulchra exposita ; or an account of the opening of some barrows... in the neighbourhood of Audley End. *Saffron Walden,* 1848
Account of excavations near the Fleam Dyke, Apr. 1852. (*Arch. Journ.,* IX.) (*London,* 1852)
NEW Display of the Beauties of England. 2 vols. 3rd ed.
London, 1776
NEW Theatre. *See* Theatre.
NEWCASTLE (*Duke of*) Ode performed in the Senate House, Cambridge, July 1, 1749, at the Installation of His Grace the Duke of Newcastle, Chancellor of the University. By Mr Mason, Fellow of Pembroke. 4º 1749
Carmina ad...Thomam Holles, Ducem de Newcastle...cum Academiam Cantabrigiensem Bibliothecæ restituendæ causa inviseret.
Fº 1755
NEWCOME (J.) The sure word of prophecy. Sermon preach'd before the University of Cambridge, 24 June, 1724. 1724
Sermon at St Margaret's, Westminster, 30 Jan. 1743. 4º 1743
NEWMAN (F.W.) The English Universities. From the German of V.A. Huber. An abridged translation, ed. by F.W. Newman. 2 vols. in 3. *London,* 1843
NEWMAN (J.H.) The office and work of Universities.
London, 1856
Mr Kingsley and Dr Newman. A correspondence on the question whether Dr Newman teaches that Truth is no Virtue ?
London, 1864
Apologia pro vita sua. *London,* 1864
See also Kingsley (C.).
NEWMARKET. *See* Acts and Bills.

NEWMARKET Hoax. *See* Causton (A. W.).

NEWNHAM College. Newnham Hall Company. Balance Sheet, etc., June 8, 1875. *n.p.* 1875

(Prospectus.) *n.p.* 1881

Girton and Newnham. By E. A. B. Hodgetts. (*Strand Mag.*, Nov. 1894.)

Report and Prospectus for Newnham College. (May, 1898.) *n.p.* 1898

NEWTON (A.) On the zoology of ancient Europe. *London and Cambridge*, 1862

The Gare-Fowl and its Historians. (*Nat. Hist. Rev.*, v.) *London*, 1865

Testimonials when a candidate for the proposed Professorship of Zoology...in the University of Cambridge. 1865

On a method of registering Natural History observations. 1870

Zoology. (Manuals of Elementary Science.) *London*, 1874

Address to Biological Section of British Association at Glasgow, Sept. 1876. *London*, 1876

The Fenland past and present. By S. H. Miller and S. B. J. Skertchly. (Review in *Zoologist*, Feb. 1879.)

Review of H. W. Elliott's *Seal-Islands*. [Corrected proof.] (*Quarterly Review*, Oct. 1883.)

Address to Biological Section of British Association at Manchester, 1887. *London*, 1887

Early days of Darwinism. (*Macmillan's Mag.*, Feb. 1888.)

Gilbert White of Selborne. Reprint of article in Dict. of Nat. Biography. 1900

Obituary notice, by A. E. Shipley. (*Proc. Linnean Soc.*) (*London*, 1908)

NEWTON (B.) Sermon, 30 Jan. 1758. 4° 1758

NEWTON (C.) Poems. 1797

NEWTON (E.) and Clark (J.W.) On the osteology of the Solitaire. (*Phil. Trans. Roy. Soc.* vol. 168.) 4° *London*, 1878

NEWTON (*Sir* I.) Some observations on the Chronology of Sir I. N. To which is prefixed his Chronology abridged by himself. 4° *London*, 1728

Four letters to Dr Bentley, containing some arguments in proof of a Deity. *London*, 1756

Correspondence of Sir Isaac Newton and Professor Cotes. With Notes by J. Edleston. *London*, 1850

An Account of Sir Isaac Newton's Philosophical Discoveries. By Colin Maclaurin. 4° *London*, 1748

A catalogue of the Portsmouth collection of books and papers written by or belonging to Sir Isaac Newton. 1888

Bibliography of Sir I. Newton. By G. J. Gray. 1888

—— 2nd ed. 4° 1907

NEXT Step (The) respectfully suggested to the Senate of the University of Cambridge. By one of its members. [On studies in the University, by A. R. Grant.] 1849

NORTHUMBERLAND (*Duke of*).

Canzone per la istallazione di sua eccel. il Duca di Northumberland, all' ufficio di Gran Cancelliere della Università di Cambridge. [By Silvio Ireneo, i.e. Marchese Spineto.]   1842

Ode performed in the Senate House, 5 July, 1842, at the first Commencement after the Installation of the Duke of Northumberland. By Tho. Whytehead.   4° 1842

NOTES on the Cambridgeshire Churches. [By G. R. Boissier.]
                London, 1827

NOURSE (P.) A sermon preached at the Public Commencement at Cambridge, July 3, 1698.   4° 1698

NUGENT (C.) The O. U. D. S. (Extracted from W. G. Elliot's *Amateur Clubs and Actors*.)   *London*, 1898

NURSES. Home and Training School for Nurses. 7th, 9th, 12th, 13th Report.   1880–6

Cambridge District Nursing Assoc. Reports 1895–1905. 1895–1905

List of donations to new Home for Nurses.   1909

NUTTALL (P.A.) *See* Fuller (T.).

O

OATHS. Considerations on the Oaths required by the University of Cambridge, at the time of taking Degrees. By a Member of the Senate. [By W. Frend.] *London*, 1787
Remarks on Oaths. *London*, 1826
Oaths. [By W. Farish.] (1833)
Historical account of Oaths and Subscriptions. [By Gilbert Ainslie.] (Two copies.) 1833
See also Subscription ; Tests.

OBSERVATION on the design of establishing annual examinations at Cambridge. [By W. S. Powell.] 1774

OBSERVATORY. Observations on the plans. By S. I. 1822
Report of the Building Syndicate on cost, 17 May, 1824. F⁰ (1824)
Regulations for management, 16 Dec. 1828. F⁰ (1828)
Special Report of proceedings in the Observatory relative to the new Planet. By J. Challis. 4⁰ 1846
Fly-sheets, etc. relating thereto, from 1847. 1847–
Letters (1–3) to the Vice-Chancellor. By R. C. Carrington.
F⁰ *n.p.* 1861

OCCASIONAL Jottings of 'Varsity vagaries. *See* True Blue.

OCCASIONAL Papers on University matters and Middle Class Education. No. 1, Dec. 1858 ; No. 2, April, 1859 ; No. 3, Dec. 1859. 1858–9

OCKLEY (S.) Oratio inauguralis...in scholis publicis Kal. Feb. 1711.
4⁰ 1712
See Ali.

O'CUTAWAY (P.) *See* Intercepted Correspondence.

ODE au Roi de la Grande Bretagne. 4⁰ 1798

OFFICERS, Examiners, Syndics, etc., from 1854. (Lists.) 1854–

OGDEN (S.) Sermons. With Life by S. Hallifax. 4th ed. 2 vols.
London, 1788

OGLE (O.) Royal Letters addressed to Oxford, and now existing in the City Archives. Ed. by O. Ogle. *Oxford*, 1892

OKES (J.) An account of some fossil remains of the Beaver found in Cambridgeshire. (*Trans. Camb. Philos. Soc.*) 4⁰ 1821

OKES (R.) Catalogue of his books, etc...to be sold, Jan. 1889. 1889
See Okes (T. V.). Account...1838.

OKES (T.V.) An account of the providential preservation of Elizabeth Woodcock. 2nd ed. 1799
—— 3rd ed. 1799
—— Repr. by R. Okes. *Eton*, 1838
Observations upon the fever lately prevalent at Cambridge. 1815

OLD Catholics. Account of the visit of Old Catholic Bishops to
England.   *London*, 1882
See also Mayor (J. E. B.), 1875.
OLD Mother Hubbard. Critica Novazealandica futura. A notable
and right marvellous edition of the Melodrame of Old Mother
Hubbord...(Two states.)   1837
OLD Schools. *See* Schools.
OLDHAM (H.Y.) A Pre-Columban discovery of America. (*Geogr.*
Journal, March, 1895.)   *London*, 1895
OLIVER (E.) Commencement Sermon, 4 July, 1784.
                                               4° *London*, 1784
OLLIVANT (A.) The introductory lecture to the course delivered
before the University of Cambridge in Lent Term, 1844. (1844)
ON legislative ignorance. Address to the Universities. *London*, 1837
ON visitatorial jurisdiction in Colleges of the Universities.
                                               4° *London*, 1785
ONLY a Daisy. A legend of St Chad.   *n.p.* 1884
OPINION of an Eminent Lawyer [P. Yorke] concerning the Right
of Appeal...supported. [Attr. to R. Hurd.]   *London*, 1751
ORDINANCES. Two Ordinances of the Lords and Commons...for
the demolishing of all organs, etc. (9 May, 1644). 4° *London*, 1644
Ordinance of the Lords and Commons...for regulating the Univ. of
Cambridge. (14 Feb. 1645.)   4° *London*, 1645
Ordinances of the Univ. of Cambridge, 1858 (14 Apr., 16 Dec.),
1860, 1861, 1863, 1871, 1874, 1877, 1880, 1885, 1888, 1892,
1896, 1901, 1904, 1908.   1858–1908
ORDINARY degree. *See* Poll degree.
ORFORD (*Lord*) Voyage round the Fens in 1774. (Ed. by J. W.
Childers.)   *Doncaster* (1868)
ORIENTATOR. Publ. by Camb. Camden Soc.   1844
ORIGINAL Poems in the moral, heroic, pathetic, and other styles.
By a Traveller (J. H.). 3rd ed. (Bowes 1680.)   1825
—— 4th ed.   1825
ORIGINAL Poetry. By a Member of Christ College, Cambridge.
                                                London, 1806
ORNITHOLOGISTS. Fourth International Congress, 20 June,
1905. Catalogue of exhibition, etc.   1905
OSBORN (H.F.) American Dinosaurs. Lecture before British
Association at Cambridge, 1904. (*Century Mag.*, Sept. 1904.)
OSBORNE (D.G.) Granta, or a page from the life of a Cantab.
[Attr. to D. G. Osborne.]   1836
OSLER (W.) Thomas Linacre. (Linacre Lecture, 1908.)   1908
O'SULLIVAN (S.) College Recollections. [? By S. O'Sullivan.]
                                                London, 1829
OTLEY (J.) J. Otley, the Geologist and Guide. By J. Clifton Ward.
(With letters by A. Sedgwick.) (*Trans. Cumb. Assoc.*, Pt 2,
1876–7.)   *Carlisle*, 1877
OTTER (W.) Life and Remains of E. D. Clarke. 4° *London*, 1824
—— Another ed. 2 vols.   8° *London*, 1825

OUR College. Leaves from an Undergraduate's " Scribbling-Book."
[By J. D. Lewis.] *London*, 1857
OVERTON (J.) Building and dedication of Second Temple.
(Seatonian Prize Poem for 1825.) 1826
OVINGTON. Poll for election of a Rector, Oct. 24, 1810.
(E. Simons elected.) 1810
—— May 10, 1865. (C. J. Evans elected.) 1865
—— Jan. 25, 1883. (S. J. Prior elected.) 1883
—— May 22, 1883. (A. T. Crisford elected.) 1883
OWEN (C.) Carmen Pindaricum in Theatrum Sheldonianum
recitatum Julii die 9° 1669. 4° *Oxonii*, 1669
OWEN (J.) Subordination considered on the grounds of reason and
religion. A sermon preached in Great St Mary's, 5 Aug. 1794.
1794
OWEN (*Sir* R.) On the classification and distribution of the Mammalia.
(Rede Lecture.) *London*, 1859
OWENS College : its foundation and growth. By J. Thompson.
Manchester, 1886
OXFORD. Account of the...new buildings of Queen's College in
Oxford. 4° *n.p.* 1718
Terrae filius, or the secret history of the University of Oxford. [By
N. Amhurst.] *London*, 1726
The new Oxford Guide. 6th ed. 12° *Oxford* [? 1768]
Considerations on...degrees in the University of Oxford. [By J.
Napleton.] *n.p.* 1773
Catalogue of graduates in the University of Oxford, 1659–1800.
Oxford, 1801
Oxford Prize Poems. 3rd ed. *Oxford*, 1808
Reply (–Second Reply) to the calumnies of the Edinburgh Review
against Oxford. [By E. Copleston.] *Oxford*, 1810
Observations on the architecture of Magdalen College. [By J.
Buckler.] *London*, 1823
Handbook for visitors to Oxford. *Oxford*, 1847
Oxford Tradesmen versus the Insolvent Jennings. *Oxford* (1847)
Letter to the V.-C. of Oxford on Proctorial power. *Oxford*, 1847
Statutes of the Colleges. 3 vols. *Oxford*, 1853
Recommendations respecting College statutes as adopted by the
Tutors' Association, March, 1854. *Oxford*, 1854
Historical handbook and guide to the City and University of Oxford.
Oxford, 1871
Notice by Board of Studies for Natural Science School. *Oxford*, 1872
Handbook for visitors. New ed. *Oxford*, 1875
Statutes made for the University under the Act of 1877. *Oxford*, 1882
The Visitor's Guide to Oxford. New ed. *Oxford*, 1885
Student's Handbook to the Univ. of Oxford. 11th ed. *Oxford*, 1891
The Visitor's Guide. *Oxford*, 1897
Tercentenary of the Bodleian Library. Proceedings. F° *Oxford*, 1902
—— Programmes, Invitations, Reports, etc. 4° 1902
—— *See also* Nicholson (E. W. B.) ; Savage (E. A.).

OXFORD.
Statement of the needs of the University.   *Oxford*, 1902
Catalogue of a loan collection of portraits.   *Oxford*, 1904
Historical Pageant.   *Oxford*, 1907

Oxford and Cambridge Magazine. Nos. 1, 2, 3, 5, 6. *London*, 1856
Oxford and Cambridge Miscellany Poems. (Ed. by E. Fenton.)
                                                    London [1709]
Oxford and Cambridge Nuts to Crack. 2nd ed.   *London*, 1835
Oxford and Cambridge Review. July, 1845–Dec. 1846. 3 vols.
                                                    London, 1845–6
Oxford and Cambridge Schools Examination Board. Regulations.
                                                    1874
—— Examinations for certificates, July, 1894.   1894
Oxford Architectural Society. Visit to Cambridge, 28 May, 1880.
  Itinerary.   (1880)
—— Visit to Cambridge, 19 June, 1889.   (1889)
Oxford Declaration (1864). Papers relating thereto. 1864
Oxford Essays, 1855, 1857.   *London*, 1855–7
Oxford Historical Society. Prospectus and statements.
                                          4° *Oxford*, 1883–1900
Oxford University Dramatic Society. Twelfth Night, 1886 ; Julius
  Caesar, 1889 ; Two Gentlemen of Verona, 1893. Programmes,
  etc.   (*Oxford*, 1886–93)
—— *See also* Aristophanes; Carr (P.) ; Nugent (C.).

P

PACKE (C.)   Charles Packe.   By Comte Henry Russell.   *Pau*, 1896
PAGET (F.E.)   A tract upon tomb-stones.   *Rugeley*, 1843
PAGET (*Sir* G.E.)   The President's address at the meeting of the British
    Association at Cambridge.   *London*, 1864
PAGET (*Lady*)   Wise Texts from the Ancients.   1893
PALEY (F.A.)   The ecclesiologist's guide to the Churches within a
    circuit of seven miles round Cambridge.   1844
—— Another ed.   *London*, 1844
    Cuttings concerning his supposed connection with Mr Morris's
    secession to Rome.   Oct. and Nov. 1846.
    The Anglican system as exhibited in the Universities.   (*Dolman's*
    Magazine, May, 1847.)
    Religious Tests and National Universities.   *London*, 1871
PALEY (W.)   Sermon before the University...5 July, 1795.
                              4º *London*, 1795
    Analysis of Paley's Evidences.   By J. Joyce.   4th ed.   *Harlow*, 1810
    Analysis of Paley's Principles.   By C. V. Le Grice.   7th ed.
                                    London, 1820
PALFREY (D.)   An address to the Members of the Senate, in the
    matter of D. Palfrey.   [By J. Tomkyns.]   (1827)
PALMER (E.H.)   Ye hole in ye walle.   A legende of Walthamstowe
    Abbey.   4º 1860
    Testimonials.   *Hertford*, 1867
    Catalogue of the Oriental MSS. in the library of King's College,
    Cambridge.   (*Royal Asiatic Soc.*)   (*London*, 1867)

    The expedition of Prof. Palmer, Captain Gill, and Lieut. Charrington.
    (Newspaper cuttings, 18 Oct.–27 Nov. 1882.)
    Correspondence concerning the murder of Prof. Palmer, Capt. Gill, and
    Lieut. Charrington.   (Blue Book.)   Fº *London*, 1883
    The life and achievements of E. H. Palmer.   By Walter Besant.
                                      London, 1883
    An interpreter's account of the search expedition, in manuscript.   [1883 ?]
    Review of *Man-hunting in the Desert: being a narrative of the Palmer search*
    expedition.   (*Athenæum*, 21 Nov. 1884.)

PALMER (J.)   Abstract of his diary.   By J. B. Pearson.   1899
PANDECT.   A Quarterly Magazine.   No. 1.   1843
PANTON (D.M.) and Blakeney (E.H.)   Poems by two friends,
    E. H. Blakeney and D. M. Panton.   1892
PAPER Lantern for Puseyites.   By "Will o' the Wisp."   *London*, 1843
PARAVICINI.   *See* De Paravicini.
PARKER (J.H.)   The Ashmolean Museum.   *Oxford*, 1870

PARKER (R.)   A View of Cambridge.   (*In* The History and
Antiquities of the University of Cambridge.)   *London*, 1721
—— Another ed.   *London* [1721]
PARKER'S London Magazine.   Nos. 1–2.   Jan.–Feb. 1845.   [The
Close-Arnold controversy.]   *Oxford*, 1845
PARKIN (C.)   An answer to, or remarks upon, Dr Stukeley's *Origines
Roystonianae*.   4º *London*, 1744
PARLIAMENTARY Representatives.   *See* Representatives.
PARNASSUS Plays.   The Pilgrimage to Parnassus with the...Return
from Parnassus.   Ed. W. D. Macray.   *Oxford*, 1886
PARNE (T.)   A sermon preached in Trinity College Chapel in
Cambridge, Dec. 21, 1721.   In commemoration of the Founders
and Benefactors.   *London*, 1722
PARROT.   Nos. 1, 2.   9, 10 June, 1893.   [By W. Peacock, Trin.]
4º 1893
PARRY (*Sir* C.H.H.)   Eton.   An Ode by A. C. Swinburne.   Set to
music.   4º *London* (1891)
See also Greek Plays performed at Cambridge.   Birds, 1903.
PASSAGES in the life of an Undergraduate.   By Bee Bee.
London, 1887
PASTOR of Dulichium.   By "A Bird."   [On J. T. Sheppard, King's,
and *The Birds* of 1903.]   1903
PASTORAL for the Times, after the manner of Virgil's Pollio.   By
a Cambridge Undergraduate.   Revised with notes by a Cambridge
Graduate.   1869
PATRICK (S.), *Bp of Ely*.   Sermon preached at the funeral of John
Smith...1652...with a short account of his life.   *See* Smith (J.).
Select Discourses.   4th ed.   1859.
Brief Account of the new sect of Latitude-Men.   By S. P.
[? S. Patrick].   4º *London*, 1662
PATTESON (*Sir* J.)   Rating of the Colleges.   Sir J. Patteson's
award.   Fº 1855
Report of Syndicate to obtain Act of Parliament to confirm Sir J.
Patteson's award.   4º (1855)
Bill to confirm Sir J. Patteson's award.   Fº *London*, 1856
—— As amended in Committee.   Fº *London*, 1856
Act to confirm Sir J. Patteson's award (5 June, 1856).
Fº *London*, 1857
See also Rating.
PATTISON (M.)   Suggestions on Academical organisation with
especial reference to Oxford.   *Edinburgh*, 1868
Memoirs.   *London*, 1885
PATTISON (W.)   Poetical Works.   *London*, 1728
PAUL (C.K.)   Stories of old Eton Days.   (*Nineteenth Century*, October,
1892.)
PAULOPOSTPRANDIALS.   [By O. Seaman, H. C. Monro, and
L. Speed.]   3rd ed.   4º 1883
PAUW (J.C.de)   Philargyrii Cantabrigiensis emendationes in Me-
nandri...reliquias.   *Amstelodami*, 1711

PAVING and Drainage.   Notes by G. F. Cobb, 17 May, 5 June.
1878
PAVING and Lighting.   *See* King's College, 1831.
PAYN (F.W.)   Trumpington's Wave.   A 'Varsity poem.   1896
PAYN (J.)   Poems.   1853
  The Foster Brothers.   *London*, 1859
  Some literary recollections.   *London*, 1884
PEACE.   A narrative of the celebration of peace at Cambridge...
  July 12, 1814.   1814
PEACE in War.   In Memoriam L[ouisa] R[yder].   [By G. W.
  Blunt.]   1856
PEACOCK (G.)   Observations on plans for New Library.   By a
  Member of the First Syndicate [G. P.].   1831
  Remarks on Replies to *Observations*, etc.   By a Member of the First
  Syndicate [G. P.].   1831
  Observations upon the Report made by a Syndicate appointed to
  confer with the Architects who were desired to furnish the
  University with designs for a New Library.   1835
  Observations on the Statutes of the University of Cambridge.   1841
  Oratio...12 Nov. 1852.   4° 1859

  Strictures on certain parts of Peacock's Algebra.   By a Graduate.   1837
  Mathematical and scientific works, being a portion of the Library of the
    late G. P....to be sold, Dec. 7, 1858.   1858
  Funeral Sermon.   By W. H. Thompson.   1858
  Peacock Memorial.   (Circular.   Issued by H. Goodwin.)   1860

PEARCE (E.S.)   A sermon...14 March, 1824.   *London*, 1824
PEARCE (Z.)   Epistolae duae.   4° *London*, 1721
  A friendly letter to Dr Bentley.   *London*, 1732
PEARSON (A.C.)   Testimonials when a candidate for the Vicarage of
  Ilketshall St Margaret.   1893
PEARSON (E.)   A sermon preached before the University of Cam-
  bridge, Nov. 5, 1793.   (1793)
  Letter to a Member of the Senate.   1799
  Cautions to the hearers and readers of...Simeon's Sermon, entitled,
  Evangelical and Pharisaical righteousness compared.
                                              Broxbourn (1810)
  See also Simeon (C.), 1810.
PEARSON (G.)   The danger of abrogating Religious tests.   1834
  The Doctrine of Tradition...Sermon preached before the University
  of Cambridge, 11 March, 1838.   1838
PEARSON (J.B.)   Letter to the Vice-Chancellor on Library Catalogue.
1863
  On the observance of Sunday in England.   1867
  Index to English books before 1700 in Emmanuel College Library.
1869
  A biographical sketch of the Chaplains to the Levant Company,
  maintained at Constantinople, Aleppo, and Smyrna, 1611–1706.
1883

PEARSON (J.B.)
Abstract of the diary of John Palmer, M.A.   1899
The Church of Chulmleigh, N. Devon. (*Trans. Devon. Assoc.*)
                                                 (*Plymouth*) 1907
PEARSON (K.) The Trinity. A nineteenth century Passion-Play.
                                                              1882
PEAT (J.) Congratulatory lines on the Installation of H.R.H. Prince
    Albert at Cambridge, July, 1847.   4° (1847)
PECKARD (P.) Memoirs of the life of Nicholas Ferrar.   1790
PEDANTIUS. Comoedia olim Cantabrig. acta in Coll. Trin.
    [? By T. Beard.] [Wants title.]   12° *London*, 1631
    —— Ed. by G. C. M. Smith.   *Louvain*, 1905
PEED (W.) Notice of first meeting of his creditors, 18 Oct. 1897
PEEP under the Hood. By Bo-Peep, of Oxford.   *London*, 1843
PEERS (C.) Christ's lamentation over Jerusalem. (Seatonian Prize
    Poem for 1805.)   4° 1805
PEILE (J.) Christ's College. (College histories.)   *London*, 1900
PELL (A.) Reminiscences. Ed. by T. Mackay.   *London*, 1908
PEM. Nos. 1–13. New series: nos. 1–9.   1893–1908
PEMBERTON (C.) The Scapegoat. By Leo [i.e. C. Pemberton].
    2 vols.   *London*, 1869
PEMBERTON (T.P.) Sermon preached in the Chapel of Trin. Coll.
    Camb. on the occasion of the commemoration of benefactors on
    9 Dec. 1902.   1902
PEMBROKE College. List of books presented...in 14th and 15th
    centuries. By G. E. Corrie. (*C.A.S.*)   1860
    Statutes, approved by the Queen in Council, 29 June, 1882.   1882
    Descriptive catalogue of the MSS. By M. R. James. With a
    hand list of the Printed Books to the year 1500. By E. H. Minns.
                                                              1905
PENNY (F.H.) Buried Oxford unearthed.   *Oxford*, 1899
"PEPYS (Samuel)" Diary while an Undergraduate at Cambridge.
    [By C. R. W. Cooke, Emm.]   1864
    —— 2nd ed.   1866
PERCEVAL (C.S.) On seals attached to documents in the Muniment
    Room, Trin. Coll. (*Proc. Soc. Ant.*)   (*London*) 1869
PERCIVAL (E.F.) Statutes of Merton Coll., Oxford. *London*, 1847
PERCIVAL (J.) Syllabus of course of twelve lectures on the elemen-
    tary principles of Chemistry.   1891
PEREGRINATIONS of Parafine. By Tilleul.   [1906]
PERIODICAL PUBLICATIONS.

    ₊ Fuller particulars will be found under the various titles.

Academica.	Basileona.
Agenda.	Bear.
Alma Mater.	Beldragon.
Anti-Snarl.	Benedict.
Appointments Gazette.	Blue 'Un.
Armadillo.	Brass Halo.

PERIODICAL PUBLICATIONS.

Bubble.
Caian.
Cam.
Cambridge A. B. C.
Cambridge Annual.
Cambridge Christmas Annual.
Cambridge Chronicle.
Cambridge Fortnightly.
Cambridge Journal.
Cambridge Magazine.
Cambridge Meteor.
Cambridge Observer.
Cambridge Quarterly Review.
Cambridge Review.
Cambridge Tatler.
Cambridge Terminal Magazine.
Cambridge University Almanac.
Cambridge University Calendar.
Cambridge University Gazette.
Cambridge University Magazine.
Cambridge University Register.
Cambridge University Reporter.
Cantab.
Christ's College Magazine.
Dial.
Eagle.
Ecclesiologist.
Emmanuel College Magazine.
Etonian (s.v. Eton, 1822).
Etonian (s.v. Eton, 1904).
Fellow.
Fitzwilliam Hall Magazine.
Gadfly.
Galvanist.
Gownsman.
Granta.
Half Blue.
Hospital Inkstand.
Individual.
Inspector.
Jack-Daw.
K.P.
Lady Clare Magazine.
    See also Marillier (H. C.).

Lantern of the Cam.
Leys Fortnightly.
Light Blue.
Light Green.
Lion.
Loiterer.
May Bee.
Mayfly.
Microcosm.
Miniature.
Momus.
Moslem in Cambridge.
Mushroom.
Oxford and Cambridge Magazine.
Oxford and Cambridge Review.
Pandect.
Parker's London Magazine.
Parrot.
Pem.
Perse School Christmas Annual.
Persean Magazine.
Pheon.
Pink.
Punch in Cambridge.
Ralph's Bottle.
Reflector.
St Peter's World.
Screed.
Sex.
Silver Crescent.
Snarl.
Snob.
Student.
Sunflower.
Tatler.
Toby in Cambridge.
Trident.
Tripos.
True Blue.
University Extension.
Wasp.
Working Men's College Magazine.
Wrangler.

PEROWNE (E.H.)   Oratio Latina.   (Members' Prize.)   1852
    Corporate responsibility.   A sermon preached before the University
    of Cambridge, at the Commemoration of Benefactors, June 15,
    1862.   1862

PEROWNE (E.H.).
  Counsel to Undergraduates on entering the University. A sermon preached in the Chapel of Corpus Christi College, Cambridge, Oct. 25, 1863.   1863
PEROWNE (J.J.S.) Remarks on Dr Donaldson's Book, entitled *Jashar*.   *London*, 1855
See Donaldson (J. W.) ; Thirlwall (C.).
PEROWNE (T.T.) Sermon preached in St Michael's Church, 17 April, 1853, the Sunday after the funeral of the Rev. J. Schole-field.   1853
  The duty of recognising a paramount object in life. A sermon preached in the Chapel of Corpus Christi College, Oct. 21, 1866.
                                                                      1866
PERRY (C.), *Bp of Melbourne*. Clerical education.   *London*, 1841
  A farewell sermon preached at St Paul's Church, Cambridge, May 23, 1847.   1847
  The Christian's light shining to God's glory. A sermon preached... July 4, 1847.   1847
  The character of the writings of the Rev. F. D. Maurice, shown by an examination of his sermon on the Sacrifices of Cain and Abel.
                                                                Geelong, 1859
PERRY (S.) A letter to the Duke of Gloucester...on the necessity of an enquiry into the conduct of the Bishop of London towards... Ten Year Men.   *London*, 1825
  A letter to the Public Orator, on the ordination of Non-Graduates under the Ten Year Divinity Statute.   *London*, 1825
See also Ten Year Men.
PERSE School. Christmas Annual, 1878, 1879.   1878-9
  The Perse School, Cambridge. Notes from Admission Registers of Gonville and Caius College, etc. By J. Venn and S. C. Venn.
                                                                      1890
PERSE Trust. Scheme for management, 26 June, 1873.   1873
PERSEAN Magazine. II. 11-18; III. 19-24; IV. 30.   1897-1904
PERSIUS (Peter), *pseud.* The Cambridge Odes.   12° [183-]
—— 2nd ed.   12° [183-]
PESHALL (*Sir* J.) *See* Wood (A. à). Antient and present state of the city of Oxford, 1773.
PETERHOUSE. An account of a late rustication from Peterhouse, in the University of Cambridge. (By R. Hopper.) *London*, 1776
A Postscript to same. (By R. Hopper.)   *London*, 1776
An account of a late dispute between the Bishop of Ely [J. Yorke] and the Fellows of Peterhouse, concerning the election of the Master of that College.   [? 1788]
—— 2nd ed.   [? 1788]
Additions and amendments to the draft of Statutes proposed for St Peter's College. By William Jack.   1860
Sexcentenary of Peterhouse. Invitation Cards, Programme, etc. 1884
Sexcentenary. The former days. A sermon preached by the Bp of Ely [J. R. Woodford] in the Chapel, Dec. 22, 1884. 1885

PETERHOUSE.
St Peter's World. Vol. I. Nos. 1–3 ; Vol. II. Nos. 1–2. 1889–90
The Sex. Magazine of the Peterhouse Sexcentenary Club. Nos. 1–40.
1897–1910
Catalogue of the MSS. in the Library of Peterhouse. By M. R. James.
With an essay on the history of the Library, by J. W. Clark. 1899
Peterhouse. By T. A. Walker. (College histories.) *London*, 1906
Sermon preached at the commemoration of benefactors by the Bp of
Ely [F. H. Chase]. 1907
Peterhouse Library, Cambridge. By J. W. Clark. (*Country Life*,
9 Feb. 1907.)
See also Hotham (C.).
PETITION of the University to H. of Commons against the Bill to
restrain the disposition of lands, whereby they become inalienable.
F° 1736
PEYTON (A.) " Peyton and Tithes." (1835)
PHALARIS. Epistolæ. Ed. C. Boyle. *Oxford*, 1695
—— Another ed. *Oxford*, 1718
Epistles. Transl. by T. Francklin. *London*, 1749
See also Bentley (R.), 1697, etc.
PHEAR (S.G.) Reply to letter of enquiries addressed by the University
Commissioners to certain members of the University. 1878
PHELPS (R.) Letter [to Provost of King's College] on the Gas
Company and Lighting, 12 June, 1868. 1868
College endowments and the Philosophers. 1872
Correspondence with the Universities Commission. 1873
College and University at Cambridge. Nos. 7, 8, 9, 12, 13, 14, 15,
16, 17, 22. 4° and 8° 1875–7
PHEON. Sidney Sussex College Magazine. Tercentenary edition.
Feb. 14, 1896. 1896
PHILALETHES *Cantabrigiensis*. Letter to the...Quarterly Review...
London, 1819
PHILARET. Bede, an Idyll. By Philaret. 1900
PHILARGYRIUS *Cantabrigiensis*. *See* Pauw (J. C. de).
PHILELEUTHERUS *Cantabrigiensis*. Animadversions upon the
University's proceedings against Dr Bentley. *London*, 1722
PHILIP'S (St) Parish. Report and Accounts for 1906. 1907
PHILLIMORE (W.P.W.) Cambridgeshire Parish Registers. Mar-
riages. Ed. by W. P. W. Phillimore, C. J. B. Gaskoin, and
E. Young. Vols. 1, 2, 3. *London*, 1907–9
PHILLPOTTS (H.), *Bp of Exeter*. Speech on occasion of a petition
from certain members of the Senate of Cambridge, April 21, 1834.
London, 1834
Letter to Dr Phillpotts containing strictures on his Speech...
London, 1834
See also Sellon (L.).
PHILO-UNION, or Cambridge Literary Society, 1826–1888. A
record. [By R. Bowes, W. Cockerell, and Harry Johnson.] 1890
PHILOGRANTUS, *pseud*. *See* Monk (J. H.).

PHILOSOPHICAL Society. (Papers and Notices of the formation
of the Society, Oct.–Nov. 1819.)   4° 1819
Regulations.   [? 1820]
List of Members.   4° 1820
Address read at the first meeting. By E. D. Clarke.   4° 1821
Notice of Publication of Vol. 1. of the Transactions, 28 Feb. 1821.
(Signed: A. Sedgwick.)   4° 1821
Rules and List of the Society, May 6, 1822.   4° 1822
Officers, etc.   4° [1827 ?]
Charter and Bye-Laws.   1832
Statement by President and Secretaries soliciting subscriptions for
new house, 7 April, 1832.   F° 1832
List of Members [between 1832 and 1835].   4° [1832–5]
Catalogue of collection of British Quadrupeds and Birds in the
Museum of the Society.   12° 1836
Balance sheets for 1836, 1837.   F° 1836–7
Circular advocating the establishment of a Reading Room.   1856
Regulations for Reading Room.   F° n.d.
Charter and Bye-Laws.   1857
Appeal to the Camb. Philosophical Soc. By Rob. Moon.   1872
Foundation and early years. By J. W. Clark. (*Camb. Phil. Soc.
Proc.*)   1891
PHILPOT (C.) Faith, a Vision. (Seatonian Prize Poem for 1790.)
                                                         4° 1790
PHILPOTT (H.), *Bp of Worcester*. Remarks on the question of
adopting the regulations recommended by the Syndicate appointed,
Feb. 9, 1848. (University studies.)   (1848)
Documents relating to St Catharine's College in the University of
Cambridge.   1861
See also Endowments.
PHOTOGRAPHIC Convention of the United Kingdom. Oxford
Meeting, 8–13 July, 1901.   *Oxford*, 1901
—— Cambridge Meeting, 7–12 July, 1902.   1902
PHRONTISTERION. Scenes from an unfinished drama entitled
Phrontisterion. [By H. L. Mansel.] 4th ed.   *Oxford*, 1852
—— 5th ed.   *Oxford*, 1861
PHYSIOLOGICAL Laboratory. Studies from the Physiological
Laboratory in the University of Cambridge. 3 parts.   1873–7
PICTURES at Play, illustrated by H. Furniss.   *London*, 1888
PICTURESQUE Cambridge.   12° *London* [1909 ?]
PIGOTT (W.G.F.) *See* Abington Pigotts.
PILGRIMAGE to Cambridge in the year 1900. By Ignotus Ignoramus
Muddlehead.   1881
PINK. Monday, June 5, 1899.   4° 1899
PINK (J.) Catalogue of Cambridge books, etc. in Free Library. 4 pts.
                                                         1874–99
After fifty years. Retrospect of the Free Library.   1905
PINNOCK (W.H.) An analysis of Ecclesiastical History. 2nd ed.
                                                          1848

PINNOCK (W.H.).
  An analysis of Scripture History. 4th ed.   1850
  An analysis of New Testament History.   1850
PIPE (The), and how to use it. By a Cantab.   1856
PIPE Lights for the Piper. By A[mbrose] E[lton].   1891
PITT Club. Rules, etc. October Term, 1885, 1893, 1899. 1885–99
PITT Press. *See* Press (University).
PLAIN account of the nature and end of the Sacrament [by B. Hoadly]
  contrary to Scripture. [By Susannah Newcome.]   1738
PLAIN and friendly Address to the Under-Graduates of Cambridge.
          London, 1786
PLAN for an Amphitheatre for Music and Publick Lectures. F° (1768)
PLATE. Catalogue of loan collection, Cambridge, 1895.   1895
  Illustrated catalogue of loan collection, 1895.   4° 1896
PLATITUDE (Peter) Letters on Cambridge and the Cantabs.
  Pts 1, 2.   1841–2
PLATO. A poem. (Unsuccessful Prize Poem, 1843.)   1843
  See also Maine (*Sir* H. J. S.).
PLAYTIME with a Pen. [By G. H. Powell.]   1891
PLEA for Cambridge. (Reprinted from the *Quarterly Review*, April,
  1906.)   *London,* 1907
PLEA for the Private Tutors, or Alumnus in search of a dodge.
          Oxford, 1843
PLUMIAN Professorship. The Deed of Foundation of Dr T. Plume
  for the establishing his Professorship in Astronomy and Experimental
  Philosophy.   (1818)
  Regulations, 16 Dec. 1828.   F° 1828
PLUMPTRE (J.) Osway : a tragedy.   4° *Norwich,* 1795
  Ecloga Sacra. Ed. altera.   4° 1796
  Four discourses on...the Stage, preached at Great St Mary's Church.
          1809
  The way in which we should go. Sermon preached in St Botolph's
    Church, Cambridge, 11 Dec. 1808, for the benefit of the new
    school, established on Dr Bell's and Mr Lancaster's system of
    education.   1809
  Forbidding to marry, a departure from the faith. A sermon preached
    before the University of Cambridge, Nov. 8, 1812.   1812
PLUMPTRE (R.) Hints respecting some of the University officers,
  its jurisdiction, its revenues, etc.   1782
POEM attempting something upon the rarities of the most renowned
  University of Cambridge.   4° *London,* 1673
POEM in answer to a Lampoon which was wrote on the Cambridge
  Ladies.   F° *London,* 1731
POEMS. A collection of Poems. By the author of a Poem on the
  Cambridge Ladies.   1733
POEMS. By the Bard of the Forest [i.e. W. Wickenden].   1823
POEMS of early years, in nine chaplets. By a Wrangler.
          London, 1851
POETS in Pupil Room. By Themselves, or practically so. *Eton,* 1908

POLICE Force. Regulations and instructions for the guidance of the Cambridge Police Force.   1857
See also Burdakin (J.).

POLITICAL Economy. Address of H. D. Macleod, Oct. 8, 1863.
Fº (1863)

Thoughts on the election of a Professor. By H. D. Macleod. 1863

Poll for the Election of Professor, 27 Nov. 1863. (H. M. Fawcett elected.)   Fº 1863

POLL degree. *See* Burn (R.); Girdlestone (W. H.); Latham (H.); Mayor (J. B.); Stephen (*Sir* L.).

POLLOCK (*Sir* F.) The methods of Jurisprudence.   *London*, 1882

Personal reminiscences. 2 vols.   *London*, 1887

POLLOCK (F.J.) Lord Acton at Cambridge. (*Indep. Rev.*, April, 1904.)

POLYCEPHALUS (Hydra), *pseud.* The Galvanist, 1–11.   [1804]

POOR Laws. Letter to the Electors of Cambridge touching...the Poor-Laws.   1837

POOR Man's Case against the Church-Rate Abolition Bill.   1837

POOR Rate. Argument in the case of the Poor's Rate charged on the Colleges of Christ and Emmanuel, 1768. [By Sir J. Marriott.]
(1768)

POPE (*Sir* T.) Life. By Thomas Warton.   *London*, 1780

PORSON (R.) Letter to Archdeacon Travis.   *London*, 1790

Tracts and Miscellaneous Criticisms. Ed. T. Kidd.   *London*, 1815

Prælectio in Euripidem recitata...1792.   1828

Account of his last illness. By J. Savage.   *London*, 1808

A short account of the late R. Porson. By an Admirer of a great Genius [S. Weston].   *London*, 1808

A Vindication of the character of the late Prof. Porson. By Crito Cantabrigiensis [T. Turton].   1827

Letter to the Rev. Thomas Benyon...in reply to a Vindication of...Prof. Porson, by Crito Cantabrigiensis [Thomas Turton]. By T. Burgess.
Salisbury, 1829

Vice Chancellor's notices of foundation of his Scholarship, 3 June, 19 Oct. 1846.   Fº (1846)

Literary anecdotes and contemporary reminiscences of Professor Porson and others. From the MS. papers of the late E. H. Barker. 2 vols.
London, 1852

Porson. By H. R. Luard. (Cambridge Essays.)   *London*, 1857

Life. By J. S. Watson.   *London*, 1861

See also Euripides.

PORSON Prize. *See* Prolusiones.

PORTER (J.) On compulsory attendance at Professors' lectures.
1877

Catalogue of books...furniture, etc. sold Dec. 1900.   1900

PORTEUS (B.) The character of David, King of Israel. A sermon preached 29 Nov. 1761.   1761

PORTEUS Medal. *See* Deck (J.).

PORTRAITS. *See* Antiquarian Society, 1884–5 ; Oxford, 1904.
POSIE of Poesies.   1839
POSTGATE (J.P.) Testimonials when a candidate for the Chair of
    Latin in University College, London.   1880
Latin Translation of " God save the King." (*Class. Rev.*, June, 1902.)
POSTGRADUATES : a suggestion for a comic opera. By R. H.
    F[orster].   1895
POTTER (M.C.) Testimonials when candidate for Chair of Botany
    in the Owens College, Manchester.   4° *Newcastle*, 1892
POTTINGER (H.A.) University Tests. A short account of the
    contrivances by which the Acts of Parliament abolishing Tests
    have been evaded at Oxford.   *London*, 1873
POTTS (A.H.) Verses on the Queen's visit to Trinity College,
    Cambridge, 25 Oct. 1843.   4° (1843)
Ode on the 300th Anniversary of Trin. Coll., 22 Dec. 1846.
                                                        4° 1846
Recollections of the Installation.   F° 1847
Sketches of Character, and other pieces in verse.   1849
Simple Poems.   12° 1852
POTTS (R.) A few brief remarks on the scheme proposed for the
    future management of the University Press.   1854
Liber Cantabrigiensis. An account of aids to poor students.... 2 vols.
                                                        1855–63
Letter to Members of the Senate on compulsory Celibacy. 4° 1857
Remarks on some points connected with sections xxiii–xxvi of the
    Cambridge University Act.   (1857)
Names of Members of the Senate in support of petition against Irish
    Church bill, June, 1869.   1869
A few brief remarks on Cambridge University and College reform.
                                                         1870
Greek as an optional subject. (*Indep. Press*, 1 Feb. 1873.)   (1873)
Account of the settlement of the Rifle Prize Fund.   1881
A few brief remarks on the recent legislation for the Colleges and
    University of Cambridge.   *London*, 1882
See Edward VI., *King of England* ; Sherlock (W.) ; Turner (W.) ;
    Wyclif (J.).
POWELL (B.) The present state and future prospects of mathematical
    and physical studies in the University of Oxford.   *Oxford*, 1832
POWELL (E.) The rising in East Anglia in 1381.   1896
POWELL (G.H.) Playtime with a Pen.   1891
POWELL (W.S.) Heads of a course of lectures in experimental
    philosophy.   1753
A defence of the Subscriptions required in the Church of England.
    A sermon preached before the University of Cambridge, Com-
    mencement Sunday, 1757. 2nd ed.   *London*, 1758
——— 3rd ed.   *London*, 1759
——— 4th ed.   4° *London*, 1772
Remarks on Dr Powell's Sermon in defence of Subscriptions. [By
    Fra. Blackburne.]   *London*, 1758

POWELL (W.S.)

The hardship and danger of Subscriptions...in a letter to Dr Powell. With Remarks upon his Sermon.   *London*, 1758

Defence of his Observations on the first chapter of a book [by E. Waring] called *Miscellanea analytica*.   *London*, 1760

A Charge delivered to the Clergy of the Archdeaconry of Colchester, June, 1772.   1772

An observation on the design of establishing annual examinations at Cambridge.   1774

POWER (J.) Index to the Baker MSS. [By J. P. and others.]   1848

POWIS Medal. *See* Prolusiones.

POYNDER (A.J.) Our College grounds (St John's). (*Eagle*.)   1882

PRAED (W.M.) The Ascent of Elijah. (Seatonian Prize Poem for 1830.)   1831

Poems: with memoir by Rev. D. Coleridge. 2 vols.   *London*, 1864

Essays: collected and arranged by Sir G. Young.   *London*, 1887

Political and Occasional poems: ed. Sir G. Young.   *London*, 1888

PRAELECTIONS delivered before the Senate of the University of Cambridge, 25, 26, 27 January, 1906. [*See* Adam, J.; Headlam, W.; Jackson, H.; Ridgeway, W.; Verrall, A. W.]   1906

PRESCOT (K.) St Paul at Athens.   1770

PRESCOTT (G.F.) Unity of design in successive dispensations recorded in the Scriptures. (Burney Prize Essay for 1850.)   1850

PRESENTATION to University livings. Fly-sheets and candidatures relating thereto, from 1866.   1866–

PRESS (University) Facts and observations relative to the state of the University Press. By I. Milner and J. Wood.   (1809)

Reply of R. Watts, to the Report of Dr Milner and Mr Wood, relative to the University Press affairs.   4° 1809

Observations on some recent University buildings, together with remarks on the management of the Public Library and Pitt Press. By Francis Bashforth.   1853

A few brief remarks on the scheme proposed for the future management of the University Press. By R. Potts.   1854

Fly-sheets, reports, etc. from 1855.   1855–

Correspondence in reference to arrangement of the Church services first introduced in Cambridge editions of 1871.   1876

Notes on the Cambridge University Press (1701–1707). By R. Bowes. (*C. A. S.*)   1887

Catalogue of books published...1889, 1890, 1891, 1892, 1895, 1901–2, 1904, 1905, 1907.   1889–1907

Specimens of printing types and ornaments. (With a note by J. W. Clark.)   1901

The Cambridge University Press. (*British Printer*, vol. XVII., 1904.)

Partnership, 1904. Fly-sheets relating thereto.   4° 1904

Bulletin. Nos. 1–21.   4° 1904–10

Prospectus of Cambridge English Classics.   1907

Encyclopaedia Britannica. 11th ed. Descriptive pamphlet. (1910)

PRESTON (J.)　The New Covenant, or the Saints Portion.　7th ed.
4º *London*, 1631

The life of the renowned Doctor Preston, writ by his pupil, Master
Thomas Ball.　Ed. by E. W. Harcourt.　*Oxford*, 1885

PREVIOUS Examination.　Proposals to institute, 8 March, 1822.
Fº (1822)

Interpretation of Regulation viii, passed 13 March, 1822.　3 May,
1823.　Fº (1823)

Publication by Vice-Chancellor of extracts from the Rules, in conse-
quence of irregular attendance, 20 March, 1828.　Fº (1828)
Fly-sheets, etc. from 1856.　1856–
See also Greek ; Hudson (W. H. H.).

PRICE (Bonamy)　Oxford Reform.　*Oxford*, 1875
PRICKETT (M.)　Some account of Barnwell Priory, Cambridge.　1837
See Fuller (T.).　History of the University of Cambridge, 1840.
PRIESTLEY (J.)　A letter to the Rt Hon. W. Pitt...on the subjects
of Toleration and Church Establishments.　2nd ed.　*London*, 1787
PRIME (G.)　*See* Pryme (G.).
PRIMROSE (P.)　Hints on Examinations.　1822
PRIOR (S.J.)　Testimonials when a candidate for the Rectory of
Ovington, Norfolk.　(With his Address to the Senate and a List
of his supporters.)　1883
PRITCHARD (C.)　Vindiciae Mosaicae.　A letter to the Rt Rev.
Bp Colenso.　*London*, 1863
PRIZE Poems.　*See* Prolusiones ; Seatonian Prize Poems.
PRIZES.　An alphabetical list of the several gentlemen who have
gained honors and prizes in the University of Cambridge to the
year 1836.　1836
See also Sertum Cantabrigiense.
PROCTER (J.)　A plain statement of facts, addressed to the Members
of the Senate, in reply to a pamphlet by the Master of Christ's
College, entitled, *An Examination of Calumnies*, etc.　1810
Remarks on two pamphlets lately published at Cambridge, the first
entitled *An Examination of Calumnies*, etc. by the Master of
Christ's College ; the second entitled *A plain Statement of Facts*,
by the Master of Catharine Hall.　*London*, 1811
See also Browne (T.), *Master of Christ's College*.
PROCTORS.　A letter to the Vice-Chancellor of Oxford, containing
a few remarks on Proctorial power, with reference to a late event
at Cambridge.　*Oxford*, 1847
Remarks on the bearing of the proposed Statute " De electione
Procuratorum," etc.　By J. S. Wood.　1857
Correspondence between the Vice-Chancellor and the late Pro-Proctors
relative to the proceedings in a recent case of immorality.　1859
The Proctorial system.　(Reprint from the *Daily Telegraph*, Feb. 7,
1860.)　s. sh. *n.p.* 1860
The Proctorial system.　Letters by J. H. Titcomb and J. Scott.
n.p. 1860

PROFESSORS.   Lectures.   Notices from 1804.   1804–
   Candidatures, fly-sheets, and other papers connected with the
   Professorships from 1825.   1825–
Return to an Order of the House of Commons, dated 27 Jan. 1846,
   for information relative to certain Professors, with explanations by
   R. Tatham, V.-C.   1846
Grace to appoint Syndicate to consider how studies for which Pro-
   fessorships have been founded may be encouraged, 4 Feb. 1848.
                                                          (1848)
Propositions submitted to this Syndicate.   (1848)
Report of this Syndicate, 16 Oct. 1848.   (1848)
Programme of lectures and regulations issued by V.-C., 6 June, 1849.
                                                      F^o (1849)
Programme of lectures, with places of delivery, 1849–1872.
                                                  F^o (1849–1872)
Graces for new statutes for Professorships offered to the Senate,
   26 Nov. 1857.   With account of their reception.   (*Camb. Chron.*)
Statutes for Regius Professorships, 10 May, 1860.   1860
Statutes for certain Professorships in the University of Cambridge.
   June and October, 1860.   F^o 1860
Professors' Fees.   Queries to Professors and other papers.   1862
Observations on the proposals of the Syndicate for establishing a
   " Professors' and Public Teachers' Fund."   By W. Johnson [Cory].
                                                          (1870)
Compulsory attendance at Professors' Lectures.   Letters, Papers, etc.
   1875–77.   F^o 1875–7
Return to House of Commons of Professors' duties and salaries.
                                                       F^o 1876
   See also the separate Professorships.
PROGRESS to B.A.   A poem by a Member of the University. 1830
   —— 2nd ed.   1830
PROJECTE conteyninge the state, order, and manner of govern-
   mente of the University of Cambridge : as now it is to be seene
   in the three and fortieth year of the raigne of our...Lady Elizabeth.
   Ed. by M. Lort.   4° 1769
PROLUSIONES.
   Greek Ode ; Latin Ode ; Greek Epigram ; Latin Epigram (= Sir
   William Browne's Medals).   Porson Prize (from 1817).
                                                      1796–1826

   Sir William Browne's Medals were first adjudged in 1775.   The
   successful exercises in that and succeeding years were written out by
   the prizemen themselves in a series of folio volumes preserved in the
   Registry.   The printing of exercises depended at first on the pleasure
   of the prizeman.   The above series is not quite continuous.   The
   names of the successful candidates, in each year, for the various prizes
   here mentioned will be found in the Cambridge University Calendar.

   Chancellor's English Medal.   1813–1826
      Both the above series were then merged in :

PROLUSIONES.
Prolusiones Academicae praemiis annuis dignatae et in Curia Canta-
brigiensi recitatae Comitiis Maximis A.D. 1827(–1829, 1831–1910).
1827–1910
The contents of each yearly volume are as follows :
Chancellor's English Medal.
Camden Medal (1841–66).
Greek Ode; Latin Ode; Greek Epigram ; Latin Epigram (= Sir
William Browne's Medals).
Powis Medal (from 1867).
Porson Prize.
Prolusiones [as above] A.D. 1830 (1832, 1833).   1830–3
In 1830 an enlarged edition of the Prolusiones was published which
contained, besides the usual exercises, the Members' Latin Essay Prizes.
In 1832 and 1833 editions were published containing the Members'
Latin Essay Prizes only.
Musae Cantabrigienses, seu carmina quaedam numismate aureo
Cantabrigiae ornata.   *London*, 1810
Prize Poems, being a complete collection of the English Poems which
have obtained the Chancellor's Gold Medal.   *London*, 1818
—— 2nd ed.   *London*, 1819
—— 3rd ed.   *London*, 1820
—— Another ed. 1813–1893. 2 vols.   *London*, 1859, 1894
The Greek and Latin Prize Poems from 1814–1832.   1833
The Greek and Latin Prize Poems from 1814–1837.   1837
See also Amos (S.), 1858; Bayley (H. V.), 1802 ; Butler (H. M.), 1854 ;
Cole (W.), 1780, 1811 ; Foster (J.), 1758 ; Frere (B.), [1798] ;
Frere (W.), [1797]; Gent (M.), 1855; Hankinson (T. E.), 1826–7;
Hopkins (B.), [1825] ; Hughes (T. S.), 1806 ; Lawson (M.), 1814,
1816 ; Maine (*Sir* H. J. S.), 1894; Mathias (T. J.), 1775;
Perowne (E. H.), 1852 ; Robertson (D. H.), 1910; Shilleto (R.),
1831 ; Smith (R. H.), 1857 ; Stoneham (T.), 1832 ; Sumner (J.B.),
1800 ; Trevelyan (R.), 1806, 1817; Tweddell (J.), 1789, 1793;
Waddington (H.), 1815; Woodham (H. A.), 1837–40.
Bannockburn ; Birth of the Prince of Wales ; Delphi ; Empire of
the Sea ; Expedition of Napoleon into Russia ; Napoleon's Invasion
of Russia ; Plato ; Taking of Jerusalem ; Timbuctoo.
PROTHERO (G.W.) Fellowships and Lectureships. (King's.) 1877
Lectures on the English Revolution of the seventeenth century.
Bishop's Stortford, 1878
The Historical Library. (*Camb. Review.*)   1884
The Abbeys of Croyland and Thorney. A sketch of their history.
Spalding, 1885
Memoir of Henry Bradshaw.   *London*, 1888
Testimonials when a candidate for Professorship of History in Uni-
versity of Edinburgh.   1894
Why should we learn History ? Inaugural lecture. *Edinburgh*, 1894
Presidential Address to the Royal Historical Society ; delivered
19 Feb. 1903.   (*London*, 1904)

PROVIDENT Bank.   Regulations.   F° [? 1822]

PRUNIÈRES (M. Villetard de).   *See* Villetard de Prunières (M.).

PRYME (A. de la)   Diary.   Ed. by C. Jackson.   (*Surtees Soc. publ.*)
Durham, etc., 1870

PRYME (C. de la)   The Roman Embassy.   A letter to Viscount
Palmerston.   3rd ed.   *Rome*, 1847
Martin Thackeray.   (*Gentleman's Magazine*, Sept. 1864.)
(*London*, 1864)
The statue of Byron in the Library of Trin. Coll.   (*Notes and Queries*,
1881.)   (*London*, 1881)

PRYME (G.)   Ode to Trinity College, Cambridge.   *London*, 1812
Syllabus of a course of lectures on principles of Political Economy.   1816
—— 2nd ed.   (In Introductory lecture, see below.)   1819
—— 3rd ed.   1852
An introductory lecture and syllabus, to a course delivered in the
University of Cambridge, on the principles of Political Economy.
1819
—— Another ed.   1823
A letter to the Freemen and Inhabitants of the Town of Cambridge,
on the state of the Borough.   1823
Jephthah.   *London*, 1838

Memoir.   (Extract from magazine.)   (1869)
Autobiographic recollections.   Ed. by his daughter.   1870

PRYME (J.T.) and Bayne (A.)   Memorials of the Thackeray family.
London, 1879

PRYNNE (G.R.)   *See* Sellon (L.).

PRYOR (F.R.) and Speed (L.)   The Oedipus Tyrannus.   A record of
the performance in Nov. 1887.   4° (1888)

PUBLIC Orator.   Poll at Election, 4 Feb. 1836.   (C. Wordsworth
elected.)   1836
—— 27 Apr. 1836.   2nd ed.   (T. Crick elected.)   1836
Fly-sheets, candidatures, etc. from 1836.   1836–
Poll at Election, 26 Oct. 1848.   (2 states.)   (W. H. Bateson elected.)
1848
—— 2 Nov. 1869.   (R. C. Jebb elected.)   1869
—— 19 Oct. 1876.   (J. E. Sandys elected.)   1876

PULLEINE (J.J.)   Adam Sedgwick.   A sermon preached at Dent,
Feb. 14, 1890.   *Sedbergh*, 1890

PULLEN (J.)   A lecture on astronomy delivered before the Grand
Gresham Committee, Nov. 28, 1833.   1833
The true Patriot.   A sermon preached Nov. 21, 1852, the Sunday
following the funeral of the Duke of Wellington.   1852
God's people afflicted.   A sermon preached in the parish church of
St Benedict, 21 March, 1855, being the day appointed for a
National Fast.   1855

PULLING (J.)   Catalogue of his sale.   9 May.   (Priced.)   1879
PULLING (W.)   A course of lectures on the French, Italian, Spanish,
and Portuguese languages.   1834

PUNCH in Cambridge.   Vols. 1, 2, 3.   Feb. 7, 1832–Dec. 23, 1834.
                                                            4º 1832–34
PUNCHARD (E.G.)   Cromwell and the old house at Ely.   *Ely*, 1906
PUNNETT (R.C.)   Mendelism.   2nd ed.   12º 1907
PURCHAS (J.)   Ode upon the death of the Marquis Camden,
    Chancellor of the University of Cambridge.   (1840)
    Schoolboy Reminiscences.   1844
    The Priest's dream.   An allegory.   1856
PURKIS (W.)   The influence of the present pursuits in learning, as
    they affect religion.   A sermon...2 July, 1786.   4º 1786
    The evils which may arise to the constitution of Great Britain from
    the influence of a too powerful nobility, considered in a sermon...
    29 May, 1789.   4º *London*, 1790
    Review of English literature as it respects moral and religious
    inquiry.   A Sermon, 25 Oct. 1789.   4º *London*, 1790
PURKISS (H.J.)   Injustice of *The Times*.   Statement by Jas. Hough
    respecting his conduct when H. J. Purkiss (Trin.) was drowned,
    17 Sept. 1865.   1865
PURNELL (E.K.)   Magdalene College.   (College histories.)
                                                     London, 1904
PURTON (J.S.)   The establishment of an examination before Matricu-
    lation considered.   1854
PYCROFT (J.)   The Collegian's guide : or recollections of College
    days.   *London*, 1845
    —— 2nd ed.   *London*, 1858
PYCROFT (J.W.)   The Oxford University Commission.   Letter to
    Sir R. H. Inglis.   2nd ed.   *Oxford*, 1851
PYCROFT (S.)   Brief enquiry into Free-Thinking...   1713
    Reflections upon the nature of contentment : and rules apply'd to
    particular circumstances of life.   1714

Q

QUAESTIONES philosophicae in usum juventutis collectae et digestae.
1732

QUEENS' College. The defence of the Rev. Reginald Bligh, of Queens' College, Cambridge, A.B., against the Fellows of that Society, who rejected him as an improper person for a Fellow, 12 Jan. 1780. *London* (1780)

Letters which passed between the Rev. Reginald Bligh, and others, on account of his being rejected as a Fellow of Queens' College, Cambridge, on pretence of his want of scholarship, etc.
London, 1781

The case of the President of Queens' College, Cambridge determined in the High Court of Chancery. Ed. by C. Bowdler.
London, 1821

Statuta Collegii Reginalis apud Cantab. 1559 a Regiis Commissariis reformata. (Ed. by G. C. Gorham.) 4° 1822

A Form for the Commemoration of Benefactors. 4° 1823

Catalogue of the Library. By T. H. Horne. 2 vols. *London*, 1827

Order of service for the dedication of the Chapel, 13 Oct. 1891

"The Beauty of Holiness." A sermon preached at the opening of a new organ in the Chapel of Queens' College...Sept. 27, 1892. By W. M. Campion. 1892

Sketch of the history of Queens' College. By J. W. Clark. 4° 1898

Queens' College. By J. H. Gray. (College histories.) *London*, 1899

Catalogue of the Western Manuscripts in the Library. By M. R. James. 1905

QUERELA Cantabrigiensis : or a remonstrance by way of apologie, for the banished Members of the late flourishing University of Cambridge. [By John Barwick.] 1647

—— (1685). *See* Mercurius Rusticus, 1723.

[QUERY] ? June, 1907. 4° 1907

QUIET Supper (with songs) at the rooms of X. Y. B., St Andrew's College, Cambridge. [Attr. to J. P. Wright.] 1864

QUIS desiderio sit pudor aut modus tam cari capitis ? [On the memorial to the Chancellor. By W. Selwyn.] 1862

R

RADCLYFFE (C.) Memorials of Eton College.   F° *Eton*, 1844
RAIKES (R.)   Oratio habita in scholis philosophicis.   4° 1767
RALEIGH (*Sir* W.)   Samuel Johnson.   The Leslie Stephen Lecture,
  delivered in the Senate House, Cambridge, 22 Feb. 1907.
                                                    Oxford, 1907
RALPH'S Bottle ; a choice collection of choice spirits.   (By a Cantab.)
  Nos. 1–4.   1840
RAMSDEN (R.)   The right to life.   A sermon preached before the
  University of Cambridge, Nov. 29, 1795.   1795
  Reflections on War.   Sermon...12 March, 1800.   1800
RAMSDEN Sermon, 1852.   On the subject of Church extension over
  the colonies and dependencies of the British Empire, 23 May.   By
  J. J. Blunt.   1852
  1853. Sermon, 22 May. By W. H. Mill.   1853
RANDALL (E.)   Freedom of election, the law of the land.   1802
RANDOLPH (J.)   *See* Marsh (H.).   Letters, 1802.
RANDOLPH (T.)   Poems, with the Muses Looking-Glasse and
  Amyntas.   3rd ed., whereunto is added The Jealous Lovers.
                                                    London, 1643

  The Muses Looking-Glasse, Amyntas, and The Jealous Lovers are separate
  books, as follows :

    The Muses Looking-Glasse. By T. R.   *London*, 1643
    Amyntas, or the Impossible Dowry. A pastorall acted...at White-
      Hall. By T. R.   *Oxford*, 1640
    The Jealous Lovers. A Comedie presented to their Majesties at
      Cambridge, by the Students of Trinitie-Colledge.   1640
  Poetical and dramatic works. Ed. by W. C. Hazlitt. 2 vols.
                                                    London, 1875
RANGER (W.)   Report to the General Board of Health, on...the
  Sewerage of Cambridge.   *London*, 1849
RANNIE (D.W.)   Oriel College, Oxford.   (College histories.)
                                                    London, 1900
RAPE of the Whisker.   An heroic poem.   With a dedication to all
  gentlemen who wear whiskers. [By Ch. Tindal.] 2nd ed.   1838
RASHDALL (H.)   The Universities of Europe in the Middle Ages.
  2 vols. in 3.   *Oxford*, 1895
  Rashdall (H.) and Rait (R.S.)   New College, Oxford.   (College
  histories.)   *London*, 1901

RATING.   Report of Borough Rating Committee.   F⁰ 1850
Reports of conferences on Rating, in the *Camb. Chron.*, Feb.–June.
                                                       1855
Broadsheet in favour of proposed Rating Bill, 24 Dec. 1896.
See also Patteson (*Sir* J.).

RATLAND Feast, an historico-ludicro-comico poem.   Translated from
   the Latin of M. V. Martialis, by Martinus Scriblerus, jun.   1820

RAVEN (J.J.)   The Church Bells of Cambridgeshire. *Lowestoft*, 1869

RAWDON (F.A.)   Anthem...performed in Great St Mary's Church,
   June 30, 1811.   Composed by G. H. Polegreen Bridgtower.
   (Words.)   1811

RAWSON (J.)   Concio ad clerum...28 Jan. 170⅛.   4⁰ *Londini*, 1709

RAY (J.)   Philosophical Letters between...Mr Ray and...his...corre-
   spondents.   Publ. by W. Derham.   *London*, 1718
   Travels through the Low Countries, etc.   2 vols.   *London*, 1738
   Select Remains, with his life by W. Derham.   Publ. by G. Scott,
   M.A.   *London*, 1760

RAY Club.   The Cambridge Ray Club.   (Account of the Club, List
   of Members, etc., by C. C. Babington.)   1857
—— Another ed.   1887

READE (J.)   Oratio habita Cantabrigiae in Coll. Regali.   4⁰ (1742)
   Gratulatio in adventum J. Sumner Coll. Regal. Praepositi.   4⁰ (1756)

REASONS for altering the method used at present in letting Church
   and College leases.   By the Senior Fellow of a College in Cambridge [John Colbatch].   1739

REASONS for declining to subscribe the Thirty-Nine articles.
                                                   London, 1836

REBELLION of the Beasts.   By a late Fellow of St John's College.
   2nd ed.   *London*, 1825

REDE (*Sir* R.)   Sir Robert Rede.   By T. Brocklebank.   (*C. A. S.*)
                                                         1859
   Proposed memorial to the founder of the Rede lecture.   1870

REDE Lecture, 1859.   On the classification and distribution of the
   Mammalia.   By Richard Owen.   *London*, 1859
   1863.   The correlation of the Natural History sciences.   By D. T.
   Ansted.   *London*, 1863
   1875.   The effects of observation of India on modern European
   thought.   By Sir H. S. Maine.   *London*, 1875
   1890.   Erasmus.   By R. C. Jebb.   1890.
   1892.   The Microscope's contributions to the earth's physical
   history.   By T. G. Bonney.   1892
   1894.   Libraries in the Medieval and Renaissance periods.   By J. W.
   Clark.   1894
   1900.   Byzantine History in the early Middle Ages.   By F.
   Harrison.   *London*, 1900

REDFERN (W.B.)   Old Cambridge.   4⁰ 1876
   Redfern (W.B.) and Clark (J.W.)   Ancient wood and iron work in
   Cambridge.   (Prospectus.)   [? 1881]
   Ancient wood and iron work in Cambridge.   F⁰ 1886

REES (A.) The Doctrine of Christ......Two Sermons preached at Cambridge, 27 June, 1790, on occasion of the death of Rev. R. Robinson.   *London*, 1790

REFLECTIONS, discriminative and pacificatory, on recent events in our Church, and our elder University. By a Graduate.
                                                    London, 1845

REFLECTIONS on the cælibacy of Fellows of Colleges.   1798

REFLECTIONS on the contentions and disorder of the Corporation of Cambridge.   *London*, 1789

REFLECTIONS on the late Elections in the County of Cambridge.
                                                    London, 1803

REFLECTOR. Vol. i. Nos. 1–4. Jan. 1, 1888—Jan. 22, 1888. (Ed. by J. K. Stephen.)   4° *London*, 1888

REFORM. Fly-sheets, etc. on the Reform movement of 1871 and following years.   1871 etc.

Fly-sheets, etc. on University Reform, 1908–10.   1908–10

REFORM Club Papers, 1872–3.   1873

REGISTER of Members of the Senate, 1859–1910.   1859–1910

REGISTRARY. Poll at election, 24 Oct. 1816. (W. Hustler, Jesus, elected.)   1816

Poll at election, 23 March, 1832. (J. Romilly, Trin., elected.) 1832

Fly-sheets, candidatures, etc. 1861–2.   1861–2

Poll at election, 29 Jan. 1862. (H. R. Luard, Trin., elected.) 1862

REGISTRY. List of documents in the Registry, 1266–1544. By H. R. Luard. (*C. A. S.*)   1876

REGRETS of a Cantab. [By J. Cowling.] (*London Mag.*, 1 Dec. 1825.)

REGULATIONS (1750–2).

An Occasional Letter to Dr Keen. [Attr. to P. Chester.]
                                                    London (1750)

Considerations on the expediency of making...the late Regulations at Cambridge. [Attr. to J. Green.]   *London*, 1751

David's Prophecy relating to Cambridge. [By W. Waller.]   1751

Free Thoughts upon University Education. Pt 1.   *London*, 1751

Friendly and honest advice of an Old Tory to the Vice-Chancellor.
                                                    London, 1751

See also Academic ; Appeal ; Fragment ; Westminster Club.

REID (T.W.) Life of Lord Houghton. 2nd ed. 2 vols.
                                                    London, 1890

REID (W.) The rise of the United States. Local Lectures. Summer meeting, 1906. Opening address.   *London*, 1906

RELHAN (R.) Flora Cantabrigiensis, exhibens plantas agro Cantabrigiensi indigenas.   1785

—— Supplementum.   1786

—— Supplementum alterum.   1788

—— Supplementum tertium.   1793

REMARKS on Clerical education. By Rusticus.   *London*, 1841

REMARKS on the Academic [of J. Green ? Attributed to S. Squire].
                                                    London, 1751

REMARKS on the actual state of the University of Cambridge.
London, 1830
REMARKS on the enormous expence in the education of young men
in the University of Cambridge.   *London,* 1788
REMARKS [by J. Mainwaring] on the Pursuits of Literature [of T. J.
Mathias].   1798
REMARKS on two pamphlets, 1811.   *See* Browne (T.).
RENDALL (G.H.) Inaugural address delivered at the opening of
University College, Liverpool, Jan. 14, 1882.   1882
RENDEL (J.M.) Report on the drainage of the Nene Valley.
Northampton, 1848
—— Another ed.   *Northampton* (1849)
RENNELL (T.) Commencement Sermon, 1 July, 1798. *London* (1798)

Some account of his life and writings. (By J. L[onsdale].) *London,* 1824

REPLY to Granta.   By a Member of the University.   1838
REPLY to the...Edinburgh Review against Oxford. (+Second Reply...)
[By E. Copleston.]   *Oxford,* 1810
REPRESENTATIVES. *Borough.* Poll...June 18, 1818, and speeches.
4º 1818

Election of 1832.   Register of Freemen.   1832
Election of 1832.   Speech of Mr Spring Rice, 26 June.   1832
Poll...Dec. 11, 12, 1832. [With note in the Conservative interest.]
1833
Poll...Dec. 11, 12, 1832. [With letter printed for Mr Spring Rice.]
1833
Election of 1834.   Register of Freemen.   1834
Poll...June 11, 12, 1834. [Pr. for T. Stevenson.]   1834
—— By C. H. Cooper.   1834
Poll, Jan. 7, 8, 1835.   1835
Poll, 26 July, 1837. [Pr. by C. E. Brown.]   1837
—— By C. H. Cooper.   1837
An alphabetical list of the Cambridge tradesmen who supported the
Conservative candidates at the election in July, 1837.   (1837)
A letter to the electors of Cambridge, touching Mr Knight, Mr Sutton,
and the Poor Laws.   1837
Poll. Sept. 5, 1839.   1839
Poll. May 22, 1840.   *London,* 1840
Alphabetical list of the Cambridge tradesmen who supported the
Conservative candidates at the election in July 1837—Sept. 1839—
May 1840.   (1840)
A plain statement relative to the Cambridge Election Petition....By
Edward Scott.   1840
Register of Electors, 1840–1.   1840
Poll. July 15, 1845.   1845
Poll. July 30, 1847.   1847
Poll. July 8, 1852.   1852
Poll. August 17, 1854.   By W. Cockerell.   1854
—— [Pr. by C. W. Naylor.]   1854

REPRESENTATIVES. *Borough.*
Poll. March 30, 1857.   1857
Poll. April 29, 1859.   1859
Poll. February 11, 1863.   1863
Poll. April 24, 1866.   1866
Account of the Liberal victory, 1880. (*Camb. Indep. Press,* April 3.)
Buckmaster and Paget, 1906. Addresses, etc.   1906
REPRESENTATIVES. *County.* Poll. May 24, 1705. F° (1705)
Poll. Sept. 14, 1780.   (1780)
Poll. May 5–10, July 12–13, 1802.   (1802)
Poll. Aug. 10–14, 1830.   (1830)
Speeches during Election of 1830.   1830
Poll. Oct. 27–31, 1831.   1831
Poll. 1868.   1868
REPRESENTATIVES. *University.* Poll. Sept. 9, 1780.   1780
Poll. April 3, 1784.   1784
Poll. June 17, 1790.   1790
Poll. Feb. 7, 1806.   1806
Poll. May 8, 1807.   1807
Poll. March 27, 1811.   1811
Addresses, circulars, fly-sheets, etc.   4° 1820–1906
Election of 1822. The claims of the different candidates considered.
                                                                            (1822)
Poll. Nov. 26, 27, 1822.   1822
Poll. June 13–16, 1826.   1826
Letter to the electors of the University of Cambridge. By one of
  their body.   1827
Poll. May 9–11, 1827.   1827
Poll. June 16–18, 1829.   1829
Poll. May 3–6, 1831.   1831
Election of 1847. Dissenters' Chapel Bill. By G. R. Clarke. (1847)
Poll. July 29–Aug. 3, 1847 (Mr Law's issue).   1847
—— (Lord Feilding's issue.)   1847
—— By H. Gunning.   1847
Poll. Feb. 7–9, 1856.   1856
Papers dealing with the riot in connection with the Poll, Feb. 1856.
                                                                        4° 1856
Poll. Feb. 19, 1868. (A. J. B. Beresford Hope and A. Cleasby.)
                                                                        4° 1862
Circulars, Addresses, and squibs on the election of 1868.   1868
Poll. Nov. 1882. (H. C. Raikes, C., and J. Stuart, L.)   1888
—— Circulars, fly-sheets, etc.   4° 1882
RESIDENTS in the University. Lists. 1845–94 (with gaps). (An
  annual card.)   12° 1845–94
RESTORATION in East Anglia. No. 1.   *London,* 1879
REYNER (G.F.) The new Chapel of St John's College.   4° 1869
RHYME the leading principle of Latin versification.   1829
RHYMES on Matrimony. By an University Bachelor. With other
  poems.   *London,* 1829

RICARDO (T.W.)   How little Winks took his friends to see the Cambridge Anatomical Museum.   (Repr. from the *Light Blue*.)
1882
RICE (J.)   The Cambridge Freshman.   *London*, 1878
—— Another ed.   *London*, n.d.
RICE (T. Spring)   *See* Spring Rice.
RICHARDS (A.B.)   The Royal University Commission.
London (1850)
RICHARDS (G.P.)   Collegium Bengalense.   Carmen praemio a rev. viro Cl. Buchanan S.T.P. Etonensibus proposito dignatum.
4º 1805
RICHARDS (W.)   The history of Lynn.   2 vols.   *Lynn*, 1812
RICHARDSON (R.)   Historical notes concerning the power of the Chancellor's Court at Cambridge.   (*Archaeologia*, VII.)
4º (*London*, 1785)
RICKMAN and Hutchinson.   Specification of work and materials to be used in the completion of the new buildings of St John's College, Cambridge.   *Birmingham*, 1827
Answer to *Observations on the Plans for the New Library*.   Being a defence of a design presented by Messrs R. and H.
Birmingham, 1831
RIDDING (G.)   A letter to the Rev. H. Latham, in reply to his Observations on the Propositions made by the Head Masters of Schools to the University of Cambridge.   *Winchester*, 1871
A letter to E. Bowen, M.A., in reply to a pamphlet entitled " The proposed control of the Public Schools by the Universities."
Winchester, 1872
Examination in theory *v.* normal schools as the training for Teachers.
Winchester, 1882
RIDDINGE (Amias) = King (W.).   *See* Fragment.
RIDGEWAY (W.)   Testimonials when a candidate for the Disney Professorship.   1892
Are the Cambridgeshire Ditches referred to by Tacitus ?   (*Arch. Journ.*)   (*London*, 1892)
The Supplices of Aeschylus.   (*Praelections*.)   1906
RIDGWAY (J.)   Oxford examinations of those who are not members of the University.   *Oxford*, 1858
RIDLEY (N.)   Brief declaration of the Lord's Supper.   Reprinted by H. C. G. Moule.   *London*, 1895
RIFLE Club.   Reports, 1, 2, 4, 6, 7, 8.   1860–7
Meeting to consider sale of Rifle Range, 2 May.   1871
Final Report.   1872
Account of settlement of Rifle Prize Fund.   1881
See also Volunteers.
ROBERTS (E.S.)   On the dates of Tripos Examinations.   1892
ROBERTS (J.)   Circulars to Members of the Senate on the title A.C. 2 March, 7 March.   1860
ROBERTS (R.D.)   The University Extension Scheme as the basis of a system of National Higher Education.   *Aberystwith*, 1887

ROBERTSON (C.G.) All Souls' College, Oxford. (College histories.)
London, 1899
ROBERTSON (D.H.) After Novara. Poem which obtained Chancellor's Medal for English verse, 1910.   1910
ROBERTSON (J.) Some Sermons preached in the Chapel of Jesus College.   1862
Sermon preached in Harrow School Chapel, Advent Sunday, 1883.
Harrow (1883)
ROBES. *See* Academical Dress.
ROBINSON (C.K.) *See* Catharine's (St) College.
ROBINSON (M.) Autobiography. Ed. by J. E. B. Mayor. (Cambridge in the xviith century, ii.)   1856
ROBINSON (R.) Arcana : or the principles of the late Petitioners to Parliament for relief in the matter of Subscription. In viii letters to a friend.   1774
—— New ed.   *Nottingham* [181–]
A plea for the Divinity of our Lord Jesus Christ.   1776
A lecture on a becoming behaviour in religious assemblies...Jan. 10, 1773, at the Meeting House, in St Andrew's Cambridge.   1776
Christianity a system of humanity. Sermon, 3 March, 1779.   1779
The General Doctrine of Toleration applied to the particular case of Free Communion.   1781
Slavery inconsistent with the spirit of Christianity. A sermon preached at Cambridge, Feb. 10, 1788.   1788
The nature and necessity of early piety. A sermon preached at Willingham, Jan. 1, 1772. New ed.   *Leeds*, 1799
Two original Letters...   *London*, 1802

Funeral Sermon, by A. Rees, 8 June 1790.   *London*, 1790

ROBINSON (T.), † 1813. Funeral Sermon, by T. Webster, 4 April, 1813.   *London*, 1813
ROBINSON (T.), † 1873. On the study of oriental literature.   1838
The character of St Paul the model of the Christian ministry. Four sermons preached before the University of Cambridge, Feb. 1840.
1840
ROBINSON (W.) The sin of conformity. 3rd ed.   *London*, 1863
ROBY (H.J.) Remarks on College Reform.   1858
Reply to Mr Clarke's attack on the Board of Moral Sciences.   1861
ROGERS (A.) Testimonials when candidate for Librarianship of the London Institution.   (1886)
ROGERS (G.F.) Testimonials. (Assistant Surgeon, Addenbrooke's Hospital.)   4° (1897)
ROGET (J.L.) Cambridge Customs and Costumes.   Obl. 4° 1851
A Cambridge Scrap-book. (Bowes 2336.)   Obl. 4° 1859
ROLLESTON (G.) Reasons for appointing a Medical Inspector to hold office during the carrying out of our Drainage scheme.
Oxford, 1871
ROMAN Catholic Church. The Church of Our Lady and the English Martyrs. [By Ch. Sayle and Christopher Scott.]   1890

ROMAN Catholic Church.
Sermon at opening of the Church, by Bp Hedley. 15 Oct. 1890.
London, 1890
Blessing of the Bells. (Service.) 17 Dec. 1890. *London*, n.d.
ROMILLY (J.) *See* Graduati, 1856.
ROSE (Henry John) An answer to *The case of the Dissenters*, with some
remarks on the Cambridge Petition. *London*, 1834
ROSE (Hugh James) The duty of maintaining the Truth. A sermon
preached before the University of Cambridge, May 18, 1834. 1834
ROSS (J.) Discourse before the University, 4 July, 1756. 4° 1756
ROTHERHAM (T.), *Abp of York*. Life. By H. L. Bennett.
Lincoln, 1901
ROTHMAN (R.W.) Observations on the climate of Italy and other
countries in ancient times. *London*, 1848
ROUND Church. Observations on...the Round Church. By Ja.
Essex. 4° *London*, 1782
Church of the Holy Sepulchre. [From Britton's *Archit. Antiq.*, 3.]
4° (*London*, 1805)
A history of the Church of the Holy Sepulchre, or Round Church,
Cambridge. 2nd ed. 12° 1847
A talk with the congregation about the Round Church. By
R. Sinker. (1898)
The Round Church. By L. N. Badenoch. (*Archit. Rev.*, Oct. 1899.)
See also Camden Society.
ROUSSEAU (J.J.) Letters on the elements of Botany. Transl., with
additional Letters, by Thomas Martyn. 8th ed. *London*, 1815
ROUTH (E.J.) Obituary notice of Sir George Airy. (*Proc. Roy.
Soc.*) *London*, 1892

Obituary notice by A. R. Forsyth. (*Proc. Lond. Math. Soc.*, ser. II.
vol. 5, pt 7.) *London*, 1907

ROW (C.A.) Letter to Sir R. H. Inglis, in reply to his speech on
University Reform, April 23, 1850. *London*, 1850
Letter to Lord John Russell...on the constitutional defects of the
University and Colleges of Oxford. *London*, 1850
ROWE (J.T.) Town and Gown. Some five years of work in
St George's, Camberwell. 4° 1891
ROWE (R.C.) The late R. C. Rowe. By Sedley Taylor. (*Camb.
Rev.*) 1884
ROWE (R.R.) Memoir of the late Alderman Richard Rowe. (Repr.
from *Camb. Chron.*, 21 Dec. 1878.) 1878
ROWING. *See* Aquatic Notes ; Armytage (H.) ; Boat Race.
ROWNTREE (G.W.) The Martyrdom of St Stephen. (Seatonian
Prize Poem for 1891.) 1891
Jeremiah. (Seatonian Prize Poem for 1892.) 1892
ROWSELL (T.J.) English Universities and English Poor. Sermons.
1859
ROY (C.S.) Physiological bearing of waist-belts and stays. By J. G.
Adami and C. S. Roy. (*National Rev.*, Nov. 1888.)

ROYAL Agricultural Society. The first two country meetings...
Oxford, 1839; Cambridge, 1840. By Ernest Clarke.

London, 1894

Journal. (Camb. Meeting, 1894.) *London,* 1894

Cambridge Meeting, 1894. Special Service, June 24, 1894, in the
Showyard. Words. *London,* 1894

ROYAL Archaeological Institute. *See* Archaeological Institute.

ROYAL Society for Prevention of Cruelty to Animals. Cambridge
Branch. Report 1896. 1897

ROYSTON. Palaeographia Britannica...No. 1. Origines Roystonianae. By W. Stukeley. 4° *London,* 1743

—— Another ed. 1795

—— No. 2. Origines Roystonianae. Pt 2...against C. Parkin.

4° *Stamford,* 1746

An answer to, or remarks upon Dr Stukeley's Origines Roystonianae. By Charles Parkin. 4° *London,* 1744

Origines Roystonianae. An account of the cave or oratory at
Royston. *Royston,* 1825

The origin and use of the Royston Cave. By J. Beldam.

Royston, 1858

RUFUS Hickman of St Botolph's. (Extract from a magazine.) (1879)

RUGGLE (G.) Ignoramus. Comœdia. Editio sexta.

12° *Westminster,* 1731

—— Nunc denuo in lucem edita...accurante J. S. Hawkins.

Londini, 1787

An English prologue and epilogue to the Latin comedy of Ignoramus.
Performed by members of the University before King James in
1614...With preface. By Geo. Dyer. *London,* 1797

RUHEMANN (S.) *See* Dewar (*Sir* J.).

"RUSH (*Friar*)" The Jolly Bachelors: a cantata. (*Puck,* May 9,
1844.) F° *London,* 1844

RUSKIN (J.) Address to the Cambridge School of Art (29 Oct. 1858)
and Report of speeches of Redgrave and Cruikshank. 1858

Inaugural Address. Camb. Sch. of Art, 29 Oct. 1858. 1858

RUSSELL (A.T.) In what respects the Law is a schoolmaster to
bring men to Christ. (Hulsean Prize Essay, 1825.) 1826

Remarks on Keble's Sermon, *Primitive tradition recognised in Holy
Scripture.* 1837

RUSSELL (*Sir* C.) Sir Charles Russell's address to the Cambridge
University Liberal Club, Feb. 26, 1890. *London,* 1890

Dinner in Downing College to the Lord Chief Justice of England
(Lord Russell of Killowen), Nov. 11, 1897. 1897

RUSSELL (H.) Charles Packe. *Pau,* 1896

RUSSELL (*Lord* J.) *See* Commission.

RUSSELL (J.F.) Letter to H. Goulburn, M.P. on the morals and
religion of the University of Cambridge. 1833

RUSSIAN Lectureship, 1899–1900. Report of Council of Senate
3 May, 1899, Graces, Fly-sheets, etc. E. H. Minns *v.* A. P.
Goudy—the latter elected. 4° 1899–1900

RUST (J.C.) Antioch. (Seatonian Prize Poem for 1879.)   1879
RUSTAT (T.) Memoirs. By William Hewett.   *London,* 1849
RUSTICUS, *pseud. See* Maurice (F. D.) ; Remarks, 1841.
RUSTON (A.S.) The Fen Country. (*Journal of the Farmers' Club,*
    November, 1870.)   *London,* 1870
RUTHERFORD (H.W.) Catalogue of the Library of C. Darwin.
    1908
RUTHERFORTH (T.) Determinatio quaestionis theologicae post
    gradum doctoratus hab. Cantab. in scholis publicis.   4° 1746
    Discourse on Miracles...29 Aug. 1751.   4° 1751
    A letter to the Rev. Mr Kennicott.   1761
    Answer...by B. Kennicott.   *London,* 1762
    Four Charges.   1763
    Defence of a Charge concerning Subscriptions.   1767
    Sermon...27 June, 1771.   4° 1771
RUTT (J.T.) *See* Calamy (E.).
RUTTER (F.) Varsity Types.   *London,* 1903
RYLE (H.E.) Sermon in King's College Chapel on Sunday, 6 March,
    1892, being the day after the funeral of Miss Clough.   12° 1892
RYMER (T.) Essay concerning Critical and Curious Learning.
    London, 1698
    Answer to the Essay.   *London,* 1698
    Vindication of the Essay.   *London,* 1698
RYVES (B.) *See* Mercurius Rusticus.

S

SABRINAE Corolla, in hortulis Regiae Scholae Salopiensis contexuerunt
tres viri floribus legendis.   *Londini*, 1850
ST AUBYN (Alan), *pseud.* [Mrs F. Marshall.] Trollope's Dilemma.
                                                                Bristol, 1889
A Fellow of Trinity.   *London*, 1891
The Junior Dean. New ed.   *London*, 1892
ST PETER'S World. Vol. I. Nos. 1–3 ; Vol. II. Nos. 1–2. 1889–90
SALMON (T.) The Foreigner's Companion through the Universities
of Cambridge and Oxford.   12° *London*, 1748
SALTER (J.W.) Catalogue of collection of Cambrian and Silurian
fossils contained in Geological Museum of University of Cambridge.
With a preface by Adam Sedgwick, LL.D.   4° 1873

This copy contains extracts from minutes of Council of Geological Soc.
made by J. W. Clark when writing Sedgwick's life.

SALVIN (O.) A catalogue of the collection of birds formed by the
late H. E. Strickland.   1882
SANCROFT (W.) Life. By George D'Oyly. 2 vols. *London*, 1821
SANDYS (C.) A critical dissertation on Prof. Willis's Architectural
history of Canterbury Cathedral.   *London*, 1846
SANDYS (*Sir* J.E.) Oratio Latina praemio annuo dignata (Members'
Prize).   1866
Speeches on presenting S. M. Schiller–Szinessy and Eiríkr Magnússon
for degrees.   1876
In Memoriam : W. H. Bateson. (*Eagle*, LXV.)   1881
The South of France and the Riviera. (*Eagle*, LXVII., LXVIII.) 1882
Testimonials when a candidate for the Professorship of Greek in the
University of Edinburgh.   1882
Obituary notice of Ch. Merivale. (*Eagle*, CIII.)   1894
Honorary Degrees. (*Camb. Rev.*, June 9, 1898.)   1898
Harvard Lectures on the revival of learning.   1905
Orationes et epistolae Cantabrigienses, 1876–1909.   4° 1910
SANDYS (W.D.) A Narrative of the late W. D. Sandys of Trinity
College. By his Father.   12° *London*, 1815
SANSKRIT Professorship, 1867. *See* Aufrecht (T.) ; Cowell (E. B.).
SARGENT (J.) Memoir of Henry Martyn. 3rd ed. *London*, 1819
—— 10th ed.   *London*, 1830
SARSON (L.) Analysis of 1 Timoth. i. 15.   4° 1645
SATOW (*Sir* E.) An Austrian diplomatist [Hübner] in the fifties.
(Rede lecture, 1908.)   1908

SAUNDERSON (N.) Memoirs of the Life of Dr N. Saunderson. (Extracted from his *Elements of Algebra*, 1740.)   4° 1740

SAURIN (J.) Sermons, translated from the original French. 4 vols.
1775–82

SAVAGE (E.A.) The Bodleian Library. (*Nineteenth Century*, Sept. 1902.)

SAVAGE (J.) An account of the last illness of Richard Porson, M.A.
London, 1808

SAWSTON. *See* Clarke (E. D.), 1817.

SAYLE (C.E.) Bertha.   *Oxford*, 1885
Wiclif. An historical drama.   *Oxford*, 1887
Erotidia.   *Rugby*, 1889
The Church of Our Lady and the English Martyrs. [By C. Sayle and C. Scott.]   1890
Bibliotheca loquitur. Notes on St John's College Library. (*Eagle*, 1892.)   1892
Hand-list of Early English Books in the University of Cambridge. (Prospectus.)   4° 1892
Musa Consolatrix.   *London*, 1893
The Vatican Library. (*Library*.)   *London*, 1895
The University Library, Cambridge.   1895
—— 2nd ed.   1905
Early English Printed Books in the University Library, Cambridge (1475–1640). 4 vols. and suppl.   1900–1907
Initial letters in Early English Printed Books. (*Bibl. Soc.*)
4° *London*, 1904
Sayle (C.E.) and Williamson (G.C.) Portraits, Prints, and Writings of John Milton.   4° 1908
—— 2nd ed.   4° 1908
—— Special ed.   4° 1908
Application by C. Sayle for post of Chief Librarian in the Univ. of Edinburgh.   1910
See Ali, 1902.

SCARGILL (D.). The recantation of D. S. publickly made before the University of Cambridge, in Gt St Maries, July 25, 1669. 4° 1669

SCENE from Alma Mater. By B.A.   12° 1830

SCENES from an unfinished drama, entitled Phrontisterion, or Oxford in the nineteenth century. [By H. L. Mansel.] 4th ed.
Oxford, 1852
—— 5th ed.   *Oxford*, 1861

SCHARF (G.) Artistic notes on the windows of King's College Chapel, Cambridge. (*Archaeol. Journ.* XII., XIII.) *London*, 1855–6

SCHOLARSHIPS. Statutes for certain scholarships proposed by the Council of the Senate. (*Camb. Chron.*, 28 Nov. 1857.)
See also Endowments.

SCHOLEFIELD (J.) St Paul and St James reconciled. A sermon preached before the University of Cambridge.   1828
An argument for a Church-Establishment. A sermon, 24 Nov. 1833. 2nd ed.   1833

SCHOLEFIELD (J.)
A reply to Prof. Scholefield's pamphlet, entitled, An argument for Church Establishments.   *London,* 1834
A zealous ministry the safeguard of a nation. A sermon preached... on the occasion of the death of Charles Simeon.   1836
—— 2nd ed.   1836
—— Another ed. (*Pulpit,* xxix.)   *London,* 1837
Scriptural grounds of Union, considered in five sermons preached before the Univ. of Cambridge, Nov. 1840.   1841
The Christian Altar. A sermon preached...23 Oct. 1842.   1842
Remarks on the Christian Altar. By F. W. Collison.   1842
Some further Remarks. By F. W. Collison.   1843
The Lord's Table the Christian Altar, in some remarks upon Prof. Scholefield's late Sermon. By C. Warren.   1843

A sermon preached in St Michael's Church 17 April, 1853, the Sunday after the funeral of the Rev. J. S. By T. T. Perowne.   1853
Memoir. By his widow. With notices of his literary character, by W. Selwyn.   *London,* 1855
Scholefield Prize. Report of meeting, etc.   1856
Catalogue of his library...sold Nov. 5, 6, 1862.   1862
See also Collison (F. W.).

SCHOOL of Art. Inaugural soirée. Mr Ruskin's address, and report of the speeches of Mr Redgrave and Mr Cruikshank.   1858
Inaugural address, by John Ruskin.   1858
SCHOOL of Cookery. Annual Report, 1881, 1882, 1883.   1881–3
SCHOOL of Pythagoras. An account of Pythagoras's School in Cambridge. [By J. Kilner.]   F° (1790)
SCHOOLBOY Reminiscences. A Poem. By an Undergraduate [J. Purchas, Chr.].   1844
SCHOOLS. Report of the Old Schools of Cambridge, 1857, 1871.   1857, 1871
Abbey District, Barnwell. Appeal for new premises.   1857
Church of England Primary Schools. Report, 1882; 1884–5; 1890–1; 1892–3; 1893–4; 1894–5; 1895–6; 1899–1900.   1882–1901
SCHULHOF (J.M.) "Attic," "Ionic," and "Tragic."   1899
The present position of Moral Philosophy.   1900
SCIENTIFIC Instrument Company. Descriptive list of instruments manufactured and supplied.   1891
SCOFFOCLES. The Suppliants of Scoffocles.   [1883]
SCORE of Lyrics. [By W. G. Clark.]   1849
SCOTT (A.) Testimonials in favour of A.S., Jacksonian Demonstrator of Chemistry in the University of Cambridge, a candidate for the Professorship of Chemistry at St Andrew's.   (1884)
SCOTT (C.B.) Age, concitate cantus, etc. Verses for tercentenary of Trinity College, 22 Dec. 1846.   4° 1846
The Greek Kingdoms of Bactria and its vicinity. (Le Bas Prize Essay for 1849.)   1849

SCOTT (C.B.)
Further remarks on the Master of Trinity's Criticism of Aristotle's
    Account of Induction.   4° 1850
See also Bernard (H. H.) ; Mason (P. H.).
SCOTT (E.)   A plain statement relative to the Cambridge Election
    Petition.   1840
SCOTT (*Sir* G.G.)   On King's College Chapel.   (From his *History
    of English Church Architecture.*)   *London,* 1881
SCOTT (James)   Heaven : a vision.   (Seatonian Prize Poem for 1760.)
    2nd ed.   4° 1761
    An hymn to Repentance.   (Seatonian Prize Poem for 1762.)   4° 1762
    A sermon preached at the Court End of the Town and in the City...
    on the King's Accession...25 Oct. 1772.   Dedicated to Mr Garrick.
                                                        London, 1773
SCOTT (John)   Letter on Proctorial jurisdiction.   1860
SCOTT (Joseph)   A new system for draining the Fens, etc.
                                                      Wisbech [1809 ?]
SCOTT (R.F.)   The meeting of Henry VII. and the King of Castile.
    (*Eagle,* March 1889.)   1889
    Notes from the College Records.   2 ser.   (*Eagle.*)   1890–1906
See John's (St) College.   Admissions.   Pt III. 1903.
SCRAPS, or essays, serious and comic, in prose and verse.   By a
    Cantab.   1795
SCREED.   No. 1.   Nov. 11, 1899.   6*d.*   4° 1899
—— 2nd ed.   3*d.*   4° 1899
SCRIBE (A.E.) and Legouvé (G.J.B.E.W.)   The Ladies' Battle.
    Transl. and acted at Cambridge, March, 1905.   1905
SCRIBLERUS (Martinus), jun.   The Ratland Feast.   1820
SCRIBLERUS Redivivus.   A new art teaching how to be plucked.
    [Attr. to E. Caswall.]   2nd ed.   *Oxford,* 1835
—— 7th ed.   *Oxford,* 1837
SEALE (J.B.)   An analysis of the Greek Metres for the use of
    students at the Universities.   1784
—— 2nd ed.   1789
—— New ed.   *Oxford,* 1812
—— 8th ed.   1820
SEAMAN (O.)   Paulopostprandials.   [By O. Seaman, H. C. Monro,
    and L. Speed.]   3rd ed.   4° 1883
    Oedipus the Wreck, or "To trace the Knave."   4° 1888
    Poetry and teaching of Robert Browning.   Syllabus of Lectures.
                                                        London, 1889
    In Cap and Bells.   *London,* 1900
SEARLE (C.E.)   The Clerical Fellow's Stewardship.   A sermon.
                                                               1878
SEARLE (W.G.)   The illuminated manuscripts in the Library of
    the Fitzwilliam Museum.   1876
    List of Cambridge Books.   (Proofs of a work never completed.)
                                                            [188–]
See Grace Book Γ.

SEATONIAN Prize Poems.

Collections.

Musae Seatonianae. A complete collection, 1750–1770.

London, 1772

—— 1750–1806. 2 vols.   1808

Separate Poems.

₊ When a title is printed in italics, the poem in question is not included in the Clark Collection; those poems marked with an asterisk will, however, be found elsewhere in the University Library. It has been considered desirable to record the whole series, but when no date of publication is given no copy of the poem in question has been examined or found described.

1750. On the Eternity of the Supreme Being. By C. Smart. 2nd ed.
     4° 1752

1751. On the Immensity of the Supreme Being. By C. Smart. 2nd ed.
     4° 1753

1752. On the Omniscience of the Supreme Being. By C. Smart.
     4° 1752

1753. On the Power of the Supreme Being. By C. Smart. 4° 1754

1754. The Justice of the Supreme Being. By G. Bally. 4° 1755

1755. On the Goodness of the Supreme Being. By C. Smart.
     4° 1756

—— 2nd ed.   4° 1756

1756. The Wisdom of the Supreme Being. By G. Bally. 4° 1756

1757. The Day of Judgment. By R. Glynn. 3rd ed. 4° 1758

—— Another ed.   1800

1758. The Providence of the Supreme Being. By G. Bally. 4° 1758

1759. *Death. By B. Porteus.*   4° 1759

1760. Heaven : a Vision. By J. Scott. 2nd ed.   4° 1761

1761. *Purity of Heart. By J. Scott.*   4° 1761

1762. An Hymn to Repentance. By J. Scott.   4° 1762

1763. The Redemption. By John Hey.   4° 1763

1764. The Conversion of St Paul. By J. Lettice.   4° 1765

1765. *The Crucifixion. By T. Zouch.*   4° 1765

1766. No prize adjudged. Subject : The Gift of Tongues.

1767. *The Gift of Tongues. By C. Jenner.*   4° 1767

1768. The Destruction of Nineveh. By C. Jenner.   4° 1768

1769. No prize adjudged.

1770. *The Dedication of the Temple of Solomon. By W. Hodson.*
     4° 1770

1771. No prize adjudged. Subject : Conscience.

1772. Conscience. By William Gibson.   4° 1772

1773. Charity. By C. P. Layard.   4° 1773

1774. No prize adjudged. Subject : Duelling.

1775. {*A poetical essay on Duelling. By C. P. Layard.*   4° 1775
{*Duelling. By S. Hayes.*   4° 1775

1776. Prophecy. By S. Hayes.   4° 1777

SEATONIAN Prize Poems.

1777.	Prayer. By S. Hayes.	4° 1777
1778.	The Nativity of our Saviour. By S. Hayes.	4° 1778
1779.	No prize adjudged. Subject: The Ascension.	
1780.	The Ascension. By Tho. Hughes.	4° 1780
1781.	Jerusalem Destroyed. By W. Gibson.	4° 1781
1782.	*The Call of the Gentiles. By S. Madan.	4° 1782
1783.	Hope. By Samuel Hayes.	4° 1783
1784.	Creation. By Samuel Hayes.	4° 1784
1785.	*The Exodus. By Samuel Hayes.	4° 1785
1786–1788.	No prize adjudged. Subject: The Resurrection.	
1789.	*The Deluge. By John Roberts.	4° 1789
1790.	Faith: a vision. By Charles Philpot.	4° 1790
1791.	*Humility. By Ch. Philpot.	4° 1791
1792–1793.	No prize adjudged. Subject: The Restoration of the Jews.	
1794.	The Restoration of the Jews. By F. Wrangham.	4° 1795
1795.	*The Destruction of Babylon. By A. W. Trollope.	4° 1795
1796.	No prize adjudged. Subject: The Mercy of God.	
1797.	Miracles. By William Bolland.	4° 1797
1798.	The Epiphany. By William Bolland.	4° 1799
1799.	*Saint Paul at Athens. By W. Bolland.	4° 1800
1800.	The Holy Land. By F. Wrangham.	4° 1800
1801.	No prize adjudged. Subject: St Peter's denial of Christ.	
1802.	St Peter's denial of Christ. By W. Cockburn.	4° 1802
1803.	Christ raising the daughter of Jairus. By W. Cockburn.	4° 1803
1804.	*Moses viewing the Promised Land. By C. Hoyle.	4° 1804
1805.	Christ's Lamentation over Jerusalem. By Charles Peers.	4° 1805
1806.	Paul and Barnabas at Lystra. By C. Hoyle.	4° 1806
1807.	*The Shipwreck of St Paul. By C. J. Hoare.	4° 1808
1808.	The Holy Wars. By B. T. H. Cole.	
1809.	The Conquest of Canaan. By G. Pryme.	
1810.	No prize adjudged. Subject: The Death of Abel.	
1811.	The Sufferings of the Primitive Martyrs. By F. Wrangham.	4° 1812
1812.	Joseph made known to his Brethren. By F. Wrangham.	4° 1812
1813.	Death of Saul and Jonathan. By E. Smedley.	London, 1814
1814.	Jephthah. By E. Smedley.	London, 1814
1815.	Jonah. By J. W. Bellamy.	London, 1815
1816.	Hezekiah and Sennacherib. By C. H. Terrot.	1816
1817.	Belshazzar's Feast. By T. S. Hughes.	1818
1818.	*Deborah. By A. Dicken.	1818
1819.	No prize adjudged. Subject: Moses receiving the Tables of the Law.	
1820.	The Omnipresence of the Supreme Being. By E. B. Elliott.	1821

SEATONIAN Prize Poems.

1821. No prize adjudged. Subject : The Old Age of St John the Evangelist.

1822. *Antiochus Epiphanes. By E. B. Elliott. London, 1825

1823. No prize adjudged. Subject : Cornelius.

1824. The Death of Absalom. By H. S. Beresford. 1825

1825. The Building and Dedication of the Second Temple. By J. Overton. 1826

1826. No prize adjudged. Subject : The Transfiguration.

1827. *The Marriage in Cana. By E. Smedley. London, 1828

1828. *Saul at Endor. By E. Smedley. London, 1829

1829. *The Finding of Moses. By J. H. Marsden. 1829

1830. {*The Ascent of Elijah. By R. Parkinson. 1830
{The Ascent of Elijah. By W. M. Praed. 1831

1831. David playing the Harp before Saul. By T. E. Hankinson. 1831

1832. The Plague Stayed. By T. E. Hankinson. 1832

1833. St Paul at Philippi. By T. E. Hankinson. 1833

1834. Jacob. By T. E. Hankinson. 1834

1835. {*Ishmael. By T. E. Hankinson. 1835
{Ishmael. By J. Gorle.

1836. No prize adjudged. Subject : The Conversion of Constantine the Great.

1837. No prize adjudged. Subject : St Paul at Ephesus.

1838. Ethiopia stretching out her hands unto God. By T. E. Hankinson. 1838

1839. Gideon. By John Murray. 1839

1840. *The Ministry of Angels. By T. E. Hankinson. 1840

1841. The Call of Abraham. By T. E. Hankinson. 1841

1842. The Cross planted upon the Himalaya Mountains. By T. E. Hankinson. 1842

1843. Faith, Hope, and Charity. By T. R. Birks. 1843

1844. *Esther. By T. R. Birks. 1844

1845. *The Loosing of the Euphratean Angels. By J. M. Neale. 1845

1846. The Curse upon Canaan. By R. W. Essington. 1846

1847. No prize adjudged. Subject : The Famine in Samaria (II Kings, 6, 7).

1848. No prize adjudged. Subject : John the Baptist.

1849. Edom. By J. M. Neale. 1849

1850. Nineveh. By G. Birch. 1850

1851. *Samson. By G. Birch. 1851

1852. Mammon. By J. M. Neale. 1852

1853. No prize adjudged. Subject : The Universal Dominion and Providence of God.

1854. *Ezechiel. By E. H. Bickersteth. 1854

1855. No prize adjudged. Subject: The Plurality of Worlds.

1856. Judith. By J. M. Neale. 1856

1857. Sinai. By J. M. Neale. 1857

SEATONIAN Prize Poems.

1858. {Egypt.   By J. M. Neale.   1858
      {*Egypt. By T. Walker.   1858
1859. The Disciples at Emmaus.   By J. M. Neale.   1859
1860. Ruth. By J. M. Neale.   1860
1861. No prize adjudged. Subject : Christ among the Doctors.
1862. King Josiah. By J. M. Neale.   1862
1863. The Seven Churches of Asia. By J. M. Neale.   1863
1864. Capernaum. By W. Saumarez Smith.   London, 1865
1865. Joshua. By H. R. Dodd.   1865
1866. The Disciples in the Upper Room. By W. S. Smith. 1866
1867. St Paul on the Appian Way. By C. Stanwell.   1867
1868. John the Baptist. By Jackson Mason.   1868
1869. Christian Self-denial. By H. C. G. Moule.   1869
1870. The Beloved Disciple. By H. C. G. Moule.   1870
1871. Tyre. By H. C. G. Moule.   1871
1872. The Gospel in Polynesia. By H. C. G. Moule.   1872
1873. The Brazen Serpent. By H. C. G. Moule.   1873
1874. The Holy Sepulchre. By E. A. Beck.   Brighton [1874]
1875. No prize adjudged. Subject : The Death of St Stephen.
1876. The Victory that overcometh the World. By H. C. G.
      Moule.   1876
1877. Judas Maccabæus. By J. W. Mills.   London, 1877
1878. No prize adjudged. Subject : "The Mind of Christ"
      (1 Cor. ii. 16).
1879. Antioch. By J. C. Rust.   1879
1880. St Paul and Felix. By E. W. Bowling.   1880
1881. "Then He arose," etc. (Matt. viii. 26). By E. W. Bowling.
                                                     1881
1882. The Transfiguration. By G. E. Freeman.   1883
1883. Jordan. By F. S. Arnold.   1884
1884. No prize adjudged. Subject : Gethsemane.
1885. The Dream of Jacob (Gen. xxviii.). By A. W. W. Dale.
1886. "The Message to the Angel of the Church in Sardis."
      (Rev. iii. 1–6.) By E. W. Bowling.   1887
1887. "On Earth Peace." By E. W. Bowling.   1888
1888. Jericho. By G. E. Freeman.   1889
1889. The Vision of the Holy Waters. (Ezechiel xlviii.) By A. S.
      Newman.   1889
1890. Samuel. By H. A. Birks.   1891
1891. The Martyrdom of St Stephen. By G. W. Rowntree. 1891
1892. Jeremiah. By G. W. Rowntree.   1892
1893. Damascus. By G. E. Freeman.   1894
1894. The Broad and the Narrow Way. By G. E. Freeman. 1895
1895. *Mount Zion. By G. W. Rowntree.   1896
1896. Polycarp. By G. W. Rowntree.
1897. *The Mount of Olives. By J. H. Lupton.   1898
1898. SS. Perpetua and Felicitas. By G. W. Rowntree. 1898
1899. St Augustine, Bp of Hippo. By John Hudson.   1900

SEATONIAN Prize Poems.

1900.	*Bede. By F. A. Hibbert.	1900
1901.	Elijah. By P. J. Loseby.	1902
1902.	*Cyrus and the Restoration of the Jews. By J. Hudson.	1902
1903.	St Aidan. By G. W. Rowntree.	
1904.	Ἐν τούτῳ νίκα. By F. H. Wood.	1904
1905.	St Columba. By A. C. Deane.	1905
1906.	The Woman of Samaria. By G. W. Rowntree.	
1907.	Barnabas. By P. J. Loseby.	1908
1908.	St Alban. By Claud Field.	London, 1909
1909.	Paul before Nero. By J.E.G.de Montmorency.	London, 1910
1910.	*St John in Patmos. By H. E. Currey.	1911

See also Hankinson (T. E.),1847; Hayes (S.), 1781; Myers (F. W. H.), 1867; Neale (J. M.), 1864; Sinai; Smedley (E.), 1815.

SECONDARY Education. Address on Secondary Education, delivered at the Social Science Congress, Birmingham. By O. Browning.
1884

Report of Conference held in the Senate House, 21 and 22 April, 1896.
1896

Conversazione at the Fitzwilliam Museum on the occasion of the Conference on Secondary Education, April 21, 1896.
1896

SEDGWICK (Adam), *Professor of Geology.* A syllabus of a course of lectures on Geology.
1821

—— 2nd ed.
1832

—— 3rd ed.
1837

A reply to an Address to the Senate (published by the Master of Jesus College, W. French).
1823

Remarks on the Observations of Dr French : with an argument on the law of Elections to Offices created by the Senate.
1824

A letter to Henry Goulburn, Chancellor of the Exchequer [on the University representatives].
4° 1829

An address delivered at the annual meeting of the Geological Society of London, 19 Feb. 1830.
London, 1830

Addresses delivered at the anniversary meeting of the Geological Society of London, 18 Feb. 1831.
London, 1831

A discourse on the studies of the University.
1833

—— 2nd ed.
1834

—— 3rd ed.
1834

—— 4th ed.
1835

—— 5th ed.
1850

Review of *A discourse on the studies of the University,* by A. Sedgwick. 3rd ed. By George Combe.
1834

Copy of a letter published in the *Times* of April 10, and the *Cambridge Chronicle* of April 11 (1834) and Postscript. (Religious Tests.)
4° (1834)

Copy of a letter (dated April 18, 1834) to the Editor of the *Independent Press,* Cambridge. (Religious Tests.)
4° 1834

Cambridge Petition (Religious Tests). Seventeen reasons for adopting the prayer of the Petition...
F° (1834)

SEDGWICK (Adam), *Professor of Geology.*
Review of R. Chambers's *Vestiges of the Natural History of Creation.*
(*Edinb. Rev.* July, 1845.)
Geology of the Lake District of Cumberland, Westmorland, and
Lancashire. (Author's copy.)   *Kendal,* 1853
—— Another ed. *See* Wordsworth (W.), 1853.
A lecture on the strata near Cambridge and the Fens of the Bedford
Level. (With suppl. containing map.)   1861
A memorial by the Trustees of Cowgill Chapel.   1868
The memorial of the Trustees of Cowgill Chapel. With appendix
and supplement.   1870
Another copy of the Supplement.   1870

Eminent living Geologists. Adam Sedgwick. (By H. Woodward.) (*Geol.
Mag.*, Apr. 1870.)
Memoir. By the Duke of Argyll, President of the Geological Society,
London (21 Feb. 1873).   (*London,* 1873)
God our Refuge. A sermon preached...Feb. 2, 1873, being the Sunday
after the death of the Rev. A. Sedgwick. By R. Burn.   1873
Purity and Light. Funeral Sermon by A. P. Stanley.   London, 1873
Adam Sedgwick. By Harvey Goodwin. (*Macmillan's Mag.*, Ap. 1880.)
Biographical notice of A. Sedgwick. By T. McKenny Hughes. *n.p.* 1883
Reminiscences of A. Sedgwick. By W. Carus. (*Churchman*, Feb. 1889.)
Life and Letters. By J. W. Clark and T. McK. Hughes. 2 vols. 1890
Review in *Church Quarterly*, July, 1890.
Review by A. Jessopp in *Nineteenth Century*, Aug. 1890.
Professor Adam Sedgwick of Cambridge. By James Macaulay. (Review.)
(*Leisure Hour*, Oct. 1890.)
Adam Sedgwick. Sermon preached at Dent, 14 Feb. 1890. By J. J.
Pulleine.   *Sedbergh,* 1890
See Beverley (R. M.); Cockburn (W.), 1849; Cole (H.), 1834; French (W.);
Otley (J.), 1877; Salter (J. W.), 1873.

SEDGWICK Memorial Museum. *See* Woodwardian Museum.
SEDGWICK Prize Essay. 1876. Post-tertiary deposits of Cambridge-
shire. By A. J. Jukes Browne.   1878
1883. The classification of the Cambrian and Silurian rocks. By
J. E. Marr.   1883
SEDGWICK (Adam), *Professor of Zoology. See* Morphological Labor-
atory; Zoology.
SEDGWICK (J.) Sermon preached at St Marie's, May 1, 1653.
                                          4° *London,* 1653
Learning's necessity to an able minister of the Gospel.
                                          4° *London,* 1653
SEELEY (*Lady*) *See* Heitland (W. E.).
SEELEY (H.G.) On the gravel and drift of the Fenlands. (*Geol.
Mag.* III. 19 Nov. 1866.)
SEELEY (*Sir* J.R.) From the Cambridge Lecture-Rooms: Bonaparte.
(*Macmillan's Mag.*, July, 1881.)
SELBIE (W.B.) Remember the Days of Old. A sermon. 4° 1906

SELLON (L.) Miss Sellon and the "Sisters of Mercy." An ex-
posure...by the Rev. James Spurrell, Vicar of Great Shelford.
London, 1852
—— 2nd ed. *London*, 1852
Reply to a tract by the Rev. J. Spurrell...By the Superior of the
Society. *London*, 1852
—— 2nd ed. *London*, 1852
A Rejoinder to the Reply to a pamphlet by the Rev. J. Spurrell.
By the Same. *London*, 1852
The Anglo-Catholics of Plymouth. A few Remarks upon Miss
Sellon's "Reply" to the Rev. J. Spurrell's "Exposure." By the
Rev. Henry T. J. Bagge, B.A. *London*, 1852
A Letter to the Rev. James Spurrell on the subject of a pamphlet
published by him...By a Member of the University of Cambridge.
London and Camb. 1852
A Letter to "A Member of the University of Cambridge," being
Remarks on his Letter to the Rev. James Spurrell. By a Presbyter
of the Church of England. 1852
A Letter to Miss Sellon, Superior of the Society of Sisters of Mercy,
at Plymouth. By Henry [Phillpotts] Lord Bishop of Exeter.
London, 1852
Sisters of Mercy, Sisters of Misery : or Miss Sellon in the Family ;
with some Remarks on "A Reply to the Rev. James Spurrell," etc.
By the Rev. W. M. Colles, A.B. *London*, 1852
An Address delivered to the Members of the Congregation of
S. Peter's Church, Plymouth, March 15, 1852, in consequence
of some statements...by the Rev. James Spurrell. By George
Rundle Prynne, B.A., Incumbent of S. Peter's. *London*, 1852
Miss Sellon, and the Sisters of Mercy. Further Statement of the...
working of the Society...By Diana A. G. Campbell, a Novice
lately seceded. *London*, 1852
Miss Sellon and the Sisters of Mercy. A Contradiction of the alleged
acts of cruelty exercised by Miss Sellon...By Commander Sellon, R.N.
London, 1852
—— 3rd ed. *London*, 1852
A Letter to the Archbishop of Dublin on the nature...of Miss Sellon's
establishment at Devenport...By the Rev. W. G. Cookesley.
2nd ed. *London*, 1853
SELWYN College. Selwyn Memorial. List of subscribers, etc. 1878
—— Later issue. 1878
Prospectus and list of Subscribers. (1880)
Form of service to be used at the laying of the foundation stone of
Selwyn College, June 1, 1881. (1881)
Foundation and Charter. Statements, Fly-Sheets, etc. 1881–82.
1881–82
Prospectus, etc. 1882
Sermon preached at opening of Selwyn College, 10 Oct. 1882
May Term Concert, June 3, 1885. Book of words. (1885)
Appeal for funds. 4° 1886

SELWYN College.
   Calendar. 1894–1903.   1894–1903
   List of subscribers to portrait of A. T. Lyttelton, given to the
     College, Dec. 3, 1894.   (1894)
   Order for the Dedication of the Chapel of Selwyn College, Cambridge,
     on St Etheldreda's Day, 1895.   (1895)
   Selwyn College. By A. L. Brown. (College histories.) *London,* 1906
   Report on Hall and Combination Room and Subscription List.
                                            [1909 ?]
SELWYN (A.L.) Memorials of four Brothers—W. Selwyn, G. A.
   Selwyn, T. K. Selwyn, C. J. Selwyn.   *Richmond* (1885)
SELWYN (G.A.) Are Cathedral institutions useless ? A practical
   answer to this question, addressed to W. E. Gladstone.
                                       London, 1838
   The work of Christ in the World. Four Sermons.   1855

   Memorial Sketch of Bishop Selwyn, and of his various diocesan works. By
    Mrs E. A. Curteis.   *Newcastle-under-Lyme* (1878)

SELWYN (W.) The doctrine of Types. (Norrisian Prize Essay
   for 1829.)   *London,* 1830
   Extracts from the College examinations in Divinity for the last four
    years.   1834
   Attempt to investigate the true principles of Cathedral Reform. 1839
   The Battle of the Epigrams, Nov. 30, 1857.   1858
   Oxford and Cambridge Mission to Central Africa. A speech,
    May 17, 1859.   1859
   Quis desiderio sit pudor aut modus tam cari capitis ? (On the
    Memorial to Prince Albert as Chancellor.)   1862
   Verses against Ball in the Fitzwilliam Museum on 7 May, 1864.
                                        4° (1864)
   Winfrid, afterwards called Boniface, A.D. 680–755.   4° 1864
   Waterloo. A lay of Jubilee for June 18, 1815. 2nd ed.   4° 1865
   Prof. Selwyn's Latin lines on his convalescence, with an English
    version.   *London,* 1867
   A letter to His Holiness Pope Pius IX.   *Dublin,* 1868
   John Hambden to his Countrymen.   4° 1869
   The New Chapel of St John's College. 6 May, 1861.   4° 1869
   "In domo procerum." Latin verses. 20 July.   4° 1869
   Genevieve—Genoveva.   4° [1869 ?]
   Speeches at Cambridge on various occasions.   4° *London,* 1875
   Pastoral Colloquies on the South Downs.   4° *London,* 1875
   See Scholefield (J.), 1855.
SELWYN (*Mrs* W.) Cousin Carl. [Transl. from the Swedish by
   Mrs Selwyn, for performance at the Deanery, Ely.] 4° *n.p.* [1866]
SENATE. The Cambridge Senate before Whitgift's Statutes. [By
   J. Edleston.]   1855
   See also Council of the Senate ; Register.
SENATE House. Papers on the Senate House Controversy, 1883.
                                           (1883)

SENDALL (*Sir* W.J.)   *See* Calverley (C. S.), 1885.
SENILE odium.   *See* Hausted (P.).
SENIOR Wranglers.   List by C. M. Neale.   *Bury St Edmunds*, 1907
SENTINEL Manufacturing Company scheme, signed by Hor. Darwin, M.A. and others.   F° 1899
SEPULCHRE'S (St) Church.   *See* Round Church.
SERMONS.   University Sermons.   *See* Mary's (St) the Great.
SERTUM Cantabrigiense; or the Cambridge Garland.   [By F. Wrangham.]   *Malton*, 1824
SETTLE (S.) Life.   By Thomas Hervey.   (Privately pr.)   *Colmer*, 1881
SEWAGE.   Report to the General Board of Health, on a preliminary enquiry into the sewerage, etc. of the town of Cambridge.   By William Ranger.   *London*, 1849
   Fly-sheets on the Sewage question from 1871.   1871–
   The Sewage of Cambridge.   By G. F. Cobb.   (*Camb. Chron.*) F° 1884
   Report of Mr Anson.   F° *n.p.* 1885
SEX.   Magazine of the Peterhouse Sexcentenary Club.   Nos. 1–40.
   1897–1910
SEXAGENARIAN.   [By W. Beloe.]   2 vols.   *London*, 1817
SEYMOUR (Gordon), *pseud.*   *See* Waldstein (C.).
SHAKESPEARE (W.)   Richard the Second.   Act I.   Specimen of proposed new edition, by W. G. Clark and H. R. Luard.   1860
   See also Amateur Dramatic Club, 1886.
"SHALL I be an Evangelical?"   A letter to an Undergraduate, in answer to the above question.   By Cassander.   1840
—— Sequel to above.   1840
SHARPE (W.)   Course of Sermons before the University.   April 1816.   2nd ed.   1816
SHARWOOD-SMITH (E.)   In Black and Red.   Cambridge Verses and School Songs.   1899
SHAW (Vero)   The Crooked Billet.   (Two states.)   *London* [*ab.* 1887]
SHEEPSHANKS (R.)   Correspondence respecting the Liverpool Observatory between Mr John Taylor and R.S.   (With Supplement.)   *London*, 1845
   A reply to Mr Babbage's letter to the *Times* on the Planet Neptune.   *London*, 1847
   A letter to the Board of Visitors of the Greenwich Royal Observatory.   With Correspondence prefixed.   *London*, 1854–60
   Memoir of R. Sheepshanks.   *London*, 1856
SHEEPSHED.   Poll for election of a Clerk to the Vicarage, 11 March, 1875.   (H. C. Turner elected.)   1875
SHELLEY (P.B.)   Adonais.   An elegy on the death of John Keats.   (Ed. by Lord Houghton and A. H. Hallam.)   1829
SHEPHERD (A.)   Heads of a course of Lectures in Experimental Philosophy which will begin at Christ College...Nov. 23, 1763.   (Date altered with pen to Feb. 29, 1768.)   1763
SHERIDAN (R.B.)   *See* Amateur Dramatic Club, 1864, 1868, 1882, 1895, 1908; Smyth (W.).

SHERLOCK (T.) The Proceedings of the Vice-Chancellor and the University of Cambridge against Dr Bentley, stated and vindicated. In a letter to a noble Peer. [By T. Sherlock.]   F⁰ *London*, 1719
SHERLOCK (W.) Dissertation concerning a Judge of Controversies. Ed. by R. Potts. (Old Tracts...1.)   1851
SHERMAN (J.) Historia Collegii Jesu Cantabrigiensis. Ed. J. O. Halliwell. (3 copies, corrected by J. W. Clark.)   *Londini*, 1840
SHERWILL (Th.) The degeneracy of the present age...June 25, 1704. A sermon.   4⁰ 1704
Church-conformity asserted...A sermon upon the Feast of St Simon and St Jude.   4⁰ 1704
Sermon before the University of Cambridge, March 8, 170⅝.
    London (1709)
SHILLETO (R.) Unsuccessful verses for Porson Prize, 1831. 1831
Fragmentum incerti ex 'Ηθικοφυσικολήροις. (With English version by T. Fremantle, Balliol College, Oxford.)   1848
Verses on the Master of Trinity's criticism of Aristotle's account of Induction. (With the original MS.)   4⁰ 1850
Thucydides or Grote?   1851
Few Remarks on *Thucydides or Grote*. [By J. Grote.]   1851
Greek verses on contested election for University Representative.
    4⁰ 1856
Latin elegiacs on the death of the *Caput Senatus*.   1856
Lines on the title A.C. proposed to be given by the Local Examinations.   1860
Testimonials when a candidate for the Greek Professorship in the University of Durham.   1862
SHIPLEY (A.E.) and Marr (J.E.) Handbook to the Natural History of Cambridgeshire.   1904
Shipley (A.E.) and Roberts (H.A.) A plea for Cambridge. (*Quarterly Review*, April, 1906.)
The same, reprinted.   *Edinburgh*, 1907
The late Professor Sir Michael Foster. (*Proc. Linnean Soc.*)
    (*London*, 1907)
Biographical sketch of John Samuel Budgett.   4⁰ 1908
Obituary notice of Professor A. Newton. (*Proc. Linnean Soc.*)
    (*London*, 1908)
Brit. Assoc. 1909, Winnipeg. Address to Zoological section. 4⁰ 1909
SHORT inquiry into the tendency of Chapel.   [? 182–]
SHUCKBURGH (E.S.) Laurence Chaderton, D.D. — Richard Farmer, D.D. An essay.   1884
Emmanuel College. (College histories.)   *London*, 1904
Memorial article by J. Adam.   (1906)
SHUDY CAMPS. Auctioneers' description of Shudy Camps Hall.
    F⁰ *London*, 1903
SIBERCH (J.) *See* Bowes (R.).
SIDGWICK (A.) Tennyson. Trin. Coll. 19 Oct. 1909.
    London, 1909

SIDGWICK (H.) On the Classical Tripos Examination.   (1866)
    The Ethics of Conformity and Subscription.   *London*, 1870

    In memory of Henry Sidgwick. By F. W. H. Myers.   *London*, 1900
    A memoir. By A. Sidgwick and E. M. Sidgwick.   *London*, 1906
    Henry Sidgwick Memorial Lecture. Decadence. By A. J. Balfour. 1908

SIDGWICK (*Mrs*) University Education of Women.   1897
SIDNEY Sussex College. The trial of F. Kendall, for setting fire to
    Sydney College.   1813
    The Pheon. Sidney Sussex College Magazine. Tercentenary ed.
    Feb. 14, 1896.   (1896)
    Sidney Sussex College. By G. M. Edwards. (College histories.)
    London, 1899
    See also Acts and Bills, 1823.
SIEVEKING (A.F.) *See* Worke for Cutlers.
SILVER Crescent. The "Hall" Magazine. Nos. 10, 11, 33, 34,
    39, 42, 43, 45, 47, 48.   1893–1907
SIMEON (C.) The danger of neglecting the Great Sacrifice. Assize
    Sermon, Aug. 22, 1797.   1797
    The Churchman's Confession. Sermon...1 Dec. 1805.   (1805)
    The Fountain of Living Waters. Sermon...14 May, 1809. (1809)
    Evangelical and Pharisaic Righteousness. Sermon...26 Nov. 1809.
    (1809)
    Fresh cautions to the public ; or a letter to the Rev. Edw. Pearson,
    D.D. Feb. 7, 1810.   (1810)
    —— 2nd ed.   (1810)
    Christ Crucified. Sermon. 17 Mar. 1811.   1811
    —— 3rd ed. (In The Excellency of the Liturgy, 3rd ed.)   1816
    The Excellency of the Liturgy. Four discourses preached before the
    University, Nov. 1811. [With] an Answer to Dr Marsh's
    Inquiry, dated 25 March, 1812.   1812
    —— 2nd ed.   1813
    —— 3rd ed.   1816
    Dr Marsh's fact ; or a congratulatory address to the Church Members
    of the British and Foreign Bible Society.   1813
    An appeal to men of wisdom and candour. Four discourses preached
    before the University, Nov. 1815.   *London*, 1816
    —— Another ed.   *London*, 1820
    The true test of Religion in the Soul. Sermon...9 March, 1817.
    1817
    The Conversion of the Jews. Two discourses preached before the
    University of Cambridge, Feb. 18 and 25, 1821.   *London*, 1821
    Pastoral admonition to an affectionate flock, 1 Oct. 1832.
    London, 1832
    Evangelical Religion. A sermon preached before the University of
    Cambridge.   1837
    Substance of an address delivered at a meeting of Undergraduates in
    Cambridge...Oct. 27, 1834.   *London*, 1837

SIMEON (C.)

Funeral Sermons. By W. Dealtry, G. Hodson, W. Mandell, J. Scholefield,
S. Thodey, T. Webster.   *Cambridge and London*, 1836
Biography and account of his funeral. (*Pulpit*, xxix.)   *London* [1837]
Memoirs of the life of C. Simeon. Ed. by W. Carus. 2nd ed. *London*, 1847
A brief memoir of the Rev. C. Simeon. By J. Williamson. *London*, 1848
Memorial of the late C. Simeon. Report.   1856
Recollections of the conversation parties of the Rev. C. Simeon. By A. B.
Brown.   *London*, 1863
Charles Simeon. By H. C. G. Moule. (English Leaders of Religion.)
London, 1892

See also Pearson (E.).

SIMEON (S.) Itineraria S. Simeonis et Willelmi de Worcestre. Ed.
J. Nasmith.   1778
SIMPKINSON (J.N.) An oration delivered in Trinity College
Chapel, at the Commemoration, Dec. 15, 1838.   (1838)
SIMPSON (J.C.) Testimonials. Assistant Surgeon, Addenbrooke's
Hospital.   1897
SINAI. Written for the Seatonian Prize Poem. By an unsuccessful
Candidate.   1858
SINKER (R.) A catalogue of the fifteenth century printed books in
the library of Trinity College, Cambridge.   1876
The statue of Byron in the Library of Trinity College, Cambridge.
(*Notes and Queries*, Nov. 26, 1881.)   (*London*, 1881)
The Library of Trinity College, Cambridge.   1891
A talk with the congregation about the Round Church.   (1898)
Descriptive catalogue of editions of printed text of versions of
Testamenta xii. Patriarcharum.   1910
SITES. Purchase of sites. Fly-sheets, reports, etc., relating thereto,
from 1896.   1896–
SIZAR (The) A rhapsody. No. 1.   1799
SIZAR MacSandy. A legend of St Bede's College. By Melissa.
1885
SKEAT (W.W.) A Student's Pastime, being Articles reprinted from
Notes and Queries.   *Oxford*, 1896
Place names of Huntingdonshire.   1902
Notes on some examples of the occurrence of initial W in written
English. (*Trans. Camb. Phil. Soc.*)   1904
SKELTON (J.) Pietas Oxoniensis, or records of Oxford Founders.
4° *Oxford*, 1828 [1831]
Oxonia antiqua restaurata. 2nd ed. By E. J. Carlos.
4° *London*, 1843
SKENE (W.B.) Handbook of certain Acts affecting the Universities
of Oxford and Cambridge, and the Colleges therein. *London*, 1894
SKERTCHLY (S.B.J.) and Miller (S.H.) The Fenland past and
present.   *Wisbech*, 1878
SKETCHES from Cambridge. By a Don [Leslie Stephen].
London, 1865

SKITS. By an Undergraduate [R. Jeffcoat, Caius].   1894
SKYNNER (J.) Speech at the laying of the first stone of the front of
    the Library, 30 April, 1755. (In Carmina ad...Ducem de New-
    castle inscripta.)   Fº 1755
SLADE Professorship of Fine Art.   Deed of Foundation.   (1869)
SLEEPERS (The) By M.P.   1909
SLIP in the Fens. [By Jane Sexey.] New ed.   London, 1885
SMART (C.) On the Eternity of the Supreme Being. 2nd ed.
    (Seatonian Prize Poem for 1750.)   4º 1752
  On the Omniscience of the Supreme Being. (Seatonian Prize Poem
    for 1752.)   4º 1752
  On the Immensity of the Supreme Being. 2nd ed. (Seatonian Prize
    Poem for 1751.)   4º 1753
  On the Power of the Supreme Being. (Seatonian Prize Poem for
    1753.)   4º 1754
  On the Goodness of the Supreme Being. (Seatonian Prize Poem for
    1755.)   4º 1756
  —— 2nd ed.   4º 1756

    Bibliography of the writings of Christopher Smart, with biographical refer-
    ences, by G. J. Gray.   4º London, 1903

SMEATON (J.) Report concerning the drainage of the North Level
    of the Fens, 22 Aug. 1768.   4º n.p. 1768
SMEDLEY (E.) A few verses English and Latin.   London, 1812
  The death of Saul and Jonathan. (Seatonian Prize Poem for 1813.)
                                                           1814
  Jephthah. (Seatonian Prize Poem for 1814.)   1814
  Jonah. A poem. (Written for the Seatonian Prize and commended.)
                                                   London, 1815
  Farewell to Harold ! [Attack on Byron.]   n.p. 1816
  Prescience ; or the secrets of divination. A poem.   London, 1816
  Poems, with a selection from his correspondence, and a memoir of
    his life.   London, 1837

    The Tribute. Edited by Lord Northampton (for E. Smedley's benefit).
                                                   London, 1837

SMEDLEY (F.E.) Frank Fairlegh.   London, 1863
SMITH (A.L.) F. W. Maitland. A bibliography.   Oxford, 1907
  Frederic William Maitland. Two lectures and a bibliography.
                                                   Oxford, 1908
SMITH (A.R.) See Catalogue.
SMITH (G.) Oxford and her Colleges.   12º London, 1894
SMITH (G.C.M.) Syllabus of lectures on the English poets of the
    modern school.   1889
  The College days of William Wordsworth. (Eagle, March, 1891.)
                                                           1891
  John Gibson's manuscript. (Eagle, June, 1892.)   1892
  Lists of past and present occupants of rooms in St John's College.
                                                           1895

SMITH (G.C.M.)
Marlowe at Cambridge. (*Mod. Lang. Review*, Jan. 1909.)   1909
See Club Law, 1907 ; Hymenaeus, 1908 ; Laelia, 1910 ; Pedantius,
1905.
SMITH (*Sir* H.B.) Simla flowers.   4° *Simla*, 1899
SMITH (J.), †1652 Select discourses. 4th ed. By H. G. Williams.
1859
SMITH (J.), *of Smith Hall, pseud. See* Lewis (J. D.).
SMITH (*Sir* J.E.) Considerations respecting Cambridge, more par-
ticularly relating to its Botanical Professorship.   *London*, 1818
A defence of the Church and Universities of England, against such
injurious advocates as Professor Monk.   *London*, 1819
See also Monk (J. H.), 1818–19.
SMITH (J.J.) The Cambridge Portfolio. 2 vols. in 1. (Bowes
1993.)   4° *London*, 1840
A few words on the last publication of the Cambridge Camden
Society [i.e. Church enlargement and Church arrangement]. 1843
Considerations on the disposal of the new Botanical Garden ground.
1845
Further considerations on the disposal of the new Botanical Garden
ground.   1845
Catalogue of Coins in the Museum of the C.A.S.   1847
Reply to Some reasons against the expediency of instituting a public
examination of students previous to their residence in the Uni-
versity. (6 Dec.)   1847
A letter to the Vice-Chancellor on the late rejection by the Caput of
a Grace respecting an examination previous to residence. (14 Dec.)
1847
Reply to Mr Harper's Remarks. [On the University system of
education.]   1848
Index to the Baker MSS. [By J. J. Smith and others.]   1848
A Catalogue of the Manuscripts in the library of Gonville and Caius
College, Cambridge.   1849
Suggestions for an Athenae Cantabrigienses.   [1851 ?]
Pictorial illustrations of the Catalogue of Manuscripts in Gonville and
Caius College library.   4° 1853
Statement of proceedings taken with reference to the election of
Master in Gonville and Caius College in 1852.   1854
SMITH (J.P.) University Representation.   *London*, 1883
SMITH (R.) A Compleat System of Opticks. 2 vols.   4° 1738
Harmonics.   1749
See Cotes (R.), 1747.
SMITH (R.H.) The connexion between religion and morality,
amongst the ancient Greeks and Romans. (Members' Prize Essay.)
1857
SMITH (T.) The life and death of Mr William Moore, late Fellow
of Caius Colledge, and Keeper of the University Library. (+ The
last words which were writ by Dr Hammond...) (Ed. by
C. Bertie.)   1660

SMITH (W.)   The annals of University College.
Newcastle-on-Tyne, 1728
SMITH (W.R.)   Baptism for the dead, an evidence of the Resurrection.
London, 1838
SMITH (W.S.)   Capernaum.   (Seatonian Prize Poem for 1864.)
London, 1865
The Disciples assembled in the Upper Room at Jerusalem after our
Lord's Ascension. (Seatonian Prize Poem for 1866.) *London,* 1866
SMYTH (W.), *Bp of Lincoln.*   Life.   By R. Churton.   *Oxford,* 1800
SMYTH (*Prof.* W.), †1849.   List of books recommended or referred
to in lectures on modern history.   1815
—— Another edition.   1817
—— Another edition.   1823
—— Another edition.   1828
Ode performed in the Senate-House, 29 June, 1811, at the installa-
tion of the Duke of Gloucester.   1811
Memoir of Mr Sheridan.   *Leeds,* 1840
Lady Morley's Lecture.   *Leeds,* 1840
SNARL.   Nos. 1 and 2.   Oct. 31, Nov. 14, 1899.   4° 1899
SNELL (J.C.)   A poetical address to the ladies of the Isle of Ely.
London [*ab.* 1780]
A poetical address to the ladies of Cambridgeshire. *London* [*ab.* 1780]
SNOB.   Nos. 3–6, 9–11.   (Bowes 1742–1744.)   1829
SNOBS' Trip to Paris; or the humours of a Long Vacation. A
fiction founded on fact.   2nd ed.   [183–]
—— 3rd ed.   *See* Fits of Folly (1832).
SNODGRASS (*Rev.* J.)   *See* Granta.
SOCIETY for opposing the endowment of research.   First publ.
London, 1881
SOCIETY for the prevention of cruelty to Undergraduates.   *See*
Trinity College, 1838.
SOCIETY for the suppression of mendicity at Cambridge.   F° 1819
SOCIUS.   *See* Cambridge Tart; Facetiae Cantabrigienses; Oxford
and Cambridge Nuts to crack.
SOHAM.   *See* Gisburne (J.).
SOLEY (T.L.)   Sermon preached in King's College Chapel.   1868
SOME considerations on the necessity of an Appeal in the University
of Cambridge.   [By M. Hodgson.]   *London,* 1752
SOME married Fellows.   [By S. C. Venn.]   2 vols.   *London,* 1893
SOMERSHAM.   An account of the Somersham water in the County
of Huntingdon.   By D. P. Layard.   *London,* 1767
SOMERVELL (R.)   Letters to a Cambridge Freshman. *London,* 1884
SOMNIUM Cantabrigiense, or a Poem upon the death of the late
King, brought to London by a Post to the Muses.   4° *London,* 1650
SPALDING (W.P.)   Street and general Directory of Cambridge.
1881
Handbook of Cambridge.   1882, 1883, 1885, 1893, 1897, 1905, 1907.
1882–1907
SPEDDING (J.)   Apology for the...xixth century.   (1830)

SPEED (L.) and Pryor (F.R.)   The Oedipus Tyrannus.   A record of
the performance in Nov. 1887.   4° (1888)
SPENCER (O.L.)   Life of H. Chichelé, Abp of Canterbury.
                                                   London, 1783
SPENCER (W.H.)   *See* Natural Science Society.
SPINETO (*Marchese*)   Syllabus of a plan of lectures on the literature
and languages of Modern Europe.   1822
Lectures on the elements of hieroglyphics and Egyptian antiquities.
                                                   London, 1829
Per l'istallazione del nobilissimo Signor Marchese di Camden.   1835
Canzone per la istallazione di sua Eccellenza il Sig. Duca di
Northumberland.   1842
Quartine in occasione della visità di...Regina Vittoria con...Principe
Alberto.   1843
Per l'inaugurazione di...Principe Alberto all' officio di Cancelliere...
canzone.   1847
SPINNING-HOUSE.   Extracts from newspapers on a death after
imprisonment in the Spinning-House.   1846
Rules for Government.   F° n.d.
Dietary for Prisoners.   F° n.d.
See also Proctors (1860).
SPRAY.   [By R. M. Bingley.]   1859
SPRING RICE (T.)   Speech at a Public Meeting of the electors of
the town of Cambridge, June 26, 1832.   1832
Speech, on presenting a petition from the University of Cambridge,
in favour of the claims of the Dissenters, in the House of Commons,
March 24, 1834.   *London*, 1834
See also Flanagan (L.).
SPROTT (T.)   Chronica.   Ed. Th. Hearnius.   *Oxonii*, 1719
SPURRELL (J.)   *See* Sellon (L.).
SQUIRE (S.)   Commencement Sermon, 2 July, 1749.   4° *London*, 1749
See also Academic.
STALLAN (J.)   Funeral sermon on J. S., who was executed for
arson, at Cambridge, Dec. 7, 1833.   By James Baines.   1833
—— Another ed.   1834
STANFORD (*Sir* C.V.)   Words to Opera "Savonarola," composed
by C. V. Stanford.   *London*, 1884
Eden.   An Oratorio, by R. Bridges.   Set to music by C. V. Stanford.
                                           12° *London*, 1891
Installation Ode for the Duke of Devonshire.   By A. W. Verrall
and C. V. Stanford.   1892
Requiem.   Performed in King's Coll. Chapel by Dr Mann's Festival
Choir, 9 June, 1898.   1898
Words to Opera "Much ado about nothing," composed by C. V.
Stanford.   *London*, 1901
STANHOPE (G.)   The perfection of Scripture stated.   A sermon...
at the Public Commencement...July 4, 1697.   4° *London*, 1697
STANLEY (A.P.)   Suggestions for an improvement of the Examina-
tion Statute.   [By B. Jowett and A. P. Stanley.]   *Oxford*, 1848

STANLEY (A.P.)

A letter to the Bishop of London on the state of Subscription in the Church of England, and in the University of Oxford. *Oxford,* 1863

Purity and Light. A sermon preached before the University of Cambridge, Feb. 2, 1873, being the Sunday following the funeral of A. Sedgwick. *London,* 1873

Charles Kingsley. A sermon preached in Westminster Abbey, Jan. 31, 1875, being the Sunday after the funeral of Charles Kingsley. *London,* 1875

See also Thirlwall (C.), 1881.

STANLEY (W.) Catalogus librorum manuscriptorum in bibliotheca Collegii Corporis Christi quos legavit M. Parkerus. F⁰ *Londini,* 1722

STANTON (V.H.) The province of Christian ethics. Introductory lecture as Ely Professor of Divinity. *London,* 1890

Some makers of Trinity College. Sermon preached, 9 Dec. 1898.
1898

STANWELL (C.) St Paul on the Appian Way. (Seatonian Prize Poem for 1867.) 1867

STATUTES.

*** For College Statutes see under the several Colleges concerned.

An argument to prove that the xxxixth section of the Lᵗʰ Chapter of the Statutes given by Queen Elizabeth to the University of Cambridge, includes the old Statutes of that University. [By J. Burford.] 4⁰ *London,* 1727

Excerpta è Statutis Academiae Cantabrigiensis...aliaque ad scholarium officium spectantia. 1732

—— Another edition. 1748

—— Another edition. 1770

—— Another edition. 1793

—— Another edition. 1815

—— Another edition. 1847

The Statutes of Queen Elizabeth for the University of Cambridge.
London, 1838

Collection of Statutes for the University and Colleges of Cambridge. (Ed. by J. Heywood.) (pp. 359.) *London,* 1840

—— Another copy to p. 279, with MS. corrections. *London,* 1840

Statuta Academiae Cantabrigiensis. (21 Apr. 1849.) (1849)

—— (31 May–2 Dec. 1851.) (1851)

—— (10 Dec. 1851.) (1851)

—— (30 Nov. 1852.) (1852)

—— (27 May, 1854.) (1854)

Early Cambridge University and College Statutes, in the English language. Collected by James Heywood. *London,* 1855

Statuta Academiae Cantabrigiensis. (16 Dec. 1856.) (1856)

—— (6 Feb. 1857.) (1857)

—— (13 March, 1857.) (1857)

—— (30 April, 1857.) (1857)

—— (21 Oct. 1857.) (1857)

STATUTES.
Reports of meetings to discuss Statutes (Nov. 1857) with other pieces
on the same subject (Nov.–Dec. 1857).   Fᵒ 1857
Statuta Academiae Cantabrigiensis.   (25 March 1858.)   (1858)
—— (31 July, 1858.)   (1858)
—— Another edition.   1859
Statutes framed by the Commissioners, 1860.   (Ordered by House of
Commons to be printed, 15 Feb. 1861.)   n.p. 1861
Statuta Academiae Cantabrigiensis.   1870
—— Another edition.   1874
Memorials and other papers on the proposed new Statutes, 1879–80.
                                                           1879–80
Statutes of the University of Cambridge.   Draft for consideration.
5 October, 1882.   1882
Statutes of the University of Cambridge.   1882
Statutes for the University and Colleges under the Act of 1877.
(Ed. by H. Bradshaw.)   1883
Statutes of the University of Cambridge.   Ed. by J. W. Clark. 1896
—— Another edition.   1904
See also Peacock (G.); Professors.
STATUTES Revision Syndicate.   Grace to appoint, 14 Feb. 1849.
                                                           Fᵒ (1849)
Second form of this, 7 March, 1849.   Fᵒ (1849)
Reports dated 10 Dec. 1851, 23 March, 1852, 28 May, 1852 (two
editions), 30 Nov. 1852.   Notice of Grace to confirm recommenda-
tions, 11 March and 10 Dec. 1852.   Fᵒ (1851–52)
Reasons for refusing to sign the Report...dated Dec. 10, 1851.   By
A. H. Wratislaw.   1852
Report, 27 May, 1854.   Fᵒ (1854)
STEBBING (H.)   Defence of Confirmation.   1729
See Fragment.
STEERE (E.)   See Universities' Mission.
STEPHEN (Caroline E.)   The Basis of Christian Science; corres-
pondence between C. E. S. and Mrs Butler.   1905
STEPHEN (Sir G.)   The Jesuit at Cambridge.   2 vols.
                                                    London, 1847
STEPHEN (Sir J.)   Letter to Sir J. Stephen on his Essays in Ecclesi-
astical Biography.   By Lucius Arthur.   n.p. 1852
Extracts from Essays in Ecclesiastical Biography, placed in contrast
with the statements of the Church which they are supposed to
impugn.   4ᵒ n.p. [1852]
Letters, with biographical notes by his daughter, Caroline Emelia
Stephen.   Gloucester, 1906
STEPHEN (J.K.)   Lapsus Calami.   1891
—— New ed.   (L. P.)   1891
Quo Musa Tendis?   (L. P.)   1891
The Living Languages.   Defence of compulsory Greek.   1891
Lapsus Calami and other verses.   (With memoir.)   1896
See also Reflector.

STEPHEN (*Sir* L.)   The Allelein-Horn.   (*Notes of Travel in* 1860.)
London, 1860

The Poll Degree from a third point of view. 1863
Sketches from Cambridge.   By a Don. *London*, 1865
Life of Henry Fawcett.   2nd ed. *London*, 1885

Life and Letters.   By F. W. Maitland. *London*, 1906
The Leslie Stephen Lecture.   Samuel Johnson.   By W. Raleigh.
Oxford, 1907

STEPHENSON (*Mrs* Guy)   Eustace Talbot. 4° 1908
STEVENS (H.W.P.)   Downing College.   (College histories.)
London, 1899
STEVENS (T.)   Two sermons on Stedfastness in the Christian faith.
1771
STEVENS (W.), †1807.   Strictures on a sermon...May, 1776, by
    R. Watson. 1777
STEVENS (W.)   Memoirs of the life and martyrdom of John Bradford.
London, 1832
STEVENSON (W.)   A supplement to the second edition of
    Mr Bentham's History and antiquities of the Cathedral and
    Conventual Church of Ely. 4° *Norwich*, 1817
STEWART (D.J.)   Liber Eliensis.   Vol. I.   Ed. by D. J. Stewart.
London, 1848

On the architectural history of Ely Cathedral. *London*, 1868
Ely Cathedral, with plans, etc.   (*Builder*, 2 Apr. 1892.)
STIRBITCH.   *See* Sturbridge.
STOCKTON (O.)   The true dignity of St Paul's Elder, exemplified
    in the life of O. S., sometime Fellow of Gonvile and Caius
    Colleges in Cambridge.   To which is added his Funeral Sermon.
    By John Fairfax.   1681.   (Reprint.) *London*, 1826
STOKES (*Sir* G.G.)   Address as President of the British Association.
1869

Religious benefits from recent science and research.   Paper at Church
    Congress, 1879. *London*, 1879
Evidence of Missionaries as to the practical effect of presenting
    Christianity to the heathen. 1882
The Harmony of Science and Faith. *London*, 1882
The Church in relation to State questions. *London*, 1886
Literature of the day, and its attitude towards Christianity.
London, 1889

"I."   Lecture on the Immortality of the Soul. *London*, 1890
The Divine Personality. *London*, 1891
Science and Faith. *London*, 1893
Is the Soul of Man by its nature Immortal? *London*, 1893
The Inductive method in Theology. *London*, 1897

List of guests attending his Jubilee, 1, 2 June, 1899. 1899
Catalogue of Mathematical books for sale by Heffer & Sons, Petty Cury,
    including the library of Sir G. G. Stokes. 1903

STOKES (*Sir* G.G.)

List of his Mathematical, Physical and Theological Papers...on sale by Heffer & Sons.   1903

Statement of proceedings in connection with the placing of a memorial to him in Westminster Abbey, 7 July, 1904.   4° 1904

STOKES (H.P.)   Corpus Christi College.   (College histories.)

London, 1898

STOKES (Hudleston)   Testimonials.   Candidate for the Rectory of Stapleton.   1894

STOKES (L.)   *See* Thirlwall (C.), 1881.

STONECROSS, and other matter of fact Rhymes, by M. K.   1900

STONEHAM (T.)   The Taking of Jerusalem in the first Crusade. (Unsuccessful Prize Poem.)   1832

STONEY (T.U.)   The Tears of Granta.   By an Undergraduate.

4° 1812

Ode on quitting the University.   1813

STORER (J. and H.S.)   Illustrations of the University of Cambridge. Two series.   (Bowes 1713, 1713 b.)   4° [1827–32]

Cantabrigia illustrata; a series of forty-four views of the principal buildings in the University and Town of Cambridge.   (Bowes 1713 c.)   4° 1835

Collegiorum portæ apud Cantabrigiam a J. et H. S. Storer delineatæ et insculptæ.   (Bowes 1713 d.)   4° [183–]

Delineations of Trinity College, Cambridge.   (Bowes 1713 e.)

4° [183–]

Delineations of the Chapel of King's College.   Engr. title and four plates; description with vignette.   4° [183–]

STOURBRIDGE.   *See* Sturbridge.

STRACHEY (R.)   Lectures on geography delivered before the University of Cambridge during the Lent Term, 1888.

London, 1888

STRAIGHTFORWARD (Timmy), *pseud.*   Election flights, etc.

4° *London* [1780]

Second letter to his Mother.   4° *London* [1780]

STRICKLAND (H.E.)   A catalogue of the collection of birds formed by the late H. E. S.   By Osbert Salvin.   1882

STRICTURES upon the Discipline of the University of Cambridge.

London, 1792

—— 2nd ed.   1794

STRINGER (J.)   A Cantab's leisure.   2 vols. in 1.   *London*, 1829

STRUGGLES of a Poor Student through Cambridge.   [By S. Atkinson.]   (*Lond. Mag.*, April 1, 1825.)

STUART (J.)   A letter on University extension.   1871

STUBBS (C.W.)   Historical memorials of Ely Cathedral.   *London*, 1897

Ely Cathedral Handbook.   20th ed.   *Ely* (1898)

—— 21st ed.   *Ely*, 1904

The Acts of S. Audrey.   The Octagon Sculptures in Ely Cathedral.

Ely [1904?]

The story of Cambridge.   *London*, 1905

STUDD (A.) Exhibition of paintings. Catalogue. *London* [1909]
STUDENT, or the Oxford and Cambridge Monthly Miscellany, Vols. 1, 2. (+ The Inspector. Nos. 1–3.) Jan. 31, 1750–July 3, 1751. (Bowes 1194.)   *Oxford*, 1750–1
STUDENT'S guide to the school of "Litterae Fictitiae," commonly called Novel-literature. 2nd ed.   *Oxford*, 1855
STUDENT'S Guide to the University of Cambridge.   1863
——— 4th ed.   1880–82
——— 5th ed.   1893
STUDENT'S Handbook to the University of Cambridge. By A. P. Humphry.   1877
STUDENT'S Handbook to the University and Colleges of Cambridge. (Ed. by J. R. Tanner.)   1902
——— 4th ed.   1905
——— 8th ed.   1909
"STUDIES," and other verses. By "Undergraduate." *Ipswich*, 1904
STUDIES Syndicate. Fly-sheets, reports, etc., from 1854.   1854–
See also Whewell (W.), 1853.
STUKELEY (W.) Palæographia Britannica. Nos. 1, 2.
                          4º *London, Stamford*, 1743–46
STURBRIDGE. Sermon preached at St Maries...to the Universitie, Sept. 6, 1668, the Sunday before Sturbridge Fair.   4º 1668
Nundinae Sturbrigienses, anno 1702. Authore T. H[ill] Cantab.
                                        Dublinii (1702)
——— Another edition.   *Londini*, 1709
——— Another edition (+ Tunbrigialia, authore P. Causton; Incendium Palatinum).   *Londini*, 1709
The history and antiquities of Barnwell Abbey, and of Sturbridge Fair. [By J. Nichols.]   4º *London*, 1786
Sturbridge Theatre. Play-bills, 1786–1803.   1786–1803
Antiquities of St Mary's Chapel, Stourbridge. By J. S. Cotman.
                                    4º *Yarmouth*, 1819
Some account of Stirbitch Fair. By a Septuagenarian. (*The Mirror*, Sept. 27, 1828.)
Appeal for funds for restoration of Stourbridge Chapel.   (1865)
SUBSCRIPTION. Articles to be subscribed by every person admitted to any degree in the University of Cambridge.   Fº n.d.
Defence of Subscriptions in the Church of England. Sermon. By W. S. Powell. 2nd ed.   4º *London*, 1758
——— 3rd ed.   *London*, 1759
——— 4th ed.   *London*, 1772
Remarks on Dr Powell's Sermon in defence of Subscriptions. [By F. Blackburne.]   *London*, 1758
The hardship and danger of Subscriptions...in a letter to Dr Powell. With Remarks upon his Sermon.   *London*, 1758
Three sermons preached before the University of Cambridge, occasioned by an attempt to abolish Subscription to the Thirty Nine Articles. By S. Hallifax. 2nd ed.   4º 1772
——— 3rd ed.   1772

SUBSCRIPTION.

A letter to Dr Hallifax, upon the subject of his three discourses. By Samuel Blackall.   2nd ed.   4° 1772

Letter to House of Commons respecting the petition for relief in the matter of Subscription...By R. Watson.   *London*, 1772

Letters on the...Subscription to the Liturgy and Articles of the Church of England. [By John Jebb.]   *London*, 1772

Arcana : or the Principles of the late petitioners to Parliament for relief in the matter of Subscription. In eight letters to a friend. [By R. Robinson.]   1774

—— Another edition.   *Nottingham*, *n.d.*

Considerations on the propriety of requiring a Subscription to Articles of Faith. [By E. Law.]   1774

A letter to the Caput of the University of Cambridge on the rejection of the Grace abolishing Subscription. By a Member of the Senate.
                                                      London, 1788

Pamphlets in defence of the Oxford usage of Subscription to the xxxix Articles at Matriculation.   *Oxford*, 1835

Subscription no bondage. By Rusticus [F. D. Maurice].
                                                      Oxford, 1835

Reasons for declining to subscribe the Thirty Nine Articles. By an Undergraduate of Trinity College, Cambridge.   *London*, 1836

A letter to the Bishop of London on the state of Subscription in the Church of England and in the University of Oxford. By A. P. Stanley.   *Oxford*, 1863

The Ethics of Conformity and Subscription. By H. Sidgwick.
                                                      London, 1870

See also Tests.

SUGGESTIONS respecting the conditions under which University education may be made more available for clerks.   *Oxford*, 1854

SUMNER (J.B.) Mysorei tyranni mors. (Latin Ode which obtained Sir W. Browne's Medal, 1800.)   (1800)

An essay tending to show that the prophecies, now accomplishing, are an evidence of the truth of the Christian religion. (Hulsean Prize Essay for 1801.)   1802

SUMNER (R.) Concio ad clerum, habita Cantabrigiae, xj Kal. Apr. 1768.   *Londini*, 1768

SUNDAY. An address to the Senate of the University of Cambridge, relative to certain Academic proceedings which occasionally take place therein on the Lord's Day. [By W. Farish.]   1823

Notice of Grace to appoint a Syndicate to consider whether business transacted in the Senate House on Sunday may not be deferred, Dec. 8, 1823 ; Report of this Syndicate, April 27, 1824.   1823–4

The Sunday question settled, with reference to the late proceedings at the Union Society. By a member of Trinity College.   1834

SUNDAY Thoughts. [By W. Whewell.]   1847

SUNFLOWER Magazine. No. 3. Jan. 1885.   *n.p.* 1885

SUPPLIANTS of Scoffocles.   (1883)

SUTTON (*Sir* Richard) Life. By R. Churton.   *Oxford*, 1800

SWAFFHAM BULBECK.   *See* Hailstone (E.).
SWAINSON (C.A.)   The College Chapel and the University Church.
1850

Catalogue of the library of Dr Swainson...sold Nov. 8, 9, 1887.   1887

SWANSTON (C.T.)   An essay on " The conditions which must exist
among a people to admit of the successful working of a consti-
tutional monarchy."   1853
SWEETING (W.D.)   The Cathedral Church of Ely.   *London,* 1901
SWETE (H.B.)   On the Bull Apostolicae Curae.   1896
SWIFT (J.)   The Tale of a Tub, etc.   5th ed.   (3 copies.)
London, 1710
Miscellaneous Works.   *London,* 1720
The Battle of the Books.   Ed. A. Guthkelch.   12º *London,* 1908
SYKES (A.A.)   The Case of Dr Bentley truly stated.   *London,* 1719
The Case of Dr Bentley farther stated.   *London,* 1719
SYMONDS (J.)   Observations upon the expediency of revising the
present English version of the Four Gospels, etc.   4º 1789
Observations upon the expediency of revising the present English
version of the Epistles in the New Testament.   4º 1794
SYMPOSIUM.   *See* Cambridge University Magazine, 1840–3.

T

TAKING of Jerusalem in the first Crusade. (Unsuccessful Prize
Poem.) " Jerusalem, lone City." 1832
—— " In that fair clime." 1832
—— " Fair is the Twilight." 1832
—— " Oh ! for the Voice." 1832
TAKINGS ; or the life of a Collegian. A poem. Illustrated by
R. Dagley. 1821
TALBOT (E.) Eustace Talbot. Some recollections. (By Mrs Guy
Stephenson, W. M. Fletcher, and M. R. James.) 4° 1908
TARVER (F.) Acting at Eton. (Elliot's *Amateur Clubs and Actors.*)
(*London*, 1898)
TATHAM (E.) Address on proposed new statute respecting public
examination in Univ. of Oxford. 2nd ed. 4° *Oxford*, 1807
Second address [on same subject]. 2nd ed. 4° *Oxford*, 1807
TATLER in Cambridge. Nos. 1–80. April 26, 1871–June 5, 1872.
(Bowes 2578.) 4° 1871–72
TAYLER (H.C.A.) Testimonials when a candidate for the principal-
ship of Cheltenham College. 1862
TAYLOR (A.) Papers in relation to the antient topography of the
Eastern Counties of Britain. 4° *London*, 1869
TAYLOR (J.) Oratio habita...in templo Beatæ Mariæ die solenni
martyrii Caroli primi Regis, A.D. 1730. *London*, 1730
The Music Speech [and Ode for Music] at the Public Commence-
ment in Cambridge, July 6, 1730. *London*, 1730
—— Another ed., with R. Long's Music Speech of 1714. Ed. by
J. Nichols. 1819
Marmor Sandvicense cum commentario et notis Jo. Taylori.
4° 1743
TAYLOR (J.P.) Considerations on Paley's Evidences. 1898
TAYLOR (S.) The so-called " Real Objective Presence " in the
Lord's Supper no doctrine of the Church of England. 1867
The system of Clerical Subscription in the Church of England.
London, 1869
On French and German as substitutes for Greek in University Pass
Examinations. *London*, 1870
On Profit-sharing between Capital and Labour. 1882
The late R. C. Rowe. (*Camb. Rev.*, Oct. 15, 1884.) 1884
Coutts Trotter. In Memoriam. 1888

TAYLOR (S.)
A record of the Cambridge Centenary Commemoration, Dec. 4, 5, 1891, of W. A. Mozart. Ed. by S. Taylor. *London*, 1892
A Song of Trinity. Words by A. E. Collins, music by Sedley Taylor. 4° 1907
TEA. The art of making Tea. A poem. 1797
TEACHERS Training Syndicate. Examination for Certificates.
London, 188c
TEARS of Granta; a satire, addressed to Undergraduates in the University of Cambridge. By an Undergraduate [T. U. Stoney]. 4° 1812
TEDDER (H.R.) *See* Library, 1880–1.
TEESDALE (F.D.) Mexico. A prize poem recited in the Theatre, Oxford, June 21, 1865. *Oxford*, 1865
TELEGRAM and Telegrapheme...in a friendly correspondence between A. C. and H., both M.A.'s of Trinity College. *London*, 1858
TEMPERANCE Union. Report of University conference on Intemperance...under the direction of the University Temperance Union, 5 March, 1873. 1873
TEMPLER (J.) The Reason of Episcopall Inspection. Sermon.
4° 1676
TEN minutes advice to Freshmen. 1785
TEN Year Men. A letter to John [Kaye], Bishop of Bristol, respecting an additional examination, or total abolition, of Ten Year Men in the University of Cambridge. By Philotheologus. 1825
See also Perry (S.).
TENNANT (S.) Some account of the late S. Tennant, Professor of Chemistry in the University of Cambridge. (Repr. from *Annals of Philosophy*.) *London*, 1815
TENNYSON (Alfred, *Lord*) Letter from Lord Monteagle, offering a bust of Tennyson to Trinity College. 1859
Sermon...in reference to the death of Lord Tennyson. By H. M. Butler. 1892
Tennyson. By Arthur Sidgwick. (On the occasion of the unveiling of the statue of Tennyson by Thornycroft.) *London*, 1909
TERRAE Filius, or the secret history of the University of Oxford. [By N. Amhurst.] *London*, 1726
TERROT (C.H.) Hezekiah and Sennacherib. (Seatonian Prize Poem for 1816.) 1816
TESTS. Dissenters University Admission Bill. A letter to Dr Phillpotts, Bp of Exeter, containing strictures on a speech delivered by him in the House of Lords, on the Second Reading of the...Bill. By a Member of the University of Cambridge. *London*, 1834
The Cambridge Petition examined; or reasons against admitting Dissenters to graduate in the Universities. *London*, 1834
Letter on Mr Bouverie's Bill for admitting Dissenters to Fellowships, 8 May, 1866. 1866
Letters, Papers, Fly-sheets, etc. on the Oxford and Cambridge Tests Bill, 1868–1870. 1868–1871

TESTS.

Report from the Select Committee of the House of Lords on University Tests.   F⁰ 1870

Memorial against the University Tests Bill.   *n.p.* 1871

University Tests, and the Bill for their abolition.   [1870 ?]

See also Acts and Bills, 1834; Beresford Hope (A. J.); Clayton (C.); Coleridge (*Sir* J. D.); Dalby (W.); Frend (W.); Guest (E.); Inglis (*Sir* R. H.); Lee (S.); Moberly (G.); Paley (F. A.); Pearson (G.); Pottinger (H. A.); Rose (H. J.); Sedgwick (A.); Spring Rice (T.); Subscription; Thirlwall (C.); Turton (T.); Whewell (W.); Wordsworth (C.), *Bp of Lincoln*; Young (*Sir* G.).

TEW (E.) Resignation no Proof. A letter to Mr Jebb; with occasional remarks on his Spirit of Protestantism. By a member of the University of Cambridge [E. Tew].   *London*, 1776

THACKERAY family. Memorials of the Thackeray family. By J. T. Pryme and A. Bayne.   *London*, 1879

THACKERAY (F. St J.) Eton College Library.   4⁰ *Eton*, 1881

Memoir of E. C. Hawtrey.   *London*, 1896

THACKERAY (W.M.) Etchings while at Cambridge, illustrative of University life, etc.   *London*, 1875

THANATOS, a poem, by the Ghost of Macaulay.   1878

THEATRE. The New Theatre. (Architect's description.)   1896

The New Theatre, Cambridge, Limited.   1896

The New Theatre. Articles of Association; with account of opening performance (*Camb. Daily News*, 21 Jan. 1896).   4⁰ *London and Cambridge*, 1896

THEOLOGICAL Society. Rules and recommendations of the Cambridge University Theological Society.   12⁰ 1857

See also Confraternity of the Most Holy Trinity.

THEOLOGY. Fly-sheets, reports, etc. on theological studies in the University, from 1841.   1841–

Theological Papers. Ed. by A. P. Moor.   1848

The Theological Tripos scheme in its relation to scholarship. By H. M. Gwatkin and F. Watson.   1871

A list of Members of the Senate who are also Graduates in Theology.   1875

—— Another edition.   1892

Theological Tripos, 1896. Fly-sheets called forth by Reports (8 June, 29 Oct. 1896) of the Special Board for Divinity.   4⁰ 1896

THIRLBY (S.) The University of Cambridge vindicated.   *London*, 1710

Answer to Mr Whiston's Seventeen Suspicions.   1712

THIRLWALL (C.) Primitiae; or essays and poems on various subjects.   *London*, 1809

Circular to Fellows of Trinity College respecting the conduct of the Master, and his own.   4⁰ 1834

A letter to the Rev. T. Turton, on the admission of Dissenters to Academical degrees.   1834

Remarks on Mr Thirlwall's Letter. By W. Whewell.   1834

THIRLWALL (C.)
Letter to Rev. T. Turton. 2nd ed., to which is added a second
letter.   1834
A second letter to the Rev. T. Turton...on the admission of Dis-
senters to Academical degrees.   1834
Additional Remarks on Mr Thirlwall's Letters. By W. Whewell.
1834
A letter to the Rev. Rowland Williams in answer to his Earnestly
respectful letter to the Bp of St David's.   London, 1860
A letter to the Editor of the *Spectator*, April 20, 1861.   n.p. (1861)
Essays, speeches, and sermons. Ed. by J. J. S. Perowne.
London, 1880
Letters to a friend. Ed. by A. P. Stanley.   London, 1881
Letters, literary and theological. Ed. by J. J. S. Perowne, and
L. Stokes.   London, 1881
See also Williams (R.).
THODEY (S.) The honour attached to eminent piety and useful-
ness. A sermon preached at Downing Street Meeting House,
Cambridge, Nov. 20, 1836, on the occasion of the death of the
Rev. C. Simeon.   London, 1836
THOMPSON (A.H.) Cambridge and its Colleges.   London, 1898
THOMPSON (D.W.) A catalogue of books and papers relating to
the fertilisation of flowers.   London, 1883
THOMPSON (H.L.) Christ Church, Oxford.   London, 1900
THOMPSON (H.Y.) *See* American Lectureship.
THOMPSON (J.) The Owens College.   *Manchester*, 1886
THOMPSON (W.H.) "Old things and new." A sermon preached
in the Chapel of Trinity College, Dec. 15, 1852, being Com-
memoration Day.   1853
On the genuineness of the Sophista of Plato, and on some of its
philosophical bearings. (*Camb. Phil. Soc.*)   4° 1858
A sermon preached in Ely Cathedral, Nov. 14, 1858, being the
Sunday next after the funeral of the Rev. G. Peacock.   1858
Preface to the Gorgias of Plato (in its uncorrected form, as a College
lecture).   4° 1871
Platonica. (*Journ. of Philol.*, v.)   1874
Introductory remarks on the Philebus. (*Journ. of Philol.*, xi.)   1882
Euripides. (*Journ. of Philol.*, xi.)   1882
Babriana. (*Journ. of Philol.*, xii.)   1883
On the Nubes of Aristophanes. (*Journ. of Philol.*, xii.)   1883
H. A. J. Munro. (*Journ. of Philol.*, xiv.)   1885

The late Master of Trinity. By A. C. Benson. (*Macmillan's Mag.*, Nov.
1886.)
The late Master of Trinity. By J. S. Prior. (*Temple Bar*, Dec. 1886.)
Notices, etc. of his death.   (1886)
The late Master of Trinity. By Harvey Goodwin. (*Macmillan's Mag.*,
March, 1887.)
Catalogue of his library, sold May 23–26, 1887.   1887

THORESBY (R.) Diary. Now first published by Joseph Hunter.
2 vols.   *London*, 1830

THORN (G.) A letter to the Burgesses of Cambridge, on the
approaching municipal elections.   1835

THORNEY Abbey. Architectural notes on Thorney Abbey. By
C. Lynam. (*Journ. Brit. Arch. Assoc.*, xxxv.)   (*London*, 1878)
The history of Thorney Abbey, Cambridgeshire. By R. H. Warner.
                                                      Wisbech, 1879
The Abbeys of Croyland and Thorney. A sketch of their history.
By G. W. Prothero.   *Spalding*, 1885
Farren's Crowland and Thorney. (Etchings.)   Fº 1889

THORNHILL (W.J.) *See* King (E.).

THORP (T.) The Commemoration sermon preached in the Chapel
of Trinity College, Cambridge, Dec. 16, 1830.   1831
On Obsolete Rules. A Sermon preached in the University Church,
13 April, 1834.   1834
College Chapel. A sermon delivered in the Chapel of Trinity
College, Cambridge, on Easter Day, 1834. 2nd ed.   1834
Three letters to his pupils.   4º 1835
Commemoration sermon preached in the Chapel of Trinity College,
Dec. 14, 1835.   1836
Four Sermons preached before the University of Cambridge in May,
1838.   1838
Two Charges delivered at the general Visitations of the Archdeaconry
of Bristol held July 1839 and July 1840.   1840
The Student's walk. A sermon preached in the Chapel of Trinity
College, Cambridge, Oct. 18, 1840.   1840
A few words to Freshmen.   1841
—— No. 2.   1841
—— Another ed. of the two tracts.   1842
The Round Church, Cambridge. Pp. 4. (*Camden Soc.*)   1844
The Church of the Holy Sepulchre. Pp. 26. (*Camden Soc.*)   1844

THOUGHTS on the nature of true devotion, with reflections on the
late Fast. Addressed to the British nation.   [1794]

THREE Dialogues. From Cambridge. [By J. F. Mortlock.] 1868

THRING (E.) A few remarks on the present system of Degrees at
King's College, Cambridge.   1846
Further remarks on Statutes, and the present system of King's
College, Cambridge.   1848

The Maker of Uppingham. (*The Month*, Feb. 1899.)   *London*, 1899

TILLEY (A.A.) Handlist of trees and shrubs grown in the gardens
and grounds of King's College.   4º 1904

TIMBUCTOO. ("It comes! it comes!...") (Unsuccessful Prize
Poem.)   [? 1829]

TITCOMB (J.H.) A Prince and a great man is fallen in Israel.
A sermon preached Sept. 19, 1852, on occasion of the death of the
Duke of Wellington.   1852
Letter on Proctorial jurisdiction.   1860

TOBY in Cambridge. Vols. 1–4. Oct. 1832–Sept. 12, 1836.
4° 1833–36
TODHUNTER (I.) Audi alteram partem. (*Macmillan's Mag.*,
May, 1872.)
William Whewell. An account of his writings. With selections
from his correspondence. 2 vols.   *London*, 1876
In memoriam: Isaac Todhunter. By J. E. B. Mayor. (*Camb. Review.*)
1884
See also Lund (T.).
TOLL Cause. Brett v. Beales. A full report of the important Toll
Cause of Brett v. Beales, tried in the Court of King's Bench,
Westminster...By Weston Hatfield.   (1826)
A letter to H. J. Adeane, on the subject of the Cambridge Toll
Cause.   1827
Brett v. Fisher and others. Lord Tenterden's summing up.
London, 1827
TOMKIS (J.) *See* Albumazar.
TOMLINE (W.E.P.) A speech on the character of the Rt Hon.
William Pitt, delivered in Trin. Coll. Chapel. Dec. 17, 1806.
4° 1806
TORR (C.) The portraits of Christ in the British Museum.
London, 1898
TORRY (A.F.) College Economy and University Extension. 1868
On the accommodation of Undergraduate members of the University.
1878
Founders and benefactors of St John's College, Cambridge.   1888
TOTTENHAM (H.R.) Cluvienus his thoughts.   1895
TOUR through Great Britain. *See* Defoe (D.).
TOURIST'S Souvenir. [Views.]   *London* [*ab.* 1858]
TOWNSEND (G.) Poems.   *London*, 1810
TOYNBEE Hall. *See* Universities' Settlement.
TRACT upon Tomb-Stones. (By F. E. Paget.)   *Rugeley*, 1843
TRAMWAYS. Prospectus, etc.   1879
TRAVIS (G.) *See* Marsh (H.), 1795.
TREHERNE (G.G.T.) and Goldie (J.H.D.) Record of the Uni-
versity Boat Race, 1829–1880.   4° *London*, 1883
TRENCH (R.C.) The fitness of Holy Scripture for unfolding the
spiritual life of men. (Hulsean Lectures for 1845.)   1845
Christ the Desire of all Nations. (Hulsean Lectures for 1846.) 1846
Five sermons preached before the University of Cambridge.
London, 1857
Letters and memorials. By the author of "Charles Lowder"
[Maria Trench]. 2 vols.   *London*, 1888
TREVELYAN (*Sir* G.O.) The Cambridge Dionysia. A classic
dream.   1858
Horace at the University of Athens.   1861
—— 2nd ed.   1862
Ladies in Parliament, and other pieces. New ed.   *London*, 1888
Interludes in verse and prose.   *London*, 1905

TREVELYAN (R.)   Ode Graeca.   (Written for a Buchanan Prize.)
1804
Mors Nelsoni.   Poema aureo dignatum numismate, quod ex judicio
dedit Gul. Turton, M.D....sub auspiciis Georg. Aug. Val. Princ.
1806
Prolusiones partim Græce partim Latine scriptæ.   1806
—— Editio altera.   *Londini*, 1817
TRIBUTE.   A collection of miscellaneous unpublished poems.   (Ed.
by Lord Northampton, for the benefit of Rev. E. Smedley.)
London, 1837
TRIDENT.   (Trin. Coll. Magazine.)   Vol. 1.   June 1889–Dec.
1891.   1889–91
TRINITY (The)   A nineteenth century Passion-Play.   The Son ;
or Victory of Love.   [By Karl Pearson.]   1882
TRINITY Church.   Brief account of Holy Trinity Church, by
H. L. C. V. de Candole.   1910
—— The same.   Penny ed.   1910
TRINITY College.   The Present State of Trinity College.   By
R. Bentley.   *London*, 1710
—— 2nd ed.   *London*, 1710
Some Remarks upon...The Present State...By E. Miller.
London, 1710
The True State of Trinity College.   [By J. Paris and S. White.]
London, 1710
—— 2nd ed.   *London*, 1710
Some Considerations...on...The Present State...[By J. N.]
London [1710]
Full View of Dr Bentley's Letter.   By T. Blomer.   *London*, 1710
The Rights of the Scholars of Trinity College asserted.   [By J. N.]
London [1710]
True Copy of the Articles against Dr Bentley exhibited...by many
of the Fellows of Trinity College.   *London*, 1710
—— 2nd ed.   *London*, 1713
True and Impartial Account of the present differences between the
Master and Fellows of Trinity College.   [Attr. to J. Paris.]
London, 1711
Some Account of Horace at Trinity College.   [Attack on Bentley
by W. King.]   [*London*, 1712]
Answer to some objections that have been made to the conduct of
Dr B.   Together with a Dialogue...concerning Trinity College.
London, 1713
An Humble and Serious Representation of the Present State of
Trinity College.   *London* [1716]
True Account of the Present State of Trinity College.   [By
C. Middleton.]   *London*, 1720
The case of Trinity College in Cambridge.   Whether the Crown or
the Bishop of Ely be the General Visitor.   [By R. Bentley.]
4° *London*, 1729
A defence of the Bishop of Ely's visitatorial jurisdiction over Trinity

TRINITY College.
College in general, and over the Master thereof in particular.
[By J. Colbatch.] 4° *n.p.* 1732
A vindication of the Bishop of Ely's visitatorial jurisdiction over
Trinity College in general, and over the Master thereof in
particular. [By J. Colbatch.] 4° *London,* 1732
Oratio habita in sacello Coll. Trin. Cant. festo S.S. Trinitatis
redeunte, 1779. By T. J. Mathias. 4° 1779
Ode to Trinity College, Cambridge. [By Geo. Pryme.]
London, 1812
Trin. Coll. Book Club. List pasted into *The Velvet Cushion,* 2nd ed.
Lond., 1814. [*Ab.* 1814]
Statutes, 1560. (Fifth Report of Select Committee on Education.)
F° *London,* 1818
Plan of Tables, etc. at entertainment given to Duchess of Gloucester,
1819. 1819
The case of the Senior Graduate in Divinity among the Fellows of
Trinity College, Cambridge, as to his right of Præ-Option to
College Livings. With other papers connected with the case of
J. D. Hustler. (1822)
Erection of the New Court. Circular, List of Subscriptions, Order
of Ceremonial, etc. F° 1823
Greek Inscriptions from the Marbles in the Library of Trinity
College, Cambridge. By P. P. Dobree. [1824]
Delineations of Trinity College. By J. and H. S. Storer. (Bowes
1713 *e.*) 4° [183–]
A statement respecting the lectures at present given on the subject
of the New Testament, in Trinity College, Cambridge. By
R. W. Evans. 4° 1834
Society for the Prevention of Cruelty to Undergraduates. Attendance
of Fellows at Trin. Coll. Chapel for the week ending Feb. 17,
1838 (–March 24, 1838). With several sets of verses (printed and
in manuscript) which appeared at the time. 4° *n.p.* 1838
Comparative table of the number of students admitted and of the
number of graduates who received testimonials for Deacon's
Orders, in Trinity College, from 1831 to 1840. (1840)
An earnest appeal to the Master and Seniors of Trinity College, on
the revision of the Statutes. By Two of the Fellows. *London,* 1840
Trinity College Prize Essay for 1839, on the Colonial policy of the
Ancients. By W. J. Butler. 1840
Statuta. (2 copies.) 4° 1844
Tercentenary. Dinner cards and copies of verses composed for the
occasion by W. G. Humphry, A. A. Van Sittart, C. B. Scott,
C. Evans, and A. H. Potts. 1846
Account of the celebration of the Tercentenary, 22 Dec. 1846.
(From *Cambridge Chronicle,* 26 Dec.)
An index of such English books printed before the year MDC., as
are now in the Library of Trinity College, Cambridge. By
E. Cranwell. 1847

TRINITY College.

Undergraduate memorial on the dinner in Hall, 28 Jan. 1854.

4° 1854

Reform of Trinity College. Fly-sheets, letters, etc. 1854–60

On Mr Edleston's Remarks on the tenure of the Lucasian Professorship. By F. Martin. 1857

Remarks on the...passage in Bp Monk's Life of Dr Bentley (p. 610, 4to ed. Vol. II. p. 352, 8vo ed.) relating to words occurring in the 40th Chapter of the Statutes of Trinity College. By Francis Martin. 1857

On Mr Clark's proposal (1) That the vacant Sizarships be competed for by persons not yet resident. (2) That the Subsizarships be abolished. (3) That in the Statutes (cap. xv. line 3) after 'sedecim' the words 'ad minimum' be added. By Francis Martin. 1857

Report at a meeting of the Governing Body, on the Revising of the Statutes, June 9, 1857. (1857)

The proposed conditions of the tenure of Fellowships in Trinity College. By J. Ll. Davies. 1857

Letter to J. Ll. Davies on tenure of Fellowships. 1857

On the proposal that the Fellowships be open to all B.A.'s of the College, who have obtained a place in the First Class of any of the Honour Triposes...By H. R. Luard. 1857

Remarks on the proposed changes in the Statutes. By W. Whewell. (23 Sept., 18 Oct., 22 Oct.) 1857

Remarks on Mr Grote's Proposal. By W. Whewell. 2 pts. 1857

Remarks on the Master's Second Paper. (Statutes.) By C. J. Vaughan. 1857

Outline of Letter in answer to proposed Statutes. By J. L. Hammond. 1857

Communications to the Commissioners in regard to revenues, with other pieces bearing on the subject. F° 1858

On the College Statutes. By E. M. Cope. 1858

Remarks on the Cambridge University Commissioners' draft of proposed new Statutes for Trinity College. By H. R. Luard. 1858

On the draft of the Statutes for Trinity College. By W. Whewell. 1858

On the draft of proposed new Statutes for Trinity College. By G. B. Airy. 1859

A few words on Statute XVIII. of the new body of Statutes. By J. Grote. 1859

Remarks on new Statutes. By F. Martin and J. Grote. March–May, 1859. F° 1859

Statutes. 1861

Table of the number of Students who were matriculated and of the number who took the Degree of B.A....in Trinity College, Cambridge, 1831–1840. By Fra. Martin. (1862)

On the proposed change in the hour of dinner in Hall. By J. W. Clark. 1862

TRINITY College.

TRINITY College.

Proposed extension in paddocks. By James Ward and R. T. Glazebrook; A. N. Whitehead; R. St J. Parry. (3 pieces.)   1895

College Building Fund. Circulars, etc. June–Dec. 1896. (6 pieces.)
   1896

Proposed extension. Some observations by the Master.   1897

Ordinances, 1 Jan. 1897.   1897

Letter on formation of an Amalgamation Club. By W. W. Rouse
Ball. 10 Nov. 1898.   1898

Trinity Foot Beagles. Song by H. S. G[ladstone].   1898

Notes on the history of Trinity College, Cambridge. By W. W.
Rouse Ball.   *London*, 1899

Report of Committee on Amalgamation. (30 May, 1899.)   1899

The Roof-Climber's Guide to Trinity. [By G. W. Young.]   1899

Remarks on the value of the Mastership and Fellowships. By
G. H. Darwin.   1900

Inscriptions from the Chapel of Trinity College. Ed. by A. E.
Bernays.   4° 1900

Benefices in the gift of Trinity College, 1902.   1902

Trinity College, by J. W. Clark. (*Country Life*, 4 Nov. 1905.)

Trinity College. By W. W. Rouse Ball.   *London*, 1906

Memoranda, by the Master, on the proposed new Combination
Room.   1906

Statutes made by the University of Cambridge Commissioners,
19 March, 1881...with the Amending Statutes since approved by
order in Council.   1906

History of the First Trinity Boat Club. By W. W. R. Ball.   1908

Fifty MSS. exhibited in the Library. List.   1909

Tennyson. By Arthur Sidgwick. (On occasion of unveiling of the
statue of Tennyson by Thornycroft.)   *London*, 1909

Alterations of Statutes, 7 Nov. 1908, approved by King in Council,
28 June, 1909.   1909

TRINITY College Commemoration.

1717. Sermon. Dec. 19. By John Colbatch.   1718

1721. Sermon. Dec. 21. By Thomas Parne.   *London*, 1722

1793. Sermon. Dec. 19. By R. E. Garnham.   (1793)
      —— 2nd ed.   1794

1798. Oration. Dec. 17. By W. Lamb, 2nd Viscount Melbourne.
   4° *London*, 1799

1801. Essay. Dec. 16. By W. A. Garratt.   4° *London* (1801)

1806. Speech. Dec. 17. By W. E. P. Tomline.   4° 1806

1817. Sermon. Dec. 16. By J. H. Monk.   (1817)

1825. Sermon. Dec. 20. By R. Ward.   1826

1827. Sermon. By G. Waddington.   1828

1828. Sermon. Dec. 17. By W. Whewell.   1828

1830. Speech. By J. Spedding.   (1830)

1830. Sermon. Dec. 16. By Th. Thorp.   1831

1831. Oration. Dec. 16. By A. H. Hallam.   1832

1832. Oration. Dec. 17. By F. Garden.   1833

TRINITY College Commemoration.

1833.	Oration.	Dec. 16.	By T. R. Birks.	1834
1834.	Sermon.	Dec. 16.	By J. A. Jeremie.	1835
1835.	Sermon.	Dec. 14.	By Th. Thorp.	1836
1837.	Oration.		By C. J. Vaughan.	(1837)
1837.	Sermon.	Dec. 17.	By William Carus.	1837
1838.	Oration.	Dec. 15.	By J. N. Simpkinson.	(1838)
1838.	Sermon.	Dec. 15.	By W. Whewell.	(1838)
1839.	Sermon.	Dec. 16.	By J. W. Blakesley.	1839
1840.	Oration.	Dec. 14.	By A. J. Beresford Hope.	1840
1841.	Sermon.	Dec. 16.	By J. W. Blakesley.	1842
1842.	Sermon.	Dec. 13.	By J. A. Jeremie.	1842
1845.	Sermon.	Dec. 16.	By J. A. Frere.	1846
1846.	Sermon.	Dec. 22.	By J. A. Jeremie.	1847
1847.	Declamation.	Dec. 16.	By A. Barry.	1848
1848.	Sermon.	Dec. 15.	By J. Grote.	1849
1849.	Sermon.	Dec. 14.	By J. A. Jeremie.	1850
1850.	Sermon.	Dec. 14.	By A. R. Grant.	1851
1851.	Oration.		By E. W. Benson.	1851
1852.	Sermon.	Dec. 15.	By W. H. Thompson.	1853
1854.	Oration.		By H. M. Butler.	1854
1856.	Sermon.	Dec. 15.	By L. Hensley.	1857
1860.	Sermon.	Dec. 15.	By J. B. Lightfoot.	1861
1864.	Sermon.	Dec. 15.	By H. J. Hotham.	1865
1868.	Sermon.	Dec. 15.	By B. F. Westcott.	London, 1869
1871.	Sermon.	Feb. 2.	By E. W. Blore.	1871
1877.	Sermon.	Dec. 13.	By J. Ll. Davies.	London, 1877
1885.	Sermon.	Dec. 10.	By H. W. Watson.	1886
1889.	Sermon.	Dec. 9.	By A. Barry.	1889
1898.	Sermon.	Dec. 9.	By V. H. Stanton.	1898
1900.	Sermon.	Dec. 11.	By B. F. Westcott.	1901
1902.	Sermon.	Dec. 9.	By T. P. Pemberton.	1902
1907.	Sermon.		By H. C. G. Moule.	1907

TRINITY Hall. The Silver Crescent. The "Hall" Magazine.
Nos. 10, 11, 33, 34, 39, 42, 43, 45, 47, 48.   1893–1907
The Brass Halo. Oct. 1893; Lent Term, 1894; Lent Term, 1895.
1893–5
Trinity Hall. By H. E. Malden. (College histories.) *London*, 1902
Descriptive Catalogue of the MSS. in the Library. By M. R. James.
1907
Trinity Hall Library, Cambridge. By J. W. Clark. (*Country Life*,
16 Oct. 1909.)
TRIPOS. Nos. 1, 2. Dec. 19 [1838], Feb. 10 [1839].   [1838–9]
TRIPOS Examinations. Memorials respecting dates, and asking for
radical alteration.   F° 1892
TRIPOSES. *See* Sertum Cantabrigiense; *see also* under separate
triposes.
TRIST (L.J.M.) Mr Trist's statement to the public [with regard to his
alleged complicity in the poisoning of race-horses]. (*London*, 1812)

TRISTRAM (H.B.) and Williams (G.)   The Bible as illustrated by
   modern science and travel.   *London* (1868)
TROLLOPE (W.)   The Expedients to which the Gentile philosophers
   resorted in opposing the progress of the Gospel. (Hulsean Disserta-
   tion for 1821.)   *London*, 1822
TROTTER (C.)   On Cambridge University examinations.   1877
   On some questions of University Reform.   1877
   —— Further consideration.   1877
   Replies to questions from the Secretaries to the Cambridge University
     Commission.   1877
   Remarks on the proposed Statutes for the University.   (1880)
   College taxation for University purposes.   (1880)
   Terms and Vacations.   (1880)
   Examinations for Medical and Surgical Degrees.   (1880)
   The Thirlwall Professorship.   (1880)
   A sermon preached in the Chapel of Trinity College, Cambridge,
     April 26, 1885, on the reassembling of the College after the deaths
     of H. A. J. Munro and H. J. Hotham.   1885
   In memoriam : H. J. Hotham.   (1885)
   University finance and new buildings.   1885

   In memoriam : Coutts Trotter.   By M. Foster, J. W. Clark, S. Taylor.
                                      1888

TRUE Blue.   Ed. by G. M. Maxwell (Trin.).   Vol. I., Nos. 1, 2.
                                      1883
TUCKER (W.H.)   Eton of old, or eighty years since, 1811–1822.
   (+ Eton of today, by A. C. Benson.)   *London*, 1892
TUDWAY (T.)   *See* Anthems.
TUKER (M.A.R.)   Cambridge.   4° *London*, 1907
TURK'S Head Coffee-House.   *See* Matthew and Son.   Café.
TURNER (B.N.)   Dr Johnson's visit to Cambridge in 1765.   (*New
   Monthly Magazine*, Dec. 1818.)
TURNER (C.)   The main drainage scheme for Cambridge.   1886
TURNER (H.C.)   *See* Sheepshed.
TURNER (J.)   The Middle Way.   Discourse containing two Sermons
   preached at St Mary's, Cambridge.   *London*, 1683
TURNER (W.), †1568.   The huntyng and fyndyng out of the Romish
   Fox.   Ed. by R. Potts.   1851
   A short and succinct history of the principal birds noticed by
   Pliny and Aristotle.   First published 1544.   Ed. with transl.
   by A. H. Evans, M.A.   1903
TURTON (T.)   Vindication of...Professor Porson from the animad-
   versions of T. Burgess.   By Crito Cantabrigiensis [T. T.].   1827
   The Text of the English Bible, as now printed by the Universities,
   considered with reference to a Report by a Sub-Committee of
   Dissenting Ministers.   1833
   —— 2nd ed.   1833
   A sermon on the death of the Duke of Gloucester.   Dec. 11, 1834.
                                      (1834)

TURTON (T.)
Thoughts on the admission of persons without regard to their
religious opinions to certain Degrees in the Universities of England.
1834
—— 2nd ed., corrected and enlarged. 1835
See also Burgess (T.); Lee (S.).
TUTORS. A plea for the private tutors; or Alumnus in search of
a dodge. *Oxford*, 1843
TWEDDELL (J.) Greek Ode and Greek and Latin epigrams.
(Sir W. Browne's Medals.) 4° 1789
Prolusiones juveniles præmiis academicis dignatæ. *Londini*, 1793
Narrative of the literary remains of J. Tweddell. By Philip Hunt.
London, 1816
Remains of John Tweddell. 2nd ed., by R. Tweddell.
4° *London*, 1816
TWIGUM (Christopher), *pseud.* Cambridge in the Long Vacation.
12° *London*, 1830
TYPES. [By O. F. Hollebone, Trin.] 1894
TYRWHITT Hebrew Scholarships. Regulations, 6 March, 1826.
F° (1826)
Regulations, 22 Apr. 1830. F° 1830
TYSON (M.) An account of an illuminated manuscript in the
Library of Corpus Christi College, Cambridge. (*Archaeologia*, II.)
4° (*London*, 1773)
Account of the Horn belonging to Corpus Christi College, Cambridge.
(*Archaeologia*, III.) 4° (*London*, 1775)

U

UFFENBACH (Z.K. von) Merkwürdige Reisen durch Niedersachsen, Holland, und Engelland. 3 vols. *Ulm*, 1753-4
Visit to Cambridge, etc. (Ed. by J. E. B. Mayor in *Cambridge under Queen Anne.*) [1870-1]
UNDERGRADUATE (The), or College life in five phases. A satire. By B.A., Cantab. [Gavin F. James, Cai.]. [1885]
UNDERGRADUATE Papers. No. 1. Dec. 1, 1857. *Oxford*, 1857
UNDERGRADUATES. A plain and friendly address to the Undergraduates of the University of Cambridge, particularly to those of Trinity College. By a late Under-graduate. *London*, 1786
Listen ! or a few words to Undergraduates. *London*, 1862
UNION Society. A statement regarding the Union, an Academical Debating Society, which existed from Feb. 13, 1815 to March 24, 1817, when it was suppressed by the Vice-Chancellor. 1817
Laws and Transactions, 1823. 1823
—— Revised and corrected to July, 1824. 1824
—— Revised and corrected to July, 1825. 1825
—— Revised and corrected to March, 1829. 1829
—— Revised and corrected to January, 1830. 1830
The Union Debating Society at Cambridge, in the years 1830-31; a satire. 1831
Lines addressed to the author of a satire, entitled, " The Union Debating Society." 1831
The Sunday Question settled, with reference to the late proceedings at the Union Society. By a member of Trinity College. 1834
List of subscribers to the Building Fund. First List. [1864 ?]
Inaugural Proceedings. (Ed. by G. C. Whiteley.) *London*, 1866
Business (?) at the Bunion. By a Speaker [A. J. A. Ball, Trin.] [1882]
Union Echoes. By " A Light that Failed." 1891
Annual Report, 1893-4 ; 1894-5. 1894-5
Debates. Vol. 1., Nos. 1, 2. 1900
See also Mary's (St) the Great, 1840.
UNITED Christian Association and Home for Young Women. Annual Reports. 5th, 8th, 12th. 1879-86
UNITED Sisters Friendly Society. Report of meeting...held at Cambridge, Oct. 1894. 1894

UNIVERSITIES. Letters to the English public on the condition, abuses, and capabilities of the national Universities. Nos. 1, 2. By a Graduate of Cambridge.   *London*, 1836

The Independence of the Universities and Colleges of Oxford and Cambridge. By a Layman.   *Oxford*, 1838

An apology for the Universities. By Oxoniensis.   *Oxford*, 1841

The Universities and the Church of England. By a Cambridge man.   1854

Return to the House of Commons relating to the Universities of Oxford and Cambridge.   Fo *London*, 1886

UNIVERSITIES' Commission. *See* Commission.

UNIVERSITIES' Mission to Central Africa. Report of a meeting in the Senate-House on All Saints' Day, 1859   *London*, 1859

An appeal to members of the University of Cambridge.   1875

Report, 1905, 1906, 1907.   *London*, 1906–8

David Livingstone and Cambridge. A record of three meetings in the Senate-House.   *London*, 1908

UNIVERSITIES' Settlement Association. Work for University men in East London. (With subscription-list, etc.)   1884

—— 8th Annual Report.   *London*, 1892

UNIVERSITY of Cambridge.

*** For Cambridge Societies, Institutions, etc., see under the first important word of their respective titles, not being 'Cambridge' or 'University,' *e.g.* Antiquarian Society; Chess Club; Female Refuge; Library; Mary's (St) the Great; Observatory; Press; Union Society; Volunteers.

UNIVERSITY Association. Report of Meeting, Jan. 31, 1899.   1899

Statement of needs prepared by Heads of Departments.   4° 1899

Statement of needs of University. 3 parts.   1899

List of Members, Subscriptions, etc.   1900

New buildings at Cambridge. (Three articles from the *Times*, 24, 27, 29 Feb. 1904.)   1904

A plea for Cambridge. [By A. E. Shipley and H. A. Roberts.] (*Quarterly Rev.*, April, 1906.)

The same, reprinted.   *Edinburgh*, 1907

UNIVERSITY Commission. *See* Commission.

UNIVERSITY Extension. Nos. 1, 2. Nov. 1904, Feb. 1905.   4° *London*, 1904–5

UNIVERSITY Queries. In a Gentle Touch by the By.   4° 1659

UNIVERSITY Taxation. By a Member of the late Syndicate. 1848

USSHER (J.) *See* Dillingham (W.).

V

VANCOUVER (C.)   General view of the agriculture in the County
   of Cambridge.   (+ Appendix.)   4° *London*, 1794
General view of the agriculture in the County of Essex.
                                                  4° *London*, 1795
VANSITTART (A.A.)   Verses for tercentenary of Trinity College,
   Dec. 22, 1846.   4° 1846
VANSITTART (N.)   Letter to Dr Marsh, occasioned by his Address
   to the Senate of the University.   *London*, 1811
   —— Another ed., in Farish's *Report*.   1812
See also Marsh (H.).
VARENNE (G.)   Regrets of Alma Mater on the Roman Catholic
   petition.   4° 1816
'VARSITY Bloods.   By "Growler" [B. B. Watson, Trin.].   1900
'VARSITY Eclogue.   By "Whif."   1878
'VARSITY Sketches.   By H. G. M.   1903
'VARSITY Snap-Shots, by myself and my camera.   [1899]
'VARSITY Verses.   By C. G.   1878
'VARSITY Verses.   By H. D. C[atling].   1901
VAUGHAN (C.J.)   An oration delivered in Trinity College Chapel,
   at the Commemoration, 1837.   (1837)
Sermon on the death of the Rev. Henry Keary.   *London*, 1852
Four Sermons preached before the University of Cambridge.   1861

Funeral Sermon.   By H. M. Butler.   1897

VAUGHAN (D.J.)   A few words about Private Tuition.   1852
Remarks on the Master of Trinity's Second Paper.   (Marriage of
   Fellows.)   1857
VAUGHAN (E.T.)   Dissertatio Latina.   [Members' Prize.]   1833
'VAUGHAN (Herbert)'   [i.e. A. H. Vaughan Morgan].   The
   Cambridge Grisette.   *London*, 1862
VENABLES (E.)   Annals of the Church of St Mary the Great.
   (*Journal of Arch. Inst.*)   *London*, 1856
VENN (H.)   Academical studies subservient to the edification of the
   Church.   A sermon preached in the Chapel of Queens' College,
   Cambridge, March 2, 1828.   1828

Memoir.   By William Knight.   *London*, 1880

VENN (J.)   Admissions to Gonville and Caius College in the University of Cambridge, March, 1558–9 to Jan. 1678–9.
                                                London, 1887

VENN (J.)
Venn (J.) and Venn (S.C.) Notes on the Perse School, from the
  Admission Registers of Gonville and Caius College, etc.   1890
Biographical History of Gonville and Caius College, 1349–1897.
  3 vols.   1897–1901
Caius College. (College histories.)   *London*, 1901
Annals of a Clerical Family. (The Venns.)   *London*, 1904

Catalogue of books on Logic presented to the University Library by John
  Venn.   1889

VERRALL (A.W.) Sanctae Trinitatis Collegii apud Cantabrigienses
  Carmen Familiare.   4° 1888
Installation Ode for the Duke of Devonshire. Latin Text. With
  music by Prof. Stanford. (Large Paper.)   4° 1892
Installation Ode for the Duke of Devonshire. Latin and English.
                                                              1892
Iphigenia in Tauris. As performed at Cambridge, Nov. 30, Dec.
  1–5, 1894. With translation by A. W. Verrall.   1894
The Vote of Athena. (*Praelections.*)   1906
Sir Richard Jebb as Scholar and Critic. (In Lady Jebb's *Life and
  Letters of Sir R. C. Jebb.*)   1907
VERSATILE verses on the 'Varsity, etc. By Two Bachelors [H. D.
  Catling and A. W. Burke Peel].   1896
VERSE Translations from the German. [By W. Whewell.]
                                     London and Cambridge, 1847
VERSES. Συνωδια, sive...congratulatio ad...Regem Carolum de quintâ
  sua sobole...(On the birth of the Princess Anne, who died young.)
  (Bowes 58*.)   4° 1637
Voces Votivæ ab Academicis Cantabrigiensibus pro novissimo Caroli
  et Mariæ principe filio emissae. (Prince Henry born, 8 July,
  1640.) (Bowes 2894.)   4° 1640
Oliva pacis. (Peace with Holland, Oct. 5.)   4° 1654
Musarum Cantabrigiensium luctus et gratulatio...in funere Oliveri
  Angliae...Protectoris...de Ricardi successione. (Oliver Cromwell
  died, 3 Sept. 1658.) (Bowes 108.)   1658
Academiae Cantabrigiensis Σωστρα, sive, ad Carolum II. reducem...
  gratulatio. (On the Restoration.) (Bowes 112.)   4° 1660
Threni Cantabrigienses in funere duorum Principum, Henrici Glo-
  cestrensis et Mariæ Arausionensis...Caroli II. fratris et sororis.
  (Henry, Duke of Gloucester, died, 13 Sept. 1660; and Mary,
  Princess of Orange, died, 24 Dec. 1660.) (Bowes 2897.) 4° 1661
Epithalamia Cantabrigiensia in nuptias Regis Caroli II. et illustr.
  Principis Catharinae. (Charles II. married Catherine of Braganza,
  21 May, 1662.)   4° 1662
Threni Cantabrigienses in exequiis...reginae Henriettae Mariae.
  (Henrietta Maria died, Aug., 1669.) (Bowes 137.)   4° 1669
Musarum Cantabrigiensium Threnodia in obitum...Georgii Ducis
  Albaemarlae. (George Monk, Duke of Albemarle, died, 3 Jan.
  1670.) (Bowes 2900.)   4° 1670

VERSES.

Lacrymae Cantabrigienses in obitum illustr. Principis Henriettæ Caroli I. filiae, Ducissae Aurelianensis. (Princess Henrietta Anna died, 29 June, 1670.) 4° 1670

Epicedia Cantabrigiensia in obitum illustr. Principis Annæ Ducissæ Eboracensis. (On the death of Anne, Duchess of York, 31 March, 1671.) 4° 1671

To...Prince James, Duke of Monmouth and Buccleugh, on the happy solemnity of His Grace's Inauguration in the Chancellorship of the University of Cambridge. F° *In the Savoy,* 1674

Epithalamium in...nuptiis...Guilielmi Henrici Arausii et Mariae Britanniarum ab Academia Cantabrigiensi decantatum. (On the marriage of William of Orange and Princess Mary, 4 Nov. 1677.) 4° 1677

Hymenæus Cantabrigiensis. (On the marriage of Prince George of Denmark and the Princess Anne of York.) (Bowes 170-1.) 4° 1683

Moestissimae ac laetissimae Academiae Cantabrigiensis affectus, decedente Carolo II. succedente Jacobo II. (Charles II. died, 6 Feb. 1685.) (Bowes 174-5.) 4° 1684⅚

Illustrissimi Principis Ducis Cornubiae...Genethliacon. (On the birth of the Old Pretender.) (Bowes 183-4.) 4° 1688

Musae Cantabrigienses...Wilhelmo et Mariae...publicae salutis ac libertatis vindicibus, haec officii et pietatis ergo d.d. (On the accession of William and Mary, 13 Feb. 1689.) (Bowes 190-1.) 4° 1689

Lacrymae Cantabrigienses in obitum...Reginae Mariae. (Queen Mary died, 28 December, 1694.) (2 copies.) (Bowes 199.) 4° 1694⅚

Mœstissimae ac lætissimae Academiae Cantabrigiensis carmina funebria et triumphalia. Illis Reginam Annam morte abreptam deflet. His Regi Georgio Britannicum solium ascendenti gratulatur. (Queen Anne died, 1 Aug. 1714.) (Bowes 395.) F° 1714

Gratulatio Academiae Cantabrigiensis auspicatissimas Friderici Walliae Principis et Augustae...nuptias celebrantis. (Frederick Prince of Wales married Augusta of Saxe-Gotha, 26 April, 1736.) (Bowes 452.) F° 1736

Pietas Academiae Cantabrigiensis in funere principis Wilhelminae Carolinae et luctu Georgii II. (Queen Caroline died, 20 Nov. 1737.) (Bowes 454.) F° 1738

Gratulatio Academiae Cantabrigiensis de reditu Georgii II. post pacem et libertatem Europae restitutam anno 1748. (On the Peace of Aix-la-Chapelle.) (Bowes 484.) F° 1748

Academiae Cantabrigiensis luctus in obitum Frederici Walliae principis. (Frederick Prince of Wales, died, 20 March, 1751.) (Bowes 499.) F° 1751

Carmina ad Thomam Holles ducem de Newcastle inscripta...Kal. Maias, 1755. (On laying the first stone of the new façade of the Library.) (Bowes 515.) F° 1755

VERSES.
Academiae Cantabrigiensis luctus in obitum Regis Georgii II. et gratulationes in Georgii III. inaugurationem. (George II. died, 25 Oct. 1760.) (Bowes 537.)   Fº 1760
Gratulatio Academiae Cantabrigiensis Georgii III. et Charlottæ principis de Mecklenburgh-Strelitz nuptias celebrantis. (George III. married Sophia Charlotte of Mecklenburg-Strelitz, 8 Sept. 1761.) (Bowes 546.)   Fº 1761
Gratulatio Academiae Cantabrigiensis natales Georgii Walliæ principis...celebrantis. (George Prince of Wales was born, 12 Aug. 1762.) (Bowes 556.)   Fº 1762
Gratulatio Academiæ Cantabrigiensis in pacem Georgii III. auspiciis Europae restitutam anno 1763. (On the Peace of Fontainebleau.) (Bowes 564.)   Fº 1763
VICTORIA (*Queen*) Order of Procession on occasion of her visit. (Dated 24 Oct. 1843.)   Fº (1843)
Accounts of her visit, 25–26 Oct. 1843. (*Camb. Advertiser*, 28 Oct. 1843; *Camb. Chron.* 28 Oct.; *Punch*, 4 and 11 Nov.)   (1843)
Verses on the occasion of her visit. By A. H. Potts.   4º (1843)
Trifolium Caianum in adventum Reginae et Principis, VIII. Kal. Nov. 1843.   4º (1843)
Quartine in occasione della visità di Regina Vittoria...alla Università di Cambridge. [By Marchese Spineto.]   1843
The Progresses of Queen Victoria and Prince Albert.
                                                          4º *London*, 1844
Memorial service at Gt St Mary's for Queen Victoria.   1901
Memorial sermons by A. H. F. Boughey, W. Cunningham, and H. C. G. Moule.   1901
See also Albert (*Prince*); Coronation, 1838; Jubilee, 1887, 1897.
VILLETARD DE PRUNIÈRES (M.) Universités d'Oxford et de Cambridge.   *Paris*, 1879
VINCE (S.) Heads of a course of lectures on Experimental Philosophy.
                                                                    1779
The credibility of Christianity vindicated.   1798
——— 2nd ed.   1809
Heads of a course of lectures on Experimental Philosophy.   1804
Confutation of Atheism.   1807
VINCE (S.B.) The propagation of Christianity was not indebted to any secondary causes. (Hulsean Prize Essay for 1806.)   1807
VINCENT (N.) The Right Notion of Honour: as it was delivered in a sermon before the King at Newmarket, Oct. 4, 1674. (2 copies.)   4º *London*, 1685
VINCENT (W.) Letter to the Rev. Richard Watson. *London*, 1780
VINES (S.H.) Botany as an Academic Study.   *Oxford*, 1888
VISION and Pass of Death. An apology for a Cambridge Prize Poem. By a modern Pythagorean.   *London*, 1838
VISITORS' Chronicle. May Term, 1888.   1888
VOLUNTEERS. Address in support of Volunteer movement, signed: A Cambridge Volunteer. 15 Aug. 1803.   Fº (1803)

VOLUNTEERS.
    Report of establishment and accounts of Band of University Volun-
        teers, 1860–61.   1861
    University Volunteers.   Report for 1865, 1867.   (1866–8)
    Proceedings at the dinner given by the Officers of the C.U.R.V.,
        May 4, 1888.   1888
    Thirty-seventh annual Report.   1896
    See also Baker (J.); Rifle Club.
VOTE (A) for the Pink 'un ; or Pottinger and the Prince of Dark-
    ness.   1882
VYVYAN (T.G.)   The Letter and the Spirit.   A sermon preached
    in the Chapel of Gonville and Caius College, Cambridge, March 15,
    1863.   1863

W

WACE (A.J.B.) Catalogue of Greek embroideries exhibited at the Fitzwilliam Museum. 1905

WADDINGTON (G.) A sermon delivered in the Chapel of Trinity College, Cambridge, on the Commemoration Day in December, 1827. 1828

WADDINGTON (H.) Wallace. A poem. (Written for the Chancellor's Medal.) 1815

WADHAM (D.) Letters. Ed. by R. B. Gardiner. *Oxford*, 1904

WAIDESON (R.) *See* Arrowsmith (J.).

WAINEWRIGHT (L.) The literary and scientific pursuits which are encouraged and enforced in the University of Cambridge, briefly described and vindicated. *London*, 1815

The studies and pursuits of the University of Cambridge stated and vindicated. By L. Wainwright, 1815. (*British Critic*, Jan. 1826.)

WAKEFIELD (G.) A sermon preached on July 29, 1784, the day appointed for a General Thanksgiving on account of the Peace.
London, 1784

An Address to the inhabitants of Nottingham. *London*, 1789

A general reply to the arguments against the enquiry into public worship. *London*, 1792

Memoirs. Written by himself. *London*, 1792

Remarks on the general orders of the Duke of York to his army, on June 7, 1794. *London*, 1794

An examination of the Age of reason, by Thomas Paine. 2nd ed.
London, 1794

The Spirit of Christianity, compared with the Spirit of the Times in Great Britain. *London*, 1794

A letter to William Wilberforce on the subject of his late publication. *London*, 1797

—— 2nd ed. *London*, 1797

Letter to Sir John Scott. *n.p.* 1798

Reply to some parts of the Bp of Llandaff's [R. Watson's] Address to the people of Great Britain. 2nd ed. *London*, 1798

WALCOTT (M.) William of Wykeham and his Colleges.
Winchester, 1852

Inventories of Religious Houses (including Barnwell Priory). (*Archaeologia*, XLIII.) 4° (*London*, 1870)

WALDSTEIN (C.) Catalogue of Casts in the Museum of Classical Archæology, Fitzwilliam Museum. *London*, 1889

Application for Disney Professorship. 4° 1892

WALDSTEIN (C.)
The study of art in Universities. Inaugural lecture. *Lonaon*, 1896
Ethics of the Surface. By Gordon Seymour [i.e. C. Waldstein].
I. The Rudeness of the Honourable Mr Leatherhead.
II. A Homburg Story.
12° *London*, 1897
WALE (H.J.) My grandfather's (T. Wale's) Pocket-Book. From
1701 to 1796. *London*, 1883
WALKER (J.) and Mylne (W.S.) *See* Fens, 1825.
WALKER (R.) A letter to the Vice-Chancellor on improvements in
the present examination statute. *Oxford*, 1848
WALKER (S.S.) Leaves gathered from a Curate's sermons delivered
during a ministry of nearly ten years. 1864
WALKER (T.A.) Peterhouse. (College histories.) *London*, 1906
WALKER (W.S.) Poetical remains. Ed. by J. Moultrie.
London, 1852
WALKEY (C.E.) The Church and the Universities. *Exeter*, 1847
WALL (A.) An account of the different ceremonies observed in the
Senate House of the University of Cambridge. 1798
—— New ed. By H. Gunning. 1828
WALLER (W.) David's Prophecy relating to Cambridge. [Con-
cerning the Westminster Club.] 1751
WALMISLEY (T.A.) *See* Whytehead (T.).
WALSH (B.D.) An historical account of the University of Cambridge
and its Colleges. *London*, 1837
WANDERING Planet. n.d.
WARBURTON (C.) Syllabus of a course of lectures on injurious
insects. 1891
WARD (A.W.) Suggestions towards the establishment of a History
Tripos. 1872
Royal Historical Society. Presidential Address. 1900
See Worke for Cutlers, 1904.
WARD (G.R.M.) Statutes of Magdalen Coll., Oxford. *Oxford*, 1840
Statutes of All Souls Coll., Oxford. *Oxford*, 1841
Statutes of Corpus Christi Coll., Oxford. *Oxford*, 1843
WARD (J.C.) Jonathan Otley, the Geologist and Guide. (With
letters of A. Sedgwick.) (*Trans. Cumb. Assoc.*, Pt II., 1876–7.)
Carlisle, 1877
WARD (R.), *Rector of Ingoldsby*. Life and Letters of Henry More.
London, 1710
WARD (R.), *Fellow of Trinity College*. Two Discourses. (12 Dec.
1822, 20 Dec. 1825.) 1826
Celebria quaedam Anglorum poemata Latine reddita.
4° *Londini*, 1860
WARDALE (J.R.) Clare College. (College histories.) *London*, 1899
See also Clare College, 1903.
WARING (E.) *See* Defence.
WARNER (R.H.) The history of Thorney Abbey, Cambs.
Wisbech, 1879

WARREN (C.) The Lord's Table the Christian Altar, in some
 remarks upon Prof. Scholefield's late Sermon. 1843
WARREN (J.) Sermon...27 June, 1776. 4° 1776
 Sermon in St Paul's Cathedral, 14 May, 1778. 4° *London* (1778)
WARREN (Z.S.) The Christian's character and triumph. A sermon
 on the death of J. Jowett. *Sleaford*, 1856
WARTON (T.) Life of Sir T. Pope. 2nd ed. *London*, 1780
WARWICK (W.A.) Cambridge University Register and Almanack.
 1843, 1844. 1843-4
WASP. Nos. 1-4. June 12, 1891–June 16, 1891. [By E. A.
 Newton, King's.] 4° 1891
WATERBEACH. A short account of the parish of Waterbeach.
 By a late Vicar [R. Masters]. *n.p.* 1795
WATERLAND (D.) A sermon preach'd at St Mary's Church,
 July 21, 1713, at the Assizes held at Cambridge. 4° 1713
Answer to Dr Whitby's Reply. 1720
Advice to a young Student. *London*, 1730
WATERLOO. A poetical epistle to Mr Serjeant Frere. [By John
 Wing, Pemb.] *London*, 1820
WATSON (C.K.) Was Shakspeare a Roman Catholic? (*Edinb.
 Review*, Jan. 1866.)
A Cambridge Professor of the last generation [W. Clark, M.D.].
 (*Macmillan's Mag.*, Jan. 1870.)
In Memoriam : Emma Jane Knight Watson. *London*, 1881

Sale Catalogue, 5 Nov. 1901. 1901

WATSON (F.) The Theological Tripos scheme. 1871
WATSON (H.W.) The Mathematical Tripos, with suggestions for
 the reform of the examination. *London*, 1877
A Sermon preached in the Chapel of Trinity College, Cambridge, at
 the Commemoration of Benefactors, Dec. 10, 1885. 1886
WATSON (J.S.) Life of Richard Porson, M.A. *London*, 1861
WATSON (R.) Institutionum chemicarum...pars metallurgica. 1768
Assize Sermon, March 9, 1769. 4° 1769
An essay on the subjects of Chemistry, and their general division.
 1771
A plan of a course of Chemical lectures. 1771
A letter to the members of the House of Commons respecting the
 petition for relief in the matter of Subscription. By a Christian
 Whig. 2nd ed. To which is added a second letter. *London*, 1772
The principles of the Revolution vindicated in a sermon preached
 before the University of Cambridge, May 29, 1776. 4° 1776
—— 3rd ed. 1776
 Remarks on a pamphlet, entitled, The Principles of the Revolution
  vindicated. By an Undergraduate. 4° 1776
 A vindication of Dr W——n, or, an answer to a pamphlet
  entitled, Remarks, etc. 4° 1776
 Strictures on...The principles of the Revolution vindicated. In
  a letter to a friend. [By W. Stevens.] 2nd ed. 1777

WATSON (R.)
Sermon preached before the University of Cambridge, Oct. 25, 1776.
Being the anniversary of His Majesty's accession to the throne.
4° 1776
An Apology for Christianity, in a series of letters to E. Gibbon.   1776
A letter to Dr Watson, King's Professor of Divinity in the University
of Cambridge. [By W. Vincent.]   *London*, 1780
A sermon preached before the University of Cambridge, Feb. 4,
1780, being the day appointed for a General Fast.   4° 1780
—— 2nd ed.   4° 1780
—— 4th ed.   1780
Discourse to the Clergy of the Archdeaconry of Ely, 9 and 10 May,
1780.   4° 1780
Chemical Essays.   5 vols.   1781–7
—— Another copy of vols. 1–2.   1781
Narrative of R. C[lobery] G[lyn]n, M.D. concerning the late...
frenzy of the Rev. R. Watson, D.D.   4° *London*, 1781
A letter to the Archbishop of Canterbury.   4° *London*, 1783
Address to Young Persons after Confirmation.   12° 1787
—— Another ed.   1788
A charge to the Clergy of the diocese of Llandaff, in June, 1788.
1788
Sermons on public occasions, and Tracts.   1788
A sermon preached before the Stewards of the Westminster Dis-
pensary, April, 1785.   4° *London*, 1793
Two Apologies, one for Christianity...the other for the Bible.
London, 1806
An Heroic Epistle to the Rev. R. Watson. [By T. J. Mathias.]   (Bowes,
1301.)   4° *London*, 1780
Anecdotes of his life.   Published by his son, Richard Watson.
4° *London*, 1817
—— 2nd ed.   2 vols.   *London*, 1818
A letter to the Publisher of the Quarterly Review, with remarks on the
want of candour in the comments therein made on the Life of Richard
Watson.   By Philalethes Cantabrigiensis.   *London*, 1819
Catalogue of Calgarth Park Library, sold July 15, 1909.   (2 copies, one
priced by J. W. Clark.)   *London*, 1909
Catalogue of remainder of Calgarth Park Library, sold at Bowness-on-
Windermere, Nov. 4, 1909.   *Kendal*, 1909
See Collection of theological tracts, 1785 ; Flower (B.), 1800 ; Wakefield (G.),
1798.
WATSON (W.)   An historical account of the ancient town and
port of Wisbech.   *Wisbech*, 1827
WATSON (W.D.)   Cache-Cache.   12° *London*, 1862
WATSON (W.G.)   Letters and other documents relating to the
death of W. G. Watson.   *London*, 1860
WATTS (R.)   Reply to Milner and Wood, on Univ. Press.   4° 1809
WAYNE (E.F.)   Testimonials.   Candidate for the Rectory of Staple-
ton, Salop.   (3 pieces.)   1894

WAYNFLETE (W.) Life. By R. Chandler. *London,* 1811
Memorial. By P. Heylin. Ed. J. R. Bloxam. *London,* 1851
WEBB (W.) Argument on an appeal of W. F. L. Fischer. 1849
WEBSTER (T.) Sermon on death of Rev. T. Robinson, 4 April,
1813. *London,* 1813
Memoir of the late John Escreet. *London,* 1823
God glorified in his faithful ministers. A sermon preached at
St Botolph's, Cambridge, Nov. 20, 1836, on occasion of the death
of the Rev. C. Simeon. *London,* 1836
A sermon preached at St Botolph's, Cambridge, on occasion of the
death of the Rev. W. Farish. *London,* 1837
WEIGHTS and Measures. Proclamation of the Vice-Chancellor.
4 April, 1843. F° 1843
WELLDON (J.E.C.) Address and Testimonials. Candidate for the
Head Mastership of Dulwich College. 1883
WELLER (J.) Dissertation on probable causes of neglect with which
writers of antiquity treated the Christian religion. (Hulsean Prize
Essay for 1817.) 1818
WELLINGTON (*Duke of*) *See* Blunt (J. J.); Evans (S.); Pullen (J.);
Titcomb (J. H.), 1852.
WELLS (J.) Oxford and Oxford life. Ed. by J. Wells.
London, 1892
Wadham College, Oxford. (College histories.) *London,* 1898
The Oxford Degree ceremony. *Oxford,* 1906
WELLS (S.) Letter to the Duke of Bedford on the works in the
New Bedford River. 1828
The history of the drainage of the great Level of the Fens called
Bedford Level. 2 vols. and map. *London,* 1829–1830
WELLS (W.) The drainage of Whittlesea Mere. *London,* 1860
On the treatment of the reclaimed bogland of Whittlesea Mere.
London, 1870
WESLEY (J.) The duty and advantage of early rising. 2nd ed.
1785
WESTCOTT (B.F.) The spiritual office of the Universities. A
sermon preached in the Chapel of Trinity College, Cambridge,
Dec. 15, 1868. *London,* 1869
An address to the University Church Society, March 13. 1872
Sermon preached in All Saints' Church, Cambridge, 1st Sunday after
Epiphany, 1874. *London,* 1874
From strength to strength. A sermon preached in Westminster
Abbey on St Mark's Day, at the consecration of Dr Lightfoot to
the see of Durham. *London,* 1879
The symbol of our inheritance. A sermon preached in the Chapel
of King's College, Nov. 26, 1882. 1882
Waiting for power from on high. A sermon. 1883
On some points in Browning's view of life. 1883
Faithful is he that calleth. A sermon. *London,* 1884
Sermon at the consecration of the Church of St Ignatius, Hendon,
Sunderland, July 2, 1889. *Sunderland,* 1889

WESTCOTT (B.F.)
Teacher and Scholar [J. P. Lee].   A memory and a hope.
                                              Birmingham, 1893
  Life.   A sermon at Trinity College, 11 Dec. 1900.   1901

  Sermon at his consecration as Bp of Durham, by F. J. A. Hort.   *London*, 1890

WESTLAKE (J.)   On the tenure of Fellowships.   1857
International Law.   An introductory lecture.   1888
The Transvaal War.   2nd ed.   *London*, 1899
WESTMACOTT (R.)   Lecture on Sculpture before the School of
  Art.   1863
WESTMINSTER Club.   An authentic narrative of the late extra-
  ordinary proceedings at Cambridge against the W - - - - - - r Club.
  [By T. Ansell or T. Francklin.]   *London*, 1751
  See also Waller (W.).
WESTMINSTER School.   Μαγειροπαιδομαχια.   In schola Sancti
  Petri Westmonasteriensis prid. Kal. Mart. 1865.   (1865)
WESTON (W.)   Some kinds of superstition worse than Atheism.
  Two sermons preached before the University of Cambridge. 1739
The moral impossibility of conquering England, and the absurdity of
  the dispensing power of the Pope.   Three Sermons before the
  University.   1746
WETHERELL (*Sir* C.)   Substance of speech before the Lords of
  the Privy Council, on the subject of incorporating the London
  University.   *London*, 1834
WHEATLEY (J.)   An extract of the life and death of Mr John
  Janeway, Fellow of King's College in Cambridge.
                                         12º *London*, 1775
—— Another ed.   12º *Leeds*, 1797
WHERRY (G.)   Observations on the horns of animals.   (*Brit. Med.*
  Journ.)   *London*, 1902
WHEWELL (W.)   Boadicea.   Poem which obtained the Chancellor's
  Medal.   1814
—— Another ed.   (*Class. Journal.*)   *London*, 1814
Commemoration sermon preached in Trinity College Chapel, Cam-
  bridge, Dec. 17, 1828.   1828
Account of experiments made at Dolcoath mine in Cornwall, in 1826
  and 1828, for the purpose of determining the density of the earth.
                                                             1828
Address to Members of the Senate on the want of Lecture Rooms
  and Museums.   1828
Architectural notes on German Churches.   1830
Reply to Observations on the plans for the New Library.   By a
  Member of both Syndicates [W. Whewell].   1831
Address delivered in the Senate House, Cambridge, June 25, 1833,
  on the occasion of the opening of the third General Meeting of
  the British Association.   1833
Remarks on some parts of Mr Thirlwall's letter on the admission of
  Dissenters to Academical Degrees.   1834

WHEWELL (W.)

Additional remarks on some parts of Mr Thirlwall's two letters on the admission of Dissenters to Academical Degrees. 1834

On the nature of the truth of the laws of motion. (*Trans. Camb. Phil. Soc.*) 4° 1834

Thoughts on the study of mathematics, as a part of a liberal education. 1835

A sermon preached on Trinity Monday, 1835, before the Corporation of the Trinity House. 4° *London*, 1835

Newton and Flamsteed. Remarks on an article in No. CIX. of the *Quarterly Review*. 1836

A letter to the Editor of the *Edinburgh Review*. (Inductive Sciences.) 1837

Letter to C. Babbage, Esq., Lucasian Professor of Mathematics in the University of Cambridge. 1837

On the foundations of morals. Four Sermons. 1837

On the principles of English University education. *London*, 1837

—— 2nd ed. *London*, 1838

An address delivered at the anniversary meeting of the Geological Society of London, Feb. 16, 1838. *London*, 1838

Trinity College Commemoration. Sermon preached in the College Chapel, Dec. 15, 1838. (1838)

Address at the anniversary meeting of the Geological Society of London, Feb. 15, 1839. *London*, 1839

Herman and Dorothea of Goethe translated. Obl. 8° [1839]

Nugarum Bartlovianarum epilogus. 4° *London*, 1840

Two introductory lectures to two courses of lectures on moral philosophy, delivered in 1839 and 1841. 1841

The Knight of Toggenburg. From Schiller. Printed for sale at the Shelford Bazaar. 4° 1842

Of a liberal education. *London*, 1845

—— 2nd ed. *London*, 1850–2

Indications of the Creator. *London*, 1845

—— 2nd ed. (Preface only.) *London*, 1845

Lectures on systematic morality delivered in Lent Term 1846. *London*, 1846

Sunday thoughts, and other verses. 1847

Verse translations from the German. *London and Cambridge*, 1847

English Hexameter translations from Schiller, Göthe, Homer, etc. (By W. Whewell, Sir J. Herschel, J. C. Hare, J. G. Lockhart, and E. C. Hawtrey. Ed. by W. Whewell.) Obl. 8° *London and Cambridge*, 1847

Preface to *Morality*. 2nd ed. 1848

On Hegel's criticism of Newton's *Principia*. (*Camb. Phil. Soc.*) 4° 1849

Of Induction, with especial reference to Mr J. S. Mill's System of Logic. *London*, 1849

A sermon preached before the University of Cambridge on the day of the General Thanksgiving, Nov. 15, 1849. 1849

WHEWELL (W.)

Remarks on the complete Gothic and after-Gothic styles in Germany. (*Arch. Journ.*, Sept. 1850.)   (*London*, 1850)

Criticism on Aristotle's Account of Induction.   (*Camb. Phil. Soc.*)
                                                                    4° 1850

Remarks on this Criticism, by H. A. J. Munro, C. B. Scott, and R. Shilleto, *q.v.*

The general bearing of the Great Exhibition on the progress of art and science.   *London*, 1851

Strength in trouble.   A sermon preached in the Chapel of Trinity College, Cambridge, Feb. 23, 1851.   *London*, 1851

A letter to the author of *Prolegomena Logica*.   1852

Studies Syndicate.   Remarks on the proposal that an Ordinary B.A. Degree shall be given on the ground of an examination in Classics, without any other examination except the Previous Examination. (April, 1853.)   (1853)

Further remarks on the same proposal, 26 Ap. 1853.   (1853)

Studies Syndicate.   Draft of Report for the Studies Syndicate, May 23, 1853.   1853

Of the Plurality of Worlds.   *London*, 1853

—— 4th ed.   *London*, 1855

Notes on the Oxford University Bill in reference to the Colleges at Cambridge, May 1, 1854.   (1854)

Elegiacs [on the death of Mrs Whewell].   4° 1855

Remarks on the Bill now before Parliament, 19 Apr. 1855.   (1855)

Remarks on University Reform, 11 May, 1855.   (1855)

Remarks on the proposed reform of the University of Cambridge, May 31, 1855.   (1855)

Additional remarks on the proposed reform of the University of Cambridge, 16 June, 1855.   1855

A sermon on 1 John iii. 3 preached in the Chapel of Trinity College, Feb. 3, 1856.   4° (1856)

Remarks on the proposed changes in Trinity College Statutes. (23 Sept., 18 Oct., 22 Oct., 17 Nov., 26 Nov.)   1857

Review of Spedding and Ellis's edition of the Works of Francis Bacon.   (Repr. from *Edinb. Rev.*, Oct. 1857.)   1857

On the draft of the Statutes prepared by the University Commissioners for Trinity College.   1858

Suggestions respectfully offered to the Cambridge University Commissioners.   1858

Considerations on the general principles in regard to Colleges proposed for consideration by the Cambridge University Commissioners.
                                                                     1858

Barrow and his academical times as illustrated in his Latin works. (From Barrow's *Works*, ix.)   (1859)

On the proposed alterations in Gt St Mary's Church.   1860

Additional lectures on the history of moral philosophy.   1862

Letter to Rev. W. Whewell.   By an Undergraduate.   *London*, 1843

Articles, verses, etc. on his death.   1866

WHEWELL (W.)

In memoriam. By W. G. Clark. (*Macmillan's Mag.*, Ap. 1866.)

In memory of William Whewell. A sermon preached in Trinity College Chapel, March 18, 1866. By J. B. Lightfoot.   1866

William Whewell. An account of his writings. By I. Todhunter. 2 vols.
London, 1876

The life and correspondence of W. Whewell. By Mrs Stair Douglas.
London, 1881

Mrs Stair Douglas's *Life of William Whewell.* (Review in *Macmillan's Mag.* By Harvey Goodwin.)

Relics of Whewell. Circular letter of H. M. Butler soliciting subscriptions to buy certain objects, 13 May, 1896.   4° (1896)

See Auerbach (B.); Fitzwilliam Museum, 1856.

WHIBLEY (C.) In Cap and Gown. Three centuries of Cambridge wit. Ed. by C. Whibley.   *London*, 1889

—— Third edition.   *London*, 1898

WHIBLEY (L.) Political parties in Athens during the Peloponnesian War. 2nd ed. (Camb. Hist. Essays, No. 1.)   1889

WHIF. A 'Varsity Eclogue. By Whif.   1878

WHISTON (R.) Cathedral Trusts and their fulfilment. 4th ed.
Rochester, 1850

The Reviewer reviewed; or a reply to the *Saturday Review* on Whiston's Demosthenes.   *London*, 1859

WHISTON (W.) Sermon at Trinity Church, 25 Jan. 1704–5... [when] the teachers of the Charity Schools lately erected in Cambridge appeared, with the poor children under their care. (With an account of the Schools.)   4° 1705

—— 2nd ed.   *London*, 1708

Reflexions on...A Discourse of Free-Thinking [by Anthony Collins].
London, 1713

WHITAKER (W.), *Master of St John's.* Cygnea cantio Guilielmi Whitakeri, hoc est, ultima illius concio ad clerum, habita Cantabrigiae in templo beatae Mariae, paulo ante mortem, Oct. 9, 1595.
Herbornæ Nassoviorum, 1599

WHITAKER (W.), *B.A. Lond.* Woodwardian Museum, Cambridge. List of works on the geology of Cambridgeshire.   [1873]

WHITE (E.) A dissertation on the fitness of the time when Jesus Christ came into the world. (Hulsean Prize Essay for 1819.) 1820

WHITE (H.K.) Remains, with account of his life by Robert Southey. 9th ed. 3 vols.   *London*, 1821

WHITE (T.P.) Letter offering to found a prize, with notice of Grace to accept the same, Feb. 1821.   (1821)

WHITE (W.) A Jubilee memorial of the consecration of Christ Church, Cambridge.   1889

The Railway Traveller's Walk through Cambridge. 8th ed. [1893]

—— 9th ed.   [*Ab.* 1897]

WHITEHEAD (W.) An Essay on Ridicule.   F° *London*, 1743

Atys and Adrastus.   F° *London*, 1744

Plays and Poems. 3 vols.   12° *London and York*, 1774–88

WILLIAMS (G.)

A letter to the Provost of Eton College on the election of scholars to the two foundations of King Henry VI.   *London,* 1850

Letter to the Provost of King's College.   1856

Statement of the property of King's College.   1857

Supplementary statement of the property of King's College.   1857

Memoir and correspondence of William Millington, first Provost of King's College. With notices of Robert Woodlarke, third Provost. By C. Hardwick.   1858

Correspondence between the Vice-Chancellor and the late Pro-Proctors.   1859

The Proctorial Question at Cambridge. A letter to the Vice-Chancellor.   1860

Détails sur le projet d'établir à Cambridge des hôtelleries en faveur des étrangers.   1860

A statement relative to the financial matters of King's College, in 1860.   1860

University Library extension. A letter to the Vice-Chancellor. 1862

Bishop Bekyngton. A paper read...Sept. 10, 1863. (*Gentleman's Magazine.*)   (*London,* 1863)

On the funds of the Library. 21 Nov. 1863.   (1863)

Proposal for building the West side of the Library Quadrangle. 1864

Dr Pierotti and his assailants ; or a defence of *Jerusalem Explored.*
    London, 1864

Williams (G.) and Tristram (H.B.)   The Bible as illustrated by modern science and travel.   *London,* 1868

WILLIAMS (H.G.) *See* Smith (J.), †1652. Select Discourses. 4th ed. 1859.

WILLIAMS (John), *Abp of York.* Letters with documents relating to them. Ed. by J. E. B. Mayor. (*C.A.S.*)   1866

WILLIAMS (John) Is my son likely to pass ? 2nd ed. *London,* 1864

The Public Schools and the Universities.   *London,* 1864

WILLIAMS (M.) and Burnand (F.C.) The Seventh Shot. (For performance at the A.D.C.)   1860

WILLIAMS (P.) Sermon, 11 June, 1738.   4° 1738

WILLIAMS (R.) An earnestly respectful letter to the Bp of St David's [C. Thirlwall] on the difficulty of bringing theological questions to an issue.   1860

A critical appendix upon the Lord Bishop of St David's reply. 1860

Life and Letters. Ed. by his wife. 2 vols.   *London,* 1874

WILLIAMS (W.) Oxonia depicta.   F° *London,* 1732–3

WILLIAMSON (G.C.) Trade Tokens issued in the seventeenth century. New ed. of Boyne's work. Part for Cambridgeshire.
    London, 1889

Williamson (G.C.) and Sayle (C.E.) Portraits, Prints, and Writings of John Milton.   4° 1908

—— 2nd ed.   4° 1908

—— Special ed.   4° 1908

WILLIAMSON (J.)   A brief memoir of the Rev. C. Simeon.
London, 1848
WILLIAMSON (K.)   Cambridge, a poem, etc.   (Fenlight Booklets, 1.)
Allahabad (1908)
WILLINGHAM.   Prodigium Willinghamense.   By T. Dawkes.
London (1747)
WILLIS (M.A.)   A short sketch about washing linen.   1868
—— 3rd ed.   1869
Science applied to the washing of linen.   London, 1869
A short essay on practical experimental philosophy.   Parts 1, 2.
London, 1871
WILLIS (R.)   Attempt to analyse the Automaton Chess Player of
Mr de Kempelen.   (Two copies.)   London, 1821
On the pressure produced on a flat plate, etc.   (Trans. Camb. Philos.
Soc.)   4° 1828
On the vowel sounds, and on reed organ pipes.   (Trans. Camb. Philos.
Soc.)   4° 1829
On the mechanism of the Larynx.   (Trans. Camb. Philos. Soc.)
4° 1832
Syllabus of lectures on Sound at Royal Institution, 1832.   London, 1832
Remarks on the architecture of the Middle Ages.   1835
On the Teeth of Wheels.   (Trans. Inst. of Civil Engineers.)
4° London, 1838
Syllabus of a course of experimental lectures on the principles of
mechanism.   1839
—— Another ed.   1840
—— Another ed.   1841
On the construction of the Vaults of the Middle Ages.   (Trans. Inst.
of British Architects.)   4° London, 1841
On the characteristic interpenetrations of the flamboyant style.
(Trans. Inst. of British Architects.)   4° London, 1841
Principles of mechanism.   London, 1841
—— 2nd ed.   London, 1870
Description of the cymagraph for copying mouldings.   (Civil Engineer
and Architect's Journal.)   4° London, 1842
Report on Cathedral of Hereford.   (Engineer's Journal.)
4° London, 1842
Description of the Sextry Barn at Ely.   (C.A.S.)   4° 1843
Architectural nomenclature of the Middle Ages.   (C.A.S.)   4° 1844
The architectural history of Canterbury Cathedral.   London, 1845
A critical dissertation on Prof. Willis's Architectural history of
Canterbury Cathedral.   By Charles Sandys.   London, 1846
On the history of the Great Seals of England.   (Arch. Journal.)
London, 1845
The architectural history of Winchester Cathedral.   London, 1846
Architectural history of York Cathedral.   (Read before Arch. Inst.)
London, 1846
Lecture on Ely Cathedral, before Arch. Inst. 4 Aug. 1847.   (Repr.
from Norfolk Chronicle.)   Norwich, 1847

WILLIS (R.)

Description of the ancient plan of the monastery of St Gall, in the ninth century. (*Arch. Journal.*) (*London*, 1848)

The architectural history of the Church of the Holy Sepulchre at Jerusalem. (Two copies.) *London*, 1849

Essay on the effects produced by causing weights to travel over elastic bars. (Appendix B of the Report of Commissioners appointed to enquire into the application of iron to railway structures.) F⁰ *London*, 1849

—— Another ed. appended to P. Barlow's *Treatise on the strength of Timber.* *London*, 1851

On the principles of tools for turning and planing metals. *London*, 1849

System of apparatus for the use of lecturers in Mechanical Philosophy. 4⁰ *London*, 1851

Exhibition of 1851. Classified Lists. Section II., Machinery, arranged by R. Willis. (With other pieces connected with the Exhibition.) 4⁰ 1851

On machines and tools for working in metal, wood, and other materials. (Lecture VII on results of Exhibition of 1851.) *London*, 1852

Crystal Palace Company. Grand Organ. Preliminary Report, by Sir F. A. G. Ouseley, R. Willis, and J. Donaldson. *London*, 1853

Pedal Harp. Specification. 4⁰ *London*, 1856

Paris Universal Exhibition. Report on machinery for woven fabrics. *London*, 1857

Apparatus for weighing. Specification. 4⁰ *London*, 1857

The architectural history of the University (of Cambridge). (Proc. Congr. Archit. Soc. at Cambridge, May, 1860. Repr. from *Camb. Chronicle.*) (1860)

Architectural history of Gloucester Cathedral. (*Arch. Journ.*) (*London*, 1860)

—— Another ed. (*Gentleman's Mag.*) (*London*, 1860)

A Westminster fabric roll of 1253. (*Gentleman's Mag.*) (*London*, 1860)

Memoir on foundations of early buildings recently discovered in Lichfield Cathedral. (*Arch. Journ.*) *London*, 1861

Architectural history of Chichester Cathedral. 4⁰ *Chichester*, 1861

Address delivered at the opening meeting of the British Association at Cambridge, Oct. 1, 1862. 1862

The architectural history of the Cathedral and Monastery at Worcester. (*Arch. Journ.*) *London*, 1863

The Crypt and Chapter House of Worcester Cathedral. (*Royal Inst. of British Architects.*) 4⁰ *London*, 1863

Sherborne Minster. (*Arch. Journ.*) (*London*, 1865)

The architectural history of Glastonbury Abbey. 1866

The architectural history of the conventual buildings of the monastery of Christ Church in Canterbury. *London*, 1869

Notes on Norwich Cathedral. By D. J. Stewart. (From Memoranda by the late Prof. Willis.) 2 pts. (*Arch. Journ.*, XXXII.) (*London*, 1875)

WILLIS (R.)

Willis (R.) and Clark (J.W.) The architectural history of the University of Cambridge. 3 vols. (Proofs with notes.) 1886

Proofs of Title and Introduction, corrected by H. Bradshaw.

Proofs of Schools, Library, Senate House, corrected by H. Bradshaw (Arch. hist. III.).

Essay on The Library. Proofs with notes. (Arch. hist. III.)

A volume of reviews, criticisms, letters, etc.

The late Prof. Willis. By J. W. Clark. (Repr. from *Camb. Chron.*, March 6, 1875.) (1875)

Memoir of Robert Willis. (*Proc. Inst. Civ. Engineers.*) (*London*, 1875)

WILLMOTT (R.A.) Conversations at Cambridge. [Attr. to R. A. Willmott.] *London*, 1836

WILLS. Calendar of Cambridge Wills proved in V.-C.'s Court, 1501–1765. 1907

WILSON (H.A.) Magdalen College, Oxford. (College histories.) *London*, 1899

WILSON (H.B.) Rationalism in the Pulpit of the University of Oxford, being an examination of doctrines advanced by H. B. Wilson. *London*, 1854

WILSON (Sir H.F.) Notice of a proposed representation of the *Ajax*. 1882

Carmen Pooleviense. (Repr. from the *Leaflet*.) *Rugby*, 1885

WILSON (J.) Memorabilia Cantabrigiae. *London*, 1803

WILSON (J.D.) John Lyly. (Harness Prize Essay.) 1905

WILSON (J.M.) A letter to the Master and Seniors of St John's College, Cambridge, on the subject of Natural and Physical Sciences in relation to School and College. *London*, 1867

On teaching Geology and Botany as part of a liberal education. *London*, 1872

Cambridge University Association for the promotion of purity of life. An address, Oct. 28. 1883

WIMPOLE Hall. Catalogue of the Library...to be sold, June 29, 1888. *London* (1888)

WISBECH. An historical account of the ancient town and port of Wisbech. By William Watson. *Wisbech*, 1827

The history of Wisbech, with an historical sketch of the Fens. *Wisbech*, 1834

Observations on a central Assize at Wisbech. By H. Fardell. *Wisbech*, 1848

See also Fens ; Letter (1679).

WISEMAN. A pastoral in humble imitation of Virgil and Dr Ullathorne. By Σ. 1850

WITHERS (J.J.) Register of Admissions to King's College, Cambridge, 1850–1900. *London*, 1903

WOLLASTON (F.J.H.) A plan of a course of Chemical lectures. 1794

—— Another ed. 1805

WOMEN. Higher Education of Women. Progress of the higher education of women at Cambridge. Signed : W. H. (*Monthly Journ. of Education.* No. 4. April, 1874.)

Report of a Conference of persons...interested in the Higher Education of Women, Dec. 27, 1877. (1878)

Fly-sheets, memorials, etc., relating to Women's degrees from 1880.
1880–

A brief history of the proposal to admit Women to Degrees at Cambridge, in 1887–8. By Thomas Case. *Oxford,* 1896

Women's Degrees: a report in Greek and English. By W. C. Green. 1897

Women's Degrees. By H. D. C[atling]. Verses. 1897

University Education of Women. 1897

See also Battle of Pons trium Trojanorum, 1881 ; Girton ; Ladies' Battle, 1881 ; Newnham.

WOOD (A.à) The ancient and present state of the city of Oxford.
4° *London,* 1773

The history and antiquities of the University of Oxford. With continuation by John Gutch. 4° *Oxford,* 1786

WOOD (F.H.) "'Ἐν τούτῳ νικά." (Seatonian Prize Poem for 1904.)
1904

WOOD (J.S.) Remarks on the bearing of the proposed Statute "De electione Procuratorum et Vice-Procuratorum." 1857

The position of members of the Church of England in a College in the University of Cambridge. 1882

WOOD (T.B.) Syllabus of a course of twelve lectures on plant and animal life. 1891

WOODCOCK (E.) An account of the providential preservation of E. Woodcock. By T. V. Okes. 2nd ed. 1799

—— 3rd ed. 1799

—— Another ed., by R. Okes. *Eton,* 1838

WOODFORD (J.R.) Christian sanctity. Four sermons preached before the University of Cambridge in November, 1863. 1863

Address to Churchwardens of Ely. *Ely,* 1877

The Strength of the Church. A sermon preached at the opening of Selwyn College, Cambridge, Oct. 10, 1882. 1882

Charges, Sept. and Oct. 1885. 1885

Peterhouse Sexcentenary. The former days. A sermon. 1885

In piam memoriam Jacobi Russell, Episc. Eliensis. By H. M. Luckock.
n.p. (1885)

WOODHAM (H.A.) Oratio Latina. (Members' Prize.) 1837

Oratio Latina. (Members' Prize.) 1838

Oratio Latina. (Members' Prize.) 1840

An application of heraldry to the illustration of various University and Collegiate antiquities. 2 pts. (*C.A.S.*) 4° 1841–2

WOODHOUSE (F.C.) Some account of St John's College Chapel, Cambridge. 1848

WOODHOUSE   WORDSWORTH   275

WOODHOUSE (R.) Syllabus of lectures on experimental philosophy.
1819
WOODLARK (R.)   Robert Woodlark, Founder of St Catharine's
Hall. By Charles Hardwick.   1858
WOODWARD (H.) Rev. Adam Sedgwick. (*Geol. Mag.*, April,
1870.)
WOODWARD (J.)   An essay towards a natural history of the earth,
etc. 2nd ed.   *London,* 1702
Naturalis historia telluris illustrata et aucta.   *Londini,* 1714
An attempt towards a natural history of the fossils of England.
(+ Catalogue of the foreign fossils in the collection of J. Wood-
ward...) 2 vols.   *London,* 1728–9
Part of the late Dr Woodward's Will, Oct. 1, 1727.   1778
WOODWARDIAN Museum. Report of Syndicate respecting suit-
able room.   Fº (1821)
List of works on the geology of Cambridgeshire. By William
Whitaker.   1873
Catalogue of the collection of Cambrian and Silurian Fossils. By
J. W. Salter. Preface by Adam Sedgwick.   4º 1873
The Sedgwick Memorial Museum. By T. McK. Hughes. 6 Dec.
1886.   1886
Sedgwick Memorial Museum. Fly-sheets relating thereto.   1886–
The Woodwardian Professor and the Sedgwick Memorial Museum.
By A. Newton and J. W. Clark.   1887
WOODWARDIAN Professorship. Poll, 21 May, 1818. (A. Sedgwick
elected.)   1818
1873. Testimonials of various candidates, including T. McK.
Hughes who was elected.   1873
WOOLLEY (J.) "By one offering Christ hath perfected for ever
them that are sanctified." (Norrisian Essay for 1844.)   1844
WORDSWORTH (Christopher), *Master of Trinity,* †1846. Letter of
explanation respecting use to be made of the rents of the new
buildings [Trinity], 7 June, 1823.   Fº 1823
The Ecclesiastical Commission and the Universities; a letter to
a friend.   *London,* 1837
WORDSWORTH (Christopher), *Bp of Lincoln,* †1885. On the
admission of Dissenters to graduate in the University of Cambridge.
1834
—— 2nd ed.   1834
Ode, July 7, 1835 at the first Commencement after the Installation,
and in the presence of the Marquess Camden.   4º 1835
College Statutes, College Fellowships, and College legislation.
London, 1872
The hope of glory and the future of our Universities. Two sermons
preached before the University of Cambridge.   *London,* 1882
Funeral Sermon for C. Wordsworth by John Wordsworth.   *Lincoln,* 1885
WORDSWORTH (Christopher), *Fellow of Peterhouse.* Social life at
the English Universities in the eighteenth century.   1874

WORDSWORTH (Christopher), *Fellow of Peterhouse.*
Scholae Academicae. 1877
WORDSWORTH (J.) Love and discipline. Sermon. *Lincoln,* 1885
WORDSWORTH (W.) Description of the scenery of the Lakes.
3rd ed. 12º *London,* 1822
Guide through the...Lakes...with a Description of the scenery.
5th ed. 12º *Kendal,* 1835
—— Ed. by J. Hudson. With Five Letters on the Geology of the
Lake District by A. Sedgwick. *Kendal,* 1853
Ode on the Installation of Prince Albert as Chancellor of the
University of Cambridge. 4º 1847
—— Another ed., illuminated. 4º 1847

The College Days of William Wordsworth. By G. C. M. Smith. (*Eagle,*
March, 1891.) (1891)

WORKE for Cutlers. Acted at Trinity Hall, at the instance of
A. F. Sieveking, 23 July, 1903. (1903)
—— Ed. by A. F. Sieveking, with introductory note by A. W. Ward.
4º *London,* 1904
WORKING Men's College, 1854–1904. Edited by J. L. Davies.
London, 1904
Working Men's College Magazine. Nos. 1–21. Jan. 1859–Sept.
1860. 1859–60
WORKING Men's Cottage Garden Society. 28th Annual Exhibition.
3 Aug. 1903. 1903
WORMAN (E.J.) Ernest James Worman, 1871–1909. (Ed. by
G. J. Gray.) 1910
WORSLEY (T.) The Roman martyr. A youthful essay in dramatic
verse. By Nominis Umbra [T. Worsley]. *London,* 1859
A few remarks on the outline of a scheme for the future constitution
of Downing College. 1860
A few remarks on the most fitting material and site for the memorial
statue to our late Chancellor. (1862)
Christian drift of Cambridge work. Eight lectures. 1865
See also Fitzwilliam Museum, 1856.
WORTHINGTON (T.L.) Proposal for rural settlements, 25 Oct.
1894. (*London,* 1894)
WOTTON (W.) Reflections upon Ancient and Modern Learning.
London, 1694
—— 2nd ed. *London,* 1697
—— 3rd ed. *London,* 1705
WRANGHAM (F.) The Restoration of the Jews. (Seatonian Prize
Poem for 1794.) 4º 1795
The Holy Land. (Seatonian Prize Poem for 1800.) 4º 1800
A poem on the restoration of learning in the East. (Written for
Buchanan Prize.) 4º 1805
Joseph made known to his brethren. (Seatonian Prize Poem for
1812.) 1812
Sertum Cantabrigiense. *Malton,* 1824

Y

YEATES (T.)   Collation of an Indian copy of the Hebrew Pentateuch, with notice of others, collected by Rev. C. Buchanan, D.D., 1806, and now in the Public Library, Cambridge.   4° 1812

YORKE (J.), *Bp of Ely.*   Sermon...26 May, 1785.   To which is annexed an account of the S.P.C.K.   4° *London,* 1785

See also Ely [1787 ?].

YORKE (P.)   *See* Appeal.

YOUNG (*Sir* G.)   University Tests; an apology for their assailants.
London, 1868

The Oedipus Tyrannus of Sophocles in English verse.   1887
Cookham Church.   *Reading,* 1901

See also Praed (W. M.).

Z

ZOOLOGY.   Reports, fly-sheets, etc., on the foundation of the Professorship of Zoology.   With Candidates' testimonials.   A. Newton elected.   1865–6

Poll for the election of a Professor, March 1, 1866.   1866

On the duties of a Professor of Zoology.   By W. H. Drosier.   1866

Proceedings of Fourth International Congress of Zoology, held at Cambridge, 22–27 August, 1898.   Ed. by A. Sedgwick.   1899

Miscellaneous papers relating to the Congress.   1898

Professorship.   Election of 1907.   Letters of Candidates and miscellaneous papers.   A. Sedgwick elected.   1907

See also Bridge (T.W.) and Clark (J.W.)   List of Dissections (1871); Illustrations of Comparative Anatomy, 1875.

APPENDIX

I. MANUSCRIPTS

II. PRINTS AND DRAWINGS

I. MANUSCRIPTS

The following will be fully described in the new edition, now in
preparation, of the Catalogue of Manuscripts in the University
Library ; the class-marks prefixed refer to that Catalogue.

WILLIS (R.)

Add. 5022.	Architectural drawings.
Add. 5023.	Church architecture.
Add. 5024.	Monasteries. Cathedrals.
Add. 5025.	Nomenclature : materials.
Add. 5026.	Nomenclature : materials.
Add. 5027.	Tracery.
Add. 5028.	Oxford. Monastic Colleges.
Add. 5029.	Notes. General : A—K.
Add. 5030.	—— —— : L—Z.
Add. 5031.	—— Ancient monuments, etc.
Add. 5032.	—— Descriptions of Churches.
Add. 5033.	—— Monuments, etc.
Add. 5034.	—— Saints, etc.
Add. 5035.	—— Cymagraph, etc.
Add. 5036.	—— Italian architecture, etc.

Further Notes by Prof. Willis were bought at the J. W. Clark sale
(Add. 5127–5141).

Add. 5037.	Drawings. Bottisham.
Add. 5038.	—— Chester.
Add. 5039.	—— Ely.
Add. 5040.	—— Exeter.
Add. 5041.	—— Gloucester.
Add. 5042.	—— Lichfield.
Add. 5043.	—— Peterborough.
Add. 5044.	—— Salisbury.
Add. 5045.	—— Miscellanea.

See also Appendix II and Add. 5142–4.

CAMBRIDGE.

Add. 5046.	Statuta Universitatis Cantabrigiensis.	(xvi. cent.)
Add. 5047.	Watson (Bp R.) Notes of G. Holmes's lectures.	1758 ?
Add. 5048–9.	Cambridge Garrick Club. Minute Book.	1833–9
Add. 5050.	Cambridge University. Act for B.A. degree.	1842 ?
Add. 5051.	—— Mathematical Tripos. Marking Book.	1842
Add. 5052.	Cambridge Camden Society. Resignations and Answers.	
		1845

CAMBRIDGE.

Add. 5053. Cambridge University. Societas Sanctae Crucis.
1854–5

Add. 5054. Smedley (E.A.) Correspondence with Rev. C. Knowles.
1865

Add. 5055–6. Luard (H.R.) Notes on Cambridge Graduati. 1856?

Add. 5057. Bradshaw (H.) Notes on King's College, University Library, etc.

University Library: Donors' Book. (Copy of part of MS. Oo . 7 . 52.)

WILLIS (R.) and CLARK (J.W.) Materials for the Architectural History of the University of Cambridge and of the Colleges of Cambridge and Eton, published 1886.

Add. 5058. Correspondence of R. Willis with the Vice-Chancellor.
1859

Add. 5059–60. Introduction.

Add. 5061. Peterhouse—Corpus.

Add. 5062–3. King's College. 2 vols.

Add. 5064. Eton.

Add. 5065. Eton (J. W. Clark).

Add. 5066. Queens' College.

Add. 5067. St Catharine's College—Jesus College.

Add. 5068. Christ's College—St John's College.

Add. 5069. Christ's College (J. W. Clark).

Add. 5070. St John's College Library (J. W. Clark).

Add. 5071–3. Trinity College. 3 vols.

Add. 5074. Michael House—King's Hall.

Add. 5075. Magdalene—Emmanuel—Sidney[1].

Add. 5076. Downing (J. W. Clark).

Add. 5077. Schools—Library—Senate House.

Add. 5078. Master's Lodge.

Add. 5079. Gateways—Treasury—Hall, etc.

Add. 5080. Chambers—Hostels—Wainscot.

Add. 5081. Chapel.

Add. 5082. India proofs of illustrations.

CLARK (J.W.)

Add. 5083–9. The Library. 6 vols. and Index.

Materials for The Care of Books based on the essay on The Library in the Architectural History.

Add. 5090. University Library. Annals.

Add. 5091–2. Miscellanies. 2 vols.

SEDGWICK (A.)

Add. 5093–7. Material for his Life, published in 1890 by J. W. Clark and T. McK. Hughes.

Add. 5098–9. Romilly (J.) Extracts from his diary. (For the Sedgwick life.)

[1] This volume was generously restored to the series by J. B. Peace, M.A. Emm., to whom it had been given by J. W. Clark.

SEDGWICK (A.)
    Add. 5100. Sedgwick (A.) Letters to Miss Duncan (copy).
    Add. 5101. Miscellanea.
    Add. 5102. Correspondence connected with Sedgwick's Life.
CLARK (J.W.)
    Add. 5103-5. Miscellanea.
    Add. 5106. Note Book.
    Add. 5107. Mr Buck's Book. (Transcript, corrected.)
    Add. 5108. Augustinian Friars.
    Add. 5109. Augustinian Canons.
    Add. 5110. Library Notes. Rome.
    Add. 5111. Roman Libraries.
    Add. 5112. Gilbertine Nuns. Institutiones. (Transcript.)
    Add. 5113. ——— Translation by J. W. Clark.
    Add. 5114. Caius (J.) History of the University. Translation by J. W. Clark.
    Add. 5115. Glossary.

SANCROFT (W.)
    Add. 5116. Correspondence with Emmanuel College. (Transcript.)
CLARK (J.W.)
    Add. 5117-8. A.D.C. Programmes, 1855-95.
    Add. 5122-3. Extracts from W. Cole's MSS.
MARTIN (T.)
    Add. 5125. Cambridgeshire Notes.

II. PRINTS AND DRAWINGS

In addition to the books and papers here described Mr Clark left to the University a collection of prints and drawings of the University, Town, and County of Cambridge. Besides topographical engravings and plans the collection includes a series of original pencil sketches by George Nicholson (1816); architectural drawings by Professor Willis; and photographs of University ceremonies.

It is hoped that these may be fully described in a projected comprehensive Catalogue of Cambridge Prints and Plans.

CAMBRIDGE: PRINTED BY JOHN CLAY, M.A. AT THE UNIVERSITY PRESS.

ET
LVCEM
POCVLA
HINC
SACRA

ALMA
MATER
CANTA-
BRIGIA.

For EU product safety concerns, contact us at Calle de José Abascal, 56–1°,
28003 Madrid, Spain or eugpsr@cambridge.org.